方 成 徐 芳 编著

英美诗歌经典

战争篇

A Critical Anthology of British and American Poetry: War Discourse

南京大学出版社

图书在版编目（CIP）数据

英美诗歌经典．战争篇：汉文、英文 / 方成，徐芳编著 . -- 南京：南京大学出版社，2023.3

ISBN 978-7-305-26182-4

Ⅰ．①英… Ⅱ．①方…②徐… Ⅲ．①诗歌研究–英国–汉、英②诗歌研究–美国–汉、英 Ⅳ．① I561.072②I712.072

中国版本图书馆 CIP 数据核字（2022）第 178981 号

出版发行　南京大学出版社

社　　　址　南京市汉口路22号　　邮　编　210093

出 版 人　金鑫荣

书　　　名　**英美诗歌经典：战争篇**

编　　者　方　成　徐　芳

责任编辑　董　颖　　编辑热线　025-83596997

照　　排　南京新华丰制版有限公司

印　　刷　苏州市古得堡数码印刷有限公司

开　　本　787×1092　1/16　印张37.5　字数419千

版　　次　2023年3月第1版　2023年3月第1次印刷

ISBN　978-7-305-26182-4

定　　价　118.00元

网址：http://www.njupco.com

官方微博：http://weibo.com/njupco

官方微信号：njupress

销售咨询热线：（025）83594756

Preface

Occasions of anthologizing war poetry vary greatly throughout history. The earliest attempts as such functioned to record what happened about the war as a national or communal memory, but there have been other anthologizing occasions, for instance, to launch wars, mobilize recruits, inspire morale, and constantly encourage combatants in the battle field. For the present occasion, anthologizing becomes an attitude towards the topic of all wars, reflects ourselves and others for a better humanity, and even more, evokes such sublime objectives as academic construction and examination of knowledge.

Although the genre of "war poetry" is a largely 20th century invention, the anthology of war writing in general and war poetry in particular spans over the Anglo-American history, beginning with the wars of British national formation, American colonial wars of the 18th century, and ending with the Gulf Wars or "Wars on Terror". Such anthologizing often comes at those very occasions as has been stated above, for instance, specifically at the beginning and end of the respectively American Civil War, the First World War, the Second World War, and so on. Collecting poems together is what anthologies do, and anthologies of poetic writing have played a central role in the construction and reconstruction of what has been defined as the 'war poem' and 'war poet'.

As for war-discoursing and self-reflection, there have also been many modern and contemporary attempts: there were such as Frederick Brereton's *An Anthology of War Poems* (1930), Julian Symons's *An Anthology of War Poetry* (1942), Oscar Williams's *The War Poets: An Anthology of the War Poetry of the 20th Century* (1945), Jon Silkin's *The Penguin Book of First World War Poetry* (1979); and there were also such as Jon Stallworthy's *The Oxford Book of War Poetry* (1984), Kenneth Baker's *The Faber Book of War Poetry* (1996), Lorrie Goldensohn's *American War Poetry: An Anthology* (2006), Pinaki Roy's *The Scarlet Critique: A Critical Anthology of War Poetry* (2010), and Jon Stallworthy's recent collection *The New Oxford Book of War Poetry* (2014); other numerous anthologies of different and specific wars in history including such as Lee Steinmetz's *The Poetry of the American Civil War* (1991), Tim Kendall's *Poetry of the First World War: An Anthology* (2013), Harvey Shapiro's *Poets of World War II* (2003), and a great number of anthologies of individual war poems or poets with collective identity in the war such as gender, race and class.

From the first anthology directed against 'the false glamour of war' in Bertram Lloyd's

Poems Written During the Great War 1914–1918, to Sam Hamil's *Poets Against the War*, selected from 11,000 poems and posted on <poetsagainstthewar.org> in 2003 on the eve of the US-led invasion of Iraq, war poetry had developed from conventional expressions of patriotic feeling to the expression of 'war neurosis' and critique, culminating in ferocious documentary works like Owen's 'Dulce et Decorum Est' and Sassoon's "Does it Matter?" Those celebrated lines or slogans, "The glamour from the sword is gone," "newspaper-warriors", "cheerful patriotic citizens", and "professional diplomatists, politicians and statesmen", have constantly overwhelmed the reading public with a sense of conscientious enlightenment.

As we are experiencing a world marked by unprecedented changes unseen for the past century, globalization has now encountered waves of conflicts, regional wars turned rampant, terrorism horrified the populace, and a new world order is to be conceived in looming regional, sectional, and global wars. It is now high time that we have to reflect ourselves, our history and our culture itself. It is thus also necessary to compile an anthology of Anglo-American war poetry as a tribute to the new reflection and evaluation. Called 'a critical anthology', the present efforts aim to reevaluate wars not only from a new critical perspective that will be categorized as 'A Critique of Cultural Pathology', but also from new materials of war writing that will shed new light on the horizon of contemporary cognition of this pan-historical phenomenon.

The critical anthology has originally planned to include a more comprehensive selection of war poetry, especially including those war poems that have been ignored or neglected in the past anthologies. In addition, due to the corresponding international copyright laws and those items concerned with the doctrine of 'fair use', the anthology limited its selection of the quoted excerpts in the review or criticism for purposes of illustration or comment, scholarly or technical illustration or clarification, or any summary of main ideas tip toeing on copyright issues for contemporary poets.

Another important category about poetic anthology is related with its writing mechanics or printing format. The anthology has followed the most commonly anthologized format, and when those selected poems are of digital medium, double-check and proofreading have been done by consulting with various versions of the selected. Despite all these efforts, mistakes, or even blunders, may be found here and there, requiring of its reader's apology and further examination.

Acknowledgements should at first go to those friends and colleagues concerned at Institute of International Studies, National University of Defense Technology, to whom I owe an immense debt of gratitude. Secondly, for her expertise of editorial advice and support, it gives me pleasure to acknowledge Miss Dong Ying of Nanjing University Press, with whom I have many years of happy cooperation, and to whom I am especially grateful to. I cannot mention everyone who has helped me, but it would be wrong not to mention my wife, to whom I owe a lot: Her sense and sensitivity, and her kindness and emotional generosity, have always been a source of strength inspiring me to go on with the present work.

Table of Contents

Chapter III

The Anglo-American War Poetry and the Age of Revolutions (1774–1830) ... 075

Chapter IV

War Poetry of British Imperialism (1830–1914)...................................... 161

Introduction

War discourse has been a long tradition in both British and American history and their poetic representation until the invention of "war poetry" as an independent literary genre in the early 20th century. War Poetry, or Poetry of War, witnessed an overwhelming portion of "War Writing", "War Literature", or "Literature of War". That poets have participated in a war and written about his or her experiences, or a non-combatant has composed poems about war scenarios, has been a common composition practice since time immemorial, but it is the young soldier poets of the First World War that established "War Poetry" as an autonomous literary genre. Their "voices of war" have become one of the defining texts of the 20th century minds across the transatlantic world. Today, the specific critical term has achieved a generic denotation, which can be applied to poetry of any nationality writing about any war, including, for instance, Homer's *Iliad* from around the 8th century BC, the Old English poem "The Battle of Maldon", and the poetry of the American and the Spanish Civil War, the Second World War, the Korean War, the Vietnam War, the Iraqi War, the so-called "Wars on Terror", and even the annual remembrance of wars.

War Poetry in English, or English language war poetry, or war poetry written in the English language, which mainly consists of the Anglo-American war poetry, or "British and American war poetry," is a characteristic portion of the whole body of English language war poetry. It has its origins from the Greeks and Romans, but historically begins together with the development of the English language over the course of more than 1,400 years, evolving as a distinct part of English-language literature, not only the literature of England but also that of Scotland, Wales, the Crown dependencies, and the whole of Ireland, as well as literature in English from countries of the former British Empire, including the United States and other English speaking countries. Taking war as its material and motif, war poets cherish humanity and happiness, long for love and peace, and explore in depths the larger questions of life, such as justice, liberty, identity, innocence, guilt, loyalty, courage, compassion, duty, desire, and death, responding to these larger questions as well as the relations of immediate personal experience to moments of national and international crisis. It has become an integrated part of the national and international mythology, an expression of historical consciousness, human identity and political conscience, and a legacy of humanity.

1. Defining War Poetry

The semantic interpretation of the word "War" in common dictionaries includes two main denotations: First a state, period, or techniques and procedures of open, armed, often prolonged conflict between nations, states, or parties, such military or political usage as any inter-human wars in history; second, a condition of active antagonism or contention both physical or metaphysical, or a concerted effort or campaign to combat or put an end to something considered injurious, such disciplinary or daily usage as "war of words" "price war" "the war against corona virus" "cultural wars", or "philosophical or psychological wars within the self". The selected readings in this critical anthology limited its denotation to the former, excluding those wars of cosmic conflict, such as biblical wars or wars with nature or God; those wars of metaphorical, symbolic, and allegorical conflict, such as wars of daily or personal conflict and even general or social conflict of what Thomas Hobbes has termed *bellum omnium contra omnes* ("war of all against all"). As a state of large-scale armed conflict throughout history between states, governments, societies and informal paramilitary groups such as mercenaries, insurgents and militias, war is generally characterized by extreme violence, aggression, destruction, and mortality, using regular or irregular military forces, activities and characteristics of which have not only restricted itself to purely legitimate military targets but also led to massive civilian suffering and casualties and human catastrophes.

War is one of the most important of human activities, and its place in history has always been overwhelmingly significant for it frequently reconfigures nations or national boundaries, displaces populations and ethnic proportion, devastates land or even civilization, and is even waged against each other for the sake of war that is usually "full of sound and fury", but really "signifies nothing". As humans fought, they also "wrote" about their fighting in such multifarious media and modes of representation as literature, art, music, and dance of every genre; film, television, radio, and the internet; and games of every description. In poetry, to find words to convey this massive and complex phenomenon encounters special difficulties: logical, ethical, psychological, and other myriad ones such as censorship, political expediency, and squeamishness.

The British and Americans largely inherited the culture of the Anglo-Saxons, who fought, and accordingly wrote about their fighting. Like those special difficulties other races have encountered, they have always been to find the words for war and to interrogate them at every stage. From 1914 to 1918, hundreds of their young men in uniform joined the first global "total war" and took to writing poetry as a way of striving to express extreme emotion at the very edge of experience, and their poetic production has endured to become what is called "a sacred national text", at the same time generating such a new literary genre, as stated above.

2. Theorizing War in Poetic Representation

In his posthumously published *On War* (1832), Carl von Clausewitz (1780–1831) wrote: "War is thus an act of force to compel our enemy to do our will."[1] The Clausewitzian conception of war is absolutely right in the general sense of military science, but it does not provide an ethical judgment for what war is or means. The key question is who "our enemy" is, which requires further specification in any literary criticism. There are wars and different wars: inter-national wars, in which the conflicting parties are the states; civil wars, in which the conflicting parties are domestic political entities; the so-called current "wars on terror", in which the warring parties are ambivalent, and etc. As a state activity pursued to fulfill the ends of policy, the resort to war seems to be the monopoly of the state, and warfare is therefore solely a feature of international politics. As civil conflicts conducted to define the state, whether in terms of religion, ethnicity, or governmental structure, wars have always tended to be fought with no less brutality and no less perseverance. Terrorism and violence characterized is deemed not to be wars in any normative sense, where such conception has been broadened to embrace many more levels of violence, including its use for purposes that are not strictly political, thus the adoption of the "global war on terror" (by the US, for instance) is largely oxymoronic usage.

The warring subjects have over-determined the nature of wars. To go to war, the subject has at first to create or identify its enemy by manufacturing collective identity or collective divide between "we" and "them". A state or a collective is always justified and obliged to resort to such an organized violence, as Niccolò Machiavelli (1469–1527) says in his *The Prince* (1532): "A ruler…should have no other objective and no other concern, nor occupy himself with anything else except war and its methods and practices."[2] The frequently discussed *jus ad bellum* framed in terms of a state's or political collective's decision to resort to violence has always been heavily focused, and a Marxian or Marxist conception and interpretation has been strikingly the most convincing. The Marxist theoretical tradition insists on "the state as the institution beyond all others whose function…is to maintain and defend class domination and exploitation", and in their classical formulation in the *Communist Manifesto*, Marx and Engels wrote that "the executive of the modern state is but a committee for managing the common affairs of the whole bourgeoisie."[3] Marx and Engels have offered a historicized critique of Hegel's conception of the state as the embodiment of society's general interest, and

---

1 Carl von Clausewitz, *On War*, ed. and trans. Michael Howard and Peter Paret. New Jersey: Princeton University Press, 1976, p.75.

2 Niccolò Machiavelli, *The Prince*, ed. Quentin Skinner and Russell Price. New York: Cambridge University Press, 1988, pp. 51-52.

3 Tom Bottomore, and et al, *A Dictionary of Marxist Thought*. Maiden, Massachusetts: Blackwell, 2001, p. 520.

argued for instrumentality of the state marking the hard fact that, as has been summarized, "the state is a neutral warrant of the general interest is not only an illusion handed out by corrupt political scientists, but part of the politico-philosophical folklore used by the dominant class to legitimize its dominance and to reproduce the mode of production that makes its dominance possible," and "the state is thus derivative of a particular kind of empirical state: a bourgeois state sustained by a bourgeois ideology within the same super-structural arrangement."[4]

The Marxist conception of war in its critique of the state is overwhelmingly illuminating, and can thus lead to such a conclusion: All wars in history have been resorted to legitimizing the dominants and thus reproducing the mode of production before the advent of socialism or communism that serves the interests of the people while containing the ruling or dominant. In order to launch and wage their self-interested wars whether in the name of the state or collective, the dominants have to invent a system of ideas and values that fosters a layered system of warring ideologies, in Marxian terms, a system of "false consciousness" or as Dipak K. Gupta has termed "collective madness" in his studies of "social order and political pathology". From the killing fields of the Holocaust in Europe, the massacres of the indigenous population in Latin America, the turn-of-the-century vigilantism in the United States, to frequent genocides or a violent civil wars pandemic across the globe, "human history is full of such appalling stories."[5] Perhaps, the only "therapeutic" wars to various symptoms of "collective madness" are what the Marxist tradition has called the "revolution wars", which can be ethically justified by the simple fact that "the people liberate themselves" or defend their national or collective interests against their aggressors or oppressors. This stand or standpoint will be adhered to in theorizing and interpreting literature of war in general and poetry of war in particular.

The Anglo-American war poetry is a vehicle of representing their history and ideology that can be theorized as such: those wars that the British and Americans participated as a state agent represented their ideologies of "national collective madness" except for their participation as wars of defense; those wars that take place in their respective domestic spheres dwells on how the people's interests can be clearly defined; and thus poetic representation that propagates or negates these ethical standards witnesses an urgency of specific "historicized" analysis. To proceed with such a theorization, the critical anthology will frequently make such distinctions; between the state and society as it has become blurred due to an increasing diffusion of power within societies, between collective madness and revolutionary enthusiasm as it has always been displaced for the dominants' manipulation of power; between collective identities and individual experience as a collective one moves to the extreme spectrum while individual transgression starts and thus the collective madness quickly turns catastrophic.

---

4 Jens Bartelson, The Critique of the State. Cambridge and New York: Cambridge University Press, 2001, p. 127.

5 Dipak K. Gupta, *Path to Collective Madness: A Study in Social Order and Political Pathology*. Westport, Connecticut and London: Praeger, 2001, p.8.

This Marxist scheme of war and poetic representation not only initiates a refreshed understanding and evaluation of past poets writing wars, but also generates a new requirement for the way we read and revere them in identifying what we are and what we want to be, as a critic or reader of any piece of war writing or discourse.

3. Looking for Origins and Beginnings

Perhaps, the earliest recorded war poetry is thought to be written by Enheduanna, a priestess from Sumer, the ancient land that is now Iraq, where she riled against war in about 2300 BC:

> You are blood rushing down a mountain,
> Spirit of hate, greed and anger,
> dominator of heaven and earth!

As the English people and their national identity were formulated during a long process of constant ethnic hybridization and integration, the English language evolved along a complex tapestry of insistent developments and short, sharp shocks, of isolation and mutual influences, and of borrowings and obsolescence, so is poetry representing wars accompanied with its history as an independent discipline. In Great Britain, war has always been a powerful and enduring cultural force shaping its imaginative literature. As a capacious category, British war poetry has its origins from the diverse literary activity of ancient Greece and Rome, such as Homer's *Iliad* and *Odyssey* (c. 750 BCE), poems of wars as the so-called central text of Greco-Roman literary culture, and Vergil's *Aeneid* (the late 1st century BCE) depicting adventures of Aeneas after the Trojan War with illustrious historical background for the Roman Empire. Another important origin is *The Bible*, in which those biblical wars dealing with conflicts soaked in blood has to a greater extent doomed both creeds and deeds in the English poetic tradition, as one scholar has put it: "The presence in the Western world of a Christian tradition as a continuous background, albeit a vaguely defined one without a univocal meaning, is not an element for leveling out conflicts; on the contrary, it is (or has become) a constitutive factor in promoting them, and can exacerbate them."[6] The rich varieties of classical antiquity grappling with the problem of how to depict war and its effects characterize those wars in epic, martial poems, lyrics or elegiacs, and historiography, contributes to later war literature for their formal features and thematic concerns memorializing great martial deeds, as Kate McMoughlin's edited *The Cambridge Companion to War Writing* (2009) has such a good summary: "classical war literature's legacy to Britain and America is multifarious, and goes beyond the simple analogizing of modern conflicts to ancient. The military writing of the

---

6 Gianni Vattimo, After Christianity, trans. Luca D'Isanto. New York: Columbia University Press, 2002, p. 93.

Greco-Roman world developed formal structures and motifs upon which subsequent writers have often drawn, as well as initiating methodological concerns of ongoing significance. And in the sphere of war literature, as elsewhere, the classical world continues to provide a useful foil for contemporary themes and preoccupations."[7]

Despite all those multifarious legacies, the British war poetry has its beginnings in its own historical and linguistic formation. The earliest form of English is called the Old English or Anglo-Saxon (c. AD 550–AD 1066), thus the earliest war poetry in English accordingly begins from such a historic process. As the highest achievement of Old English literature, the heroic national epic *Beowulf* may initiate a good beginning, but its denomination of the Scandinavian hero Beowulf, its lack of historical Beowulf, and more importantly its seemingly non-human or supernatural warfare may exclude itself from what is categorized as "war poetry", so is the Welsh poet Aneirin's *The Gododdin* preserved in "The Book of Aneirin" manuscript in the *Historia Brittonum* (written c. 830) for its language (translated from the Welsh by Joseph P. Clancy). *Beowulf* is believed to have been composed between AD 700 and AD 750 dealing with events of the early 6th century, and Aneirin is one of five poets renowned among the Welsh in the 6th century, relating in poetic form that at some time around AD 600, Mynyddawg Mwynfawr, a king of the North British people known as the Gododdin, assembled 300 Celtic warriors and feasted them for a year at his court in Edinburgh, before leading them southward; they encountered the English hosts at Catterick in Yorkshire, and in the ensuing battle all, or all but a handful, were killed.

The pre-historical English language was in the womb before the end of about 500 AD, the Old English was born and growing in the cradle from about AD 500 to about AD 1100, and wars taking place during the transitional period from the Old English to Middle English (c. AD 1100 – c. AD 1500) [8]are "The Battle of Brunanburh" (AD 937) and "The Battle of Maldon" (991 AD), battles before "The Battle of Hastings" (AD 1066) of the Norman Conquest, in which William, Duke of Normandy won his decisive victory and effected profound political, administrative, and social metamorphoses in the British Isles. It is for this good reason that poetry writing the former two battles can be taken as the proper beginning of the English war poetry, but this critical anthology sets *Beowulf* as a beginning only to mediate the British poetic tradition.

4. Marking Genealogy, Canonization and Periodization

Throughout history, poets have expressed contradictory ideas about their roles in wartime

---

7 Kate McLoughlin, ed., *The Cambridge Companion to War Writing*. Cambridge: Cambridge University Press, 2009, p. 79.

8 Explanatory Notes: In development periodization of the English language, different studies do use different demarcations. The main phases can be conveniently divided, but the dates attributed to the various phases are arbitrary only for convenient markers offering a general idea of the timescales involved.

and postwar reflections. To acknowledge Shelley's notion that poets are the "unacknowledged legislators of the world," Harriet Monroe once wrote: "What is the fundamental, the essential and psychological cause of war? … The feeling that war is beautiful still lingers in men's hearts, a feeling founded on world-old savageries—love of power, of torture, of murder, love of big stakes in a big game." She continued: "This feeling must be destroyed, as it was created, through the imagination. It is work for a poet."[9]

The critical anthology acknowledges Harriet Monroe's judgment of war as an insatiable "love of power, of torture, of murder, love of big stakes in a big game", leading to such a logical argument that war and especially that glorification of war can be regarded as "cultural pathology" and war poetry performs a fundamental mission of a "cultural critique" or "cultural therapy". If literature is a textually transmitted virus, then war as a cultural virus must be historically, politically, culturally or socially toxic. To this extent, war indicates a system of such a historical, political and cultural pathology.

As a scientific study of the nature of a disease and its causes, processes, development, and consequences, the scientific terminology "pathology" often deals with the structural and functional changes in abnormal physical and biological conditions, thus also called "pathobiology". It is here used as a metaphor for cultural studies in terms of the pathology of our shared ideas, values and behaviors that have constituted a communal or collective culture. In addition, pathology also conceives a broader meaning in the sciences of the study of disorders, not specifically in such a discipline as psychology, which is termed as "psychopathology," or simply "pathology," indicating disorders within its domain (mental, emotional and behavioral) to be forms of "illness" or "disease." When it is appropriated in the field of the study of collective disorders in the domain of culture, it can thus be termed as "cultural pathology" and "patho-culturology." Therefore, the terminology "cultural pathology" here basically refers to "communal" or "social" psychoses or neuroses as represented in war and war writing.

As the system of shared beliefs, values, customs, behaviors, and artifacts transmitted from generation to generation through acquisition or learning, the complex whole of culture has been incessantly contaminated by the dominant ideology that serves the very interests of a particular class at a particular time in history, and with its dominant discourse of power, its "true" but "false" consciousness, or its "imaginary relation to the real conditions of existence", it has become merely an instrument of social reproduction or social control. It is such a "lived" or "perceived" culture thus contaminated and transformed by the dominant ideology that is pathological in nature but that humans have acquired and used it to cope with the world. Thus, "cultural pathology" is proposed as a constructive approach to the study of culture in general and as an interdisciplinary study of literature and war in particular. Such a cultural pathology

---

9 Harriet Monroe wrote these words for an editorial called "The Poetry of War," which appeared in the September 1914 issue of the magazine—the first of many special war numbers *Poetry* would produce over the decades.

of war covers four categories of pathological cultures: 1) those "cultures" that disable the natural subject's physical body; 2) those that cripple the natural subject's mode of thinking or psychological wellbeing; 3) those that drag the social development into long terms of inertia and stagnancy; 4) and finally, those that plunge the whole community into a state of insanity and devastation.

Regarding genealogy, a history-toxic culture of war, concerning the reproduction of power, depends on the historical genealogy as a legitimating force. Culture is that "abode" that power is frequently exercised apart from any changes of the regimes, or power has always corrupted culture through historical genealogy. In this light, the genealogy of British and American war poetry has transmitted a diseased conception of war and at the same time a constant therapy of those "beautiful feelings" about war, especially in the modern and contemporary antiwar movements, in those poetic traditions that have questioned the legitimacy of the state, criticized the glorification of nationalism as "an imagined community" and worshipped the dominant power at all manipulating levels.

Canonization, or canon formation, is an important category for the present critical anthology. Representational exclusion has served as a basic organizing principle for all war poetry anthologies. The current principle follows the three aspects: Historically, it tries to be comprehensive, selecting as many as possible war poems from British and American history and their involvements with wars, the objective of which is to provide the Chinese reader with a comprehensive scope of war writings in English, and for the modern and contemporary war writings, it intends to select and include those marginal, left-wing, and "revolutionary" poets who have been often ignored or neglected by the Western ideologies in canon formation such as Rupert John Cornford (1915–1936), Sylvia Townsend Warner (1893–1978), and so on; Thematically, it lean heavily on those "anti-war" poetic writings, especially foregrounding our Chinese ideologies of Marxian concept of class confrontation and civilian harmony.

Periodization, or period division, has always been an ideological construction of knowledge. The anthological research leans heavily on its periodization as war-related demarcations. Poets are chronologically arranged according to the chronology of wars with Anglo-American involvements. Focusing on the poets' verse composition, a very short introduction will be positioned when the poet's war writing appears for the first time. When the poet's another piece of war writing appears, only the excerpted poem or poems are presented.

In addition to the inclusion of some Irish poets, the anthology also includes a number of Australian, Canadian, South African poets before the Second World War. The reasons are that they all belong to the Commonwealth of Nations, or formerly British Commonwealth of Nations (1931–1949). The Commonwealth is now a free association of sovereign states comprising the United Kingdom and a number of its former dependencies who acknowledge the British monarch as symbolic head of their association, and from 1965 on the Commonwealth Secretariat were established in London to organize and coordinate

Commonwealth activities.

5. War Poetry Studies and Anti-war Activities

In the United States, there is such a great project as "The Dean Echenberg War Poetry Collection". According to its self-introduction, it consists of war poetry written by men, women and children of all nationalities, languages and conflicts, who have experienced war and then wrote about their experiences in the form of poetry. The collection began in the 1960's and currently consist of over 6,500 volumes, spanning the time from the first appearance of the written word to the present day, from the war poetry of the Sumerians to the war poetry arising from nearby conflicts in the Middle East, including related anthologies, manuscripts, biographies, bibliographies, links to online resources, critical examinations, reviews and etc. It is a living collection that continues to grow with the addition not only of published texts but also with links to important online war poetry resources. Dean Echenberg was a flight surgeon during the Vietnam War who later became the director of disease control for the City of San Francisco during the first years of the AIDS crisis.

In the United Kingdom, The War Poets Association (WPA) is engaged in war poets of all periods and nationalities, with a primary focus on conflicts since 1914: mainly the First World War, Spanish War 1936–1939, the Second World War and wars in Ireland. There are already many societies dedicated to individual war poets; one of the WPA's aims is to work with these and others to help promote joint activities and events of mutual interest.

One of the most important global movements is the "War and Worldwide Action to Stop Wars". Poets have their special missions and responsibilities. The Global Movement of Poets is as such: "Poets against the War" that erupted in February 2003, protested the invasion of Iraq by the Bush administration. Within a few weeks, the movement ballooned into an international phenomenon, with over 13,000 poets submitting their poetry to the web site to protest the war. The movement inspired the 2004 documentary film *Voices in Wartime*, and then the Voices Education Project, with its mission to amplify the voices of veterans and civilian witnesses to war, in order to heal the wounds of war and lay the basis for a more peaceful world. Andrew Himes was co-founder of "Poets Against the War" (with Sam Hamill and Emily Warn), executive producer of *Voices in Wartime*, and founder of *Voices*, which has now become the education program of the Charter for Compassion.

Voices in Wartime began in 2004 as a feature-length documentary that sharply etches the experience of war through powerful images and the words of poets – unknown and world-famous. Soldiers, journalists, historians and experts on combat interviewed in "Voices in Wartime" add diverse perspectives on war's effects on soldiers, civilians and society. In *Voices in Wartime*, poets around the world, from the United States and Colombia to Britain and Nigeria, to Iraq and India, share their views and experiences of war that extend beyond national borders and into the depth of the human soul. The film and its curricula are now a project of "The Charter for Compassion".

As history has already loomed into the new millennium, technological advancements, particularly in military technology, have developed more powerful ways to massacre millions of people and even wipe out the whole humanity. The rapidly increasingly destructive consequences of modern warfare has apparently brought a hideous pattern of terror over a long time, while Albert Einstein once stated with a particular concern for the consequences and costs of the newly developed atom bomb: "I know not with what weapons World War III will be fought, but World War IV will be fought with sticks and stones." Should humanity have a desire to survive, it calls for the poets or all artists' mission to "stop all wars".

Contemporary studies of war poetry multiplied together with the atmosphere that studies of wars exploded. Anti-war voices and activities are loud enough to be heard all over the globe. It is under this "significant" context that the present critical anthology wishes to take a part.

Chapter I

Poetry of British Classical Wars from National Formation to the

English Revolution (The Beginnings –1651)

From the beginnings of its national formation to the "Civil Wars" (1642–1651), Britain had witnessed waves of ethnic immigration and integration, constant conquests and naturalization by such aliens as the Romans, the Vikings and the Normans, until a unified national identity was established in the 11th century and the national sovereignty characteristic of the modern state was accomplished in the middle of the 17th century. While the pre-historical British wars have not been clearly recorded, the English nationality was born in a series of alien invasions and conquests, making its national identity characteristically bellicose or belligerent and a national culture inherently pathological: Conquerors has become the ethnic fathers. In 55 BCE, the Romans led by Julius Caesar sailed across the English Channel and conquered Britain, and nearly 100 years later, in AD 43, the Roman emperor Claudius invaded Britain again, making part of the island a province of their huge empire called "Britannia". Beginning from the 5th century and as the Roman rule got weaker, the Germanic tribes known as the Angles, the Saxons, the Jutes, and Frisians invaded the former Roman colony with a fresh influx of foreign settlers, bringing with them their language, their paganism, and their distinctive warrior traditions. Such a national origin, as has been now claimed by the "Anglo-Saxon Britain" (AD 600–AD 900), in fact cherishes a displaced genealogy from native fathers to alien invaders.

The Anglo-Saxons are illiterate, and the earliest of their records are only inventive lists of rulers who established separate kingdoms: the Saxons in the south and west; the Angles in the east and north; and the Jutes on the Isle of Wight and the mainland opposite. It is left for the literary to restore this cultural genealogy, in which those legendary stories of King Arthur retold again and again across the British history seem to have been serving as the misplaced cure: King Arthur must be a very brave warrior around the year AD 450, or AD 500, or AD 525, though not even named Arthur, or a figure of imagination or a real person, leads the remnants of Romanized British resistance against a steady onslaught of these foreign pagan invaders, who have later become the ancestors of the British nationalities.

Conquests and being conquered constantly change their roles. What King Arthur has restored is the legacy of Romanized Britain rather than native Britain, and thus has identically inherited a misplaced "father". So is Alfred the Great (AD 849–AD 899). When Britain was robbed by the Danish Vikings who came from Norway and Denmark, King Alfred defended as such until Britain first became one single kingdom under his great-grandson, Edgar, in 959. The next 100 years seems to be in order and stability until the Norman Conquest of 1066 that results ultimately in profound political, administrative, and social changes in the British Isles. Starting from the Battle of Hastings (1066), Britain entered one of the largest sections of the Nation, spanning over three centuries of the so-called "the Middle Ages" to the late 15th century, which were rampant with wars with France such as the Hundred Years War (1337–1453) and the Wars of the Roses (1455–1487). From the Renaissance and Reformation to the Revolution and Restoration, Britain witnessed the Tudor Re-conquest of Ireland in the 1540s, the Defeat of the Spanish Armada in 1588, the Thirty Years War (1618–1648), and the British Civil Wars (1642–1651). As the demarcation line from the classic to the modern period, the British Civil Wars polarised society largely along class lines: Parliament forces, called "Roundheads", drew most of its support from the middle classes, while the king's army, called "Cavaliers", was supported by the nobility, the clergy, and the peasantry. It greatly shook England, Wales, and Scotland with a struggle for power until its final solution by the "Glorious Revolution".

As warfare is a constant of political and civic life during this long period of about 1000 years' history, the prevalence of war both as a theme and form has been remarkable in such national epics focusing on human-supernatural conflicts as *Beowulf* (?– the late 8th century), such heroic poems as *The Battle of Brunanburh*[1] in *The Anglo-Saxon Chronicle* (compiled in around AD 890. at the command of King Alfred the Great), such heroic, lyrical or elegiac poems as *The Battle of Maldon* (the late 10th century), such legendary romances as *King Horn* (c.1250)[2], *Guy of Warwick* and *Beves of Hampton* (in the 14th century Auchinleck manuscript)

---

1 "Brunanburh" is the old name for "Bromborough" used until about 1732, and the Battle of Brunanburh was fought in 937, which is one of the bloodiest battles ever fought on British soil and the greatest single battle in Anglo-Saxon history before the Battle of Hastings (1066). The poem celebrates the victory of the West-Saxon king Athelstan (the grandson of Alfred the Great) and his brother Edmund over the allied forces of Scots, Picts, Welsh, and Vikings.

2 *King Horn* is frequently called the earliest English-language romance, which contains about 1,500 lines, based on an Anglo-Norman romance, telling the story of a heroic Scottish prince's successful fight to regain his kingdom after his expulsion by invaders.

and those various versions of heroic exploits of King Arthur and the Round Table, e.g., *Morte Arthure* (the 14th century).

A peculiar feature of these earliest war writing or poems is their anonymity. As the long night of medieval darkness became less dark and bright prospect of the English Renaissance loomed large along the horizon, not only did history become clearly recorded, but authorship became individually marked. Geoffrey Chaucer's (circa 1343–1400) great Trojan romance *Troilus and Criseyde* (circa 1382–1386) writes the war topic, and in his *The Canterbury Tales* (circa 1375–1400), he brings together legendary and contemporary warfare in the figure of the Knight and his tale, which has long been characteristic of the Medieval war poetry.

The English Renaissance began in about 1500 and spanned through the first few decades of the next century, characterised by increased affluence for the nation, civil unrest associated with the War of the Roses (1455–1487), and changes in popular thinking and cultural standards among the populace. Queen Elizabeth I was credited with spurring literature and theatre in the years of the English Renaissance. Homer was not known until the rediscovery of Greek texts in the Renaissance, alongside Vergil's *Aeneid*. Other great events include the Protestant Reformation and the establishment of the Church of England orchestrated by King Henry VIII. Renaissance philosophers and artists revisited the ideas, learning and artistic conventions of antiquity, as a more secular view of human nature and life itself began to take hold in European culture. William Shakespeare wrote his many plays, and his ten English history plays are where he engaged most profoundly with the experience and recording of early modern warfare.

The English Reformation was a series of events in the 16th century England by which the Church of England broke away from the authority of the Roman Catholic Church. It had begun as an assertion of English nationhood under a monarch who saw himself as head, protector, and arbiter of a national Church, but ended as a challenge to the idea of monarchy itself. The English Revolution (the English Civil Wars), also respectively categorised as the "Great Rebellion", "Puritan Revolution", or "English Bourgeois Revolution", was the discrediting of the idea of the divine right of kings, the belief that parliament was supreme in political matters, and that the English monarch had to rule in a manner which was limited by the idea of a constitutional monarchy. Charles I was executed, and Oliver Cromwell (1599–1658) became Lord Protector. Oliver Cromwell led parliamentary forces in the English Civil Wars and served as the lord protector of England, Scotland, and Ireland (1653–1658) during the republican Commonwealth, and helped to enlarge and sustain a Puritan attitude of mind, both in Great Britain and in North America, which continued to influence political and social life until modern times.

Here in this critical anthology, the "British Classical Wars" refers to those wars before the British Civil Wars whether taking place in the British Isles or outside and with the Anglo-Saxons race involved, including the Anglo-Saxons wars, Medieval and Early modern wars, characteristics of which serve as the foundation of the English national identity and its genealogy, which is, of course, evident in that war poetry before the British Civil Wars had been influenced by *The Bible* and Classical Greek or Roman war literature.

1. Inventing National Genealogy in Old English War Poetry

National genealogy is an important instrument of legitimating dominant power. Patriotic "imagined community" constructed national consciousness, fabricated collective identity, and all these contributed to the formation of the ideological state apparatus. These ancient war poems provided an account of ideal legendary warriors in order to establish the core heroic values of bravery and patriotism. Such heroic poetry had been supported and strengthened by their cultures or civilisations over time. To sacrifice one's life and what is best for someone consequently became the intensely wanted attribute for each soldier to fight. Whereas the Middle Ages had its glorious tales of self-sacrifice and martyrdom, the spirited behaviour of warring parties had dramatically altered by the 17th century. To some extent, the English national formation goes closely together with the linguistic formation of the *Old English*, the language spoken from about AD 500 to AD 1100, one of the Germanic languages derived from a prehistoric Common Germanic originally spoken in southern Scandinavia and the northernmost parts of Germany.

Anonymous: Excerpts from *Beowulf* (c. the late 8th century)

Written in the Old English dialect sometime between the first part of the 8th century and the 10th century, the poem was considered to be the earliest English epic with some of its old linguistic and storytelling roots. Preserved in late 10th century manuscript, it was probably composed by an anonymous Anglo-Saxon poet following the versification and style of Germanic oral poetry. Beowulf, who fought two monsters, Grendel and his mother, ruled a kingdom with courage and wisdom, and killed a dragon in his last battle. Built on an alliterative, strong-stress pattern, in which each line normally contains four strongly stressed syllables, the poem deals with the Germanic forebears of the English people, specifically the Danes, who inhabited the Danish island of Zealand, and the Geats of southern Sweden. It mixes elements of the Christian tradition with the heroic ideals of a pagan, warrior society. The excerpt is from the modern standard version of Craig Williamson's translation version[3]: Lines 3137–3182, depicting the magnitude of the loss of Beowulf's funeral, which provides the last chance for his retainers and subjects to mourn together in an attempt to reaffirm their love for their lord and their sense of shared values:

> The old battle-warrior. The Geats prepared
> His funeral pyre, a splendid hoard

---

3 Craig Williamson, ed. and trans., *Beowulf and Other Old English Poems*. Philadelphia: University of Pennsylvania Press, 2011.

Hung with helmets, battle-shields,
Bright mail-coats, as Beowulf had asked.
In the middle they laid their battle-lord,
Lamenting their leader, mourning the man.
There on the barrow they woke the flame,
The greatest of funeral fires, stoking the pyre.
The wood-smoke rose to the sound of wailing
In the curling fire. The blaze was fierce,
Its fury twisted with the sound of keening.
The wind died down—the fire had ravaged
Beowulf's bone-house, hot at the heart.
Sad in spirit, they mourned their prince;
Likewise a lonely old woman of the Geats,
With her hair bound up, wove a sad lament
For her fallen lord, sang often of old feuds
Bound to fester, a fearful strife,
The invasion of enemies, the slaughter of troops,
Slavery and shame. Heaven swallowed the smoke.
Then the Geats built a barrow, broad and high,
On the sea-cliff to be seen by seafarers.
It took ten days to build that beacon,
A hero's monument. The pyre's remains,
The fire's offering of ashes and dust,
They wrapped in walls for the great warrior,
As beautiful as craftsmen knew how to build.
In that best of barrows, the Geats buried
Rings and gems, ornaments and heirlooms,
All they had hauled from the worm's hoard.
They returned to earth its ancient treasure,
The gifts of men now gold in the ground,
Where it still lies useless, unloved, unliving.

Then around Beowulf's barrow twelve
Battle-warriors rode, mourning their prince,
Keening for the king, shaping their praise
For a precious man. They spoke of sorrow,
They sang of courage, of great words and deeds,
Weaving glory with a weft of power.
When a lord's life lifts from its body-home,

It's only fitting to mourn and remember,

To lament and praise. So the Geats recalled

His great heart and lamented his fall,

Keening and claiming that of all the kings,

He was the kindest of men, most generous and just,

Most desiring of praise, most deserving of fame.

Anonymous: Excerpts from *The Battle of Brunanburh* (937)

The Battle of Brunanburh is one of the most representative national poems that defined Great Britain, of which people today know as England, Scotland and Wales for the battle was the greatest one ever fought in England. In 937, when the battle took place, Britain was a divided nation, ruled by several Kings and Earls, all vying for land and power: In the far north, there were the Celts, divided into two main Kingdoms; Alba (mainly in Scotland) led by Constantine, and Strathclyde (nowadays SW Scotland, Cumbria and parts of Wales) ruled by Owain. The poem is recorded in four manuscript copies of *The Anglo-Saxon Chronicle*, and in fact serves as the entry for the year 937, although it is entirely unclear as to whether it was written specifically for *The Anglo-Saxon Chronicle*, or an entirely independent work that was simply incorporated into later manuscript copies. *The Anglo-Saxon Chronicle* is a collection of interrelated texts that have a similar core but considerable local variations, beginning as early as the time of Julius Caesar, but most of the entries range from the 5th century to the 11th or the 12th century. Originally written in the Old English, the poem represents the battle as the continuation of a tradition of heroic action, creates an unbroken tradition of national and racial heroic glory extending from the earlier kings in the Anglo-Saxon royal genealogy of a national kingdom, and has become a poetic tradition that later poets continue to relate the topic, such as Alfred Lord Tennyson's (1809–1892) translated poem of the same title.[4]

In this year King Athelsta, ruler of earls,

Ring-giver of men, and his brother Edmund,

A proud prince won lifelong glory

At a fierce battle near Brunanburh—

Bold brothers wielding sharp, bitter swords,

Offering their enemies the edge of destruction.

The sons of Edward gave no respite—

They hacked through the shield-wall,

Splintering the hand-held, sheltering wood,

Brought death with the gift the forge-hammer left,

A whistling steel, a deadly strike.

---

4 The poem is selected from Craig Williamson, ed. and trans., *The Complete Old English Poems*. Philadelphia: University of Pennsylvania Press, 2017.

Their family legacy was firm: fight the foe,
Protect the heritage of land and treasure,
Hoard and home. Enemies perished—
Scots and seafarers, Viking pirates.
The battlefield was flattened with heavy bodies
And saturated with blood from the day's dawn—
When the star-fire sun knifed through the dark,
God's bright candle lifting its light,
Gliding high over earth's broad plains—
To the day's darkening down at long last,
As the shaping radiance slipped to its rest.
Warriors lay wounded, a multitude of men,
Their unshielded flesh in unwaking sleep.
Norsemen and Scots lay dead on the field,
Gutted by spears thrust over the shield- wall,
All of them battle-weary, sated with slaughter.
The warriors of Wessex dogged the enemy
All day long, hacking and hewing from behind
The hostile heathens with whetted swords.
Nor did the Mercians make any concessions.
They refused no hard hand-play of swords
With the savage Vikings who landed in hordes
With their leader Anlaf from across the ocean.
They rode in the belly of wood over rough waves,
A sea-steed stuffed with daring warriors
Doomed in battle. Five young kings
Were camped on the battlefield, all cold,
Tucked into a final rest with ravaging swords,
A blade's quick kiss, an unseen swipe.
Seven of Anlaf's earls, countless Scots,
And seafaring Vikings shared that bed,
Broken bodies in unbroken sleep.
Then the Norse leader was forced to flee,
Seeking protection at the ship's prow
With his paltry remnant. The sea-floater
Set sail, angling on the ocean, driven out
On the dusky waves, saving the king.
Crafty Constantine, king of the Scots,
Also fled north to his native land.

The gray-haired warrior had no need to boast

Of sword-strike and blade-play

Since his kinsmen were cut down

In the fiercest of battles. He lost many friends,

Left them sleeping in the field of slaughter.

Also his young son, savagely undone,

Went weary to bed with bitter wounds.

The crafty old king had no cause to brag

Or have sung the story of great battle-deeds.

Anlaf also sailed home, humbled.

His scop was silent, his song unsung.

With the small remnant left, they had no need

To laugh or exult over their accomplishments

In the spear-clash and battle-crush,

In that savage meeting of men and standards,

The sword-conflict with the sons of Edward.

The Norsemen sailed off in their nailed ships,

Skulking home on the sea with their battle-shame,

A hacked host of what the Saxon swords left.

They sailed on the waves of Dingesmere Sea,

Over deep water home to Dublin, humiliated.

The victorious brothers, both king and prince,

Went home to Wessex, exulting in triumph.

They left behind them a feast of corpses,

Carrion comfort for the savage scavengers,

The dark-feathered raven, his horny beak

Ravenous, the gray-feathered eagle

With his white tail, a greedy war-hawk,

And that gray stalker, the wolf in the wood.

Books tell us that never before on this island

Has there ever been such a slaughter

Of warriors struck down by the sword's edge—

Never since the Angles and Saxons came sailing

Across the broad sea, seeking Britain,

Proud warriors and battle-craftsmen

Who overcame the Welshmen, conquering their country?

They were bold in battle, eager for fame.

Anonymous: Excerpts from *The Capture of the Five Boroughs* (942)

The poem is also recorded in *The Anglo-Saxon Chronicle*. With a continuation of the Old English poetic convention to shape a sense of national cohesion and purpose, it relates that King Edward fights as a Christ-like warrior to rid Mercia of its heathen Norse invaders and free the enslaved Danes who had earlier settled there and had come to consider themselves natives.

> In this year King Edmund, lord of the English,
> Beloved protector of people, famous for great deeds,
> Conquered Mercia, overran all the boundaries,
> From Dore to Whitwell Gap and the River Humber,
> That broad stream, seizing the five boroughs—
> Leicester, Lincoln, Nottingham, Derby, and Stamford.
> The Danes living there had long been held
> In cruel captivity, heathen bondage,
> By the fierce Norsemen until finally freed
> By the brave deeds of Edmund, son of Edward,
> The worthy protector of warriors, the conquering,
> Righteous king who rescued and released them.

Anonymous: Excerpts from *The Battle of Maldon* (991)

It is an Old English heroic poem, describing a historical skirmish between the East Saxons and Viking (mainly Norwegian) raiders. The Battle took place at Maldon along the shores of the River Blackwater in Essex, where a small force of the East Saxons was cut down by the Viking invaders in AD 991. Composed in the oral tradition of Old English alliterative verse, the poem *The Battle of Maldon*, only part of which survives, takes a heroic stand by the Anglo-Saxons against the Viking invasion, which ended in utter defeat for Brithnoth and his men, offering a mournful and ambiguous celebration of heroism in its narrative of the defeat of the English. What it celebrates is not victory, but failure, a failure so heroic that the losers are remembered long after the victors are forgotten. Brithnoth is thus a caricature of British heroism that conceives a peculiarly British character.

> Then Byrhtnoth ordered every warrior to dismount,
> Let loose his horse and go forward into battle
> With faith in his own skills and bravery.
> Thus Offa's young son could see for himself
> That the earl was no man to suffer slackness.
> He sent his best falcon flying from his wrist
> To the safety of the forest and strode into the fight;

The boy's behaviour was a testament

That he would not be weak in the turmoil of battle.

Eadric too was firmly resolved to follow his leader

Into the fight. At once he hurried forward

With his spear. He feared no foe

For as long as he could lift his shield

And wield a sword: he kept his word

That he would pierce and parry before his prince.

Then Byrhtnoth began to martial his men.

He rode about, issuing instructions

As to how they should stand firm, not yielding an inch,

And how they should tightly grip their shields

Forgetting their qualms and pangs of fear.

And when he had arrayed the warriors' ranks

He dismounted with his escort at a carefully chosen place

Where his finest troops stood prepared for the fight.

Then a spokesman for the Vikings stood on the river bank

And aggressively shouted

A message from the seafarers

To Byrhtnoth, the earl, on the opposite bank.

"The brave seafarers have sent me to say to you

That they will be so good as to let you give gold rings

In return for peace. It is better for you

To buy off our raid with gold

Than that we, renowned for cruelty, should cut you down in battle.

Why destroy one another? If you're good for a certain sum,

We'll settle for peace in exchange for gold.

If you, most powerful over there, agree to this

And wisely decide to disband your men,

Giving gold to the seafarers on their own terms

In return for a truce,

We'll take to the sea with the tribute you pay

And keep our promise of peace."

Then Byrhtnoth spoke. He grasped his shield

And brandished his slender ashen spear,

Resentful and resolute he shouted his reply:

'Can you hear, you pirate, what these people say?

They will pay you a tribute of whistling spears,

Of deadly darts and proven swords,

Weapons to pay you, pierce, slit and slay you in storming battle.

Listen, messenger! Take back this reply:

Tell your people the unpleasant tidings

That over here there stands a noble earl with his troop—

Guardians of the people and of the country,

The home of Ethelred, my prince—who'll defend this land

To the last ditch. We'll sever the heathens' heads

From their shoulders. It would be much to our shame

If you took our tribute and embarked without battle

Since you've intruded so far

And so rudely into this country.

No! You'll not get your treasure so easily.

The spear's point and the sword's edge, savage battle-play,

Must teach us first that we have to yield tribute.'

Then Byrhtnoth gave word that all his warriors should walk

With their shields to the river bank.

The troops on either side could not get at one another,

For there the flood flowed after the turn of the tide;

The water streams ran together. Waiting seemed like passing years,

Waiting to cross and clash their spears.

The East-Saxons and the Ship-army

Stood beside the River Panta in proud array.

But no warrior could work harm on another

Except by the flight of a feathered arrow.

The tide ebbed; the pirates stood prepared,

Many bold Vikings ready for battle.

Then Byrhtnoth, brave protector of his men, ordered

A warrior, Wulfstan by name, to defend the ford.

He was Ceola's son, outstanding for his courage amongst courageous men

He struck the first seafarer with his spear

Who stepped intrepidly on to the ford.

Two experienced warriors stood with Wulfstan,

Ælfere and Maccus, both brave men.

Nothing could have made them take flight at the ford.

They would have defended it

For as long as they could wield their weapons.

But as it was, the Danes found the dauntless guardians

Of the ford too fierce for their liking…

The hateful strangers began to use guile

And asked if they could cross,

Leading their warriors over the water.

Then, in foolhardy pride, the earl permitted

Those hateful strangers to have access to the ford.

The son of Byrhthelm began to call out

Across the cold water (the warriors listened):

"Now the way is clear for you. Come over to us quickly,

Come to the slaughter. God alone can say

Who of us that fight today will live to fight again."

Then the wolvish Vikings, avid for slaughter,

Waded to the west across the River Panta;

The seafarers hoisted their shields on high

And carried them over the gleaming water.

Byrhtnoth and his warriors awaited them,

Ready for battle: he ordered his men

To form a phalanx with their shields, and to stand firm

Against the onslaught of the enemy. Then was the battle,

With its chance of glory, about to begin. The time had come

For all the doomed men to fall in the fight.

The clamour began; the ravens wheeled and the eagle

Circled overhead, craving for carrion; there was shouting on earth.

They hurled their spears, hard as files,

And sent sharp darts flying from their hands.

Bow strings were busy, shield parried point,

Bitter was the battle. Brave men fell

On both sides, youths choking in the dust.

Byrhtnoth's sister's son, Wulfmær, was wounded;

Slashed by the sword, he decided

To sleep on the bed of death.

This was violently requited, the Vikings were repaid in kind.

I was told that Eadweard swung his sword

So savagely—a full-blooded blow—

That a fated warrior fell lifeless at his feet.

Byrhtnoth shouted out his thanks to him,

His chamberlain, as soon as he had a chance to do so.

The brave men stood resolute, rock firm.

Each of them eagerly hunted for a way

To be first in with his spear,

Winning with his weapons the life
Of a doomed warrior; the dead sank down to the earth.
But the rest stood unshaken and Byrhtnoth spurred them on,
Inciting each man to fight ferociously
Who wished to gain glory against the Danes.
Then a brave seafarer raised up his spear,
Gripped his shield and advanced towards Byrhtnoth.
The resolute earl advanced towards the churl;
Each had evil designs on the other.
The Viking was the quicker—he hurled his foreign spear
Wounding the lord of the warriors.
Byrhtnoth broke the shaft with the edge of his shield;
The imbedded spear-head sprang out of his wound.
Then he flung his spear in fury
At the proud Viking who dared inflict such pain.
His aim was skilful. The spear
Slit open the warrior's neck.
Thus Byrhtnoth put paid to his enemy's life.
Then, for safety's sake, he swiftly hurled another
Which burst the Viking's breastplate, cruelly wounding him
In the chest; the deadly spear pierced his heart.
The brave earl, Byrhtnoth, was delighted at this;
He laughed out loud and gave thanks to the Lord
That such good fortune had been granted to him .
But one of the seafarers sent a sharp javelin
Speeding from his hand
That pierced Byrhtnoth's body, the noble thane of Ethelred.
By his side stood a young warrior,
Wulfmær by name, Wulfstan's son,
Who without a moment's hesitation
Drew out the blood-red javelin from Byrhtnoth's side
And hurled it back as hard as he could
At the man who had grievously injured his prince.
The sharp point struck home; the Viking sagged, and sank into the dust.
Another seafarer advanced on the earl, meaning to make
Short work of him and snatch away his treasures—
His armour and his rings and his ornamented sword.

2. Legitimating Dominant Power in Medieval War Poetry

The conception of the "Middle Ages" or the "Medieval Period" varies according to different categories or locations. In European history, whether it indicates a period dated from AD 476 to AD 1453 between the 5th and the 15th century (between the decline of the Roman Empire and the Renaissance), or in Great Britain, the period between approximately AD 1000 and AD 1400, covering over three centuries from the Norman Conquest to the beginning of the Tudor dynasty under Henry VII, it has been a time of legitimating power of the dominants, those kings, lords, or masters. It has often been said the period was that of the chivalric tradition with cavaliers and knights struggling for power: All men in medieval times were instructed to know how to fight and were expected to readily serve their kings at any moment; soldiers were basically medieval knights, foot soldiers, and archers. As the composition and re-composition of Arthurian legends have shown, the old conception of holy power has collapsed, and the logic of "fighting for the state power and ruling the country", as initiated from *Beowulf*, continued to be strengthened.

Layamon (the 12th century): Excerpts from *Brut* (c. 1190)

The chivalric tradition relating legends of cavaliers and knights is one of the most striking features of English medieval literature, but more of which were written in the prose romance. Layamon, the 12th century English poet and priest, made it into the poetic form by adapting Wace's *Roman de Brut*[5] into Middle English alliterative verse and thus providing the earliest version of the Arthurian story in English. His *Brut* (c. 1190) runs to 16,095 lines, expanding on Wace and adding much new material. Composed with a long alliterative line that goes back to Old English poetry, he had the two halves of a poetic line linked by rhyme as well as by alliteration, thus revealing his close ties with Germanic literary tradition.

The topic of Arthur's legendary return is conceived in a recurrent myth about a leader or hero who has not really died, or lived in some state of suspended life and will return to save his people. The narrative goes in such that after winning the continental campaign against Lucius, Arthur is forced to return to Britain upon learning that his nephew, Mordred, whom he had left behind as regent, has usurped Arthur's throne and queen; when he was mortally wounded, he was carried off to the island of Avalon to have his wounds treated, giving over the crown to his cousin Constantine, the son of Duke Cador in the year 542; evidently, the Bretons and Welsh developed this myth about Arthur in oral tradition long before it turns up in medieval chronicles.

---

5 Wace (circa 1110–1180) was a Norman cleric, born on the island of Jersey in the English Channel, then part of the dukedom of Normandy. All works, including saints' lives, *Le Roman de Brut* (1155), and *Le Roman de Rou*, were written in French verse for a lay audience, of which the former is a very free translation in eight-syllable couplets of Geoffrey of Monmouth's Latin prose *History of the Kings of Britain*.

Arthur was mortally wounded, grievously badly;

To him there came a young lad who was from his clan,

He was Cador the Earl of Cornwall's son;

The boy was called Constantine; the king loved him very much.

Arthur gazed up at him, as he lay there on the ground,

And uttered these words with a sorrowing heart:

"Welcome, Constantine; you were Cador's son;

Here I bequeath to you all of my kingdom,

And guard well my Britons all the days of your life

And retain for them all the laws which have been extant in my days

And all the good laws which there were in Uther's days.

And I shall voyage to Avalon, to the fairest of all maidens,

To the Queen Argante, a very radiant elf,

And she will make quite sound every one of my wounds,

Will make me completely whole with her health-giving potions.

And then I shall come back to my own kingdom

And dwell among the Britons with surpassing delight."

After these words there came gliding from the sea

What seemed a short boat, moving, propelled along by the tide

And in it were two women in remarkable attire,

Who took Arthur up at once and immediately carried him

And gently laid him down and began to move off.

And so it had happened, as Merlin said before:

That the grief would be incalculable at the passing of Arthur.

The Britons even now believe that he is alive

And living in Avalon with the fairest of the elf-folk,

And the Britons are still always looking for when Arthur comes returning.

Yet once there was a prophet and his name was Merlin:

He spoke his predictions, and his sayings were the truth,

Of how an Arthur once again would come to aid the English.

Anonymous: Excerpts from *Sir Gawain and the Green Knight* (c. 1400)

The Arthurian narrative poem goes on in the Anglo-Norman tradition. After the Norman Conquest, alliterative verse continued to be recited by oral poets though composed in England in the Anglo-Norman dialect with the French vernacular. To strengthen the new order, there was a movement toward a more solitary religious life and a more personal encounter with God in the 12th and 13th centuries. The 14th century produced two great English poets, Geoffrey Chaucer and the anonymous poet who wrote the *Pearl, Purity, Patience, Sir Gawain and the Green Knight*, and *St. Erkenwald*. During the late 14th century there was a renewed flowering of alliterative poetry, especially in the north and west of Britain, while *Sir Gawain and the Green Knight*, probably written around 1400, belongs to the so-called "Alliterative Revival". The poetic lines are longer and do not contain a fixed number or pattern of stresses like the classical alliterative meter of Anglo-Saxon poetry, but it still uses internal rhyme or alliteration: the words in each line rhyme with each other; the metrical form is called the "bob and wheel", where each stanza ends with a short half-line of only two syllables (the bob), followed by a mini-stanza of longer lines which rhyme internally (the wheel).The poem focuses on the young Gawain, who is a knight at the legendary court of King Arthur, relating a story of knightly deeds, sexual enticement and wild landscapes. The excerpt is the denouement of the poem.[6] In addition, the Arthurian is retold again and again throughout English history, for instance, another version in the same period, the alliterative *Morte Arthure*, which is a 4346-line Middle English alliterative poem, retelling the latter part of the legend of King Arthur, weaving together actual, legendary, and mythic notions of war not only to celebrate heroism, but also to convey tragedy and suffering. Dating from about 1400, it is preserved in a single copy, in the early 15th century Lincoln Thornton Manuscript.

> So he winds through the wilds of the world once more,
> Gawain on Gringolet, by the grace of God,
> under a roof sometimes and sometimes roughing it,
> and in valleys and vales had adventures and victories
> but time is too tight to tell how they went.
> The nick to his neck was healed by now;
> thereabouts he had bound the belt like a baldric—
> slantwise, as a sash, from shoulder to side,
> laced in a knot looped below his left arm,
> a sign that his honor was stained by sin.
> So safe and sound he sets foot in court,
> and when clansmen had learned of their comrade's return
> happiness cannoned through the echoing halls.
> The king kissed his knight and so did the queen,
> and Gawain was embraced by his band of brothers,
> who made eager enquiries, and he answered them all
> with the tale of his trial and tribulations,
> and the challenge at the chapel, and the great green chap,
> and the love of the lady, which led to the belt.
> And he showed them the scar at the side of his neck,
> confirming his breach of faith, like a badge of blame.

---

6 Selected from Simon Armitage, *Sir Gawain and the Green Knight: A New Verse Translation*. New York and London: W. W. Norton and Company, 2007. Lines: 2479-2531.

He grimaced with disgrace,

he writhed in rage and pain.

Blood flowed towards his face

and showed his smarting shame.

"Regard," said Gawain, grabbing the girdle,

"through this I suffered a scar to my skin—

for my loss of faith I was physically defaced;

what a coveting coward I became it would seem.

I was tainted by untruth and this, its token,

I will drape across my chest till the day I die.

For man's crimes can be covered but never made clean;

once entwined with sin, man is twinned for all time."

The king gave comfort, then laughter filled the castle

and in friendly accord the company of the court

allowed that each lord belonging to their Order—

every knight in the brotherhood-should bear such a belt,

a bright green belt worn obliquely to the body,

crosswise, like a sash, for the sake of this man.

So that slanting green stripe was adopted as their sign,

and each knight who held it was honored forever,

as all meaningful writings on romance remind us:

an adventure which happened in the era of Arthur,

as the chronicles of this country have stated clearly.

Since fearless Brutus first set foot

on these shores, once the siege and assault at Troy had ceased,

our coffers have been crammed

with stories such as these.

Now let our Lord, thorn-crowned,

bring us to perfect peace. AMEN.

HONY SOYT QUI MAL PENCE[7]

Geoffrey Chaucer (circa 1343–1400)

Known as the first English author or the "Father of English literature", Geoffrey Chaucer wrote in English at a time when Latin was considered the *grammatica* and most of the upper-

---

7 The Latin idiom for "Shamed be he who thinks evil" or "Shame be to the man who has evil in his mind." This is the motto of the Order of the Garter, founded c. 1350, apparently a copyist of the poem associated this order with the one founded to honor Gawain.

class English spoke French. That he chose the language of the lower-class Saxons rather than Norman nobility has perplexed readers and scholars for centuries. In 1359, he joined the English army's invasion of France during the Hundred Years' War (1337–1453) and was taken prisoner. The War dominated life in England and France for well over a century. His earliest poems, *The Book of the Duchess* (circa 1368–1369) and *The Parliament of Birds* (circa 1378–1381), rest on a heavy French base. His transitional works such as *Anelida and Arcite* (c. 1379), *Parlement of Foules* (c. 1382), and *Troilus and Criseyde* (c. 1385) shows his writing of the Italian influence, of which the latter can be considered as the first English novel because of the way its main characters are always operating at two levels of response, verbal and intellectual.

Chaucer's most famous work is *The Canterbury Tales* (circa 1375–1400). According to the original plan of 120 tales in which each of thirty pilgrims tells four, he never finished all, among which the composition of none of the tales can be accurately dated. He draws on the technique of the frame tale as practised by Boccaccio in his *The Decameron* (1349–1351), contributes to many recognisably "modern" novelistic techniques, including psychologically complex characters running the spectrum of the middle class from the Knight to the Pardoner and the Summoner, and subtle distinctions of the class become the focal point of the narrative. Various wars are most typically presented in *The Knight's Tale*, relating the romance in 2,350 lines, which Chaucer had written before beginning *The Canterbury Tales*, representing one of the 29 archetypes of late-medieval English society with insight and humour. The excerpt concerns a briefing of the Knight's deeds in "The Prologue", hybridising legendary and contemporary warfare in the figure of the Knight and his tale: the Knight's many crusading battles against the Muslims in Spain, North Africa, and the Near East; and with Teutonic knights against pagans in the Baltic.

Excerpts from *The Knight's Tale*

But none the less, while I have time and space,
Before my story takes a further pace,
It seems a reasonable thing to say,
What the condition was, the full array
Of each of hem, as it appeared to me,
According to profession and degree,
And what apparel they were riding in:
And at a Knight, I therefore will begin.
A knight there was, and he a worthy man,
Who, from the moment that he first began
To ride about the world, loved chivalry,
Truth, honour, freedom and all courtesy.

Full worthy was he in his liege-lord's war,
And therein had he ridden, no man more,
As well in Christendom as heathen places,
And ever honoured for his noble graces.

       When we took Alexandria, he was there,
He often sat at the table in the chair
Of honour, above all nations' knights in Prussia.
In Latvia raided he, and Russia,
No christened man so often of his degree.
In far Granada the siege was he
Of Algeciras, and in Belmarie.
At Ayas was he and at Satalye
When they were won; and on the Middle Sea
At many a noble meeting chanced to be.
Of mortal battles he had fought fifteen,
And he'd fought for our faith at Tramissene
Three times in lists, and each time slain his foe.
This self-same worthy knight had been also
At one time with the lord of Palatye
Against another heathen in Turkey:
And always won he sovereign fame for prize.
Though so illustrious, he was very wise
And bore himself as meekly as a maid.
He never yet had any vileness said,
In all his life, to whatsoever might.
He was a truly perfect, gentle knight.

       But now, to tell you all of his array,
His steeds were good, but yet he was not gay.
Of simple fustian wore he a jupon
Sadly discoloured by his habergeon;
For he had lately come from his voyage
And now was going on this pilgrimage.

     …

But in the dome of mighty Mars the red
With different figures all the sides were spread;
This temple, less in form, with equal grace,
Was imitative of the first in Thrace:
For that cold region was the loved abode
And sovereign mansion of the warrior god.

The landscape was a forest wide and bare,

Where neither beast nor humankind repair;

The fowl that scent afar the borders fly,

And shun the bitter blast, and wheel about the sky.

A cake of scurf lies baking on the ground,

And prickly stubs, instead of trees, are found;

Or woods with knots and knares deformed and old;

Headless the most, and hideous to behold:

A rattling tempest through the branches went,

That stripped 'em bare, and one sole way they bent.

Heaven froze above, severe; the clouds congeal,

And through the crystal vault appeared the standing hail.

Such was the face without: a mountain stood

Threatening from high, and overlooked the wood;

Beneath the lowering brow, and on a bent,

The temple stood of Mars armipotent:

The frame of burnished steel, that cast a glare

From far, and seemed to thaw the freezing air.

A strait, long entry to the temple led,

Blind with high walls, and horror overhead:

Thence issued such a blast and hollow roar,

As threatened from the hinge to heave the door.

In through that door, a northern light there shone;

'Twas all it had, for windows there were none.

The gate was adamant; eternal frame!

Which, hewed by Mars himself, from Indian quarries came,

The labour of a god; and all along

Tough iron plates were clenched to make it strong.

3. Secularizing Power in the English Renaissance War Poetry

Like the Renaissance in other parts of Europe, the English Renaissance also witnessed a sudden new growth of activities or interests in humanity itself, as has deeply conceived in the new conception of literature and arts: The medieval synthesis collapsed before the new science, new religion, and new humanism; the strengthening of new secular ideas lead to drastic advancements in education and the growth of a strong body of secular literature; and the wide dissemination of new learning produces a literary revival that occurred in a society rife with tensions, uncertainties, and competing versions of order and authority, calling into question the newly won certainties and the older truths that they were dislodging. In short, this doubling of new possibilities and new doubts, simultaneously apprehended, gives an immediate deconstruction of the holiness of power that the dominants have attempted to contain, having provided a ready therapy to the long-existing cultural pathology.

Henry Howard (1517–1547)

Henry Howard, Earl of Surrey, is a British poet and soldier. For a poet, he continued in Sir Thomas Wyatt's (1503–1542) footsteps on the English sonnet form while the two were both often entitled with "father of the English sonnet". They established the form that was later used by Shakespeare and others, and they also introduced blank verse to English—a form that Henry Howard used in his translations of Virgil. For a soldier, he was a mighty fighter, like his father and grandfather: In October 1536, he served with his father in quelling "The Pilgrimage of Grace rebellion", which protested against the King's dissolution of the monasteries. He also served the king in Flanders with the English army on the side of Holy Roman Emperor Charles V, who was seeking to acquire the Netherlands. His major publication of poems is included in his posthumous *Tottel's Miscellany* (1557), of which of the 271 poems in the collection, 40 were by Surrey, 96 by Wyatt, and the rest by various courtier poets. The excerpted poem is usually named "An Epitaph on Clere, Surrey's Faithful Friend and Follower", which says that Henry Howard and Thomas Clere, his squire and companion, fought together in expeditions to Kelsal in Scotland, Landrecy in the Netherlands, and Boulogne in France. At the siege of Montreuil, on 19 September 1544, Clere received wounds while protecting Surrey, from which he died the following spring. He was buried at Lambeth, in the chapel assigned to the Howards.

"An Epitaph on Clere, Surrey's Faithful Friend and Follower"

Clere of the County of Cleremont though hight;
Norfolk sprang thee, Lambeth holds thee dead,
Within the womb of Ormond's race thou bred,
And saw'st thy cousin crownèd in thy sight.
Shelton for love, Surrey for Lord thou chase:
Ay me, while life did last that league was tender;
Tracing whose steps thou saw'st Kelsal blaze,
Laundersey burnt, and battered Bullen render.
At Muttrell gates, hopeless of all recure,
Thine Earl half dead gave in thy hand his Will;
Which cause did thee this pining death procure,
Ere summers four times seven thou could'st fulfil.
　　　Ah! Clere! if love had booted, care, or cost,

Heaven had not won, nor Earth so timely lost.

Edmund Spenser (1552/53–1599)

Edmund Spenser is one of the preeminent poets of the English language, who strongly extends the genealogy of English poetic culture initiated by Geoffrey Chaucer. Among his many contributions to English poetic tradition, he is the originator and namesake of the Spenserian stanza and the Spenserian sonnet, represented respectively in his classical pastoral *The Shepheardes Calendar* (1579), which marks the beginning of the English Renaissance in literature, and his great epic poem *The Faerie Queene* (1590–1596), written in honour of Queen Elizabeth I and celebration of the Tudor dynasty. With the virtuous exploits of 12 knights in the service of the mythical King Arthur, the latter is not only an epic celebration of Queen Elizabeth, the Protestant faith and the English nation, but also a chivalric romance, full of jousting knights and damsels in distress, dragons, witches, enchanted trees, wicked magicians, giants, dark caves, and shining castles. The following two excerpts are respectively from his *The Faerie Queene* and his short poem *Astrophel: A Pastorall Elegie Upon the Death of the Most Noble and Valorous Knight, Sir Philip Sidney* (1595) .[8]

Excerpts from *The Faerie Queene*

Gentle Knight was pricking on the plaine,
    Y cladd in mightie armes and siluer shielde,
    Wherein old dints of deepe wounds did remaine,
    The cruell markes of many'a bloudy fielde;
    Yet armes till that time did he neuer wield:
    His angry steede did chide his foming bitt,
    As much disdayning to the curbe to yield:
    Full iolly knight he seemd, and faire did sitt,
As one for knightly giusts and fierce encounters fitt.

But on his brest a bloudie Crosse he bore,
    The deare remembrance of his dying Lord,
    For whose sweete sake that glorious badge he wore,
    And dead as liuing euer him ador'd:
    Vpon his shield the like was also scor'd,
    For soueraine hope, which in his helpe he had:
    Right faithfull true he was in deede and word,

---

8 The poem alludes that in 1586, the Earl of Leicester unsuccessfully attempted to wrest the city of Zutphen in the Netherlands from the Spanish. Sir Philip Sidney, his thirty-two-year-old nephew, was killed in the skirmish.

But of his cheere did seeme too solemne sad;
Yet nothing did he dread, but euer was ydrad.

Vpon a great aduenture he was bond,
 That greatest *Gloriana* to him gaue,
 That greatest Glorious Queene of *Faerie* lond,
 To winne him worship, and her grace to haue,
 Which of all earthly things he most did craue;
 And euer as he rode, his hart did earne
 To proue his puissance in battell braue
Vpon his foe, and his new force to learne;
Vpon his foe, a Dragon horrible and stearne.

A louely Ladie rode him faire beside,
 Vpon a lowly Asse more white then snow,
 Yet she much whiter, but the same did hide
 Vnder a vele, that wimpled was full low,
 And ouer all a blacke stole she did throw,
 As one that inly mournd: so was she sad,
 And heauie sat vpon her palfrey slow:
 Seemed in heart some hidden care she had,
And by her in a line a milke white lambe she lad.

So pure and innocent, as that same lambe,
 She was in life and euery vertuous lore,
  And by descent from Royall lynage came
  Of ancient Kings and Queenes, that had of yore
  Their scepters stretcht from East to Westerne shore,
  And all the world in their subiection held;
  Till that infernall feend with foule vprore
  Forwasted all their land, and them expeld:
Whom to auenge, she had this Knight from far compelld.

Excerpts from *Astrophel: A Pastorall Elegie*

They stopt his wound (too late to stop it was)
And in their armes then softly did him reare:
Tho (as he wild) vnto his loued lasse,
His dearest loue him dolefully did beare.

The dolefulst beare that euer man did see,
Was *Astrophel*, but dearest vnto mee.

She when she saw her loue in such a plight,
With crudled blood and filthie gore deformed:
That wont to be with flowers and gyrlonds dight,
And her deare fauours dearly well adorned,
Her face, the fairest face, that eye mote see,
She likewise did deforme like him to bee.

Her yellow locks that shone so bright and long,
As Sunny beames in fairest somers day:
She fiersly tore, and with outragious wrong
From her red cheeks the roses rent away.
And her faire brest the threasury of ioy,
She spoyld thereof, and filled with annoy.

His palled face impictured with death,
She bathed oft with teares and dried oft:
And with sweet kisses suckt the wasting breath,
Out of his lips like lillies pale and soft.
And oft she cald to him, who answerd nought,
But onely by his lookes did tell his thought.

The rest of her impatient regret,
And piteous mone the which she for him made:
No toong can tell, nor any forth can set,
But he whose heart like sorrow did inuade.
At last when paine his vitall powres had spent,
His wasted life her weary lodge forwent.

Which when she saw, she staied not a whit,
But after him did make vntimely haste:
Forth with her ghost out of her corps did flit,
And followed her make like Turtle chaste.
To proue that death their hearts cannot diuide,
Which liuing were in loue so firmly tide.

The Gods which all things see, this same beheld,

And pittying this paire of louers trew:
Transformed them there lying on the field,
Into one flowre that is both red and blew.
It first growes red, and then to blew doth fade,
Like *Astrophel*, which thereinto was made.

And in the midst thereof a star appeares,
As fairly formd as any star in skyes:
Resembling *Stella* in her freshest yeares,
Forth darting beames of beautie from her eyes,
And all the day it standeth full of deow,
Which is the teares, that from her eyes did flow.

That hearbe of some, Starlight is cald by name,
Of others *Penthia*, though not so well:
But thou where euer thou doest finde the same,
From this day forth do call it *Astrophel*.
And when so euer thou it vp doest take,
Do pluck it softly for that shepheards sake.

Hereof when tydings far abroad did passe,
The shepheards all which loued him full deare:
And sure full deare of all he loued was,
Did thether flock to see what they did heare.
And when that pitteous spectacle they vewed,
The same with bitter teares they all bedewed.

And euery one did make exceeding mone,
With inward anguish and great griefe opprest:
And euery one did weep and waile, and mone,
And meanes deviz'd to shew his sorrow best.
That from that houre since first on grassie greene
Shepheards kept sheep, was not like mourning seen.

But first his sister that *Clorinda* hight,
The gentlest shepheardesse that liues this day:
And most resembling both in shape and spright
Her brother deare, began this dolefull lay.
Which least I marre the sweetnesse of the vearse,

In sort as she it sung, I will rehearse.

George Peele (1556–1596)

As a dramatist, historian and poet, George Peele belonged to the group of university scholars for academic literature. He employed blank-verse lines and lyric interludes of dramatic representation in ways that anticipate Shakespeare, and he also used blank verse effectively in non-dramatic poems, and many of these poems were published in *Polyhymnia* (1590) and *The Honor of the Garter* (1593), the former of which has a prologue containing his judgments on his contemporaries. The excerpt "Farewell to Arms to Queen Elizabeth" was written in 1589. It is a blank verse description of the ceremonies attending the retirement of the Queen's champion, Sir Henry Lee.

"Farewell to Arms to Queen Elizabeth"

His golden locks time hath to silver turned;
    O time too swift, O swiftness never ceasing!
His youth 'gainst time and age hath ever spurned,
    But spurned in vain; youth waneth by increasing:
Beauty, strength, youth, are flowers but fading seen;
Duty, faith, love, are roots, and ever green.

His helmet now shall make a hive for bees;
    And, lovers' sonnets turned to holy psalms,
A man-at-arms must now serve on his knees,
    And feed on prayers, which are age's alms:
But though from court to cottage he depart,
His saint is sure of his unspotted heart.

And when he saddest sits in homely cell,
    He'll teach his swains this carol for a song:
'Blest be the hearts that wish my sovereign well,
    Curst be the souls that think her any wrong.'
Goddess, allow this aged man his right,
To be your beadsman now, that was your knight.

Michael Drayton (1563–1631)

Michael Drayton is a poet, and a learned and accomplished practitioner of most Renaissance poetic genres. He was also the first to write odes in English in the manner of Horace. Among his works are *The Harmony of the Church* (1591), *Idea: The Shepherd's*

Garland (1593), *Idea's Mirror* (1594), and historical heroic poems such as *Robert, Duke of Normandy* (1596) and *Mortimeriados* (1596). Besides, his *Englands Heroicall Epistles* (1597) and *Poly-Olbion* (1612–1622) are considered to be the greatest in the celebration of the topography of Britain recording comprehensively the beauty of the countryside, the romantic fascination of ruined abbeys, and its history, legend and present life. In *The Battle of Agincourt*, he retells the story of the war in which Henry V renewed the Hundred Years War with France in 1415, laying successful siege to Harfleur. On 25 October 1415, with an army of only 14,000 men, Henry V defeated a French force numbering 50,000 in a famous battle at Agincourt.

Excerpts from *The Battle of Agincourt*

Fair stood the wind for France
When we our sails advance,
Nor now to prove our chance
Longer will tarry;
But putting to the main,
At Caux, the mouth of Seine,
With all his martial train,
Landed King Harry.

And taking many a fort,
Furnished in warlike sort,
Marcheth towards Agincourt
In happy hour;
Skirmishing day by day
With those that stopped his way,
Where the French gen'ral lay
With all his power;

Which, in his height of pride,
King Henry to deride,
His ransom to provide
Unto him sending;
Which he neglects the while,
As from a nation vile,
Yet with an angry smile
Their fall portending.

And turning to his men,
Quoth our brave Henry then,
Though they to one be ten,
Be not amazed.
Yet have we well begun,
Battles so bravely won
Have ever to the sun
By fame been raised.
And for myself (quoth he),
This my full rest shall be;
England ne'er mourn for me,
Nor more esteem me.
Victor I will remain,
Or on this earth lie slain;
Never shall she sustain
Loss to redeem me.

Poitiers and Cressy tell,
When most their pride did swell,
Under our swords they fell;
No less our skill is
Than when our grandsire great,
Claiming the regal seat,
By many a warlike feat
Lopped the French lilies.

The Duke of York so dread
The eager vaward led;
With the main Henry sped
Amongst his henchmen.
Exeter had the rear,
A braver man not there; -
O Lord, how hot they were
On the false Frenchmen!

They now to fight are gone,
Armour on armour shone,
Drum now to drum did groan,
To hear was wonder;

That with the cries they make
The very earth did shake;
Trumpet to trumpet spake,
Thunder to thunder.

Well it thine age became,
O noble Erpingham,
Which didst the signal aim
To our hid forces!
When from a meadow by,
Like a storm suddenly,
The English archery
Stuck the French horses.

With Spanish yew so strong,
Arrows a cloth-yard long,
That like to serpents stung,
Piercing the weather;
None from his fellow starts,
But, playing manly parts,
And like true English hearts,
Stuck close together.

When down their bows they threw,
And forth their bilbos drew,
And on the French they flew,
Not one was tardy;
Arms were from shoulders sent,
Scalps to the teeth were rent,
Down the French peasants went -
Our men were hardy!

This while our noble king,
His broadsword brandishing,
Down the French host did ding,
As to o'erwhelm it;
And many a deep wound lent,
His arms with blood besprent,
And many a cruel dent

Bruised his helmet.

Gloucester, that duke so good,
Next of the royal blood,
For famous England stood
With his brave brother;
Clarence, in steel so bright,
Though but a maiden knight,
Yet in that furious fight
Scarce such another.

Christopher Marlowe (1564–1593)

Christopher Marlowe is a great poet and dramatist, enjoying a life of only 29 years. His poem *Hero and Leander* concerns the Greek mythical lovers of those names concerned. He is known for his establishment of dramatic blank verse in such plays as *The Jew of Malta*, the chronicle history *Edward II*, and *The Tragical History of Doctor Faustus*, which ensured his lasting legacy. His enormously popular play *Tamburlaine the Great* (1587–1588), produced on the London stage with a sequel soon followed, used the story of the 14th century Tartar Timur-i-leng to dramatise the problems of military command and to examine popular assumptions about war as divine punishment or deliverance. The excerpt is Tamburlaine's speech in Scene II, Act I of the first part of *Tamburlaine The Great*.

Excerpts from *Tamburlaine The Great*

With what a majesty he rears his looks!—
In thee, thou valiant man of Persia,
I see the folly of thy emperor.
Art thou but captain of a thousand horse,
That by characters graven in thy brows,
And by thy martial face and stout aspect,
Deserv'st to have the leading of an host?
Forsake thy king, and do but join with me,
And we will triumph over all the world:
I hold the Fates bound fast in iron chains,
And with my hand turn Fortune's wheel about;
And sooner shall the sun fall from his sphere
Than Tamburlaine be slain or overcome.
Draw forth thy sword, thou mighty man-at-arms,
Intending but to raze my charmed skin,

And Jove himself will stretch his hand from heaven

To ward the blow, and shield me safe from harm.

See, how he rains down heaps of gold in showers,

As if he meant to give my soldiers pay!

And, as a sure and grounded argument

That I shall be the monarch of the East,

He sends this Soldan's daughter rich and brave,

To be my queen and portly emperess.

If thou wilt stay with me, renowmed man,

And lead thy thousand horse with my conduct,

Besides thy share of this Egyptian prize,

Those thousand horse shall sweat with martial spoil

Of conquer'd kingdoms and of cities sack'd:

Both we will walk upon the lofty cliffs;

And Christian merchants, that with Russian stems

Plough up huge furrows in the Caspian Sea,

Shall vail to us as lords of all the lake;

Both we will reign as consuls of the earth,

And mighty kings shall be our senators.

Jove sometime masked in a shepherd's weed;

And by those steps that he hath scal'd the heavens

May we become immortal like the gods.

Join with me now in this my mean estate,

(I call it mean, because, being yet obscure,

The nations far-remov'd admire me not,)

And when my name and honour shall be spread

As far as Boreas claps his brazen wings,

Or fair Bootes sends his cheerful light,

Then shalt thou be competitor with me,

And sit with Tamburlaine in all his majesty.

William Shakespeare (1564–1616)

William Shakespeare is the greatest figure of English literature, known for his poetry and poetic drama. He wrote more than thirty plays: histories, comedies, tragedies, and romances, a large portion of which is composed in blank verse. For his poetry, the representative is his 154 sonnets, written in the form of three quatrains and a couplet that is now recognised as the Shakespearean Sonnet, all of which focus on the inevitable decay of time, and the immortalisation of beauty and love in poetry: While sonnets 1–126 are addressed to a beloved friend and sonnets 127–152 to a malignant but fascinating "Dark Lady" whom he loves.

Shakespeare's ten English history plays are engaged most profoundly with the experience and recording of early modern warfare. *The Cambridge Companion to War Writing* (2009) makes such a good summary of his great quantities and complex formulations: "The first tetralogy (*1, 2, 3 Henry VI* and *Richard III*) traces the later Wars of the Roses up to Henry VII's accession, while the second tetralogy (*Richard II; 1, 2 Henry IV; Henry V*) goes further back in time to deal with events from the deposition of Richard II to Henry V's victory at Agincourt. Richard II (1595) investigates the figure of the warrior-king by splitting it down the middle, giving eloquence to Richard and military command to his usurper Bolingbroke (the future Henry IV). Richard's departure for war in Ireland at the end of Act 2, Scene 1 provides Bolingbroke's opportunity for the beginnings of his military coup, while false rumours of Richard's death cause the Welsh to join the rebellion, precipitating the collapse of Richard's hope in Act 3, Scene 2. The two parts of *Henry IV* (1596, 1598) and *Henry V* (1599) together make perhaps the most encompassing vision of war to be found in all of early modern English literature."[9] The following excerpts are two speeches in blank verse by Henry V from Act 4, Scene 3: The English camp of *Henry V*.

Excerpts from *Henry V*

What's he that wishes so?

My cousin Westmoreland? No, my fair cousin:

If we are mark'd to die, we are enow

To do our country loss; and if to live,

The fewer men, the greater share of honour.

God's will! I pray thee, wish not one man more.

By Jove, I am not covetous for gold,

Nor care I who doth feed upon my cost;

It yearns me not if men my garments wear;

Such outward things dwell not in my desires:

But if it be a sin to covet honour,

I am the most offending soul alive.

No, faith, my coz, wish not a man from England:

God's peace! I would not lose so great an honour

As one man more, methinks, would share from me

For the best hope I have. O, do not wish one more!

Rather proclaim it, Westmoreland, through my host,

That he which hath no stomach to this fight,

Let him depart; his passport shall be made

---

9 Kate Mcloughlin, ed., *The Cambridge Companion to War Writing*. Cambridge, New York: Cambridge University Press, 2009, p.104.

And crowns for convoy put into his purse:
We would not die in that man's company
That fears his fellowship to die with us.
This day is called the feast of Crispian:
He that outlives this day, and comes safe home,
Will stand a tip-toe when the day is named,
And rouse him at the name of Crispian.
He that shall live this day, and see old age,
Will yearly on the vigil feast his neighbours,
And say 'To-morrow is Saint Crispian:'
Then will he strip his sleeve and show his scars.
And say 'These wounds I had on Crispin's day.'
Old men forget: yet all shall be forgot,
But he'll remember with advantages
What feats he did that day: then shall our names.
Familiar in his mouth as household words
Harry the king, Bedford and Exeter,
Warwick and Talbot, Salisbury and Gloucester,
Be in their flowing cups freshly remember'd.
This story shall the good man teach his son;
And Crispin Crispian shall ne'er go by,
From this day to the ending of the world,
But we in it shall be remember'd;
We few, we happy few, we band of brothers;
For he to-day that sheds his blood with me
Shall be my brother; be he ne'er so vile,
This day shall gentle his condition:
And gentlemen in England now a-bed
Shall think themselves accursed they were not here,
And hold their manhoods cheap whiles any speaks
That fought with us upon Saint Crispin's day.

     …

I pray thee, bear my former answer back:
Bid them achieve me and then sell my bones.
Good God! why should they mock poor fellows thus?
The man that once did sell the lion's skin
While the beast lived, was killed with hunting him.
A many of our bodies shall no doubt
Find native graves; upon the which, I trust,

Shall witness live in brass of this day's work:

And those that leave their valiant bones in France,

Dying like men, though buried in your dunghills,

They shall be famed; for there the sun shall greet them,

And draw their honours reeking up to heaven;

Leaving their earthly parts to choke your clime,

The smell whereof shall breed a plague in France.

Mark then abounding valour in our English,

That being dead, like to the bullet's grazing,

Break out into a second course of mischief,

Killing in relapse of mortality.

Let me speak proudly: tell the constable

We are but warriors for the working-day;

Our gayness and our gilt are all besmirch'd

With rainy marching in the painful field;

There's not a piece of feather in our host—

Good argument, I hope, we will not fly—

And time hath worn us into slovenry:

But, by the mass, our hearts are in the trim;

And my poor soldiers tell me, yet ere night

They'll be in fresher robes, or they will pluck

The gay new coats o'er the French soldiers' heads

And turn them out of service. If they do this, —

As, if God please, they shall, —my ransom then

Will soon be levied. Herald, save thou thy labour;

Come thou no more for ransom, gentle herald:

They shall have none, I swear, but these my joints;

Which if they have as I will leave 'em them,

Shall yield them little, tell the constable.

4. Manipulation of Power in the Reformation and Revolution War Poetry

In theoretical terms, both reformation and revolution have conceived a struggle for power. As part of the 16th century European religious movements marked by rejection or modification of some Roman Catholic doctrines and practices as well as the establishment of the Protestant churches, the English Reformation indicated that the Church of England broke away from the authority of the Pope and the Roman Catholic Church. The so-called "Puritan Revolution" or "English Bourgeois Revolution" stemmed from the conflict between Charles I and Parliament over an Irish insurrection with evolving consequences such as the trial and execution of an anointed sovereign and the presence of a standing army throughout the 1650s. It was combined with the proliferation of radical religious sects that shook the very foundations of British society and ultimately facilitated the restoration of Charles II in 1660. The revolution was often regarded as "the last civil war fought on English soil", where domestic manipulation of power has been temporarily settled, but potentially initiated the subsequent waves of outward power expansion—the massive orchestration of imperial expansion and colonisation.

Sir William Davenant (1606–1668)

Sir William Davenant is a Poet Laureate, playwright and theatre manager, and Civil War hero, probably one of the most influential but neglected figures in the history of British theatre. Two important identity problems have perplexed his readers, among which the first is his relationship with William Shakespeare in that the gossip held that: the famous playwright may even have been his father; and the second is his escape of execution as a supporter of King Charles I during the Civil Wars. After the execution of Charles I, he went to aid the Royalist cause in America as lieutenant governor of Maryland, but his ship was captured in the English Channel and imprisoned in the Tower of London until 1654. Apart from his numerous dramatic works, his poetry includes *Madagascar and other Poems* (1638) and *Gondibert* (1651), a tale of chivalry in 1,700 quatrains which was never to be completed. The excerpted poem "The Soldier Going to the Field" is from his posthumous poetic publication in 1672.

"The Soldier Going to the Field"

Preserve thy sighs, unthrifty girl,
    To purify the air;
Thy tears to thread instead of pearl
    On bracelets of thy hair.

The trumpet makes the echo hoarse
    And wakes the louder drum;
Expense of grief gains no remorse
    When sorrow should be dumb.

For I must go where lazy Peace
    Will hide her drowsy head,
And, for the sport of Kings, increase
    The number of the dead.

But first I'll chide thy cruel theft:
    Can I in war delight,
Who being of my heart bereft
    Can have no heart to fight?

Thou know'st the sacred Laws of old
    Ordained a thief should pay,
To quit him of his theft, sevenfold
    What he had stolen away.

Thy payment shall but double be;
    O then with speed resign
My own seducèd heart to me,
    Accompanied with thine.

John Milton (1608−1674)

John Milton is a prose polemicist, dramatist, and poet. He attacked both the idea and the supposed enormities of English episcopacy, championing the cause of the Puritans and Oliver Cromwell with a series of pamphlets advocating radical political topics including the morality of divorce, the freedom of the press, populism, and sanctioned regicide, among the great works of which the greatest is *Areopagitica: A Speech of Mr. John Milton for the Liberty of Unlicenced Printing, to the Parliament of England* (1644), arguing for a far broader constitutional liberty. His collected volumes of verse, *Poems of Mr. John Milton, both English and Latin, Compos'd at Several Times* (1645), and his two most-remembered *Paradise Lost* (1667) and *Paradise Regained* (1671), expressed his spirit of revolt by chronicling the biblical Satan's temptation of Adam and Eve and their expulsion from Eden. The excerpted sonnet "On the Late Massacre in Piedmont" (1673) contributes to remembering the real world rebellious tragedy.[10]

"On the Late Massacre in Piedmont"

Avenge, O Lord, thy slaughtered saints, whose bones
Lie scattered on the Alpine mountains cold,
Even them who kept thy truth so pure of old
When all our fathers worshipped stocks and stones,
Forget not; in thy book record their groans

---

10 It is said that the heretical Waldensian sect inhabited in northern Italy (Piedmont) and southern France, and held beliefs compatible with Protestant doctrine; their massacre by Catholics in 1655 was widely protested by Protestant powers, including Oliver Cromwell and John Milton.

Who were thy sheep and in their ancient fold
Slain by the bloody Piedmontese that rolled
Mother with infant down the rocks. Their moans
The vales redoubled to the hills, and they
To Heaven. Their martyred blood and ashes sow
O'er all th' Italian fields where still doth sway
The triple tyrant, that from these may grow
A hundredfold, who having learnt thy way,
Early may fly the Babylonian woe.

Richard Lovelace (1618–1657)

Richard Lovelace is an English poet, soldier, and Royalist, whose graceful lyrics and dashing career made him the prototype of the perfect Cavalier with a legendary life as a soldier, lover, and courtier. Persecuted for his unflagging support of King Charles I, he died in dire poverty. His greatest poetic contribution is *Lucasta; Posthume Poems of Richard Lovelace, Esq.* (1659), from which the excerpt "To Lucasta, Going to the Wars" (1649) comes.

"To Lucasta, Going to the Wars"

Tell me not, sweet, I am unkind,
    That from the nunnery
Of thy chaste breast and quiet mind
    To war and arms I fly.

True, a new mistress now I chase,
    The first foe in the field;
And with a stronger faith embrace
    A sword, a horse, a shield.

Yet this inconstancy is such
    As you too shall adore;
I could not love thee, dear, so much,
    Loved I not honour more.

Andrew Marvell (1621–1678)

Andrew Marvell is one of the best Metaphysical Poets and a well-known politician during that turbulent period of English history. The inconsistencies and ambiguities within his work and the scarcity of information about his personal life have enlisted a lot of contemporary academic curiosity. His collection of verses *Miscellaneous Poems* was published posthumously in 1684. The poem "An Horatian Ode upon Cromwell's Return from Ireland" (1650) marks those complexities.

"An Horatian Ode upon Cromwell's Return from Ireland"

The forward youth that would appear
Must now forsake his Muses dear ,
    Nor in the shadows sing
    His numbers languishing.

'Tis time to leave the books in dust.
And oil the unusèd armour's rust,
    Removing from the wall
    The corslet of the hall.

So restless Cromwell could not cease
In the inglorious arts of peace,
    But through adventurous war
    Urgèd his active star:

And like the three-forked lightning, first
Breaking the clouds where it was nurst,
    Did thorough his own side
    His fiery way divide:

For 'tis all one to courage high,
The emulous, or enemy;
    —And with such, to enclose
    —Is more than to oppose.

Then burning through the air he went
And palaces and temples rent;
    And Caesar's head at last
    Did through his laurels blast.

'Tis madness to resist or blame
The force of angry Heaven's flame;
    And if we would speak true,
    Much to the man is due,

Who, from his private gardens, where
He lived reservèd and austere
    (As if his highest plot
    To plant the bergamot),

Could by industrious valour climb
To ruin the great work of time,
    And cast the Kingdom old
    Into another mould.

Though Justice against Fate complain,
And plead the ancient rights in vain—
    But those do hold or break
    As men are strong or weak—

Nature, that hateth emptiness,
Allows of penetration less,
    And therefore must make room
    Where greater spirits come.

What field of all the civil wars
Where his were not the deepest scars?
    And Hampton shows what part
    He had of wiser art;

Where, twining subtle fears with hope,
He wove a net of such a scope
    That Charles himself might chase
    To Car's brook's narrow case;

That thence the Royal Actor borne
The tragic scaffold might adorn:
    While round the armèd bands
    Did clap their bloody hands.

He nothing common did or mean
Upon that memorable scene,
    But with his keener eye
    The axe's edge did try;

Nor called the Gods, with vulgar spite,
To vindicate his helpless right;
    But bowed his comely head
    Down, as upon a bed.

This was that memorable hour
Which first assured the forcèd power:
    So when they did design
    The Capitol's first line,

A bleeding head, where they begun,
Did fright the architects to run;
    And yet in that the State
    Foresaw its happy fate!

And now the Irish are ashamed
To see themselves in one year tamed:
    So much one man can do
    That does both act and know.

They can affirm his praises best,
And have, though overcome, confest
    How good he is, how just
    And fit for highest trust;

Nor yet grown stiffer with command,
But still in the Republic's hand—
    How fit he is to sway
    That can so well obey!

He to the Commons' feet presents
A Kingdom for his first year's rents,
    And, what he may, forbears
    His fame, to make it theirs:

And has his sword and spoils ungirt
To lay them at the public's skirt.
    So when the falcon high
    Falls heavy from the sky,

She, having killed, no more does search
But on the next green bough to perch,
        Where, when he first does lure,
        The falconer has her sure.

What may not then our Isle presume
While victory his crest does plume?
        What may not others fear,
        If thus he crown each year?

As Caesar he, ere long, to Gaul,
To Italy an Hannibal,
        And to all States not free
        Shall climacteric be.

The Pict no shelter now shall find
Within his particoloured mind,
        But from this valour sad
        Shrinks underneath the plaid,

Happy, if in the tufted brake
The English hunter him mistake,
        Nor lay his hounds in near
        The Caledonian deer.

But thou, the War's and Fortune's son,
March indefatigably on;
        And for the last effect,
        Still keep thy sword erect:

Besides the force it has to fright
The spirits of the shady night,
        The same arts that did gain
        A power, must it maintain.

Chapter II

War Poetry of the British Colonization (1651–1773)

From "The English Bourgeois Revolution" to the Age of Revolutions, the Anglo-American, or the transatlantic English world, has witnessed constant drastic changes in the former in its expanding colonisation and the latter in its dependent national formation. The "Bourgeois Revolution", as argued in the former chapter, had been "discrediting of the idea of the divine right of kings, the belief that parliament was supreme in political matters, and that the English monarch had to rule in a manner which was limited by the idea of a constitutional monarchy." But the revolutionary in the 1640s and 1650s seemed reactionary in the 1680s. After the death of Oliver Cromwell (1599–1658), Charles II resumed the royal power and became the king in 1660, initiating those years of backlash as had been called the "The Restoration", until another national attempt to "secularise" the political power. The "Glorious Revolution", or "Revolution of 1688", or "Bloodless Revolution", results in the abolition of the absolute power of the King and establishment of the constitutional monarchy as represented by such historic documents of the English Bill of Rights, the Toleration Act, and the Mutiny Act, having accomplished the settlement of the fundamental questions of power between king and Parliament with the monarchs to respect Parliament and Parliament's laws. After 1688, the monarchy that emerged in Britain was limited by a constitution. It also created a body of ideas that were to be very influential in the development of Anglo-American political and constitutional thought in the 18th century.

Once the internal or domestic power division was balanced, Britain began to wage its wars to the outside, becoming from a once-being-colonised territory to a colonizing nation.

In fact, its colonisation had begun much earlier: Britain colonised Ireland in 1169; Queen Elizabeth I (1533–1603) established England as a fiercely independent Protestant nation and built up her navy to keep invading, while encouraging her native adventurers to sail west and set up colonies in North America; from about 1600 on, Protestant Fundamentalists to join these adventurers successively appeared in Boston, Virginia and the Caribbean, together with Bombay and Calcutta in India. In 1707, the Act of Union brought together Scotland and England to form "Great Britain"; in 1770, Captain Cook claimed Australia for Britain.

As the British Empire expanded, the first hostile factor to deter is France, while rubbing with the Spanish. From 1650 to 1750, the Empire was almost continuously fighting with the French in America and India as well as the high seas for global domination. It defeated the French in both America at Quebec in 1759, dividing North America into three: Canada to the north, the thirteen colonies on the eastern coast, and a native Indian reservation on the west. In 1776, "English" settlers in North America were much larger in number, ten times larger than the French colony in Quebec, Canada. But this did not bring fortune to the Empire. These well-educated American colonists objected to the new taxes placed on them as they had no representatives in London. They declared themselves independent while many loyalists moved north into Canada, creating the current east-west split of French and English speakers. Around 1800, The Empire continued to expand with the help of a navy that knew no boundaries, even making the Pacific Ocean an "English lake" with Australia, New Zealand, India, including Burma, and Malay added to its Empire mapping without opposition. Back with France, Britain showed its overwhelming supremacy and finally defeated France at Waterloo in 1815, making the French and English remain at peace but stay culturally very different. From the end of the 18th century, Britain had emerged as an empire dominating both the transatlantic and global territories, entering into a period of aggressive imperialism.

1. The Fantasy of the State and Legitimacy of Colonization

The conception of sovereign "state" has been one of the most complicated in modern and contemporary history. Whether as a politically organised body of people occupying a definite territory, or a political organisation of such a body of people, or a government or politically organised society having a particular character, the sovereign "state" has often been regarded as a truth marker, a moral arbiter, or beauty conceiver. It has witnessed a long time of glorification, mystification, and apotheosis. But it gradually encountered violent critique in modern discourses.

The critique of cultural pathology has grown out of two convictions: The criticism of a constitutive feature of modernity; and the state concept as the foundation of modern political discourse. As has been seen from Kant to Marx and far beyond, criticism has been the main instrument in fulfilling the promises of the modern age. By tracing those pre-modern "ghosts" out of political institutions and political critique, criticism has shown that the modern state has been envisaged as the place where expectations were to be realised, but it has also indicated that the sovereign state is unlikely to remain as a legitimate source of political authority. The Marxian conception takes the role of the state as a "monopoly of the legitimate use of physical force within a given territory", and regards any political power as merely the organised power of one class for oppressing another. What is unfortunate is that war poetry that writes about the British colonisation largely glorifies the state and tries with every means to legitimate its colonisation, such as in John Dryden and Charles Sackville. Equally, the fantasy of the state even weakens the traditional conception of "Nationalism", singing high praise of the British even as a mongrel race and taking "Patriotism" as a gesture of constant imperial expansion, such as in Daniel Defoe, Joseph Addison, and James Thomson.

John Dryden (1631–1700)

John Dryden is an English poet, dramatist, and literary critic, dominating the last four decades of the 17th century, and the literary scene of his day as "the Age of Dryden". When Sir William Davenant died in 1668, Dryden was soon appointed poet laureate in his place and royal historiographer two years later. As a poet, he is known for his two sub-genres of poetry: "Occasional", such as *Annus Mirabilis* (1667), *Religio Laici* (1682), *The Hind and the Panther* (1687), *Anne Killigrew* (1686), and *Alexander's Feast* (1697); and "Satirical", such as *Absalom and Achitophel* (1681), *Mac Flecknoe* (1682), and *The Medall* (1682). His non-dramatic poems are most typically occasional poems, written for the commemoration of particular events of a public character such as a coronation, a military victory, a death, or a political crisis, among which the longest up to date, *Annus Mirabilis*, was a celebration of two victories by the English fleet over the Dutch[1] and the fortitude of the people of London and the king during the Great Fire of 1666, both events of that being widely called "Year of Wonders". The significance lies in his gilding the royal image and reinforcing the concept of a loyal nation united under the best of kings by interpreting those trials sent by the God to punish rebellious spirits and to bind the king and his people together, in response to the enemies of Charles II who say that the God is casting his wrath on the English people signifying that the reign of an unholy king would soon come to an end. The first excerpt is from *Annus Mirabilis,* and the second can be simply named as *"To her Royal Highess the Duchess",* entitled in full as "Verses to Her Royal Highess the Duchess, on the Memorable Victory Gained by the Duke against the Hollanders, June 3 1665, and on Her Journey Afterwards into the North" with an initial greeting as "Madam".

---

1 The second of the Dutch Wars erupted in 1664; in March 1665, Charles II officially declared war on the Netherlands. The English victory at sea described here took place off the coast of Holland at North Foreland on 25 July, 1666.

Excerpts from *Annus Mirabilis*

Now van to van the foremost squadrons meet,
    The midmost battles hasting up behind,
Who view, far off, the storm of falling sleet,
    And hear their thunder rattling in the wind.

At length the adverse admirals appear:
    (The two bold champions of each country's right)
Their eyes describe the lists as they come near,
    And draw the lines of death before they fight.

The distance judged for shot of every size,
    The linstocks touch, the pond'rous ball expires:
The vig'rous seaman every port-hole plies,
    And adds his heart to every gun he fires.

Fierce was the fight on the proud Belgians' side,
    For honour, which they seldom sought before:
But now they by their own vain boasts were tied,
    —And forced, at least in show, to prize it more.

But sharp remembrance on the English part,
    And shame of being matched by such a foe:
Rouse conscious virtue up in every heart,
    And seeming to be stronger makes them so.

Nor long the Belgians could that fleet sustain,
    Which did two gen'rals' fates, and Caesar's bear.
Each several ship a victory did gain,
    As Rupert or as Albemarl were there.

Their battered admiral too soon withdrew,
    Unthanked by ours for his unfinished fight :
But he the minds of his Dutch masters knew,
    Who called that providence which we called flight.

Never did men more joyfully obey,
    Or sooner understand the sign to fly:

With such alacrity they bore away,
    As if to praise them all the states stood by.

O famous Leader of the Belgian fleet,
    Thy monument inscribed such praise shall wear
As Varro, timely flying, once did meet,
    Because he did not of his Rome despair.

Behold that navy which a while before
    Provoked the tardy English to the fight,
Now draw their beaten vessels close to shore,
    As larks die dared to shun the hobbies' flight.

Who ere would English monuments survey,
    In other records may our courage know:
But let them hide the story of this day,
    Whose fame was blemished by too base a foe.

Or if too busily they will enquire
    Into a victory which we disdain:
Then let them know, the Belgians did retire
    Before the Patron Saint of injured Spain.

Repenting England this revengeful day
    To Philip's manes did an off'ring bring:
England, which first, by leading them astray,
    Hatched up rebellion to destroy her King.

Our fathers bent their baneful industry
    To check a monarchy that slowly grew:
But did not France or Holland's fate foresee,
    Whose rising power to swift dominion flew.

In fortune's empire blindly thus we go,
    And wander after pathless destiny:
Whose dark resorts since prudence cannot know,
    In vain it would provide for what shall be.

Now on their coasts our conquering navy rides,

Waylays their merchants, and their land besets:
Each day new wealth without their care provides,
  They lie asleep with prizes in their nets.

"To her Royal Highness the Duchess"

When, for our sakes, your hero you resigned
To swelling seas, and every faithless wind;
When you released his courage, and set free
A valour fatal to the enemy;
You lodged your country's cares within your breast,
(The mansion where soft love should only rest,)
And, ere our foes abroad were overcome,
The noblest conquest you had gained at home.
Ah, what concerns did both your souls divide!
Your honour gave us what your love denied;
And 'twas for him much easier to subdue
Those foes he fought with, than to part from you.
That glorious day, which two such navies saw,
As each unmatched might to the world give law,
Neptune, yet doubtful whom he should obey,
Held to them both the trident of the sea:
The winds were hushed, the waves in ranks were cast,
As awfully as when God's people past:
Those, yet uncertain on whose sails to blow,
These, where the wealth of nations ought to flow.
Then with the Duke your Highness ruled the day:
While all the brave did his command obey,
The fair and pious under you did pray.
How powerful are chaste vows! the wind and tide
You bribed to combat on the English side.
Thus to your much-loved lord you did convey
An unknown succour, sent the nearest way.
New vigour to his wearied arms you brought,
(So Moses was upheld while Israel fought)
While, from afar, we heard the cannon play,
Like distant thunder on a shiny day.
For absent friends we were ashamed to fear,
When we considered what you ventured there.

Ships, men, and arms, our country might restore,
But such a leader could supply no more.
With generous thoughts of conquest he did burn,
Yet fought not more to vanquish than return.
Fortune and victory he did pursue,
To bring them, as his slaves, to wait on you:
Thus beauty ravished the rewards of fame,
And the fair triumphed, when the brave o'ercame.
Then, as you meant to spread another way
By land your conquests, far as his by sea,
Leaving our southern clime, you marched along
The stubborn north ten thousand Cupids strong.
Like commons the nobility resort,
In crowding heaps, to fill your moving court:
To welcome your approach the vulgar run,
Like some new envoy from the distant sun;
And country beauties by their lovers go,
Blessing themselves, and wondering at the show.
So, when the new-born Phœnix first is seen,
Her feathered subjects all adore their queen,
And, while she makes her progress through the east,
From every grove her numerous train's increased:
Each poet of the air her glory sings,
And round him the pleased audience clap their wings.

Charles Sackville (1638–1706)

Charles Sackville, Earl of Dorset, is a poet whose satires in heroic couplets anticipated and influenced the style of Alexander Pope. He was a friend of John Dryden and a well-known courtier of the reign of British king Charles II, The Merry Monarch (1630–1685), king of Great Britain and Ireland (1660–1685), in which the years of his reign are known in English history as the Restoration period. Dorset wrote "Song Written at Sea in the First Dutch War, the night before an Engagement" in 1665.[2] As the title has indicated, the First Anglo-Dutch War, or simply the First Dutch War (1652–1654), a conflict fought entirely at sea between the navies of the Commonwealth of England and the United Provinces of the Netherlands, was largely caused by disputes over trade.

---

2 From *Wit and Mirth* (1714), with the sub-title: "Written at sea, in the First Dutch War, 1665, the night before an engagement."

"Song Written at Sea in the First Dutch War, the Night before an Engagement"

To all you ladies now at land
        We men at sea indite;
But first would have you understand
        How hard it is to write:
The Muses now, and Neptune too,
We must implore to write to you—
        With a fa, la, la, la, la.

For though the Muses should prove kind,
        And fill our empty brain,
Yet if rough Neptune rouse the wind
        To wave the azure main,
Our paper, pen, and ink and we,
Roll up and down our ships at sea—
        With a fa, la, la, la, la.

Then if we write not by each post,
        Think not we are unkind;
Nor yet conclude our ships are lost
        By Dutchmen or by wind:
Our tears we'll send a speedier way,
The tide shall bring them twice a day—
        With a fa, la, la, la, la.

The King with wonder and surprise
        Will swear the seas grow bold,
Because the tides will higher rise
        Than e'er they did of old:
But let him know it is our tears
Bring floods of grief to Whitehall stairs—
        With a fa, la, la, la, la.

Should foggy Opdam chance to know
        Our sad and dismal story,
The Dutch would scorn so weak a foe,
        And quit their fort at Goree:
For what resistance can they find

From men who've left their hearts behind?—
        With a fa, la, la, la, la.

Let wind and weather do its worst,
        Be you to us but kind;
Let Dutchmen vapour, Spaniards curse,
        No sorrow we shall find:
'Tis then no matter how things go,
Or who's our friend, or who's our foe—
        With a fa, la, la, la, la .

To pass our tedious hours away
        We throw a merry main,
Or else at serious ombre play;
        But why should we in vain
Each other's ruin thus pursue?
We were undone when we left you—
        With a fa, la, la, la, la.

But now our fears tempestuous grow
        And cast our hopes away;
Whilst you, regardless of our woe,
        Sit careless at a play:
Perhaps permit some happier man
To kiss your hand, or flirt your fan—
        With a fa, la, la, la, la.

When any mournful tune you hear,
        That dies in every note
As if it sighed with each man's care
        For being so remote,
Think then how often love we've made
To you, when all those tunes were played—
        With a fa, la, la, la, la.

In justice you cannot refuse
        To think of our distress,
When we for hopes of honour lose
        Our certain happiness:

All those designs are but to prove
Ourselves more worthy of your love—
    With a fa, la, la, la, la.

And now we've told you all our loves,
    And likewise all our fears,
In hopes this declaration moves
    Some pity for our tears:
Let's hear of no inconstancy—
We have too much of that at sea—
    With a fa, la, la, la, la.

Daniel Defoe (1660–1731)

Daniel Defoe is a novelist, pamphleteer and journalist, best known for his novels of *Robinson Crusoe* (1719–1722) and *Moll Flanders* (1722), who had fundamentally shaped the novel as an emerging genre of English literature. As a staunch Dissenter and with characteristic impetuosity, he joined the rebellion of the Duke of Monmouth when the Roman Catholic James II ascended the throne in 1685. His representative poetic production includes *The True-Born Englishman* (1701), which ridicules the very conception of being "a true Englishman" in reply to attacks on the "foreign" kings[3], *Poems on Affairs of State* (1703), *Reformation of Manners* (1702), and *A Hymn to the Pillory* (1703). These poems witnessed the development of his thought, such as reform or morality and casting poems into irony. The excerpt is Part I of *The True-Born Englishman*, which can be considered as a war poem for its conception of the English race as a result of constant conquest and racial integration while another excerpt *The Spanish Descent* (1702) celebrates the military victory regarded at the time as the most momentous in over a hundred years and is thus a poem on the history of state affairs: The providential success at Vigo of Sir George Rooke's capture of the entire Spanish fleet[4] is in sharp contrast to the English failure at Cadiz during the earlier war, 1689–1697.

---

3 As a result of the Glorious Revolution of 1688, the Protestant William Prince of Orange replaced the Catholic James II on the throne of England. Not everyone was happy with this turn of events as William was a Dutchman; they objected to having a foreigner as king and extolled their own English parentage by way of comparison. Defoe composed this satirical rejoinder as a gentle reminder to those English patriots of where their true roots lay.

4 In 1702, during the War of the Spanish Succession, an unsuccessful expedition to Cadiz by the British and the Dutch was followed by a dramatic victory in the Bay of Vigo, where, without losing a single ship themselves, they were able to capture an entire fleet, including 12 Spanish galleons and 15 French men-of-war.

Excerpts from *The True-born Englishman*

WHEREVER God erects a house of prayer,
The Devil always builds a chapel there:
And 'twill be found upon examination,
The latter has the largest congregation:
For ever since he first debauch'd the mind,
He made a perfect conquest of mankind.
With uniformity of service, he
Reigns with general aristocracy.
No non-conforming sects disturb his reign,
For of his yoke, there's very few complain.
He knows the genius and the inclination,
And matches proper sins for ev'ry nation.
He needs no standing army government;
He always rules us by our own consent:
His laws are easy, and his gentle sway
Makes it exceeding pleasant to obey.
The list of his vicegerents and commanders,
Out-does your Cæsars, or your Alexanders.
They never fail of his infernal aid,
And he's as certain ne'er to be betray'd.
Thro' all the world they spread his vast command,
And death's eternal empire is maintain'd.
They rule so politically and so well,
As if they were Lords Justices of hell;
Duly divided to debauch mankind,
And plant infernal dictates in his mind.

PRIDE, the first peer, and president of hell,
To his share, Spain, the largest province fell.
The subtle Prince thought fittest to bestow
On these the golden mines of Mexico,
With all the silver mountains of Peru;
Wealth which in wise hands would the world undo;
Because he knew their genius was such,
Too lazy and too haughty to be rich:
So proud a people, so above their fate,
That, if reduced to beg, they'll beg in state:

Lavish of money, to be counted brave,

And proudly starve, because they scorn to save;

Never was nation in the world before,

So very rich, and yet so very poor.

LUST chose the torrid zone of Italy,

Where blood ferments in rapes and sodomy:

Where swelling veins o'erflow with living streams,

With heat impregnate from Vesuvian flames;

Whose flowing sulphur forms infernal lakes,

And human body of the soil partakes.

There nature ever burns with hot desires,

Fann'd with luxuriant air from subterranean fires:

Here undisturbed, in floods of scalding lust,

Th' infernal king reigns with infernal gust.

DRUNKENNESS, the darling favourite of hell,

Chose Germany to rule; and rules so well,

No subjects more obsequiously obey,

None please so well, or are so pleased as they;

The cunning artist manages so well,

He lets them bow to heav'n, and drink to hell.

If but to wine and him they homage pay,

He cares not to what deity they pray;

What god they worship most, or in what way.

Whether by Luther, Calvin, or by Rome,

They sail for heaven, by wine he steers them home.

UNGOVERN'D PASSION settled first in France,

Where mankind lives in haste, and thrives by chance;

A dancing nation, fickle and untrue,

Have oft undone themselves, and others too;

Prompt the infernal dictates to obey,

And in hell's favour none more great than they.

THE pagan world he blindly leads away,

And personally rules with arbitrary sway:

The mask thrown off, plain devil, his title stands;

And what elsewhere he tempts, he there commands;

There, with full gust, th' ambition of his mind,
Governs, as he of old in heaven design'd:
Worshipp'd as God, his Paynim altars smoke,
Imbrued with blood of those that him invoke.

THE rest by deputies he rules so well,
And plants the distant colonies of hell;
By them his secret power he firm maintains,
And binds the world in his infernal chains.

BY zeal the Irish, and the Russ by folly,
Fury the Dane, the Swede by melancholy;
By stupid ignorance, the Muscovite;
The Chinese, by a child of hell, call'd wit;
Wealth makes the Persian too effeminate;
And poverty the Tartar desperate:
The Turks and Moors, by Mah'met he subdues;
And God has given him leave to rule the Jews:
Rage rules the Portuguese, and fraud the Scotch;
Revenge the Pole, and avarice the Dutch.

SATIRE, be kind, and draw a silent veil,
Thy native England's vices to conceal:
Or, if that task's impossible to do,
At least be just, and show her virtues too;
Too great the first, alas! the last too few.

ENGLAND, unknown, as yet unpeopled lay,—
Happy, had she remain'd so to this day,
And still to ev'ry nation been a prey.
Her open harbours, and her fertile plains,
The merchant's glory these, and those the swain's,
To ev'ry barbarous nation have betray'd her;
Who conquer her as oft as they invade her,
So beauty, guarded out by Innocence,
That ruins her which should be her defence.

INGRATITUDE, a devil of black renown,
Possess'd her very early for his own:

An ugly, surly, sullen, selfish spirit,
Who Satan's worst perfections does inherit;
Second to him in malice and in force,
All devil without, and all within him worse.

He made her first-born race to be so rude,
And suffer'd her to be so oft subdued;
By sev'ral crowds of wandering thieves o'er-run,
Often unpeopled, and as oft undone;
While ev'ry nation that her powers reduced,
Their languages and manners introduced;
From whose mix'd relics our compounded breed,
By spurious generation does succeed;
Making a race uncertain and uneven,
Derived from all the nations under heaven.

The Romans first with Julius Cæsar came,
Including all the nations of that name,
Gauls, Greek, and Lombards; and, by computation,
Auxiliaries or slaves of ev'ry nation.
With Hengist, Saxons; Danes with Sweno came,
In search of plunder, not in search of fame.
Scots, Picts, and Irish from th' Hibernian shore;
And conq'ring William brought the Normans o'er.

All these their barb'rous offspring left behind,
The dregs of armies, they of all mankind;
Blended with Britons, who before were here,
Of whom the Welch ha' blest the character.

From this amphibious, ill-born mob began,
That vain ill-natured thing, an Englishman.
The customs, sirnames, languages, and manners,
Of all these nations, are their own explainers;
Whose relics are so lasting and so strong,
They've left a Shiboleth upon our tongue;
By which, with easy search, you may distinguish
Your Roman, Saxon, Danish, Norman, English.

THE great invading Norman let us know
What conquerors in after-times might do.
To every musqueteer he brought to town,
He gave the lands which never were his own;
When first the English crown he did obtain,
He did not send his Dutchmen home again.
No re-assumptions in his reign were known,
Davenant might there ha' let his book alone.
No parliament his army could disband;
He raised no money, for he paid in land.
He gave his legions their eternal station,
And made them all freeholders of the nation.
He canton'd out the country to his men,
And every soldier was a denizen.
The rascals thus enrich'd, he called them lords,
To please their upstart pride with new-made words,
And doomsday book his tyranny records.

AND here begins the ancient pedigree
That so exalts our poor nobility.
'Tis that from some French trooper they derive,
Who with the Norman bastard did arrive:
The trophies of the families appear;
Some show the sword, the bow, and some the spear,
Which their great ancestor, forsooth, did wear.
These in the herald's register remain,
Their noble mean extraction to explain,
Yet who the hero was no man can tell,
Whether a drummer or a colonel:
The silent record blushes to reveal
Their undescended dark original.

BUT grant the best. How came the change to pass;
A true-born Englishman of Norman race?
A Turkish horse can show more history,
To prove his well-descended family.
Conquest, as by the moderns 'tis express'd,
May give a title to the lands possess'd;
But that the longest sword should be so civil,

To make a Frenchman English, that's the devil.

THESE are the heroes that despise the Dutch,
And rail at new-come foreigners so much;
Forgetting that themselves are all derived
From the most scoundrel race that ever lived;
A horrid crowd of rambling thieves and drones
Who ransack'd kingdoms, and dispeopled towns;
The Pict and painted Briton, treach'rous Scot,
By hunger, theft, and rapine, hither brought;
Norwegian pirates, buccaneering Danes,
Whose red-hair'd offspring everywhere remains;
Who, join'd with Norman French, compound the breed
From whence your true-born Englishmen proceed.

AND lest, by length of time, it be pretended,
The climate may this modern breed have mended;
Wise Providence, to keep us where we are,
Mixes us daily with exceeding care;
We have been Europe's sink, the jakes, where she
Voids all her offal out-cast progeny;
From our fifth Henry's time the strolling bands,
Of banish'd fugitives from neighb'ring lands,
Have here a certain sanctuary found:
The eternal refuge of the vagabond,
Where in but half a common age of time,
Borrowing new blood and manners from the clime,
Proudly they learn all mankind to contemn,
And all their race are true-born Englishmen.

DUTCH Walloons, Flemmings, Irishmen, and Scots,
Vaudois, and Valtolins, and Hugonots,
In good Queen Bess's charitable reign,
Supplied us with three hundred thousand men:
Religion—God, we thank thee!—sent them hither,
Priests, Protestants, the devil, and all together;
Of all professions, and of ev'ry trade,
All that were persecuted or afraid:
Whether for debt, or other crimes, they fled,

David at Hackelah was still their head.

THE offspring of this miscellaneous crowd,
Had not their new plantations long enjoy'd,
But they grew Englishmen, and raised their votes,
At foreign shoals of interloping Scots;
The royal branch from Pict-land did succeed,
With troops of Scots and scabs from north of Tweed;
The seven first years of his pacific reign,
Made him and half his nation Englishmen.
Scots from the northern frozen banks of Tay,
With packs and plods came whigging all away,
Thick as the locusts which in Egypt swarm'd,
With pride and hungry hopes completely arm'd;
With native truth, diseases, and no money,
Plunder'd our Canaan of the milk and honey;
Here they grew quickly lords and gentlemen,
And all their race are true-born Englishmen.

THE civil wars, the common purgative,
Which always use to make the nation thrive,
Made way for all that strolling congregation,
Which throng'd in pious Charles's restoration.
The royal refugee our breed restores,
With foreign courtiers, and with foreign whores:
And carefully re-peopled us again,
Throughout his lazy, long, lascivious reign,
With such a blest and true-born English fry,
As much illustrates our nobility.
A gratitude which will so black appear,
As future ages must abhor to bear:
When they look back on all that crimson flood,
Which stream'd in Lindsey's, and Caernarvon's blood;
Bold Strafford, Cambridge, Capel, Lucas, Lisle,
Who crown'd in death his father's fun'ral pile.
The loss of whom, in order to supply
With true-born English nobility,
Six bastard dukes survive his luscious reign,
The labours of Italian Castlemain,

French Portsmouth, Tabby Scott, and Cambrian;
Besides the num'rous bright and virgin throng,
Whose female glories shade them from my song.
This offspring if our age they multiply,
May half the house with English peers supply:
There with true English pride they may contemn
Schomberg and Portland, new-made noblemen.

FRENCH cooks, Scotch pedlars, and Italian whores,
Were all made lords or lords' progenitors.
Beggars and bastards by this new creation
Much multiplied the peerage of the nation;
Who will be all, ere one short age runs o'er,
As true-born lords as those we had before.

THEN to recruit the commons he prepares,
And heal the latent breaches of the wars;
The pious purpose better to advance,
He invites the banish'd Protestants of France;
Hither for God's sake, and their own, they fled
Some for religion came, and some for bread:
Two hundred thousand pair of wooden shoes,
Who, God be thank'd, had nothing left to lose;
To heaven's great praise did for religion fly,
To make us starve our poor in charity.
In ev'ry port they plant their fruitful train,
To get a race of true-born Englishmen;
Whose children will, when riper years they see,
Be as ill-natured, and as proud as we;
Call themselves English, foreigners despise,
Be surly like us all, and just as wise.

THUS from a mixture of all kinds began,
That heterogeneous thing, an Englishman:
In eager rapes, and furious lust begot,
Betwixt a painted Briton and a Scot:
Whose gend'ring offspring quickly learn'd to bow,
And yoke their heifers to the Roman plough;
From whence a mongrel half-bred race there came,

With neither name nor nation, speech or fame,
In whose hot veins new mixtures quickly ran,
Infused betwixt a Saxon and a Dane;
While their rank daughters, to their parents just,
Received all nations with promiscuous lust.
This nauseous brood directly did contain
The well-extracted blood of Englishmen.

WHICH medley, canton'd in a heptarchy,
A rhapsody of nations to supply,
Among themselves maintain'd eternal wars,
And still the ladies loved the conquerors.

THE Western Angles all the rest subdued,
A bloody nation, barbarous and rude;
Who by the tenure of the sword possess'd
One part of Britain, and subdued the rest:
And as great things denominate the small,
The conquering part gave title to the whole;
The Scot, Pict, Briton, Roman, Dane, submit,
And with the English Saxon all unite:
And these the mixture have so close pursued,
The very name and memory's subdued;
No Roman now, no Briton does remain;
Wales strove to separate, but strove in vain:
The silent nations undistinguish'd fall,
And Englishman's the common name for all.
Fate jumbled them together, God knows how;
Whate'er they were, they're true-born English now.

THE wonder which remains is at our pride,
To value that which all wise men deride;
For Englishmen to boast of generation
Cancels their knowledge, and lampoons the nation,
A true-born Englishman's a contradiction,
In speech an irony, in fact a fiction:
A banter made to be a test of fools,
Which those that use it justly ridicules;
A metaphor intended to express,

A man a-kin to all the universe.

Excerpts from *The Spanish Descent*

The word's gone out, and now they spread the main
With swelling sails, and swelling hopes, for Spain:
To double vengeance pressed where'er they come,
Resolved to pay the haughty Spaniard home:
Resolved by future conduct to atone
For all our past mistakes, and all their own.
New life springs up in every English face,
And fits them all for glorious things apace:
The booty some excites, and some the cause;
But more the hope to gain their lost applause.
Eager their sullied honour to restore,
Some anger whets, some pride and vengeance more.
    The lazy minutes now pass on too slow,
Fancy flies faster than the winds can blow:
Impatient wishes lengthen out the day;
They chide the loitering winds for their delay.
But time is nature's faithful messenger,
And brings up all we wish, as well as all we fear.
    The mists clear up, and now the scout decries
The subject of their hopes and victories:
The wished for fleets embayed, in harbour lie,
Unfit to fight, and more unfit to fly.
Triumphant joy throughout the navy flies,
Echoed from shore with terror and surprise.
Strange power of noise! which at one simple sound
At once shall some encourage, some confound.
    In vain the lion tangled in the snare
With anguish roars, and rends the trembling air:
'Tis vain to struggle with Almighty Fate;
Vain and impossible the weak debate.
The mighty boom, the forts, resist in vain.
The guns with fruitless force in noise complain.
See how the troops intrepidly fall on!
Wish for more foes, and think they fly too soon.
With eager fury to their forts pursue,

And think the odds of four to one too few.

The land's first conquered and the prize attends;

Fate beckons in the fleet to back their friends:

Despair succeeds, they struggle now too late,

And soon submit to their prevailing fate:

Courage is madness when occasion's past,

Death's the securest refuge, and the last.

       And now the rolling flames come threat'ning on,

And mighty streams of melted gold run down.

The flaming ore down to its centre makes,

To form new mines beneath the oozy lakes.

       Here a galleon with spicy drugs inflamed,

In odoriferous folds of sulphur streamed.

The gods of old no such oblations knew,

Their spices weak, and their perfumes but few.

The frighted Spaniards from their treasure fly,

Loath to forsake their wealth, but loath to die.

       Here a vast carrack flies while none pursue,

Bulged on the shore by her distracted crew:

There like a mighty mountain she appears,

And groans beneath the golden weight she bears.

Conquest perverts the property of friend,

And makes men ruin what they can't defend :

Some blow their treasures up into the air

With all the wild excesses of despair.

Strange fate! that war such odd events should have;

Friends would destroy, and enemies would save:

Others their safety to their wealth prefer,

And mix some small discretion with their fear.

Life's the best gift that nature can bestow;

The first that we receive, the last which we forgo:

And he that's vainly prodigal of blood,

Forfeits his sense to do his cause no good.

All desperation's the effect of fear;

Courage is temper, valour can't despair.

       And now the victory's completely gained;

No ships to conquer now, no foes remained.

The mighty spoils exceed whate'er was known

That vanquished ever lost, or victor won:

So great, if Fame shall future times remind,

They'll think she lies, and libels all mankind.

Joseph Addison (1672-1719)

Joseph Addison is an essayist, poet, dramatist, and government official. His writing skill led to his important posts in government while the Whigs were in power. In 1695, he wrote *A Poem to his Majesty* (William III), which brought favourable notice for later services of potential use to the crown. The greatest literary achievement is his co-author, with Richard Steele, of *The Tatler* and *The Spectator*, which elevates the English essay to a degree of technical perfection never before achieved and perhaps never since surpassed. His major works also include an opera libretto *Rosamund* (1707), a prose comedy *The Drummer* (1716), and a neoclassical tragedy *Cato* (1713). The poem *The Campaign* (1705), a poem addressed to Duke of Marlborough while trumpeting his successes as a modern "Iliad," a glorious hunt accomplished with spears rather than cannon and musketry, expresses the nation's great hour of victory at the Battle of Blenheim, where the Duke of Marlborough and Prince Eugene of Savoy won one of the most important victories of the War of the Spanish Succession on 13 August 1704. The poem's title in full is *The Campaign, A Poem, To His Grace the Duke of Marlborough*.

Excerpts from *The Campaign*…

While crowds of princes your deserts proclaim,

Proud in their number to enroll your name;

While emperors to you commit their cause,

And Anna's praises crown the vast applause,

Accept, great leader, what the muse indites,

That in ambitious verse records your fights,

Fir'd and transported with a theme so new:

Ten thousand wonders op'ning to my view

Shine forth at once, sieges and storms appear,

And wars and conquests fill th' important year,

Rivers of blood I see, and hills of slain;

An Iliad rising out of one campaign.

…

Thus would I fain Britannia's wars rehearse,

In the smooth records of a faithful verse;

That, if such numbers can o'er time prevail,

May tell posterity the wondrous tale.

When actions, unadorn'd, are faint and weak,

Cities and countries must be taught to speak,

Gods may descend in factions from the skies,

And rivers from their oozy beds arise;

Fiction may deck the truth with spurious rays,

And round the hero cast a borrow'd blaze.

Marlbro's exploits appear divinely bright,

And proudly shine in their own native light;

Rais'd of themselves, their genuine charms they boast,

And those who paint 'em truest praise 'em most.

James Thomson (1700–1748)

James Thomson is a poet best known for his masterpiece, a long blank verse in four parts, called *The Seasons*: *Winter* in 1726, *Summer* in 1727, *Spring* in 1728, and the whole poem, including *Autumn*, in 1730. He is also remembered for his ambitious poem in five parts, *Liberty* (1735–36), and for *The Castle of Indolence* (1748), an allegory in Spenserian stanzas. The excerpt is his famous ode "Rule, Britannia!" from *Alfred, a Masque* (1740), giving expression to the achievements of Newtonian science and to an England reaching toward great political power based on commercial and maritime expansion, which is later adapted as the British Navy song. It can also be a glorification of British colonisation.

"Rule, Britannia!"

When Britain first, at heaven's command,
  Arose from out the azure main,
This was the charter of the land,
  And guardian angels sung this strain—
    "Rule, Britannia, rule the waves;
    Britons never will be slaves."

The nations, not so blest as thee,
  Must in their turns to tyrants fall;
While thou shalt flourish great and free,
  The dread and envy of them all.
    "Rule, Britannia, rule the waves;
    Britons never will be slaves."

Still more majestic shalt thou rise,
  More dreadful from each foreign stroke;
As the loud blast that tears the skies

Serves but to root thy native oak.
"Rule, Britannia, rule the waves;
Britons never will be slaves."

Thee haughty tyrants ne'er shall tame;
All their attempts to bend thee down,
Will but arouse thy generous flame,
But work their woe and thy renown.
"Rule, Britannia, rule the waves;
Britons never will be slaves."

To thee belongs the rural reign;
Thy cities shall with commerce shine;
All thine shall be the subject main,
And every shore it circles thine.
"Rule, Britannia, rule the waves;
Britons never will be slaves."

The Muses, still with freedom found,
Shall to thy happy coast repair:
Blest isle! with matchless beauty crowned,
And manly hearts to guard the fair.
"Rule, Britannia, rule the waves;
Britons never will be slaves."

2. The Falsehood of Patriotism and Stigma of Colonizing Wars

The false flag of the British colonisation is "patriotism". It seems "quite strange" that Samuel Johnson had always kept "opened eyes" on the British colonising war and even all wars. In his speech "The Patriot" (addressed to the electors of Great Britain, 1774), Samuel Johnson said: "A patriot is he whose publick conduct is regulated by one single motive, the love of his country; who, as an agent in parliament, has, for himself, neither hope nor fear, neither kindness nor resentment, but refers every thing to the common interest"; "Patriotism is not necessarily included in rebellion. A man may hate his king, yet not love his country. He that has been refused a reasonable, or unreasonable request, who thinks his merit underrated, and sees his influence declining, begins soon to talk of natural equality, the absurdity of 'many made for one,' the original compact, the foundation of authority, and the majesty of the people"; and finally, "A patriot is always ready to countenance the just claims, and animate the reasonable hopes of the people; he reminds them, frequently, of their rights, and stimulates them to resent encroachments, and to multiply securities." The above three quotes have spoken for the truth, which makes Samuel Johnson the only found writer and scholar requiring careful and conscientious examination in the contemporary academic arena.

Samuel Johnson (1709–1784)

Samuel Johnson is a critic, biographer, essayist, poet, and lexicographer, widely regarded as one of the greatest figures of the 18th-century life and letters. One of his greatest contributions was *The Dictionary of the English Language* (1747). His thought of patriotism, as recorded in James Boswell's *The Life of Johnson* (1791), is widely quoted: "Patriotism is the last refuge of a scoundrel. But let it be considered, that he did not mean a real and generous love of our country, but that pretended patriotism which so many, in all ages and countries, have made a cloak for self-interest." He wrote poetry throughout his life, but most of which have not in general been well known. His poetic production is best known for the long poem *London* (1738) and *The Vanity of Human Wishes* (1749), in which he, like Juvenal, the Roman Satirist whose works denounced the corruption and extravagance of the privileged classes, satirises the folly of human desires such as wealth, power, war and et al., of which the excerpt is about King Charles XII of Sweden.[5] To Samuel Johnson, war is not the test lab of "Patriotism", but the stigma of the privileged class.

Excerpts from *The Vanity of Human Wishes*

On what foundation stands the warrior's pride,
How just his hopes, let Swedish Charles decide;
A frame of adamant, a soul of fire,
No dangers fright him, and no labours tire;
O'er love, o'er fear, extends his wide domain,
Unconquered lord of pleasure and of pain;
No joys to him pacific sceptres yield,
War sounds the trump, he rushes to the field;
Behold surrounding kings their powers combine,
And one capitulate, and one resign;
Peace courts his hand, but spreads her charms in vain;
'Think nothing gained,' he cries, 'till naught remain,
On Moscow's walls till Gothic standards fly,
And all be mine beneath the polar sky.'

---

5 King Charles XII of Sweden invaded Russia in 1708, where he was disastrously defeated at Pultowa in 1709. Unsuccessful in his efforts to forge a lasting alliance against Russia with Turkey, he invaded Norway; in 1816 he was killed in the attack on Fredrikshald.

The march begins in military state,

And nations on his eye suspended wait;

Stern Famine guards the solitary coast,

And Winter barricades the realms of Frost;

He comes, nor want nor cold his course delay—

Hide, blushing Glory, hide Pultowa's day:

The vanquished hero leaves his broken bands,

And shows his miseries in distant lands;

Condemned a needy supplicant to wait,

While ladies interpose, and slaves debate.

But did not Chance at length her error mend?

Did no subverted empire mark his end?

Did rival monarchs give the fatal wound?

Or hostile millions press him to the ground?

His fall was destined to a barren strand,

A petty fortress, and a dubious hand;

He left the name at which the world grew pale,

To point a moral, or adorn a tale.

3. Colonizers' Complexities and British Colonial American War Poetry

The colonising process in North America has witnessed the representative British colonisation types, during which the colonisers launched waves of wars against the natives. In 1581, the Separatist Robert Browne published "Treatise of Reformation without Tarrying for Any", which will be the manifesto of the Puritans who found the Massachusetts Bay colony. As for these English Puritans, they created colonies at Jamestown in 1607, and Plymouth in 1620. Each of these colonies has its Indian myth. Jamestown (in Virginia) has Pocahontas. Plymouth has the Thanksgiving dinner with the Wampanoags. But in reality, there was quickly conflict with the Indian tribes in both places. There were numerous such Indian struggles in the early colonial times, for instance: King Philip's War (1675–1676), also called "Metacom's War" or "Metacom's Rebellion", is named after King Philip, chief of the Wampanoag Indians; the war began when the English executed three Native Americans for murder; it involved several Native American peoples and all the New England colonies before the tribes were defeated.

There were also other numerous wars concerned both with European colonisers and American Indians: King William's War (1689–1697) was waged by William III of Great Britain and the League of Augsburg against France under Louis XIV, while the Canadian and New England colonists divided in support of their mother countries and, together with their respective Indian allies, assumed primary responsibility for their own defence. The war is also known as the first of the four French and Indian Wars because of the large-scale Indian participation. There was Queen Anne's War (1702–1713), the second in a series of wars fought between Great Britain and France in North America for control of the continent and at the same time as the War of the Spanish Succession in Europe. The English settlements were subject to repeated raids by French forces and their Indian allies; King William's War, Queen Anne's War, and King George's War (1744–1748) serve as the three earlier phases, followed by The American phase of Nine years' war (1754–1763) and The European phase of the Seven Years' War (1756–1763) between France and Great Britain, which determined the control of the vast colonial territory of North America. After years of warlike activity with France, England officially declared war on May 18 1756, beginning the Seven Year's War in Europe. Britain's victory relieved France of its North American empire, terminating the series of conflicts.

Colonial American war poems or songs were composed in such historical contexts. Almost no poetry was published in New York and Pennsylvania before 1776. Those known poets published their poems either in England or elsewhere, including Anne Bradstreet, Michael Wigglesworth, Edward Taylor, Nathaniel Ward, Edward Johnson, Sarah Kemble, Ebenezer Cook, Richard Lewis, Benjamin Tompson, and so on, most of whom wrote either religious poems or poems of nature, often religious in theme and traditional in form. Only Benjamin Tompson seemed to have presented the war—the King Philip's War—then being fought—as a crucial event in the history of Massachusetts Bay.

Benjamin Tompson (1642–1714)

Benjamin Tompson is America's first native poet. He was most active in writing from 1666 until 1683 and again from 1695 until 1713. He is known for his only book *New Englands Crisis. Or a Brief Narrative of New Englands Lamentable Estate at Present, Compar'd with the Former (but Few) Years of Prosperity* (1676), which is the first book of verse initially published in America and later republished in England. The long poem describes many Indian surprise attacks on English settlements under the leadership of Metacomet, known to the settlers as King Philip. Some British military commentators employed the phrase "civilised warfare" to distinguish wars between recognised nation-states from the war outside Europe in the pursuit of colonial objectives. But the colonising wars are often represented as a romantic image of war or bravery to pioneer civilisations, or a combination of travelogue, big-game hunting, and exploration, with a little fighting to spice up the tale, but the reality was often much more brutal than its more fanciful depictions. The excerpt is from *New Englands Crisis*, subtitled with "On the Women Fortifying Boston Neck".

Excerpts from *New Englands Crisis*

A GRAND attempt some Amazonian Dames
Contrive whereby to glorify their names,
A ruff for Boston Neck of mud and turfe,
Reaching from side to side, from surf to surf,
Their nimble hands spin up like Christmas pyes,
Their pastry by degrees on high doth rise.
The wheel at home counts in an holiday,
Since while the mistress worketh it may play.
A tribe of female hands, but manly hearts,
Forsake at home their pastry crust and tarts,
To kneed the dirt, the samplers down they hurl,
Their undulating silks they closely furl.
The pick-axe one as a commandress holds,
While t'other at her awk'ness gently scolds.
One puffs and sweats, the other mutters why
Cant you promove your work so fast as I?
Some dig, some delve, and others' hands do feel
The little wagon's weight with single wheel.
And least some fainting-fits the weak surprize,
They want no sack nor cakes, they are more wise.
These brave essays draw forth male, stronger hands,
More like to dawbers than to marshal bands;
These do the work, and sturdy bulwarks raise,
But the beginners well deserve the praise.

Anonymous: "Lovewell's Fight"[6]

OF worthy Captain Lovewell, I purpose now to sing,
How valiantly he served his country and his king;
He and his valiant soldiers did range the woods full wide,
And hardships they endured to quell the Indian's pride.

'T was nigh unto Pigwacket, on the eighth day of May,
They spied a rebel Indian soon after break of day;
He on a bank was walking, upon a neck of land,

---

6 This ballad was said to be written soon after the battle of May 8th, 1725, but its author had been lost. As the earliest American war ballads known, it was regarded as "the most beloved song in all New England".

Which leads into a pond as we're made to understand.

Our men resolved to have him, and travelled two miles round,
Until they met the Indian, who boldly stood his ground;
Then up speaks Captain Lovewell: "Take you good heed," says he,
"This rogue is to decoy us, I very plainly see.

"The Indians lie in ambush, in some place nigh at hand,
In order to surround us upon this neck of land;
Therefore we'll march in order, and each man leave his pack;
That we may briskly fight them, when they make their attack."

They came unto this Indian, who did them thus defy,
As soon as they came nigh him, two guns he did let fly,
Which wounded Captain Lovewell, and likewise one man more,
But when this rogue was running, they laid him in his gore.

Then having scalped the Indian, they went back to the spot
Where they had laid their packs down, but there they found them not.
For the Indians having spied them, when they them down did lay,
Did seize them for their plunder, and carry them away.

These rebels lay in ambush, this very place hard by,
So that an English soldier did one of them espy,
And cried out, "Here's an Indian"! with that they started out,
As fiercely as old lions, and hideously did shout.

With that our valiant English all gave a loud huzza,
To show the rebel Indians they feared them not a straw:
So now the fight began, and as fiercely as could be,
The Indians ran up to them, but soon were forced to flee.

Then spake up Captain Lovewell, when first the fight began:
"Fight on, my valiant heroes! You see they fall like rain."
For as we are informed, the Indians were so thick
A man could scarcely fire a gun and not some of them hit.

Then did the rebels try their best our soldiers to surround,
But they could not accomplish it, because there was a pond,

To which our men retreated, and covered all the rear,
The rogues were forced to face them, although they skulked for fear.

Two logs there were behind them that close together lay,
Without being discovered, they could not get away;
Therefore our valiant English they travelled in a row,
And at a handsome distance, as they were wont to go.

'T was ten o'clock in the morning when first the fight begun,
And fiercely did continue until the setting sun;
Excepting that the Indians some hours before 't was night
Drew off into the bushes and ceased awhile to fight.

But soon again returned, in fierce and furious mood.
Shouting as in the morning, but yet not half so loud;
For as we are informed, so thick and fast they fell,
Scarce twenty of their number at night did get home well.

And that our valiant English till midnight there did stay,
To see whether the rebels would have another fray;
But they no more returning, they made off towards their home,
And brought away their wounded as far as they could come.

Of all our valiant English there were but thirty-four,
And of the rebel Indians there were about fourscore,
And sixteen of our English did safely home return,
The rest were killed and wounded, for which we all must mourn.

Our worthy Captain Lovewell among them there did die,
They killed Lieutenant Robbins, and wounded good young Frye,
Who was our English chaplain; he many Indians slew,
And some of them he scalped when bullets round him flew.

Young Fullam, too, I'll mention, because he fought so well,
Endeavoring to save a man, a sacrifice he fell:
But yet our valiant Englishmen in fight were ne'er dismayed,
But still they kept their motion, and Wymans captain made.

Who shot the old chief Pagus, which did the foe defeat,

Then set his men in order, and brought off the retreat;

And braving many dangers and hardships in the way,

They safe arrived at Dunstable, the thirteenth day of May.

Anonymous: "The Song of Braddock's Men"[7]

To arms, to arms! my jolly grenadiers!

    Hark how the drums do roll it along!

To horse, to horse, with valiant good cheer;

    We'll meet our proud foe before it is long.

Let not your courage fail you;

Be valiant, stout, and bold;

And it will soon avail you,

My loyal hearts of gold.

Huzzah, my valiant countrymen!—again I say huzzah!

'T is nobly done,—the day's our own—huzzah, huzzah!

March on, march on, brave Braddock leads the foremost;

    The battle is begun as you may fairly see.

Stand firm, be bold, and it will soon be over;

    We'll soon gain the field from our proud enemy.

    A squadron now appears, my boys;

    If that they do but stand!

    Boys, never fear, be sure you mind

    The word of command!

Huzzah, my valiant countrymen!—again I say huzzah!

'T is nobly done,—the day's our own—huzzah, huzzah!

See how, see how, they break and fly before us!

    See how they are scattered all over the plain!

Now, now—now, now, our country will adore us!

    In peace and in triumph, boys, when we return again!

    Then laurels shall our glory crown

    For all our actions told:

    The hills shall echo all around,

---

7 The old ballad wrote that Braddock was sent to America to take charge of the army there and to expel the French from their encroachments west of the Allegheny Mountains. He scorned the advice of Americans who were accustomed to border warfare while George Washington was among others, and was killed, a victim to his own obstinacy, on July 9, 1755.

My loyal hearts of gold.
Huzzah, my valiant countrymen!—again I say huzzah!
'T is nobly done,—the day's our own—huzzah, huzzah!

Chapter III

The Anglo-American War Poetry and the Age of Revolutions (1774–1830)

The "Age of Revolutions" indicates the profound and comprehensive transformations of the Anglo-American world from about the 1770s to the 1830s. In past historiography of the Western culture in general and the Anglo-American culture in particular, historical periodization has been called as such, for instance: in his epic four-volume history of the modern world, *The Age of Revolution: Europe 1789–1848*, Eric Hobsbawm defines it as a period of the death of the ancient traditions, the triumph of new classes, and the emergence of new technologies, sciences, and ideologies; in their *The Age of the Democratic Revolution: A Political History of Europe and America, 1760–1800*, R. R. Palmer and et al. wrote that the period from 1760 to 1800 was the great revolutionary era, marking the advent of the modern democratic state, showing that the American, French, and Polish revolutions…were manifestations of similar political ideas, needs, and conflicts, and clearly illustrating that the clash between an older form of society characterized by legalized social rank and hereditary or self-perpetuating elites is transformed into a new form of society placing a greater value on social mobility and legal equality; in his *The Age of Revolution: A History of the English-Speaking Peoples*, Winston Churchill regards "the Age of Revolution" as characteristic of the American and French Revolutions, which have transformed the political structure of much of the world, altered traditional political and social thought, and dissolved most traditional European notions of political authority, and most importantly, the global conception of power.

In addition to varieties of political revolutions, the more profound and comprehensive is the "Industrial Revolution"[1], which, taking place across the Atlantic world, began in Britain in the late 18th century and from there spread to other parts of the world and had gradually forced an agrarian and handicraft economy to one dominated by industry. The main features were technological, socioeconomic, and cultural.

The final solution to the Age of Revolutions is a new chart of the world power with the British Empire as the strongest, in spite of its surrender in America and acknowledgement of its independence in 1783. As it has subdued the Spanish earlier, Britain terminated the French dominance during The Napoleonic Wars (1803–1815), in which an array of European powers formed into various coalitions and financed and usually led by the United Kingdom fighting with France. As for changes of wars, the historian Frederic J. Baumgartner has summarised: both the American and the French Revolutions[2] drew heavily from the Enlightenment for inspiration in staging their revolutions and for the concepts of war and ideas for the new governments they created: Enlightened philosophers were sharply critical of war, regarding it as the greatest evil confronting mankind though they had little hope it could be eliminated; they combine proposals for permanent peace with a more realistic discussion of the means by which war might be limited or rendered more humane; the "civilizing of war" seemed to be a reasonable, worthwhile, and achievable undertaking.[3]

In the revolutionary periods spanning from the end of the 1800s to the middle of the 19th century, American revolutions resonated with French Revolutions and even revolutions across the whole of Europe, plunging the transatlantic world into an integrated community for "looking for better societies." Although the British and the Americans were in confrontations, they were in fact, integrated as a whole culturally as the British romanticism echoed with the legacy of American independence. Thomas Paine announced that "Society in every state is a blessing, but government, even in its best stage, is but a necessary evil" and "in its worst state an intolerable one." The "common sense" had generated a history of the "American distrust of government": Not only is the natural legitimacy of the state negated, but also the power of the dominant is to be subverted. Edmund Burke's *Reflections on the Revolution in France* (1790) had once met the rising sympathy for events in France with questions about the legitimacy and future of the state. The intellectual and political turmoil surrounding the French Revolution had set in motion intense and urgent discussion concerning the nature of society. Samuel Taylor Coleridge now conceived the design of circumventing the disastrous violence that had

---

1 Although used earlier by French writers, the term *"Industrial Revolution"* was first popularized by the English economic historian Arnold Toynbee (1852–1883) to describe Britain's economic development from 1760 to 1840. Later, the term was spreading to all of the transatlantic world.

2 The "French Revolution", or the "Revolution of 1789", is a revolutionary movement (1787–1799) that denotes the end of the "ancien régime" of political and social system of hierarchy in France, which serves to distinguish from the later French revolutions of 1830, or "July Revolution", which brought Louis-Philippe to the throne, and 1848, or "Revolutions of 1848", which indicates series of republican revolts against European monarchies, but all ended in failure and repression.

3 F. J. Baumgartner, *Declaring War in Early Modern Europe*. New York: Palgrave Macmillan, 2011, p. 147.

destroyed the idealism of the French Revolution by establishing a small society that should organise itself and educate its children according to better principles than those obtained in the society around them.

1. Poetry of the American Revolutionary Wars

In addition to essays of political debate, biographies and memoirs, epistolary correspondences, fiction, the American revolutionary bards produced verses in a wide variety of forms—the epic, the dramatic, the lyric, the narrative, and so on. Throughout the century and a half before the American Revolution, little seemed to have produced in the English colonies that may rightly be termed literature save those of religious fervor and dogmatic earnestness. In addition, none of the early American novels addressed the Revolution directly except Susanna Rowson's *Charlotte Temple*. When the three-fold struggle for religious freedom, the thirst for adventure and interest in trade had become a revolutionary fervour for the comprehensive transformation of the American colony beyond the purpose of mere independence from the British rule, American poetic production seemed to explore and maintain a long time of its explosive energy.

Anonymous: "The Battle of Trenton"[4]

On Christmas-day in seventy-six,
Our ragged troops, with bayonets fixed,
    For Trenton marched away.
The Delaware see! the boats below!
The light obscured by hail and snow!
    But no signs of dismay.

Our object was the Hessian band,
That dared invade fair freedom's land,
    And quarter in that place.
Great Washington he led us on,
Whose streaming flag, in storm or sun;
    Had never known disgrace.

---

4 In 1776, the Continental Army desperately needed a victory after months of intense fighting with several significant defeats and no major victories. Following his famous crossing of the Delaware River, General George Washington marched the Continental Army to Trenton, New Jersey, where the highly trained Hessian army was crushed in Washington's raid across the Delaware River and the Americans were invigorated by the easy defeat of the British Hessian forces.

In silent march we passed the night,

Each soldier panting for the fight,

　　　Though quite benumbed with frost.

Greene on the left at six began,

The right was led by Sullivan

　　　Who ne'er a moment lost.

Their pickets stormed, the alarm was spread,

That rebels risen from the dead

　　　Were marching into town.

Some scampered here, some scampered there,

And some for action did prepare;

　　　But soon their arms laid down.

Twelve hundred servile miscreants,

With all their colors, guns, and tents,

　　　Were trophies of the day.

The frolic o'er, the bright canteen,

In centre, front, and rear was seen

　　　Driving fatigue away.

Now, brothers of the patriot bands,

Let's sing deliverance from the hands

　　　Of arbitrary sway.

And as our life is but a span,

Let's touch the tankard while we can.

　　　In memory of that day.

Anonymous: "The Ballad of Nathan Hale" (1856)[5]

The breezes went steadily through the tall pines,

A-saying "oh! hu-ush!" a-saying "oh! hu-ush!"

As stilly stole by a bold legion of horse,

For Hale in the bush, for Hale in the bush.

"Keep still!" said the thrush as she nestled her young

In a nest by the road; in a nest by the road.

---

5 Selected from Moore F., *Songs and Ballads of the American Revolution*. Boston: D Appleton & Company
& Broadway, 1856.

"For the tyrants are near, and with them appear
What bodes us no good, what bodes us no good."

The brave captain heard it, and thought of his home
In a cot by the brook; in a cot by the brook.
With mother and sister and memories dear,
He so gayly forsook; he so gayly forsook.

Cooling shades of the night were coming apace,
The tattoo had beat; the tattoo had beat.
The noble one sprang from his dark lurking-place,
To make his retreat; to make his retreat.

He warily trod on the dry rustling leaves,
As he passed through the wood, as he passed through the wood;
And silently gained his rude launch on the shore,
As she played with the flood; as she played with the flood.

The guards of the camp, on that dark, dreary night,
Had a murderous will; had a murderous will.
They took him and bore him afar from the shore,
To a hut on the hill; to a hut on the hill.

No mother was there, nor a friend who could cheer,
In that little stone cell; in that little stone cell.
But he trusted in love, from his Father above,
In his heart, all was well; in his heart, all was well.

An ominous owl, with his solemn bass voice,
Sat moaning hard by; sat moaning hard by:
"The tyrant's proud minions most gladly rejoice,
For he soon must die; for he soon must die."

The brave fellow told them, no thing he restrained,—
The cruel general! the cruel general!—
His errand from camp, of the ends to be gained,
And said that was all; and said that was all.

They took him and bound him and bore him away,

Down the hill's grassy side; down the hill's grassy side.
'T was there the base hirelings, in royal array,
His cause did deride; his cause did deride.

Five minutes were given, short moments, no more,
For him to repent; for him to repent.
He prayed for his mother, he asked not another,
To Heaven he went; to Heaven he went.

The faith of a martyr the tragedy showed,
As he trod the last stage; as he trod the last stage.
And Britons will shudder at gallant Hale's blood
As his words do presage, as his words do presage.

"Thou pale king of terrors, thou life's gloomy foe,
Go frighten the slave; go frighten the slave;
Tell tyrants, to you their allegiance they owe.
No fears for the brave; no fears for the brave."

John Dickinson (1732–1808)

John Dickinson is an American statesman, a delegate to the Continental Congress and one of the writers of the Articles of Confederation, often referred to as the "Penman of the Revolution." His reputation in 1767–1768 came from his famous *Letters from a Farmer in Pennsylvania, to the Inhabitants of the British Colonies*. The excerpted poem, named the "Liberty Song", was printed first in the *Pennsylvania Chronicle* of July 4, 1768. In his *The American Revolution as Revealed in the Poetry of the Period: A Study of American Patriotic Verse from 1760–1783* (1915), Samuel White Patterson called it "The Words of Battle", and noted that the poem was sung to the tune of "Hearts of Oak".[6]

"Liberty Song"

Come join hand in hand, brave Americans all,
And rouse your bold hearts at fair Liberty's call;
No tyrannous acts shall suppress your just claim,
Or stain with dishonor America's name,
　　In freedom we're born, and in freedom we'll live;
　　Our purses are ready,

---

6 Samuel White Patterson, *The American Revolution as Revealed in the Poetry of the Period: A Study of American Patriotic Verse from 1760–1783*. Boston: Richard G. Badger, 1915, pp. 41-43.

Steady, Friends, steady,
Not as *slaves*, but as *freemen* our money we'll give.

Our worthy forefathers—let's give them a cheer—
To climates unknown did courageously steer;
Thro's oceans to deserts, for freedom they came,
And, dying, bequeath'd us their freedom and fame.

Their generous bosoms all dangers despis'd,
So highly, so wisely, their birthrights they priz'd;
We'll keep what they gave, we will piously keep,
Nor frustrate their toils on the land or the deep.

The tree, their own hands had to Liberty rear'd,
They lived to behold growing strong and rever'd;
With transport then cried,—"Now our wishes we gain
For our children shall gather the fruits of our pain."

How sweet are the labors that freemen endure,
That they shall enjoy al l the profit, secure,—
No more such sweet labors Americans know,
If Britons shall reap what Americans sow.

Then join hand in hand, brave Americans all,
By uniting we stand, by dividing we fall;
In so righteous a cause let us hope to succeed,
For Heaven approves of each generous deed.

All ages shall speak with amaze and applause,
Of the courage we'll show in support of our laws;
To die we can bear,—but to serve we disdain,
For shame is to freedom more dreadful than pain.

This bumper I crown for our sovereign's health,
And this for Britannia's glory and wealth;
That wealth and that glory immortal may be,
If she is but just, and we are but free.

    In freedom we're born, and in freedom we'll live;
    Our purses are ready,

Steady, Friends, steady,

Not as *slaves*, but as *freemen* our money we'll give.

Joseph Warren (1741–1775)

Joseph Warren is a physician, politician, soldier, and revolutionary, often regarded as the most notable founding figure and representative example of an involved citizen from a time before the creation of the United States of America, casting in words and actions an inspirational view for the meaning of America. He was the hero of the Battle of Bunker Hill. He went to the Battle to offer his services as a volunteer, fought valiantly, and was one of the last Americans to leave Breed's Hill, but was tragically struck in the back of the head by a musket ball and died instantly. The excerpt was printed in the *Massachusetts Newspapers* in 1774.

"Free America"

That seat of Science, Athens,

And earth's proud mistress, Rome;

Where now are all their glories?

We scarce can find a tomb.

Then guard your rights, Americans,

Nor stoop to lawless sway;

Oppose, oppose, oppose, oppose,

For North America.

We led fair Freedom hither,

And lo, the desert smiled!

A paradise of pleasure

Was opened in the wild!

Your harvest, bold Americans,

No power shall snatch away!

Huzza, huzza, huzza, huzza,

For free America.

Torn from a world of tyrants,

Beneath this western sky,

We formed a new dominion,

A land of liberty:

The world shall own we're masters here;

Then hasten on the day:

Huzza, huzza, huzza, huzza,
For free America.

Proud Albion bowed to Cæsar,
And numerous lords before;
To Picts, to Danes, to Normans,
And many masters more:
But we can boast, Americans,
We've never fallen a prey;
Huzza, huzza, huzza, huzza,
For free America.

God bless this maiden climate,
And through its vast domain
May hosts of heroes cluster,
Who scorn to wear a chain:
And blast the venal sycophant
That dares our rights betray;
Huzza, huzza, huzza, huzza,
For free America.

Lift up your hands, ye heroes,
And swear with proud disdain,
The wretch that would ensnare you,
Shall lay his snares in vain:
Should Europe empty all her force,
We'll meet her in array,
And fight and shout, and shout and fight
For North America.

Some future day shall crown us,
The masters of the main,
Our fleets shall speak in thunder
To England, France, and Spain;
And the nations over the ocean spread
Shall tremble and obey
The sons, the sons, the sons, the sons,
Of brave America.

John Trumbull (1750–1831)

John Trumbull is an American poet and jurist, widely known for his political satire. He was the leader of what has been known as the "Connecticut Wits" or "Hartford Wits". In 1772 he published his *Progress of Dullness*, a satirical verse against the current educational system and the ignorance of the clergy. His comic epic *M'Fingal* (1776–1782) mocked the British cause through the story of a Loyalist named Squire M'Fingal. The excerpt is Canto I of the poem.

Excerpts from *M'Fingal*

When Yankies, skill'd in martial rule,
First put the British troops to school;
Instructed them in warlike trade,
And new manoeuvres of parade,
The true war-dance of Yankee reels,
And manual exercise of heels;
Made them give up, like saints complete,
The arm of flesh, and trust the feet,
And work, like Christians undissembling,
Salvation out, by fear and trembling;
Taught Percy fashionable races,
And modern modes of Chevy-Chases:
From Boston, in his best array,
Great Squire M'Fingal took his way,
And graced with ensigns of renown,
Steer'd homeward to his native town.

His high descent our heralds trace
From Ossian's famed Fingalian race:
For though their name some part may lack,
Old Fingal spelt it with a Mac;
Which great M'Pherson, with submission,
We hope will add the next edition.

His fathers flourish'd in the Highlands
Of Scotia's fog-benighted islands;
Whence gain'd our Squire two gifts by right,
Rebellion, and the Second-sight.
Of these, the first, in ancient days,
Had gain'd the noblest palm of praise,

'Gainst kings stood forth and many a crown'd head
With terror of its might confounded;
Till rose a king with potent charm
His foes by meekness to disarm,
Whom every Scot and Jacobite
Strait fell in love with at first sight;
Whose gracious speech with aid of pensions,
Hush'd down all murmurs of dissensions,
And with the sound of potent metal
Brought all their buzzing swarms to settle;
Who rain'd his ministerial manna,
Till loud Sedition sung hosanna;
The grave Lords-Bishops and the Kirk
United in the public work;
Rebellion, from the northern regions,
With Bute and Mansfield swore allegiance;
All hands combin'd to raze, as nuisance,
Of church and state the Constitutions,
Pull down the empire, on whose ruins
They meant to edify their new ones;
Enslave th' Amer'can wildernesses,
And rend the provinces in pieces.
With these our 'Squire, among the valiant'st,
Employ'd his time, and tools and talents,
And found this new rebellion pleasing
As his old king-destroying treason.

Nor less avail'd his optic sleight,
And Scottish gift of second-sight.
No ancient sybil, famed in rhyme,
Saw deeper in the womb of time;
No block in old Dodona's grove
Could ever more orac'lar prove.
Nor only saw he all that could be,
But much that never was, nor would be;
Whereby all prophets far outwent he,
Though former days produced a plenty:
For any man with half an eye
What stands before him can espy;

But optics sharp it needs, I ween,

To see what is not to be seen.

As in the days of ancient fame,

Prophets and poets were the same,

And all the praise that poets gain

Is for the tales they forge and feign:

So gain'd our Squire his fame by seeing

Such things, as never would have being;

Whence he for oracles was grown

The very tripod of his town.

Gazettes no sooner rose a lie in,

But strait he fell to prophesying;

Made dreadful slaughter in his course,

O'erthrew provincials, foot and horse,

Brought armies o'er, by sudden pressings,

Of Hanoverians, Swiss and Hessians,

Feasted with blood his Scottish clan,

And hang'd all rebels to a man,

Divided their estates and pelf,

And took a goodly share himself.

All this with spirit energetic,

He did by second-sight prophetic.

Philip Freneau (1752–1832)

Philip Freneau is an American poet, essayist, and editor, widely known as the "poet of the American Revolution." He was schooled in the classics and the Neoclassical English poetry of the period, but he hunted for a fresh idiom that would be unmistakably American. In 1780, he was captured and imprisoned and treated brutally on the British prison ship *Scorpion*, and on his release, he wrote his experience of captivity in *The British Prison-Ship* (1781). His collection of *Poems Written and Published during the American Revolutionary War* (1809) appeared in two volumes.

"Emancipation from British Dependence"

Libera nos, Domine—Deliver us, O Lord, Not only from British dependence, but also,

FROM a junto that labor for absolute power,

Whose schemes disappointed have made them look sour;

From the lords of the council, who fight against freedom

Who still follow on where delusion shall lead 'em.

From groups at St. James's who slight our Petitions,
And fools that are waiting for further submissions;
From a nation whose manners are rough and abrupt,
From scoundrels and rascals whom gold can corrupt.

From pirates sent out by command of the king
To murder and plunder, but never to swing;
From Wallace, and Graves, and *Vipers*, and *Roses*,
Whom, if Heaven pleases, we'll give bloody noses.

From the valiant Dunmore, with his crew of banditti
Who plunder Virginians at Williamsburg city,
From hot-headed Montague, mighty to swear,
The little fat man with his pretty white hair.

From bishops in Britain, who butchers are grown,
From slaves that would die for a smile from the throne,
From assemblies that vote against Congress' proceedings,
(Who now see the fruit of their stupid misleadings).

From Tryon, the mighty, who flies from our city,
And swelled with importance, disdains the committee;
(But since he is pleased to proclaim us his foes,
What the devil care we where the devil he goes.)

From the caitiff, Lord North, who would bind us in chains,
From our noble King Log, with his toothful of brains,
Who dreams, and is certain (when taking a nap)
He has conquered our lands as they lay on his map.

From a kingdom that bullies, and hectors, and swears.
I send up to Heaven my wishes and prayers
That we, disunited, may freemen be still,
And Britain go on—to be damn'd if she will.

Excerpts from *The British Prison-Ship*

Four hundred wretches here, denied all light,
In crowded mansions pass the infernal night,
Some for a bed their tatter'd vestments join,
And some on chests, and some on floors recline;
Shut from the blessings of the evening air
Pensive we lay with mingled corpses there,
Meagre and wan, and scorch'd with heat, below,
We look'd like ghosts, ere death had made us so —
How could we else, where heat and hunger join'd,
Thus to debase the body and the mind,——
Where cruel thirst the parching throat invades,
Dries up the man, and fits him for the shades.

No waters laded from the bubbling spring
To these dire ships these little tyrants bring——
By plank and ponderous beams completely wall'd
In vain for water and in vain we call'd——
No drop was granted to the midnight prayer,
To *rebels* in these regions of despair!——
The loathsome cask a deadly dose contains,
Its poison circling through the languid veins;
Here, *generous* Briton, generous, as you say,
To my parch'd tongue one cooling drop convey,
Hell has no mischief like a thirsty throat,
"Nor one tormentor like your *David Sproat*."

Dull pass'd the hours, till, from the East displayed,
Sweet morn dispell'd the horrors of the shade;
On every side dire objects met the sight,
And pallid forms, and murders of the night,——
The dead were past their pain, the living groan,
Nor dare to hope another morn their own;
But what to them is morn's delightful ray?
Sad and distressful as the close of day;
O'er distant streams appears the dewy green,
And leafy trees on mountain tops are seen,
But they no groves nor grassy mountains tread,

Mark'd for a longer journey to the dead.

"Eutaw Springs"[7]

At Eutaw Springs the valiant died;
Their limbs with dust are covered o'er—
Weep on, ye springs, your tearful tide;
How many heroes are no more!

If in this wreck or ruin, they
Can yet be thought to claim a tear,
O smite your gentle breast, and say
The friends of freedom slumber here!

Thou, who shalt trace this bloody plain,
If goodness rules thy generous breast,
Sigh for the wasted rural reign;
Sign for the shepherds, sunk to rest!

Stranger, their humble graves adorn;
You too may fall, and ask a tear;
'Tis not the beauty of the morn
That proves the evening shall be clear.—

They saw their injured country's woe;
The flaming town, the wasted field;
Then rushed to meet the insulting foe;
They took the spear—but left the shield.

Led by thy conquering genius, Greene,
The Britons they compelled to fly;
None distant viewed the fatal plain,
None grieved, in such a cause to die—

But, like the Parthian, famed of old,
Who, flying, still their arrows threw,
These routed Britons, full as bold,

---

7 The poem is subtitled with "To the Memory of the Brave Americans under General Greene, in South Carolina, who fell in the action of September 8, 1781."

Retreated, and retreating slew.

Now rest in peace, our patriot band,
Though far from nature's limits thrown,
We trust they find a happier land,
A brighter sunshine of their own.

"The American Soldier"

Deep in a vale, a stranger now to arms,
Too poor to shine in courts, too proud to beg,
He, who once warred on *Saratoga's* plains,
Sits musing o'er his scars, and wooden leg.

Remembering still the toil of former days,
To other hands he sees his earnings paid;—
They share the due reward—*he* feeds on praise.
Lost in the abyss of want, misfortune's shade.

Far, far from domes where splendid tapers glare,
'Tis his from dear bought *peace* no wealth to win,
Removed alike from courtly cringing 'squires,
The great-man's *Levee*, and the proud man's grin.

Sold are those arms which once on Britons blazed,
When, flushed with conquest, to the charge they came;
That power repelled, and *Freedom's* fabrick raised,
She leaves her soldier—*famine and a name!*

Timothy Dwight (1752–1817)

Timothy Dwight is a poet, educator, clergyman and theologian. He is a grandson of Jonathan Edwards and a founding member of the first "literary school" in America, the Connecticut Wits, including such poets as a John Trumbull (1750–1831), Joel Barlow (1754–1812), David Humphreys (1752–1818), and others. He served as chaplain in the army in 1777–1778, and later in his life, he served as the eighth president of Yale in 1795, serving until 1817. Dwight followed the particular Augustan sense of poetry as a means of political or ideological reflection, a characteristic of the neoclassic period, especially of 18th-century English literature. His *The Conquest of Canaan* (1785), distinctly patriotic, is believed to be the first epic poem produced in America. He also wrote a number of songs for the soldiers of the Revolution, for instance, "Columbia", written while he was an Army Chaplain.

"Columbia"

COLUMBIA, Columbia, to glory arise,
The queen of the world, and the child of the skies!
Thy genius commands thee; with rapture behold,
While ages on ages thy splendors unfold.
Thy reign is the last, and the noblest of time,
Most fruitful thy soil, most inviting thy clime;
Let the crimes of the east ne'er encrimson thy name,
Be freedom, and science, and virtue thy fame.

To conquest and slaughter let Europe aspire;
Whelm nations in blood, and wrap cities in fire;
Thy heroes the rights of mankind shall defend,
And triumph pursue them, and glory attend.
A world is thy realm: for a world be thy laws,
Enlarged as thine empire, and just as thy cause;
On Freedom's broad basis, that empire shall rise,
Extend with the main, and dissolve with the skies.

Fair Science her gates to thy sons shall unbar,
And the east see thy morn hide the beams of her star.
New bards, and new sages, unrivalled shall soar
To fame unextinguished, when time is no more;
To thee, the last refuge of virtue designed,
Shall fly from all nations the best of mankind;
Here, grateful to heaven, with transport shall bring
Their incense, more fragrant than odors of spring.

Nor less shall thy fair ones to glory ascend,
And genius and beauty in harmony blend;
The graces of form shall awake pure desire,
And the charms of the soul ever cherish the fire;
Their sweetness unmingled, their manners refined,
And virtue's bright image, instamped on the mind,
With peace and soft rapture shall teach life to glow,
And light up a smile in the aspect of woe.

Thy fleets to all regions thy power shall display,

The nations admire, and the ocean obey;

Each shore to thy glory its tribute unfold,

And the east and the south yield their spices and gold.

As the day-spring unbounded, thy splendor shall flow,

And earth's little kingdoms before thee shall bow:

While the ensigns of union, in triumph unfurled,

Hush the tumult of war, and give peace to the world.

Thus, as down a lone valley, with cedars o'erspread,

From war's dread confusion I pensively strayed—

The gloom from the face of fair heaven retired;

The winds ceased to murmur; the thunders expired;

Perfumes, as of Eden, flowed sweetly along,

And a voice, as of angels, enchantingly sung:

"Columbia, Columbia, to glory arise,

The queen of the world, and the child of the skies."

Phillis Wheatley (1753–1784)

Phillis Wheatley is the first African American and the third woman in America to publish a book, and the first African American woman to make a living from her writings. Her only poetic collection is *Poems on Various Subjects, Religious and Moral* (1773), published in London, apart from which she also wrote about the current political events and was a strong supporter of American independence. She wrote the "To His Excellency, George Washington", paying tributes to his heroism, and was invited to George Washington's house for a private reading. Wheatley also explores the ironies of patriotic rhetoric of freedom that could not only tolerate but actually embrace racial slavery. In her poem "To the Right Honorable William, Earl of Dartmouth" (1802), she subtly weaves together the rhetoric of the Revolution with images of slavery for the American patriots had often identified British imperial policies with an attempt to enslave the colonies.

"To His Excellency, George Washington"

Celestial choir! enthron'd in realms of light,

Columbia's scenes of glorious toils I write.

While freedom's cause her anxious breast alarms,

She flashes dreadful in refulgent arms.

See mother earth her offspring's fate bemoan,

And nations gaze at scenes before unknown!

See the bright beams of heaven's revolving light
Involved in sorrows and veil of night!
The goddess comes, she moves divinely fair,
Olive and laurel bind her golden hair:
Wherever shines this native of the skies,
Unnumber'd charms and recent graces rise.

Muse! bow propitious while my pen relates
How pour her armies through a thousand gates,
As when Eolus heaven's fair face deforms,
Enwrapp'd in tempest and a night of storms;
Astonish'd ocean feels the wild uproar,
The refluent surges beat the sounding shore;
Or thick as leaves in Autumn's golden reign,
Such, and so many, moves the warrior's train.
In bright array they seek the work of war,
Where high unfurl'd the ensign waves in air.
Shall I to Washington their praise recite?
Enough thou know'st them in the fields of fight.
Thee, first in peace and honours,—we demand
The grace and glory of thy martial band.
Fam'd for thy valour, for thy virtues more,
Hear every tongue thy guardian aid implore!

One century scarce perform'd its destined round,
When Gallic powers Columbia's fury found;
And so may you, whoever dares disgrace
The land of freedom's heaven-defended race!
Fix'd are the eyes of nations on the scales,
For in their hopes Columbia's arm prevails.
Anon Britannia droops the pensive head,
While round increase the rising hills of dead.
Ah! cruel blindness to Columbia's state!
Lament thy thirst of boundless power too late.

Proceed, great chief, with virtue on thy side,
Thy ev'ry action let the goddess guide.
A crown, a mansion, and a throne that shine,
With gold unfading, WASHINGTON! be thine.

"America"

New England first a wilderness was found
Till for a continent 'twas destin'd round
From feild to feild the savage monsters run
E'r yet Brittania had her work begun
Thy Power, O Liberty, makes strong the weak
And (wond'rous instinct) Ethiopians speak
Sometimes by Simile, a victory's won
A certain lady had an only son
He grew up daily virtuous as he grew
Fearing his Strength which she undoubted knew
She laid some taxes on her darling son
And would have laid another act there on
Amend your manners I'll the task remove
Was said with seeming Sympathy and Love
By many Scourges she his goodness try'd
Untill at length the Best of Infants cry'd
He wept, Brittania turn'd a senseless ear
At last awaken'd by maternal fear
Why weeps americus why weeps my Child
Thus spake Brittania, thus benign and mild
My dear mama said he, shall I repeat —
Then Prostrate fell, at her maternal feet
What ails the rebel, great Brittania Cry'd
Indeed said he, you have no cause to Chide
You see each day my fluent tears my food.
Without regard, what no more English blood?
Has length of time drove from our English viens.
The kindred he to Great Brittania deigns?
Tis thus with thee O Brittain keeping down
New English force, thou fear'st his Tyranny and thou didst frown
He weeps afresh to feel this Iron chain
Turn, O Brittania claim thy child again
Riecho Love drive by thy powerful charms
Indolence Slumbering in forgetful arms
See Agenoria diligent imploy's
Her sons, and thus with rapture she replys
Arise my sons with one consent arise

Lest distant continents with vult'ring eyes
Should charge America with Negligence
They praise Industry but no pride commence
To raise their own Profusion, O Brittain See
By this, New England will increase like thee.

"To The Right Honorable William, Earl of Dartmouth"

Hail, happy day, when, smiling like die morn,
Fair Freedom rose New England to adorn:
The northern clime beneath her genial ray,
Dartmouth, congratulates thy blissful sway:
Elate with hope her race no longer mourns,
Each soul expands, each grateful bosom burns,
While in thine hand with pleasure we behold
The silken reins, and Freedom's charms unfold.
Long lost to realms beneath the northern skies
She shines supreme, while hated faction dies:
Soon as appear'd the Goddess long desir'd,
Sick as the view, she languish'd and expir'd;
Thus from the splendors of the morning light
The owl in sadness seeks the caves of night.

    No more America in mournful strain
Of wrongs, and grievance unredress'd complain,
No longer shalt thou dread the iron chain,
Which wanton Tyranny with lawless hand
Had made, and which it meant t' enslave the land.
Should you, my lord, while you peruse my song,
Wonder from whence my love of Freedom sprung,
Whence flow these wishes for the common good,
By feeling hearts alone best understood,
I, young in life, by seeming cruel fate
Was snatch'd from Afric's fancy'd happy seat:
What pangs excruciating must molest,
What sorrows labour in my parent's breast!
Steel'd was the soul and by no misery mov'd
That from a father seiz'd his babe belov'd.
Such, such my case. And can I then but pray
Others may never feel tyrannic sway?

For favours past, great Sir, our thanks are due,

And thee we ask thy favours to renew,

Since in thy pow'r, as in thy will before,

To sooth the griefs, which thou did'st once deplore.

May heav'nly grace the sacred sanction give

To all thy works, and thou for ever live

Not only on the wings of fleeting Fame,

Though praise immortal crowns the patriot's name,

But to conduct to heav'n's refulgent fane,

May fiery courses sweep th' ethereal plain,

And bear thee upwards to that blest abode,

Where, like prophet, thou shalt find thy God.

John Pierpont (1785–1866)

John Pierpont is an American poet and politician, but of little known origin and fame. He wrote Joseph Warren, who was commissioned by Massachusetts as a Major-General three days before the Battle of Bunker Hill, at which he fought as a volunteer. Warren was one of the last to leave the field, and as a British officer in the redoubt called to him to surrender, a ball struck him in the forehead, killing him instantly. The excerpt is often named as "Warren's Address to the American Soldiers".

"Warren's Address"

Stand! the ground's your own, my braves!

Will ye give it up to slaves?

Will ye look for greener graves?

  Hope ye mercy still?

What's the mercy despots feel?

Hear it in that battle-peal!

Read it on yon bristling steel.

  Ask it,—ye who will.

Fear ye foes who kill for hire?

Will ye to your homes retire?

Look behind you!—they're a-fire!

  And, before you, see

Who have done it!—From the vale

On they come!—And will ye quail?—

Leaden rain and iron hail

  Let their welcome be!

In the God of battles trust!
Die we may,—and die we must;—
But, O, where can dust to dust
    Be consigned so well,
As where Heaven its dews shall shed
On the martyred patriot's bed,
And the rocks shall raise their head,
    Of his deeds to tell!

William Cullen Bryant (1794–1878)

William Cullen Bryant is an American poet and editor, one of the most celebrated figures in the frieze of 19th-century, best remembered for his *Thanatopsis* (1817). His several books include *The White-Footed Deer and Other Poems* (1844), and *The Fountain and Other Poems* (1842). In the excerpt "Song of Marion's Men", Bryant wrote: the British had succeeded in defeating most of the American troops in South Carolina by 1780, and had laid waste much of that state, confiscating plantations, burning houses, and hanging "traitors" such as they termed without giving them any form of trial. General Francis Marion is a native of South Carolina, whose ancestors were Huguenot refugees. At first, his troop contained only twenty men, but more joined his band, and for three years they carried on irregular warfare, harassing the British forces more than regular soldiers could have done. Marion's men succeeded in capturing Georgetown on their third attempt, and fought in the battle of Eutaw Springs, September 8, 1781, which practically ended the British occupation of that part of the United States of America. He has always been one of the most popular heroes of the revolution, and the "Swamp Fox" well deserved his fame.

"Song of Marion's Men"

Our band is few, but true and tried,
    Our leader frank and bold;
The British soldier trembles
    When Marion's name is told.
Our fortress is the good greenwood
    Our tent the cypress-tree;
We know the forest round us,
    As seamen know the sea.
We know its walls of thorny vines,
    Its glades of reedy grass,
Its safe and silent islands
    Within the dark morass.

Woe to the English soldiery,
        That little dread us near!
On them shall light at midnight
        A strange and sudden fear:
When, waking to their tents on fire,
        They grasp their arms in vain,
And they who stand to face us
        Are beat to earth again.
And they who fly in terror deem
        A mighty host behind,
And hear the tramp of thousands
        Upon the hollow wind.

Then sweet the hour that brings release
        From danger and from toil;
We talk the battle over,
        And share the battle's spoil.
The woodland rings with laugh and shout
        As if a hunt were up,
And woodland flowers are gathered
        To crown the soldier's cup.
With merry songs we mock the wind
        That in the pine-top grieves,
And slumber long and sweetly
        On beds of oaken leaves.

Well knows the fair and friendly moon
        The band that Marion leads—
The glitter of their rifles,
        The scampering of their steeds.
'Tis life to guide the fiery barb
        Across the moonlight plain;
'Tis life to feel the night-wind
        That lifts his tossing mane.
A moment in the British camp—
        A moment—and away
Back to the pathless forest,
        Before the peep of day.

Grave men there are by broad Santee,
    Grave men with hoary hairs;
Their hearts are all with Marion,
    For Marion are their prayers.
And lovely ladies greet our band
    With kindliest welcoming,
With smiles like those of summer,
    And tears like those of spring.
For them we wear these trusty arms,
    And lay them down no more
Till we have driven the Briton,
    Forever, from our shore.

Ralph Waldo Emerson (1803–1882)

Ralph Waldo Emerson is an American philosopher, essayist, poet, the leading exponent of New England Transcendentalism, and one of America's best known and best-loved 19th-century figures. His original profession was a Unitarian minister, but he left the ministry to pursue a career in writing and public speaking. His prose works include *Nature* (1836), *The American Scholar* (1837), *Representative Men* (1850), *The Conduct of Life* (1860), and *English Traits* (1865). His two volumes are *Poems* (1846) and *May-Day* (1867), which also established his reputation as a major American poet. The poem *"Concord Hymn"* is sung at the completion of the Battle Monument on April 19, 1836: On the night April 18-19 of 1775, Paul Revere and other riders gathered a band of minute men from the Massachusetts countryside to confront advancing British troops, and battles with the British in Lexington and Concord the following day marked the beginning of the American War of Independence.

"Concord Hymn"

By the rude bridge that arched the flood,
    Their flag to April's breeze unfurled,
Here once the embattled farmers stood,
    And fired the shot heard round the world.

The foe long since in silence slept;
    Alike the conqueror silent sleeps;
And Time the ruined bridge has swept
    Down the dark stream which seaward creeps.

On this green bank, by this soft stream,

We set today a votive stone;

That memory may their deed redeem,

When, like our sires, our sons are gone.

Spirit, that made those heroes dare

To die, and leave their children free,

Bid Time and Nature gently spare

The shaft we raise to them and thee.

"Boston"[8]

The rocky nook with hill-tops three

Looked eastward from the farms,

And twice each day the flowing sea

Took Boston in its arms;

The men of yore were stout and poor,

And sailed for bread to every shore.

And where they went on trade intent

They did what freemen can,

Their dauntless ways did all men praise,

The merchant was a man.

The world was made for honest trade,—

To plant and eat be none afraid.

The waves that rocked them on the deep

To them their secret told;

Said the winds that sung the lads to sleep,

"Like us be free and bold!"

The honest waves refuse to slaves

The empire of the ocean caves.

Old Europe groans with palaces,

Has lords enough and more;—

We plant and build by foaming seas

A city of the poor;—

8 This poem was read in Faneuil Hall, on the Centennial Anniversary of the "Boston Tea-Party," at which a band of men disguised as Indians had quietly emptied into the sea the taxed tea-chests of three British ships on Dec. 16, 1773.

For day by day could Boston Bay
    Their honest labor overpay.

We grant no dukedoms to the few,
    We hold like rights and shall;—
Equal on Sunday in the pew,
    On Monday in the mall.
        For what avail the plough or sail,
        Or land or life, if freedom fail?

The noble craftsmen we promote,
    Disown the knave and fool;
Each honest man shall have his vote,
    Each child shall have his school.
        A union then of honest men,
        Or union nevermore again.

The wild rose and the barberry thorn
    Hung out their summer pride
Where now on heated pavements worn
    The feet of millions stride.

Fair rose the planted hills behind
    The good town on the bay,
And where the western hills declined
    The prairie stretched away.

What care though rival cities soar
    Along the stormy coast:
Penn's town, New York, and Baltimore,
    If Boston knew the most!

They laughed to know the world so wide;
    The mountains said: "Good-day!
We greet you well, you Saxon men,
    Up with your towns and stay!"
        The world was made for honest trade,—
        To plant and eat be none afraid.

"For you," they said, "no barriers be,
  For you no sluggard rest;
Each street leads downward to the sea,
  Or landward to the West."

O happy town beside the sea,
  Whose roads lead everywhere to all;
Than thine no deeper moat can be,
  No stouter fence, no steeper wall!

Bad news from George on the English throne:
  "You are thriving well," said he;
"Now by these presents be it known,
  You shall pay us a tax on tea;
    'T is very small,—no load at all,—
    Honor enough that we send the call."

"Not so," said Boston, "good my lord,
  We pay your governors here
Abundant for their bed and board,
  Six thousand pounds a year.
(Your highness knows our homely word,)
    Millions for self-government,
    But for tribute never a cent."

The cargo came! and who could blame
  If *Indians* seized the tea,
And, chest by chest, let down the same
  Into the laughing sea?
    For what avail the plough or sail
    Or land or life, if freedom fail?

The townsmen braved the English king,
  Found friendship in the French,
And Honor joined the patriot ring
  Low on their wooden bench.

O bounteous seas that never fail!
  O day remembered yet!

O happy port that spied the sail
Which wafted Lafayette!
Pole-star of light in Europe's night,
That never faltered from the right.

Kings shook with fear, old empires crave
The secret force to find
Which fired the little State to save
The rights of all mankind.

But right is might through all the world;
Province to province faithful clung,
Through good and ill the war-bolt hurled,
Till Freedom cheered and the joy-bells rung.

The sea returning day by day
Restores the world-wide mart;
So let each dweller on the Bay
Fold Boston in his heart,
Till these echoes be choked with snows,
Or over the town blue ocean flows.

Let the blood of her hundred thousands
Throb in each manly vein;
And the wit of all her wisest
Make sunshine in her brain.
For you can teach the lightning speech,
And round the globe your voices reach.

And each shall care for other,
And each to each shall bend,
To the poor a noble brother,
To the good an equal friend.

A blessing through the ages thus
Shield all thy roofs and towers!
God with the fathers, so with us,
Thou darling town of ours!

James Russell Lowell (1819–1891)

James Russell Lowell is an American poet, critic, essayist, editor, and diplomat, a highly influential man of letters in his day. Along with Longfellow and Whittier, Lowell belongs to the group of writers called the "Fireside Poets", known for their conservative, traditional forms, strict attention to rhyme and meter, and conservative moral and political themes. As an ardent abolitionist, he published widely in many anti-slavery newspapers. His early collection *The Biglow Papers, First Series* (1848) was a series of satirical verses written in opposition to the Mexican War. His other collections include *The Biglow Papers, Second Series* (1867), *Under the Willows and Other Poems* (1869), *The Cathedral* (1870), *Three Memorial Poems* (1877), *Early Poems* (1887), and *Heartsease and Rue* (1888). The excerpt "George Washington" is a fragment from the ode for the centenary of Washington's command of the American army at Cambridge.

"George Washington"

Soldier and statesman, rarest unison;
High-poised example of great duties done
Simply as breathing, a world's honors worn
As life's indifferent gifts to all men born;
Dumb for himself, unless it were to God,
But for his barefoot soldiers eloquent,
Tramping the snow to coral where they trod,
Held by his awe in hollow-eyed content;
Modest, yet firm as Nature's self; unblamed
Save by the men his nobler temper shamed;
Never seduced through show of present good
By other than unsetting lights to steer
New-trimmed in Heaven, nor than his steadfast mood
More steadfast, far from rashness as from fear,
Rigid, but with himself first, grasping still
In swerveless poise the wave-beat helm of will;
Not honored then or now because he wooed
The popular voice, but that he still withstood;
Broad-minded, higher-souled, there is but one
Who was all this and ours, and all men's—WASHINGTON.

Francis Miles Finch (1827–1907)

Francis Miles Finch was an American judge, poet, and academic associated with the early years of Cornell University. He wrote poetry throughout his life, but declined a chair in rhetoric literature at Cornell. "Nathan Hale" is a memorial to the hero thus named, who was captured by the British in New York City and hanged for espionage on September 22, 1776, during the American revolutionary war, as one witness has recorded his characteristic dying words: "I only regret that I have but one life to lose for my country."

"Nathan Hale"[9]

To drum-beat and heart-beat,
    A soldier marches by:
There is color in his cheek,
    There is courage in his eye,
Yet to drum-beat and heart-beat
    In a moment he must die.

By starlight and moonlight,
    He seeks the Briton's camp;
He hears the rustling flag,
    And the armed sentry's tramp;
And the starlight and moonlight
    His silent wanderings lamp.

With slow tread and still tread,
    He scans the tented line;
And he counts the battery guns
    By the gaunt and shadowy pine;
And his slow tread and still tread
    Gives no warning sign.

The dark wave, the plumed wave,
    It meets his eager glance;
And it sparkles 'neath the stars,
    Like the glimmer of a lance—
A dark wave, a plumed wave,
    On an emerald expanse.

A sharp clang, a steel clang,

---

9 After the retreat from Long Island, Washington needed information as to the British strength. Captain Nathan Hale, a young man of twenty-one, volunteered to get this. He was taken, inside the enemy's lines, and hanged as a spy, regretting that he had but one life to lose for his country.

And terror in the sound!
For the sentry, falcon-eyed,
        In the camp a spy hath found;
With a sharp clang, a steel clang,
        The patriot is bound.

With calm brow, steady brow,
        He listens to his doom;
In his look there is no fear,
        Nor a shadow-trace of gloom;
But with calm brow and steady brow
        He robes him for the tomb.

In the long night, the still night,
        He kneels upon the sod;
And the brutal guards withhold
        E'en the solemn Word of God!
In the long night, the still night,
        He walks where Christ hath trod.

'Neath the blue morn, the sunny morn,
        He dies upon the tree;
And he mourns that he can lose
        But one life for Liberty;
And in the blue morn, the sunny morn,
        His spirit-wings are free.

But his last words, his message-words,
        They burn, lest friendly eye
Should read how proud and calm
        A patriot could die,
With his last words, his dying words,
        A soldier's battle-cry.

From the Fame-leaf and Angel-leaf,
        From monument and urn,
The sad of earth, the glad of heaven,
        His tragic fate shall learn;
And on Fame-leaf and Angel-leaf

The name of HALE shall burn.

Sidney Lanier (1842–1881)

Sidney Lanier is an American musician, poet, and talented musician who utilised the rhythms of music and the thematic developments of symphonies in such fine songs as "Corn" (1875), "The Symphony" (1875), and "The Marshes of Glynn" (1878). He served in the Civil War until his capture and subsequent imprisonment at Point Lookout, Md., where he contracted tuberculosis. But the following verse is a fragment of the "Psalm of the West" about the war that initiated the American Revolution.

"The Battle of Lexington"[10]

Then haste ye, Prescott and Revere!
Bring all the men of Lincoln here;
Let Chelmsford, Littleton, Carlisle,
Let Acton, Bedford, hither file—
Oh, hither file, and plainly see
Out of a wound leap Liberty.

Say, Woodman April! all in green,
Say, Robin April! hast thou seen
In all thy travel round the earth
Ever a morn of calmer birth?
But Morning's eye alone serene
Can gaze across yon village-green
To where the trooping British run
        Through Lexington.
Good men in fustian, stand ye still;
The men in red come o'er the hill,
Lay down your arms, damned rebels! cry
The men in red full haughtily.
But never a grounding gun is heard;
The men in fustian stand unstirred;
Dead calm, save maybe a wise bluebird
Puts in his little heavenly word.
O men in red! if ye but knew
The half as much as bluebirds do,

---

10 The skirmish at Lexington and the fight at Concord on April 19, 1775 closed all political bickering between Great Britain and her colonies and began the War of the Revolution.

Now in this little tender calm

Each hand would out, and every palm

With patriot palm strike brotherhood's stroke

Or ere these lines of battle broke.

O men in red! if ye but knew

The least of all that bluebirds do,

Now in this little godly calm

Yon voice might sing the Future's Psalm—

The Psalm of Love with the brotherly eyes

Who pardons and is very wise—

Yon voice that shouts, high-hoarse with ire,

  Fire!

The red-coats fire, the homespuns fall:

The homespuns' anxious voices call,

Brother, art hurt? and Where hit, John?

And, Wipe this blood, and Men, come on,

And Neighbor, do but lift my head,

And Who is wounded? Who is dead?

Seven are killed. My God! my God!

Seven lie dead on the village sod.

Two Harringtons, Parker, Hadley, Brown,

Monroe and Porter,—these are down.

Nay, look! stout Harrington not yet dead.

He crooks his elbow, lifts his head.

He lies at the step of his own house-door;

He crawls and makes a path of gore.

The wife from the window hath seen, and rushed;

He hath reached the step, but the blood hath gushed;

He hath crawled to the step of his own house-door,

But his head hath dropped: he will crawl no more.

Clasp Wife, and kiss, and lift the head,

Harrington lies at his doorstep dead.

But, O ye Six that round him lay

And bloodied up that April day!

As Harrington fell, ye likewise fell—

At the door of the House wherein ye dwell;

As Harrington came, ye likewise came

And died at the door of your House of Fame.

2. Poetry of the War of 1812

"The War of 1812" broke out thirty years after the American Revolution and lasted until mutual ratifications of the Treaty of Ghent in 1814. Often called "the last war with Great Britain", it was largely derived from the French Revolutionary (1792–1799) and Napoleonic Wars (1799–1815). It was a "small war", but it had shaped the American identity, as American had finally decided to be completely separated and stepped upon its self-isolation until its entry into World War I. A great number of American patriots and their followers wrote verses about this historic event. The first three excerpted, "The 'United States' and 'Macedonian'" (1812), "The Wasp's Frolic" (1813), and "Yankee Thunders" (1813), all anonymous, are selected from various sources, written roughly at the beginning and during the War.

Anonymous: "'The United States' and 'Macedonian'"

The banner of Freedom high floated unfurled,

While the silver-tipt surges in low homage curled,

Flashing bright round the bow of Decatur's brave bark,

In contest, an "eagle"—in chasing a "lark".

   The bold *United States*,

   Which four-and-forty rates,

Will ne'er be known to yield—be known to yield or fly,

Her motto is "Glory! we conquer or we die."

All canvas expanded to woo the coy gale,

The ship cleared for action, in chase of a sail;

The foemen in view, every bosom beats high,

All eager for conquest, or ready to die.

   The bold *United States*,

   Which four-and-forty rates,

Will ne'er be known to yield—be known to yield or fly.

Her motto is "Glory! we conquer or we die."

Now havoc stands ready, with optics of flame,

And battle-hounds "strain on the start" for the game;

The blood demons rise on the surge for their prey,

While Pity, rejected, awaits the dread fray.

The bold *United States*,
Which four-and-forty rates,
Will ne'er be known to yield—be known to yield or fly,
Her motto is "Glory! we conquer or we die."

The gay floating streamers of Britain appear,
Waving light on the breeze as the stranger we near;
And now could the quick-sighted Yankee discern
"*Macedonian*," emblazoned at large on her stern.
The bold *United States*,
Which four-and-forty rates,
Will ne'er be known to yield—be known to yield or fly,
Her motto is "Glory! we conquer or we die."

She waited our approach, and the contest began,
But to waste ammunition is no Yankee plan;
In awful suspense every match was withheld,
While the bull-dogs of Britain incessantly yelled.
The bold *United States*,
Which four-and-forty rates,
Will ne'er be known to yield—be known to yield or fly,
Her motto is "Glory! we conquer or we die."

Unawed by her thunders, alongside we came,
While the foe seemed enwrapped in a mantle of flame;
When, prompt to the word, such a flood we return,
That Neptune aghast, thought his trident would burn.
The bold *United States*,
Which four-and-forty rates,
Will ne'er be known to yield—be known to yield or fly,
Her motto is "Glory! we conquer or we die."

Now the lightning of battle gleams horridly red,
With a tempest of iron and hail-storm of lead;
And our fire on the foe we so copiously poured,
His mizzen and topmasts soon went by the board.
The bold *United States*,
Which four-and-forty rates,
Will ne'er be known to yield—be known to yield or fly,

Her motto is "Glory! we conquer or we die."

So fierce and so bright did our flashes aspire,
They thought that their cannon had set us on fire,
"The Yankee's in flames!"—every British tar hears,
And hails the false omen with three hearty cheers.
       The bold *United States*,
       Which four-and-forty rates,
Will ne'er be known to yield—be known to yield or fly,
Her motto is "Glory! we conquer or we die."

In seventeen minutes they found their mistake,
And were glad to surrender and fall in our wake;
Her decks were with carnage and blood deluged o'er,
Where welt'ring in blood lay an hundred and four.
       The bold *United States*,
       Which four-and-forty rates,
Will ne'er be known to yield—be known to yield or fly,
Her motto is "Glory! we conquer or we die."

But though she was made so completely a wreck,
With blood they had scarcely encrimsoned our deck;
Only five valiant Yankees in the contest were slain,
And our ship in five minutes was fitted again.
       The bold *United States*,
       Which four-and-forty rates,
Will ne'er be known to yield—be known to yield or fly,
Her motto is "Glory! we conquer or we die."

Let Britain no longer lay claim to the seas,
For the trident of Neptune is ours, if we please,
While Hull and Decatur and Jones are our boast,
We dare their whole navy to come on our coast.
       The bold *United States*,
       Which four-and-forty rates,
Will ne'er be known to yield—be known to yield or fly,
Her motto is "Glory! we conquer or we die."

Rise, tars of Columbia!—and share in the fame,

Which gilds Hull's, Decatur's and Jones's bright name;
Fill a bumper, and drink, "Here's success to the cause,
But Decatur supremely deserves our applause."
      The bold *United States*,
      Which four-and-forty rates,
Shall ne'er be known to yield—be known to yield or fly,
Her motto is "Glory! we conquer or we die."

Anonymous: "The Wasp's Frolic" (1813)

'Twas on board the sloop-of-war *Wasp* boys,
      We set sail from Delaware Bay,
To cruise on Columbia's fair coast, sirs,
      Our rights to maintain on the sea.

Three days were not passed on our station,
      When the Frolic came up to our view;
Says Jones, "Show the flag of our nation";
      Three cheers were then gave by our crew.

We boldly bore up to this Briton,
      Whose cannon began for to roar;
The Wasp soon her stings from her side ran,
      When we on them a broadside did pour.

Each sailor stood firm at his quarters,
      'Twas minutes past forty and three,
When fifty bold Britons were slaughter'd,
      Whilst our guns swept their masts in the sea.

Their breasts then with valor still glowing,
      Acknowledged the battle we'd won,
On us then bright laurels bestowing,
      When to leeward they fired a gun.

On their decks we the twenty guns counted,
      With a crew for to answer the same;
Eighteen was the number we mounted,
      Being served by the lads of true game.

With the Frolic in tow, we were standing,
    All in for Columbia's fair shore;
But fate on our laurels was frowning,
    We were taken by a seventy-four.

Anonymous: "Yankee Thunders" (1813)

Britannia's gallant streamers,
    Float proudly o'er the tide,
And fairly wave Columbia's stripes,
    In battle side by side.
And ne'er did bolder seamen meet,
    Where ocean's surges pour;
O'er the tide now they ride,
    While the bell'wing thunders roar,
While the cannon's fire is flashing fast,
    And the bell'wing thunders roar.

When Yankee meets the Briton,
    Whose blood congenial flows,
By Heav'n created to be friends,
    By fortune rendered foes;
Hard then must be the battle fray,
    Ere well the fight is o'er;
Now they ride, side by side,
    While the bell'wing thunders roar,
While her cannon's fire is flashing fast,
    And the bell'wing thunders roar.

Still, still, for noble England
    Bold D'Acres' streamers fly;
And for Columbia, gallant Hull's
    As proudly and as high;
Now louder rings the battle din,
    And thick the volumes pour;
Still they ride, side by side,
    While the bell'wing thunders roar,
While the cannon's fire is flashing fast,
    And the bell'wing thunders roar.

Why lulls Britannia's thunder,
    That waked the wat'ry war?
Why stays the gallant Guerrière,
    Whose streamers waved so fair?
That streamer drinks the ocean wave,
    That warrior's fight is o'er!
Still they ride, side by side,
    While the bell'wing thunders roar,
While the cannon's fire is flashing fast,
    And the bell'wing thunders roar.

Hark! 'tis the Briton's lee gun!
    Ne'er bolder warrior kneeled!
And ne'er to gallant mariners
    Did braver seamen yield.
Proud be the sires, whose hardy boys
    Then fell to fight no more:
With the brave, mid the wave;
    When the cannon's thunders roar,
Their spirits then shall trim the blast,
    And swell the thunder's roar.

Vain were the cheers of Britons,
    Their hearts did vainly swell,
Where virtue, skill, and bravery
    With gallant Morris fell.
That heart so well in battle tried,
    Along the Moorish shore,
And again o'er the main,
    When Columbia's thunders roar,
Shall prove its Yankee spirit true,
    When Columbia's thunders roar.

Hence be our floating bulwark
    Those oaks our mountains yield;
'Tis mighty Heaven's plain decree—
    Then take the wat'ry field!
To ocean's farthest barrier then
    Your whit'ning sail shall pour;

Safe they'll ride o'er the tide,
    While Columbia's thunders roar,
While her cannon's fire is flashing fast,
    And her Yankee thunders roar.

James Gates Percival (1795–1856)

James Gates Percival is one of the most promising American poets. The frequently anthologised war poem of James Gates Percival is his "Perry's Victory on Lake Erie", which writes: Throughout the war of 1812 with Great Britain, the navy was more successful than the army. In the battle on Lake Erie, Commodore Oliver Hazard Perry captured six British vessels on Sept. 10, 1813.

"Perry's Victory on Lake Erie"

Bright was the morn,—the waveless bay
Shone like a mirror to the sun;
'Mid greenwood shades and meadows gay,
The matin birds their lays begun:
While swelling o'er the gloomy wood
Was heard the faintly-echocd roar,—
The dashing of the foaming flood,
That beat on Erie's distant shore.

The tawny wanderer of the wild
Paddled his painted birch canoe,
And, where the wave serenely smiled,
Swift as the darting falcon, flew;
He rowed along that peaceful bay,
And glanced its polished surface o'er,
Listening the billow far away,
That rolled on Erie's lonely shore.

What sounds awake my slumbering ear,
What echoes o'er the waters come?
It is the morning gun I hear,
The rolling of the distant drum.
Far o'er the bright illumined wave
I mark the flash,—I hear the roar,
That calls from sleep the slumbering brave,

To fight on Erie's lonely shore.

See how the starry banner floats,
And sparkles in the morning ray:
While sweetly swell the fife's gay notes
In echoes o'er the gleaming bay:
Flash follows flash, as through yon fleet
Columbia's cannons loudly roar,
And valiant tars the battle greet,
That storms on Erie's echoing shore.

O, who can tell what deeds were done,
When Britain's cross, on yonder wave,
Sunk 'neath Columbia's dazzling sun,
And met in Erie's flood its grave?
Who tell the triumphs of that day,
When, smiling at the cannon's roar,
Our hero, 'mid the bloody fray,
Conquered on Erie's echoing shore.

Though many a wounded bosom bleeds
For sire, for son, for lover dear,
Yet Sorrow smiles amid her weeds,—
Affliction dries her tender tear;
Oh! she exclaims, with glowing pride,
With ardent thoughts that wildly soar,
My sire, my son, my lover died,
Conquering on Erie's bloody shore.

Long shall my country bless that day,
When soared our Eagle to the skies;
Long, long in triumph's bright array,
That victory shall proudly rise:
And when our country's lights are gone,
And all its proudest days are o'er,
How will her fading courage dawn,
To think on Erie's bloody shore!

Francis Scott Key (1779–1843)

Francis Scott Key is a lawyer who witnessed the daylong assault of Fort McHenry by British troops during the War of 1812. He saw the fort held during the attack in September 1814 when the British had burned the city of Washington and was inspired to write "The Star-Spangled Banner" (1814) with the original title "Defence of Fort McHenry", which was officially adopted as the national anthem by an act of Congress in 1931.

"The Star-Spangled Banner"[11]

O! say can you see, by the dawn's early light,
What so proudly we hail'd at the twilight's last gleaming,
Whose broad stripes and bright stars through the perilous fight,
O'er the ramparts we watch'd, were so gallantly streaming?
And the rockets' red glare, the bombs bursting in air,
Gave proof through the night that our flag was still there —
O! say, does that star-spangled banner yet wave
O'er the land of the free, and the home of the brave?

On the shore, dimly seen through the mists of the deep,
Where the foe's haughty host in dread silence reposes,
What is that which the breeze o'er the towering steep,
As it fitfully blows, half conceals, half discloses?
Now it catches the gleam of the morning's first beam,
In full glory reflected now shines on the stream —
'Tis the star-spangled banner, O! long may it wave
O'er the land of the free, and the home of the brave.

And where is that band who so vauntingly swore
That the havock of war and the battle's confusion
A home and a country should leave us no more?
Their blood has wash'd out their foul foot-steps' pollution,
No refuge could save the hireling and slave,
From the terror of flight or the gloom of the grave;
And the star-spangled banner in triumph doth wave
O'er the land of the free, and the home of the brave.

---

11 After the British had burned the Capitol at Washington, in August, 1813, they retired to their ships, and on September 12th and 13th, they made an attack on Baltimore. This poem was written on the morning after the bombardment of Fort McHenry, while the author was a prisoner on the British fleet.

O! thus be it ever when freemen shall stand

Between their lov'd home, and the war's desolation,

Blest with vict'ry and peace, may the heav'n-rescued land

Praise the power that hath made and preserv'd us a nation!

Then conquer we must, when our cause it is just,

And this be our motto — "In God is our trust!"

And the star-spangled banner in triumph shall wave

O'er the land of the free, and the home of the brave.

Thomas Dunn English (1819–1902)

Thomas Dunn English is an American writer and poet, and a politician of Irish Quaker heritage. He worked as a doctor, a lawyer, and a long-time politician, but it was literature that English primarily distinguished himself. One episode says that in 1843 the *New York Mirror* published what would become his most memorable poem or song, "Ben Bolt." It immediately became the most popular of popular songs in the country. *The New York Times* reported that, during English's 1890 bid for a seat in the House of Representatives, the song "was sung nightly by all the singers the Democrats could muster, and the author was literally sung into Congress."

During his remaining years, he balanced well between literature and politics. As a writer or poet, English has attracted little attention from critics, having been neglected as a writer worthy of individual study. However, as scholars continue to recover literature with important cultural associations, English may invite study as a representative of nineteenth-century magazinists and popular poets. The following two excerpts of his poetic production may serve as a good appreciation.

"The Battle of New Orleans"[12]

Here, in my rude log cabin,
    Few poorer men there be
Among the mountain ranges
    Of Eastern Tennessee.
My limbs are weak and shrunken,
    White hairs upon my brow,
My dog—lie still, old fellow!—
    My sole companion now.

---

12 The treaty of peace between Great Britain and the United States was signed at Ghent, December 14, 1814; but before the news crossed the ocean, Pakenham, with twelve thousand British veterans, attacked New Orleans, defended by Andrew Jackson with five thousand Americans, mostly militia on Jan. 8 1815. The British were repulsed with a loss of two thousand; the American loss was trifling.

Yet I, when young and lusty,
    Have gone through stirring scenes,
For I went down with Carroll
    To fight at New Orleans.

You say you'd like to hear me
    The stirring story tell
Of those who stood the battle
    And those who fighting fell.
Short work to count our losses—
    We stood and dropp'd the foe
As easily as by firelight
    Men shoot the buck or doe.
And while they fell by hundreds
    Upon the bloody plain,
Of us, fourteen were wounded,
    And only eight were slain.

The eighth of January,
    Before the break of day,
Our raw and hasty levies
    Were brought into array.
No cotton-bales before us—
    Some fool that falsehood told;
Before us was an earthwork,
    Built from the swampy mould.
And there we stood in silence,
    And waited with a frown,
To greet with bloody welcome
    The bulldogs of the Crown.

The heavy fog of morning
    Still hid the plain from sight,
When came a thread of scarlet
    Marked faintly in the white.
We fired a single cannon,
    And as its thunders roll'd
The mist before us lifted
    In many a heavy fold.

The mist before us lifted,
    And in their bravery fine
Came rushing to their ruin
    The fearless British line.

Then from our waiting cannons
    Leap'd forth the deadly flame,
To meet the advancing columns
    That swift and steady came.
The thirty-twos of Crowley
    And Bluchi's twenty-four,
To Spotts's eighteen-pounders
    Responded with their roar,
Sending the grape-shot deadly
    That marked its pathway plain,
And paved the road it travell'd
    With corpses of the slain.

Our rifles firmly grasping,
    And heedless of the din,
We stood in silence waiting
    For orders to begin.
Our fingers on the triggers,
    Our hearts, with anger stirr'd,
Grew still more fierce and eager
    As Jackson's voice was heard:
"Stand steady! Waste no powder
    Wait till your shots will tell!
To-day the work you finish—
    See that you do it well!"

Their columns drawing nearer,
    We felt our patience tire,
When came the voice of Carroll,
    Distinct and measured, "Fire!"
Oh! then you should have mark'd us
    Our volleys on them pour
Have heard our joyous rifles
    Ring sharply through the roar,

And seen their foremost columns
　　Melt hastily away
As snow in mountain gorges
　　Before the floods of May.

They soon reform'd their columns,
　　And 'mid the fatal rain
We never ceased to hurtle
　　Came to their work again.
The Forty-fourth is with them,
　　That first its laurels won
With stout old Abercrombie
　　Beneath an eastern sun.
It rushes to the battle,
　　And, though within the rear
Its leader is a laggard,
　　It shows no signs of fear.

It did not need its colonel,
　　For soon there came instead
An eagle-eyed commander,
　　And on its march he led.
'Twas Pakenham, in person,
　　The leader of the field;
I knew it by the cheering
　　That loudly round him peal'd;
And by his quick, sharp movement,
　　We felt his heart was stirr'd,
As when at Salamanca,
　　He led the fighting Third.

I raised my rifle quickly,
　　I sighted at his breast,
God save the gallant leader
　　And take him to his rest!
I did not draw the trigger,
　　I could not for my life.
So calm he sat his charger
　　Amid the deadly strife,

That in my fiercest moment
  A prayer arose from me,—
God save that gallant leader,
  Our foeman though he be.

Sir Edward's charger staggers:
  He leaps at once to ground,
And ere the beast falls bleeding
  Another horse is found.
His right arm falls—'tis wounded;
  He waves on high his left;
In vain he leads the movement,
  The ranks in twain are cleft.
The men in scarlet waver
  Before the men in brown,
And fly in utter panic—
  The soldiers of the Crown!

I thought the work was over,
  But nearer shouts were heard,
And came, with Gibbs to head it,
  The gallant Ninety-third.
Then Pakenham, exulting,
  With proud and joyous glance,
Cried, "Children of the Tartan—
  Bold Highlanders—advance!
Advance to scale the breastworks
  And drive them from their hold,
And show the staunchless courage
  That mark'd your sires of old!"

His voice as yet was ringing,
  When, quick as light, there came
The roaring of a cannon,
  And earth seemed all aflame.
Who causes thus the thunder
  The doom of men to speak?
It is the Baritarian,
  The fearless Dominique.

Down through the marshall'd Scotsmen
　　The step of death is heard,
And by the fierce tornado
　　Falls half the Ninety-third.

The smoke passed slowly upward,
　　And, as it soared on high,
I saw the brave commander
　　In dying anguish lie.
They bear him from the battle
　　Who never fled the foe;
Unmoved by death around them
　　His bearers softly go.
In vain their care, so gentle,
　　Fades earth and all its scenes;
The man of Salamanca
　　Lies dead at New Orleans.

But where were his lieutenants?
　　Had they in terror fled?
No! Keane was sorely wounded
　　And Gibbs as good as dead.
Brave Wilkinson commanding,
　　A major of brigade,
The shatter'd force to rally,
　　A final effort made.
He led it up our ramparts,
　　Small glory did he gain—
Our captives some, while others fled,
　　And he himself was slain.

The stormers had retreated,
　　The bloody work was o'er;
The feet of the invaders
　　Were seen to leave our shore.
We rested on our rifles
　　And talk'd about the fight,
When came a sudden murmur
　　Like fire from left to right;

We turned and saw our chieftain,
    And then, good friend of mine,
You should have heard the cheering
    That rang along the line.

For well our men remembered
    How little when they came,
Had they but native courage,
    And trust in Jackson's name;
How through the day he labored,
    How kept the vigils still,
Till discipline controlled us,
    A stronger power than will;
And how he hurled us at them
    Within the evening hour,
That red night in December,
    And made us feel our power.

In answer to our shouting
    Fire lit his eye of gray;
Erect, but thin and pallid,
    He passed upon his bay.
Weak from the baffled fever,
    And shrunken in each limb,
The swamps of Alabama
    Had done their work on him.
But spite of that and lasting,
    And hours of sleepless care,
The soul of Andrew Jackson
    Shone forth in glory there.

"The Yankee Man-of-War"[13]

'Tis of a gallant Yankee ship that flew the stripes and stars,
And the whistling wind from the west-nor'-west blew through the pitch-pine spars.
With her starboard tacks aboard, my boys, she hung upon the gale,
On an autumn night we raised the light on the old head of Kinsale.
It was a clear and cloudless night, and the wind blew steady and strong,
As gayly over the sparkling deep our good ship bowled along;
With the foaming seas beneath her bow the fiery waves she spread,
And bending low her bosom of snow, she buried her lee cat head.

There was no talk of short'ning sail by him who walked the poop,
And under the press of her pond'ring jib the boom bent like a hoop,
And the groaning water-ways told the strain that held her stout main tack.
But he only laughed as he glanced abaft at a white and silvery track.
The mid-tide meets in the channel waves that flow from shore to shore,
And the mist hung heavy upon the land from Featherstone to Dunmore;
And that sterling light on Tusker rock, where the old bell tolls the hour,
And the beacon light that shone so bright was quenched on Waterford tower.
The nightly robes our good ship wore were her three topsails set,
The spanker and her standing jib, the spanker being fast.
"Now, lay aloft, my heroes bold, let not a moment pass!"
And royals and topgallant sails were quickly on each mast.

What looms upon the starboard bow? What hangs upon the breeze?
'T is time our good ship hauled her wind abreast the old Saltees;
For by her ponderous press of sail and by her consorts four
We saw our morning visitor was a British man-of-war.

Up spoke our noble captain then, as a shot ahead of us passed,
"Haul snug your flowing courses, lay your topsail to the mast!"
The Englishmen gave three loud hurrahs from the deck of their covered ark,
And we answered back by a solid broadside from the decks of our patriot bark.

---

13 The naval war of 1812 was a glorious epoch in American militarey history. The achievements of the troops were very far from creditable, with a few exceptions, including, of course, the great one of the repulse of British regulars at New Orleans; but on the ocean the American sailors proved themselves quite the equal, if not more, of the English seamen, who had learned to consider themselves invincible, and despised the petty fleet of half a dozen cruisers,—not a single line-of-battle ship in the number,—which they had force enough to sweep off the seas without a struggle, and which they finally did blockade into inaction. The excerpted serves as an illustration.

"Out, booms! Out, booms!" our skipper cried, "Out, booms, and give her sheet!"
And the swiftest keel that ever was launched shot ahead of the British fleet.
And amidst a thundering shower of shot, with stunsails hoisting away,
Down the North Channel Paul Jones did steer, just at the break of day.

3. British Romanticism and War Representation

The British Romanticism, generally mapped from the political and poetic tremors of the 1780s to the 1832 Reform Act, is a historical period of inward and outward revolutions in literature, painting, music, architecture, criticism, historiography, and what is more, society and culture. As waves of revolution, Romanticism is comprehensively consequential and nothing short of a revolution in all aspects: how poets understood their art, its provenance, and its powers; how poets wrote with the revolutionary spirit, rejecting and dismantling the precepts of order, calmness, harmony, balance, idealisation, and rationality while emphasising the individual, the subjective, the irrational, the imaginative, the personal, the spontaneous, the emotional, the visionary, and the transcendental; to a great extent, British Romanticism has achieved a semantic equivalence with revolution, and its poetic representation has been filled with warring imagination, especially against the war and its generators.

John Scott (1730–1783)

John Scott, known as John Scott of Amwell, is a poet and a wealthy Quaker draper, who lives at Amwell near Ware in Hertfordshire. He wrote a lot of verses in such fashions of Thomas Gray and William Wordsworth, most of which have been forgotten. The anti-war poem "The Drum" (1782) is most remembered now.

"The Drum"

I hate that drum's discordant sound,
Parading round, and round, and round:
To thoughtless youth it pleasure yields,
And lures from cities and from fields,
To sell their liberty for charms
Of tawdry lace, and glittering arms;
And when Ambition's voice commands,
To march, and fight, and fall, in foreign lands.

I hate that drum's discordant sound,
Parading round, and round, and round:
To me it talks of ravaged plains,

And burning towns, and ruined swains,

And mangled limbs, and dying groans,

And widows' tears, and orphans' moans;

And all that Misery's hand bestows,

To fill the catalogue of human woes.

William Blake (1757–1827)

William Blake is a British poet, painter, engraver, and visionary, largely unrecognised during his lifetime and even dismissed as mad, but now considered a seminal figure and the earliest and most original of the Romantic poets. He is known for a great quantity of poetic works such as *Poetical Sketches* (1783), *Songs of Innocence* (1789), *The Marriage of Heaven and Hell* (circa 1790), *Visions of the Daughters of Albion* (1793), and *Songs of Experience* (1794). Generally, Blake brutally attacks oppressive authority in church and state. The spirit of the French Revolution captivated him, encouraging him to work on the poem *The French Revolution*. Though remaining unfinished, it celebrates the rise of democracy in France and the fall of the monarchy and offers him powerful material for works such as *America: A Prophecy* (1793) and *Europe* (1794). The excerpt is from *America: A Prophecy* (1793), a prophetic book[14] that explores the radical paradigms of political repression and revolt through a highly imaginative treatment of the American Revolution viewed as a harbinger of universal revolution, epistemological as much as political. It addresses the idea of revolution less as a commentary on the actual revolution in America as a commentary on universal principles that are at work in any revolution. The excerpted poem, "A War Song to Englishmen", speaks of the same theme.

Excerpts from *America: A Prophecy*

The shadowy Daughter of Urthona stood before red Orc,

When fourteen suns had faintly journey'd o'er his dark abode:

His food she brought in iron baskets, his drink in cups of iron:

Crown'd with a helmet and dark hair the nameless female stood;

A quiver with its burning stores, a bow like that of night,

When pestilence is shot from heaven: no other arms she need!

Invulnerable though naked, save where clouds roll round her loins

Their awful folds in the dark air: silent she stood as night;

---

14 The figure of Orc represents all revolutions: The revolution in America suggests to Blake a similar revolution in England. In the poem, the king, like the ancient pharaohs of Egypt, sends pestilence to America to punish the rebels, but the colonists are able to redirect the forces of destruction to England. Erdman suggests that Blake is thinking of the riots in England during the war and the chaotic condition of the English troops, many of whom deserted.

For never from her iron tongue could voice or sound arise,
But dumb till that dread day when Orc assay'd his fierce embrace.
"Dark Virgin," said the hairy youth, "thy father stern, abhorr'd,
Rivets my tenfold chains while still on high my spirit soars;
Sometimes an Eagle screaming in the sky, sometimes a Lion
Stalking upon the mountains, and sometimes a Whale, I lash
The raging fathomless abyss; anon a Serpent folding
Around the pillars of Urthona, and round thy dark limbs
On the Canadian wilds I fold; feeble my spirit folds,
For chain'd beneath I rend these caverns: when thou bringest food
I howl my joy, and my red eyes seek to behold thy face—
In vain! these clouds roll to and fro, and hide thee from my sight."
Silent as despairing love, and strong as jealousy,
The hairy shoulders rend the links; free are the wrists of fire;
Round the terrific loins he seiz'd the panting, struggling womb;
It joy'd: she put aside her clouds and smiled her first-born smile,
As when a black cloud shews its lightnings to the silent deep.
Soon as she saw the terrible boy, then burst the virgin cry:
"I know thee, I have found thee, and I will not let thee go:
Thou art the image of God who dwells in darkness of Africa,
And thou art fall'n to give me life in regions of dark death.
On my American plains I feel the struggling afflictions
Endur'd by roots that writhe their arms into the nether deep.
I see a Serpent in Canada who courts me to his love,
In Mexico an Eagle, and a Lion in Peru;
I see a Whale in the south-sea, drinking my soul away.
O what limb-rending pains I feel! thy fire and my frost
Mingle in howling pains, in furrows by thy lightnings rent.
This is eternal death, and this the torment long foretold."
The stern Bard ceas'd, asham'd of his own song; enrag'd he swung
His harp aloft sounding, then dash'd its shining frame against
A ruin'd pillar in glitt'ring fragments; silent he turn'd away,
And wander'd down the vales of Kent in sick and drear lamentings.

"A War Song to Englishmen"

Prepare, prepare the iron helm of war,
Bring forth the lots, cast in the spacious orb;
Th' Angel of Fate turns them with mighty hands,

And casts them out upon the darken'd earth!
Prepare, prepare!

Prepare your hearts for Death's cold hand! prepare
Your souls for flight, your bodies for the earth;
Prepare your arms for glorious victory;
Prepare your eyes to meet a holy God!
Prepare, prepare!

Whose fatal scroll is that? Methinks 'tis mine!
Why sinks my heart, why faltereth my tongue?
Had I three lives, I'd die in such a cause,
And rise, with ghosts, over the well-fought field.
Prepare, prepare!

The arrows of Almighty God are drawn!
Angels of Death stand in the louring heavens!
Thousands of souls must seek the realms of light,
And walk together on the clouds of heaven!
Prepare, prepare!

Soldiers, prepare! Our cause is Heaven's cause;
Soldiers, prepare! Be worthy of our cause:
Prepare to meet our fathers in the sky:
Prepare, O troops, that are to fall to-day!
Prepare, prepare!

Alfred shall smile, and make his harp rejoice;
The Norman William, and the learnèd Clerk,
And Lion Heart, and black-brow'd Edward, with
His loyal queen, shall rise, and welcome us!
Prepare, prepare!

William Wordsworth (1770–1850)

William Wordsworth is not only one of the founders of English Romanticism, but also one of the greatest English poets producing one of the most important and innovative works in the history of English literature. In 1795, he met the poet Samuel Taylor Coleridge, with whom he published *Lyrical Ballads* (1798). They wrote the human relationship to nature and a fierce advocate of using the vocabulary and speech patterns of common people in poetry, but with spiritual and epistemological speculation, all of which show his erudition and attachment to rural life and landscape. Another of his most famous work, *The Prelude* (1850) chronicles the spiritual life of the poet and marks the birth of a new genre of poetry—Romanticism.

He lives in the turbulent age of revolutions and wars, and such a martial context has defined his personal and political development, shaped his poetic career, and witnessed his greatest literary works: In 1793, revolutionary France declared war against England; his attitude to the Anglo-French conflict changed dramatically over time, but throughout the early and middle phases of the poet's career national combat remained a key subject of his writing.

"Character of the Happy Warrior"

Who is the happy Warrior? Who is he
Whom every Man in arms should wish to be?
—It is the generous Spirit, who, when brought
Among the tasks of real life, hath wrought
Upon the plan that pleased his childish thought:
Whose high endeavours are an inward light
That make the path before him always bright:
Who, with a natural instinct to discern
What knowledge can perform, is diligent to learn;
Abides by this resolve, and stops not there,
But makes his moral being his prime care;
Who, doom'd to go in company with Pain,
And Fear, and Bloodshed, miserable train!
Turns his necessity to glorious gain;
In face of these doth exercise a power
Which is our human-nature's highest dower;
Controls them and subdues, transmutes, bereaves
Of their bad influence, and their good receives;
By objects, which might force the soul to abate
Her feeling, render'd more compassionate;
Is placable because occasions rise
So often that demand such sacrifice;
More skilful in self-knowledge, even more pure,
As tempted more; more able to endure,
As more expos'd to suffering and distress;
Thence, also, more alive to tenderness.
Tis he whose law is reason; who depends
Upon that law as on the best of friends;

Whence, in a state where men are tempted still

To evil for a guard against worse ill,

And what in quality or act is best

Doth seldom on a right foundation rest,

He fixes good on good alone, and owes

To virtue every triumph that he knows:

—Who, if he rise to station of command,

Rises by open means; and there will stand

On honourable terms, or else retire,

And in himself possess his own desire;

Who comprehends his trust, and to the same

Keeps faithful with a singleness of aim;

And therefore does not stoop, nor lie in wait

For wealth, or honors, or for worldly state;

Whom they must follow; on whose head must fall,

Like showers of manna, if they come at all:

Whose powers shed round him in the common strife,

Or mild concerns of ordinary life,

A constant influence, a peculiar grace;

But who, if he be called upon to face

Some awful moment to which heaven has join'd

Great issues, good or bad for human-kind,

Is happy as a Lover; and attired

With sudden brightness like a Man inspired;

And through the heat of conflict keeps the law

In calmness made, and sees what he foresaw;

Or if an unexpected call succeed,

Come when it will, is equal to the need:

—He who, though thus endued as with a sense

And faculty for storm and turbulence,

Is yet a Soul whose master bias leans

To home-felt pleasures and to gentle scenes;

Sweet images! which, wheresoe'er he be,

Are at his heart; and such fidelity

It is his darling passion to approve;

More brave for this, that he hath much to love:

'Tis, finally, the Man, who, lifted high,

Conspicuous object in a Nation's eye,

Or left unthought-of in obscurity,

Who, with a toward or untoward lot,

Prosperous or adverse, to his wish or not,

Plays, in the many games of life, that one

Where what he most doth value must be won;

Whom neither shape of danger can dismay,

Nor thought of tender happiness betray;

Who, not content that former worth stand fast,

Looks forward, persevering to the last,

From well to better, daily self-surpast:

Who, whether praise of him must walk the earth

For ever, and to noble deeds give birth,

Or He must go to dust without his fame,

And leave a dead unprofitable name,

Finds comfort in himself and in his cause;

And, while the mortal mist is gathering, draws

His breath in confidence of Heaven's applause;

This is the happy Warrior; this is He

Whom every Man in arms should wish to be.

"October, 1803"

Six thousand Veterans practis'd in War's game,

Tried Men, at Killicranky were array'd

Against an equal Host that wore the Plaid,

Shepherds and Herdsmen.—Like a whirlwind came

The Highlanders, the slaughter spread like flame;

And Garry thundering down his mountain-road

Was stopp'd, and could not breathe beneath the load

Of the dead bodies. 'Twas a day of shame

For them whom precept and the pedantry

Of cold mechanic battle do enslave.

Oh! for a single hour of that Dundee

Who on that day the word of onset gave!

Like conquest would the Men of England see;

And her Foes find a like inglorious Grave.

"To the Men of Kent, October 1803"

Vanguard of liberty, ye Men of Kent,
Ye children of a soil that doth advance
Its haughty brow against the coast of France,
Now is the time to prove your hardiment!
To France be words of invitation sent!
They from their fields can see the countenance
Of your fierce war, may ken the glittering lance,
And hear you shouting forth your brave intent.
Left single, in bold parley, ye, of yore,
Did from the Norman win a gallant wreath;
Confirmed the charters that were yours before;
No parleying now! In Britain is one breath;
We all are with you now from shore to shore;
Ye Men of Kent, 'tis victory or death!

"November, 1806"[15]

Another year!—another deadly blow!
Another mighty empire overthrown!
And we are left, or shall be left alone;
The last that dare to struggle with the foe.
'Tis well! from this day forward we shall know
That in ourselves our safety must be sought;
That by our own right hands it must be wrought;
That we must stand unpropped, or be laid low.
O dastard whom such foretaste doth not cheer!
We shall exult, if they who rule the land
Be men who hold its many blessings dear,
Wise, upright, valiant; not a servile band,
Who are to judge of danger which they fear,
And honour which they do not understand.

Robert Southey (1774–1843)

Robert Southey is an English poet, and a versatile, prolific and encyclopedic writer, but he is chiefly remembered for his association with Samuel Taylor Coleridge and William

---

15 The Battle of Jena, on 14 October 1806, resulted in the complete overthrow of Prussia by the French under Napoleon.

Wordsworth. In 1813, he was appointed poet laureate through the influence of Sir Walter Scott. His poems include the epic with revolutionary overtones of *Joan of Arc* (1796; revised, 1798) and other epic poems such as *Thalaba the Destroyer* (1801) and *Madoc* (1805). The excerpt "The Battle of Blenheim" (1798) reflects his ambivalent attitude against all wars.

"The Battle of Blenheim"

It was a summer evening,
    Old Kaspar's work was done,
And he before his cottage door
    Was sitting in the sun,
And by him sported on the green
    His little grandchild Wilhelmine.

She saw her brother Peterkin
    Roll something large and round,
Which he beside the rivulet
    In playing there had found;
He came to ask what he had found,
    That was so large, and smooth, and round.

Old Kaspar took it from the boy,
    Who stood expectant by;
And then the old man shook his head,
    And, with a natural sigh,
"'Tis some poor fellow's skull," said he,
    "Who fell in the great victory.

"I find them in the garden,
    For there's many here about;
And often when I go to plough,
    The ploughshare turns them out!
For many thousand men," said he,
    "Were slain in that great victory."

"Now tell us what 'twas all about,"
    Young Peterkin, he cries;
And little Wilhelmine looks up
    With wonder-waiting eyes;

"Now tell us all about the war,
     And what they fought each other for."

"It was the English," Kaspar cried,
     "Who put the French to rout;
But what they fought each other for,
     I could not well make out;
But everybody said," quoth he,
     "That 'twas a famous victory.

"My father lived at Blenheim then,
     Yon little stream hard by;
They burnt his dwelling to the ground,
     And he was forced to fly;
So with his wife and child he fled,
     Nor had he where to rest his head.

"With fire and sword the country round
     Was wasted far and wide,
And many a childing mother then,
     And new-born baby died;
But things like that, you know, must be
     At every famous victory.

"They say it was a shocking sight
     After the field was won;
For many thousand bodies here
     Lay rotting in the sun;
But things like that, you know, must be
     After a famous victory.

"Great praise the Duke of Marlbro' won,
     And our good Prince Eugene."
"Why, 'twas a very wicked thing!"
     Said little Wilhelmine.
"Nay... nay... my little girl," quoth he,
     "It was a famous victory."

"And everybody praised the Duke

Who this great fight did win."
"But what good came of it at last?"
Quoth little Peterkin.
"Why that I cannot tell," said he,
"But 'twas a famous victory."

Thomas Campbell (1777–1844)

Thomas Campbell is a Scottish lyric poet, and one of the most popular poets of his time, though not well known today. His publication of *Pleasures of Hope* (1799) at once made him famous at the age of twenty-one, and it was read and admired everywhere. His poetic collection includes *Gertrude of Wyoming* (1809), *Lord Ullin's Daughter* (1809), *Theodric* (1824), and *The Pilgrim of Glencoe* (1842). He wrote the fine lyric of "The Battle of Hohenlinden" (1800) though he was not a spectator of the fight. His other poems include the glorious national lyric "Ye Mariners of England" (1801), "The Battle of the Baltic" (1809), and so on, all of which have made him unrivalled in his expression of patriotic feeling.

"The Battle of Hohenlinden"

On Linden, when the sun was low,
All bloodless lay the untrodden snow,
And dark as winter was the flow
Of Iser, rolling rapidly.

But Linden saw another sight,
When the drum beat, at dead of night,
Commanding fires of death to light
The darkness of her scenery.

By torch and trumpet fast arrayed,
Each horseman drew his battle blade,
And furious every charger neighed,
To join the dreadful revelry.

Then shook the hills with thunder riven,
Then rushed the steed to battle driven,
And louder than the bolts of heaven,
Far flashed the red artillery.

But redder yet that light shall glow

On Linden's hills of stainèd snow,
And bloodier yet the torrent flow
Of Iser, rolling rapidly.

'Tis morn, but scarce yon level sun
Can pierce the war-clouds, rolling dun,
Where furious Frank, and fiery Hun,
Shout in their sulph'rous canopy.

The combat deepens. On, ye brave,
Who rush to glory, or the grave!
Wave, Munich! all thy banners wave,
And charge with all thy chivalry!

Few, few, shall part where many meet!
The snow shall be their winding-sheet,
And every turf beneath their feet
Shall be a soldier's sepulchre.

"Ye Mariners of England"

Ye Mariners of England
    That guard our native seas!
Whose flag has braved a thousand years
    The battle and the breeze!
Your glorious standard launch again
    To match another foe;
And sweep through the deep,
    While the stormy winds do blow!
While the battle rages loud and long
    And the stormy winds do blow.

The spirits of your fathers
    Shall start from every wave—
For the deck it was their field of fame,
    And Ocean was their grave:
Where Blake and mighty Nelson fell
    Your manly hearts shall glow,
As ye sweep through the deep,

While the stormy winds do blow!
While the battle rages loud and long
And the stormy winds do blow.

Britannia needs no bulwarks,
No towers along the steep;
Her march is o'er the mountain-waves,
Her home is on the deep.
With thunders from her native oak
She quells the floods below,
As they roar on the shore,
When the stormy winds do blow!
When the battle rages loud and long,
And the stormy winds do blow.

The meteor flag of England
Shall yet terrific burn;
Till danger's troubled night depart
And the star of peace return.
Then, then, ye ocean-warriors!
Our song and feast shall flow
To the fame of your name,
When the storm has ceased to blow!
When the fiery fight is heard no more,
And the storm has ceased to blow.

"The Soldier's Dream"

Our bugles sang truce—for the night-cloud had lowered,
And the sentinel stars set their watch in the sky;
And thousands had sunk on the ground overpowered,
The weary to sleep, and the wounded to die.

When reposing that night on my pallet of straw,
By the wolf-scaring faggot that guarded the slain,
At the dead of the night a sweet vision I saw,
And thrice ere the morning I dreamt it again.

Methought from the battle-field's dreadful array,

Far, far I had roamed on a desolate track:
'Twas Autumn,—and sunshine arose on the way
    To the home of my fathers, that welcomed me back.

I flew to the pleasant fields traversed so oft
    In life's morning march, when my bosom was young
I heard my own mountain-goats bleating aloft,
    And knew the sweet strain that the corn-reapers sung.

Then pledged we the wine-cup, and fondly I swore,
    From my home and my weeping friends never to part
My little ones kissed me a thousand times o'er,
    And my wife sobbed aloud in her fulness of heart,

Stay, stay with us, —rest, thou art weary and worn;
    And fain was their war-broken soldier to stay;—
But sorrow returned with the dawning of morn,
    And the voice in my dreaming ear melted away.

"The Battle of the Baltic"

I

Of Nelson and the North,
Sing the glorious day's renown,
When to battle fierce came forth
All the might of Denmark's crown,
And her arms along the deep proudly shone;
By each gun the lighted brand,
In a bold determined hand,
And the Prince of all the land
Led them on.

II

Like leviathans afloat,
Lay their bulwarks on the brine;
While the sign of battle flew
On the lofty British line:
It was ten of April morn by the chime;
As they drifted on their path,
There was silence deep as death;

And the boldest held his breath,

For a time.

III

But the might of England flushed

To anticipate the scene;

And her van the fleeter rushed

O'er the deadly space between.

"Hearts of oak!" our captain cried; when each gun

From its adamantine lips

Spread a death-shade round the ships,

Like the hurricane eclipse

Of the sun.

IV

Again! again! again!

And the havoc did not slack,

Till a feeble cheer the Dane

To our cheering sent us back;—

Their shots along the deep slowly boom:—

Then ceased—and all is wail,

As they strike the shattered sail;

Or, in conflagration pale,

Light the gloom.

V

Out spoke the victor then,

As he hailed them o'er the wave;

"Ye are brothers! ye are men!

And we conquer but to save:—

So peace instead of death let us bring;

But yield, proud foe, thy fleet,

With the crews, at England's feet,

And make submission meet

To our King."

VI

Then Denmark blessed our chief,

That he gave her wounds repose;

And the sounds of joy and grief

From her people wildly rose,

As death withdrew his shades from the day.

While the sun looked smiling bright

O'er a wide and woeful sight,
Where the fires of funeral light
Died away.
            VII
Now joy, Old England, raise!
For the tidings of thy might,
By the festal cities' blaze,
While the wine-cup shines in light;
And yet amidst that joy and uproar,
Let us think of them that sleep,
Full many a fathom deep,
By thy wild and stormy steep.
Elsinore!
            VIII
Brave hearts! to Britain's pride
Once so faithful and so true,
On the deck of fame that died;—
With the gallant good Riou:
Soft sigh the winds of Heaven o'er their grave!
While the billow mournful rolls
And the mermaid's song condoles,
Singing glory to the souls
Of the brave!

Lord Byron (1788–1824)

George Gordon Noel Byron, or Lord Byron, is the most flamboyant and notorious of the English Romantic poets, whose real-life and poetic characterisation of the so-called Byronic hero make him one of the most controversial personas of the age. He most bravely champions liberty and gives all his money, time, energy, and finally his life to the Greek war of independence, proving that a poet is a soldier with his pen mightier than a sword. He has attempted nearly every genre of writing such as satire, verse narrative, ode, lyric, speculative drama, historical tragedy, confessional poetry, dramatic monologue, and seriocomic epic, and every form of poetic presentation old and new such as Spenserian stanzas, heroic couplets, blank verse, terza rima, ottava rima and vigorous prose. His poetic collection includes *Hours of Idleness* (1807), Oriental verse tales such as *The Giaour* (1813), *The Bride of Abydos* (1813), *The Corsair* (1814) and *Lara* (1814), and autobiographical poem in four cantos *Childe Harold's Pilgrimage* (1812–18), and *Don Juan* (1819–24), of which his early death prevented the completion. The poem "The Destruction of Sennacherib" was published in 1815.

"The Destruction of Sennacherib"[16]

The Assyrian came down like the wolf on the fold,
And his cohorts were gleaming in purple and gold;
And the sheen of their spears was like stars on the sea,
When the blue wave rolls nightly on deep Galilee.

Like the leaves of the forest when Summer is green,
That host with their banners at sunset were seen:
Like the leaves of the forest when Autumn hath blown,
That host on the morrow lay withered and strown.

For the Angel of Death spread his wings on the blast,
And breathed in the face of the foe as he passed;
And the eyes of the sleepers waxed deadly and chill,
And their hearts but once heaved, and for ever grew still!

And there lay the steed with his nostril all wide,
But through it there rolled not the breath of his pride:
And the foam of his gasping lay white on the turf,
And cold as the spray of the rock-beating surf.

And there lay the rider distorted and pale,
With the dew on his brow, and the rust on his mail;
And the tents were all silent, the banners alone,
The lances unlifted, the trumpet unblown.

And the widows of Ashur are loud in their wail,
And the idols are broke in the temple of Baal;
And the might of the Gentile, unsmote by the sword,
Hath melted like snow in the glance of the Lord!

---

16 Sennacherib, King of Assyria, from 709 BC to his death in 681 BC, demolished a series of Judaean cities and besieged Jerusalem. Byron based his poem on this event, in which the Assyrian army was destroyed by an angel, and Sennacherib retreated in defeat.

Excerpts from *Childe Harold's Pilgrimage*[17]

There was a sound of revelry by night,
 And Belgium's Capital had gathered then
 Her Beauty and her Chivalry, and bright
 The lamps shone o'er fair women and brave men;
 A thousand hearts beat happily; and when
 Music arose with its voluptuous swell,
 Soft eyes looked love to eyes which spake again,
 And all went merry as a marriage bell;
But hush! hark! a deep sound strikes like a rising knell!

Did ye not hear it?—No; 'twas but the wind,
 Or the car rattling o'er the stony street;
 On with the dance! let joy be unconfined;
 No sleep till morn, when Youth and Pleasure meet
 To chase the glowing Hours with flying feet—
 But hark!—that heavy sound breaks in once more,
 As if the clouds its echo would repeat;
 And nearer, clearer, deadlier than before!
Arm! Arm! it is—it is—the cannon's opening roar!

Within a windowed niche of that high hall
 Sate Brunswick's fated chieftain; he did hear
 That sound the first amidst the festival,
 And caught its tone with Death's prophetic ear;
 And when they smiled because he deemed it near,
 His heart more truly knew that peal too well
 Which stretched his father on a bloody bier,
 And roused the vengeance blood alone could quell;
He rushed into the field, and, foremost fighting, fell.

Ah! then and there was hurrying to and fro,
 And gathering tears, and tremblings of distress,
 And cheeks all pale, which but an hour ago
 Blushed at the praise of their own loveliness;

---

17 This part is probably written in 1816. The Duchess of Richmond gave a famous ball in Brussels, Wellington's headquarters, on the evening before the Battle of Waterloo. The Duke of Wellington and most of his officers were present.

And there were sudden partings, such as press

The life from out young hearts, and choking sighs

Which ne'er might be repeated; who could guess

If ever more should meet those mutual eyes,

Since upon night so sweet such awful morn could rise!

And there was mounting in hot haste: the steed,

The mustering squadron, and the clattering car,

Went pouring forward with impetuous speed,

And swiftly forming in the ranks of war;

And the deep thunder peal on peal afar;

And near, the beat of the alarming drum

Roused up the soldier ere the morning star;

While thronged the citizens with terror dumb,

Or whispering, with white lips—'The foe! They come! they come!'

And wild and high the 'Cameron's Gathering' rose!

The war-note of Lochiel, which Albyn's hills

Have heard, and heard, too, have her Saxon foes:—

How in the noon of night that pibroch thrills,

Savage and shrill! But with the breath which fills

Their mountain-pipe, so fill the mountaineers

With the fierce native daring which instils

The stirring memory of a thousand years,

And Evan's, Donald's fame rings in each clansman's ears!

And Ardennes waves above them her green leaves,

Dewy with nature's tear-drops, as they pass,

Grieving, if aught inanimate e'er grieves,

Over the unreturning brave,—alas!

Ere evening to be trodden like the grass

Which now beneath them, but above shall grow

In its next verdure, when this fiery mass

Of living valour, rolling on the foe

And burning with high hope, shall moulder cold and low.

Last noon beheld them full of lusty life,

Last eve in Beauty's circle proudly gay,

The midnight brought the signal-sound of strife,

The morn the marshalling in arms,—the day

Battle's magnificently-stern array!

The thunder-clouds close o'er it, which when rent

The earth is covered thick with other clay

Which her own clay shall cover, heaped and pent,

Rider and horse,—friend, foe,—in one red burial blent!

Excerpts from *Don Juan*[18]

The fortress is call'd Ismail, and is placed

     Upon the Danube's left branch and left bank,

With buildings in the Oriental taste,

     But still a fortress of the foremost rank,

Or was at least, unless 't is since defaced,

     Which with your conquerors is a common prank:

It stands some eighty versts from the high sea,

     And measures round of toises thousands three.

Within the extent of this fortification

     A borough is comprised along the height

Upon the left, which from its loftier station

     Commands the city, and upon its site

A Greek had raised around this elevation

     A quantity of palisades upright,

So placed as to impede the fire of those

     Who held the place, and to assist the foe's.

This circumstance may serve to give a notion

     Of the high talents of this new Vauban:

But the town ditch below was deep as ocean,

     The rampart higher than you 'd wish to hang:

But then there was a great want of precaution

     (Prithee, excuse this engineering slang),

Nor work advanced, nor cover'd way was there,

To hint at least 'Here is no thoroughfare.'

---

18 The excerpt is from Canto VII of *Don Juan*. The setting is Ismail, a Turkish fortress on the Danube, which is being besieged by the Russians. Here arrive, by steps which Byron omits, a party from Constantinople made up of Juan, Johnson, two unidentified Turkish women, and a eunuch. They are brought to General Suwarrow, the ruthless and efficient commander of the Russians.

But a stone bastion, with a narrow gorge,
  And walls as thick as most skulls born as yet;
Two batteries, cap-a-pie, as our St. George,
  Case-mated one, and t' other 'a barbette,'
Of Danube's bank took formidable charge;
  While two and twenty cannon duly set
Rose over the town's right side, in bristling tier,
Forty feet high, upon a cavalier.

But from the river the town's open quite,
  Because the Turks could never be persuaded
A Russian vessel e'er would heave in sight;
  And such their creed was, till they were invaded,
When it grew rather late to set things right.
  But as the Danube could not well be waded,
They look'd upon the Muscovite flotilla,
And only shouted, 'Allah!' and 'Bis Millah!'

The Russians now were ready to attack:
  But oh, ye goddesses of war and glory!
How shall I spell the name of each Cossacque
  Who were immortal, could one tell their story?
Alas! what to their memory can lack?
  Achilles' self was not more grim and gory
Than thousands of this new and polish'd nation,
Whose names want nothing but—pronunciation.

Still I 'll record a few, if but to increase
  Our euphony: there was Strongenoff, and Strokonoff,
Meknop, Serge Lwow, Arsniew of modern Greece,
  And Tschitsshakoff, and Roguenoff, and Chokenoff,
And others of twelve consonants apiece;
  And more might be found out, if I could poke enough
Into gazettes; but Fame (capricious strumpet),
It seems, has got an ear as well as trumpet,

4. The French Revolution and Napoleonic Wars

It seems that the 18th century wars culminated in the French Revolutionary and later

Napoleonic Wars. The so-called "war of civilisations" had led to the increasing valorisation of the army and navy as professions of intrinsic worth to the nation. War writing had taken on the following two distinctive features, as Kate Mcloughlin *The Cambridge Companion to War Writing* has summarised: The first is "to legitimate the valour of the officer and the honour of war by means of metrical romances and historical fiction that interpreted contemporary war in terms of a heroic, chivalric past", while the second is "the emergence of the military author, a sign of the legitimation and respect accorded to the profession and interest in the personal experience of the soldier and sailor."[19] But for most romantic poets or poets of other schools, war is quickly becoming an evil instrument unless it is a matter of human liberation.

Anna Laetitia Barbauld (1743–1825)

Anna Laetitia Barbauld is a minor British poetess, but with the publication of the slender volume entitled *Poems* (1773), she became a figure of eminence in the world of letters, reportedly exerting an important impact on Wordsworth and Coleridge (It is said that Coleridge once walked forty miles to meet her). As an early Romantic poet, she was rediscovered by contemporary feminists, having been again recognised as one of the important poets of her time. The excerpt from her poem *Eighteen Hundred and Eleven* (1812) comments on the wars taking place in Britain and Europe, especially those in the French Revolutionary and Napoleonic Wars. She made a striking comparison between America as with the possibility of freedom and Britain as with "faded glories" and "desolated shores", thinking that wars have turned uncontainable and no longer capable of being defined.

Excerpts from *Eighteen Hundred and Eleven*

Still the loud death drum, thundering from afar,
O'er the vext nations pours the storm of war:
To the stern call still Britain bends her ear,
Feeds the fierce strife, the alternate hope and fear;
Bravely, though vainly, dares to strive with Fate,
And seeks by turns to prop each sinking state.
Colossal Power with overwhelming force
Bears down each fort of Freedom in its course;
Prostrate she lies beneath the Despot's sway,
While the hushed nations curse him—and obey.

Bounteous in vain, with frantic man at strife,
Glad Nature pours the means—the joys of life;

---

19 Kate McMoughlin, ed., *The Cambridge Companion to War Writing*. Cambridge: Cambridge University Press, 2009, p. 121.

In vain with orange blossoms scents the gale,

The hills with olives clothes, with corn the vale;

Man calls to Famine, nor invokes in vain,

Disease and Rapine follow in her train;

The tramp of marching hosts disturbs the plough,

The sword, not sickle, reaps the harvest now,

And where the Soldier gleans the scant supply.

The helpless Peasant but retires to die;

No laws his hut from licensed outrage shield,

And war's least horror is the ensanguined field.

Fruitful in vain, the matron counts with pride

The blooming youths that grace her honoured side;

No son returns to press her widow'd hand,

Her fallen blossoms strew a foreign strand.

—Fruitful in vain, she boasts her virgin race,

Whom cultured arts adorn and gentlest grace;

Defrauded of its homage, Beauty mourns,

And the rose withers on its virgin thorns.

Frequent, some stream obscure, some uncouth name

By deeds of blood is lifted into fame;

Oft o'er the daily page some soft-one bends

To learn the fate of husband, brothers, friends,

Or the spread map with anxious eye explores,

Its dotted boundaries and penciled shores,

Asks *where* the spot that wrecked her bliss is found,

And learns its name but to detest the sound.

And thinks't thou, Britain, still to sit at ease,

An island Queen amidst thy subject seas,

While the vext billows, in their distant roar,

But soothe thy slumbers, and but kiss thy shore?

To sport in wars, while danger keeps aloof,

Thy grassy turf unbruised by hostile hoof?

So sing thy flatterers; but, Britain, know,

Thou who hast shared the guilt must share the woe.

Nor distant is the hour; low murmurs spread,

And whispered fears, creating what they dread;

Ruin, as with an earthquake shock, is here,

There, the heart-witherings of unuttered fear,

And that sad death, whence most affection bleeds,

Which sickness, only of the soul, precedes.

Thy baseless wealth dissolves in air away,

Like mists that melt before the morning ray:

No more on crowded mart or busy street

Friends, meeting friends, with cheerful hurry greet;

Sad, on the ground thy princely merchants bend

Their altered looks, and evil days portend,

And fold their arms, and watch with anxious breast

The tempest blackening in the distant West.

Joel Barlow (1754–1812)

Joel Barlow is an American poet and public official. While a Yale undergraduate, he joined with John Trumbull and Timothy Dwight and formed a circle called "Hartford wits" in the 1780s and later volunteered for the American army. His *Vision of Columbus* (1787) is a poetic paean to America in nine books, bringing him immediate fame, and his mock-heroic poem *The Hasty Pudding* (1793) is written for patriotism that led him to attempt to create national literature for the newly-born America. In 1807, he enlarged his *Vision of Columbus* to create a new edition entitled *The Columbiad*. In 1811, he was appointed U.S. ambassador to France and travelled from Paris to Vilna to negotiate a trade agreement with Napoleon. He was caught in the retreat of the French army from Russia and died near Krakow in Poland on the day before the 1812 Christmas. The poem "Advice to a Raven in Russia" was written in December 1812 before his death.

"Advice to a Raven in Russia"

Black fool, why winter here? These frozen skies,

Worn by your wings and deafened by your cries,

Should warn you hence, where milder suns invite,

And day alternates with his mother night.

You fear perhaps your food will fail you there,

Your human carnage, that delicious fare

That lured you hither, following still your friend

The great Napoleon to the world's bleak end.

     You fear, because the southern climes poured forth

Their clustering nations to infest the north,

Bavarians, Austrians, those who drink the Po

And those who skirt the Tuscan seas below,

With all Germania, Neustria, Belgia, Gaul,
Doomed here to wade through slaughter to their fall,
You fear he left behind no wars, to feed
His feathered cannibals and nurse the breed.

Fear not, my screamer, call your greedy train,
Sweep over Europe, hurry back to Spain,
You'll find his legions there; the valiant crew
Please best their master when they toil for you.
Abundant there they spread the country o'er
And taint the breeze with every nation's gore,
Iberian, Lusian, British widely strown,
But still more wide and copious flows their own.

Go where you will; Calabria, Malta, Greece,
Egypt and Syria still his fame increase,
Domingo's fattened isle and India's plains
Glow deep with purple drawn from Gallic veins.
No raven's wing can stretch the flight so far
As the torn bandrols of Napoleon's war.
Choose then your climate, fix your best abode,
He'll make you deserts and he'll bring you blood.

How could you fear a dearth? have not mankind,
Though slain by millions, millions left behind?
Has not Conscription still the power to wield
Her annual faulchion o'er the human field?
A faithful harvester! or if a man
Escape that gleaner, shall he scape the Ban?
The triple Ban, that like the hound of hell
Gripes with three jowls, to hold his victim well.

Fear nothing then, hatch fast your ravenous brood,
Teach them to cry to Bonaparte for food;
They'll be like you, of all his suppliant train,
The only class that never cries in vain.
For see what mutual benefits you lend!
(The surest way to fix the mutual friend)
While on his slaughtered troops your tribe are fed,
You cleanse his camp and carry off his dead.
Imperial scavenger! but now you know
Your work is vain amid these hills of snow.
His tentless troops are marbled through with frost

And change to crystal when the breath is lost.

Mere trunks of ice, though limbed like human frames

And lately warmed with life's endearing flames,

They cannot taint the air, the world impest,

Nor can you tear one fibre from their breast.

No! from their visual sockets, as they lie,

With beak and claws you cannot pluck an eye.

The frozen orb, preserving still its form,

Defies your talons as it braves the storm,

But stands and stares to God, as if to know

In what cursed hands he leaves his world below.

Fly then, or starve; though all the dreadful road

From Minsk to Moscow with their bodies strowed

May count some myriads, yet they can't suffice

To feed you more beneath these dreary skies.

Go back, and winter in the wilds of Spain;

Feast there awhile, and in the next campaign

Rejoin your master; for you'll find him then,

With his new million of the race of men,

Clothed in his thunders, all his flags unfurled,

Raging and storming o'er the prostrate world.

War after war his hungry soul requires,

State after state shall sink beneath his fires,

Yet other Spains in victim smoke shall rise

And other Moscows suffocate the skies,

Each land lie reeking with its people's slain

And not a stream run bloodless to the main.

Till men resume their souls, and dare to shed

Earth's total vengeance on the monster's head,

Hurl from his blood-built throne this king of woes,

Dash him to dust, and let the world repose.

Samuel Taylor Coleridge (1772–1834)

Samuel Taylor Coleridge is an English lyrical poet, critic, and philosopher. His contributions to the collaborative *Lyrical Ballads* (1798) with William Wordsworth not only heralded the English Romantic movement but also witnessed the first great work of the Romantic school of poetry. His *Biographia Literaria* (1817) serves as the most significant work of general literary criticism produced in the period. His poetic production is best represented by his "The Rime of the Ancient Mariner", a poem in seven parts that first appeared in *Lyrical Ballads*. The poem "Fears in Solitude" (1798) can be seen as an anxiety-of-empire poem, for it discloses the fact that war had become an entertainment and commodity, urgently requiring re-evaluating the bellicosity based on ignorance of war's reality.

"Fears in Solitude"

A green and silent spot, amid the hills,
A small and silent dell! O'er stiller place
No singing sky-lark ever poised himself.
The hills are heathy, save that swelling slope,
Which hath a gay and gorgeous covering on,
All golden with the never-bloomless furze,
Which now blooms most profusely: but the dell,
Bathed by the mist, is fresh and delicate
As vernal corn-field, or the unripe flax,
When, through its half-transparent stalks, at eve,
The level sunshine glimmers with green light.
Oh! 'tis a quiet spirit-healing nook!
Which all, methinks, would love; but chiefly he,
The humble man, who, in his youthful years,
Knew just so much of folly, as had made
His early manhood more securely wise!
Here he might lie on fern or withered heath,
While from the singing lark (that sings unseen
The minstrelsy that solitude loves best),
And from the sun, and from the breezy air,
Sweet influences trembled o'er his frame;
And he, with many feelings, many thoughts,
Made up a meditative joy, and found
Religious meanings in the forms of Nature!
And so, his senses gradually wrapt
In a half sleep, he dreams of better worlds,
And dreaming hears thee still, O singing lark,
That singest like an angel in the clouds !

My God! it is a melancholy thing
For such a man, who would full fain preserve
His soul in calmness, yet perforce must feel

For all his human brethren—O my God!
It weighs upon the heart, that he must think
What uproar and what strife may now be stirring
This way or that way o'er these silent hills—
Invasion, and the thunder and the shout,
And all the crash of onset; fear and rage,
And undetermined conflict—even now,
Even now, perchance, and in his native isle:
Carnage and groans beneath this blessed sun!
We have offended, Oh! my countrymen!
We have offended very grievously,
And been most tyrannous. From east to west
A groan of accusation pierces Heaven!
The wretched plead against us; multitudes
Countless and vehement, the sons of God,
Our brethren! Like a cloud that travels on,
Steamed up from Cairo's swamps of pestilence,
Even so, my countrymen! have we gone forth
And borne to distant tribes slavery and pangs,
And, deadlier far, our vices, whose deep taint
With slow perdition murders the whole man,
His body and his soul! Meanwhile, at home,
All individual dignity and power
Engulfed in Courts, Committees, Institutions,
Associations and Societies,
A vain, speech-mouthing, speech-reporting Guild,
One Benefit-Club for mutual flattery,
We have drunk up, demure as at a grace,
Pollutions from the brimming cup of wealth;
Contemptuous of all honourable rule,
Yet bartering freedom and the poor man's life
For gold, as at a market! The sweet words
Of Christian promise, words that even yet
Might stem destruction, were they wisely preached,
Are muttered o'er by men, whose tones proclaim
How flat and wearisome they feel their trade:
Rank scoffers some, but most too indolent
To deem them falsehoods or to know their truth.
Oh! blasphemous! the Book of Life is made

A superstitious instrument, on which
We gabble o'er the oaths we mean to break;
For all must swear—all and in every place,
College and wharf, council and justice-court;
All, all must swear, the briber and the bribed,
Merchant and lawyer, senator and priest,
The rich, the poor, the old man and the young;
All, all make up one scheme of perjury,
That faith doth reel; the very name of God
Sounds like a juggler's charm; and, bold with joy,
Forth from his dark and lonely hiding-place,
(Portentous sight!) the owlet Atheism,
Sailing on obscene wings athwart the noon,
Drops his blue-fringèd lids, and holds them close,
And hooting at the glorious sun in Heaven,
Cries out, 'Where is it?'
Thankless too for peace,
(Peace long preserved by fleets and perilous seas)
Secure from actual warfare, we have loved
To swell the war-whoop, passionate for war!
Alas! for ages ignorant of all
Its ghastlier workings, (famine or blue plague,
Battle, or siege, or flight through wintry snows,)
We, this whole people, have been clamorous
For war and bloodshed; animating sports,
The which we pay for as a thing to talk of,
Spectators and not combatants! No guess
Anticipative of a wrong unfelt,
No speculation on contingency,
However dim and vague, too vague and dim
To yield a justifying cause; and forth,
(Stuffed out with big preamble, holy names,
And adjurations of the God in Heaven,)
We send our mandates for the certain death
Of thousands and ten thousands! Boys and girls,
And women, that would groan to see a child
Pull off an insect's leg, all read of war,
The best amusement for our morning meal!
The poor wretch, who has learnt his only prayers

From curses, who knows scarcely words enough
To ask a blessing from his Heavenly Father,
Becomes a fluent phraseman, absolute
And technical in victories and defeats,
And all our dainty terms for fratricide ;
Terms which we trundle smoothly o'er our tongues
Like mere abstractions, empty sounds to which
We join no feeling and attach no form!
As if the soldier died without a wound;
As if the fibres of this godlike frame
Were gored without a pang; as if the wretch,
Who fell in battle, doing bloody deeds,
Passed off to Heaven, translated and not killed;
As though he had no wife to pine for him,
No God to judge him! Therefore, evil days
Are coming on us, O my countrymen!
And what if all-avenging Providence,
Strong and retributive, should make us know
The meaning of our words, force us to feel
The desolation and the agony
Of our fierce doings?
Spare us yet awhile,
Father and God! O! spare us yet awhile!
Oh! let not English women drag their flight
Fainting beneath the burthen of their babes,
Of the sweet infants, that but yesterday
Laughed at the breast! Sons, brothers, husbands, all
Who ever gazed with fondness on the forms
Which grew up with you round the same fire-side,
And all who ever heard the sabbath-bells
Without the infidel's scorn, make yourselves pure!
Stand forth! be men! repel an impious foe,
Impious and false, a light yet cruel race,
Who laugh away all virtue, mingling mirth
With deeds of murder; and still promising
Freedom, themselves too sensual to be free,
Poison life's amities, and cheat the heart
Of faith and quiet hope, and all that soothes,
And all that lifts the spirit! Stand we forth;

155

Render them back upon the insulted ocean,
And let them toss as idly on its waves
As the vile seaweed, which some mountain-blast
Swept from our shores! And oh! may we return
Not with a drunken triumph, but with fear,
Repenting of the wrongs with which we stung
So fierce a foe to frenzy!

                    I have told,
O Britons! O my brethren! I have told
Most bitter truth, but without bitterness.
Nor deem my zeal or factious or mistimed;
For never can true courage dwell with them,
Who, playing tricks with conscience, dare not look
At their own vices. We have been too long
Dupes of a deep delusion! Some, belike,
Groaning with restless enmity, expect
All change from change of constituted power;
As if a Government had been a robe,
On which our vice and wretchedness were tagged
Like fancy-points and fringes, with the robe
Pulled off at pleasure. Fondly these attach
A radical causation to a few
Poor drudges of chastising Providence,
Who borrow all their hues and qualities
From our own folly and rank wickedness,
Which gave them birth and nursed them. Others, meanwhile,
Dote with a mad idolatry; and all
Who will not fall before their images,
And yield them worship, they are enemies
Even of their country!
Such have I been deemed.—
But, O dear Britain! O my Mother Isle!
Needs must thou prove a name most dear and holy
To me, a son, a brother, and a friend,
A husband, and a father! who revere
All bonds of natural love, and find them all
Within the limits of thy rocky shores.
O native Britain! O my Mother Isle!

How shouldst thou prove aught else but dear and holy
To me, who from thy lakes and mountain-hills,
Thy clouds, thy quiet dales, thy rocks and seas,
Have drunk in all my intellectual life,
All sweet sensations, all ennobling thoughts,
All adoration of the God in nature,
All lovely and all honourable things,
Whatever makes this mortal spirit feel
The joy and greatness of its future being?
There lives nor form nor feeling in my soul
Unborrowed from my country! O divine
And beauteous island! thou hast been my sole
And most magnificent temple, in the which
I walk with awe, and sing my stately songs ,
Loving the God that made me!—
                              May my fears,
My filial fears, be vain! and may the vaunts
And menace of the vengeful enemy
Pass like the gust, that roared and died away
In the distant tree: which heard, and only heard
In this low dell, bowed not the delicate grass.

But now the gentle dew-fall sends abroad
The fruit-like perfume of the golden furze:
The light has left the summit of the hill,
Though still a sunny gleam lies beautiful,
Aslant the ivied beacon. Now farewell,
Farewell, awhile, O soft and silent spot!
On the green sheep-track, up the heathy hill,
Homeward I wind my way; and lo! recalled
From bodings that have well-nigh wearied me,
I find myself upon the brow, and pause
Startled! And after lonely sojourning
In such a quiet and surrounded nook,
This burst of prospect, here the shadowy main,
Dim-tinted, there the mighty majesty
Of that huge amphitheatre of rich
And elmy fields, seems like society—
Conversing with the mind, and giving it

A livelier impulse and a dance of thought!

And now, belovèd Stowey! I behold

Thy church-tower, and, methinks, the four huge elms

Clustering, which mark the mansion of my friend;

And close behind them, hidden from my view,

Is my own lowly cottage, where my babe

And my babe's mother dwell in peace! With light

And quickened footsteps thitherward I tend,

Remembering thee, O green and silent dell!

And grateful, that by nature's quietness

And solitary musings, all my heart

Is softened, and made worthy to indulge

Love, and the thoughts that yearn for human kind.

Charles Wolfe (1791–1823)

Charles Wolfe is an Irish poet, best known for his "The Burial of Sir John Moore after Corunna" (1817), one of the four or five best martial poems in English preeminent for simplicity, patriotic fervour, and manly pathos: Sir John Moore commanded British troops supporting the Spanish Army against Napoleon in the Peninsular War (1808–1814), which was part of the generation-long war between France, under Napoleon Buonaparte, and pretty much everyone else in Europe; forced into a 250-mile retreat by a French defeat of the Spanish, he fought valiantly at Corunna, Spain, where he won the battle against the French, but lost his own life in 1809. His collection of poetry *Poetical Remains* was published posthumously in 1825.

"The Burial of Sir John Moore after Corunna"

Not a drum was heard, not a funeral note,

    As his corse to the rampart we hurried;

Not a soldier discharged his farewell shot

    O'er the grave where our hero we buried.

We buried him darkly at dead of night,

    The sods with our bayonets turning,

By the struggling moonbeam's misty light

    And the lanthorn dimly burning.

No useless coffin enclosed his breast,

    Not in sheet or in shroud we wound him;

But he lay like a warrior taking his rest
     With his martial cloak around him.

Few and short were the prayers we said,
     And we spoke not a word of sorrow;
But we steadfastly gazed on the face that was dead,
     And we bitterly thought of the morrow.

We thought, as we hollowed his narrow bed
     And smoothed down his lonely pillow,
That the foe and the stranger would tread o'er his head,
     And we far away on the billow!

Lightly they'll talk of the spirit that's gone,
     And o'er his cold ashes upbraid him—
But little he'll reck, if they let him sleep on
     In the grave where a Briton has laid him.

But half of our heavy task was done
     When the clock struck the hour for retiring;
And we heard the distant and random gun
     That the foe was sullenly firing.

Slowly and sadly we laid him down,
     From the field of his fame fresh and gory;
We carved not a line, and we raised not a stone,
     But we left him alone with his glory.

Chapter IV

War Poetry of British Imperialism (1830–1914)

In British history, the "Victorian Era" witnessed a period between approximately 1820 and 1914, corresponding roughly (but not exactly) to the period of Queen Victoria (1837–1901) and Edward VII (1901–1910). The period was characterized by a class-based society, a growing number of people able to vote, a growing state economy, and finally, the imperialist status as the most powerful empire in the world. The period can be thus regarded as the period of "British Imperialism". From the Battle of Waterloo of 1815 in which British and Prussian forces routed the French, terminating over 15 years of European conflicts, to the beginning of the first global total war of 1914, when Britain declared war on Germany on 4 August, the Anglo-American world enjoyed a relatively long period of internal order and stability, accompanied with the British territorial or global imperial expansion.

As Queen Victoria was crowned, the British Empire expanded with such wars as the First Afghan War (1839–1842), the First Opium War (1839–1842), the Crimean War (1853–1856), the Anglo-Persian War (1856–1857), the Second Opium War (1856–1860), the Boer Wars (or the South African Wars between the British and the descendants of the Dutch settlers (Boers) in Africa, 1880–1881; 1899–1902); and finally the British Colonial Wars in Africa (1900–1915). The sinking of the Titanic in 1912 may indicate the collapse of all the westerns with Britain as its symbolic nation. As for poetic production of "The Victorians and war", John Reed once wrote: "Victorian war literature is generically varied, ranging from adventure stories to poetry to historical novels to works for children. Patriotic and imperial impulses jostle with the antiwar sentiment, often within the oeuvre of a single writer... Constructions of the man-at-war varied through the nineteenth century. Developing weapons technology–repeating rifles, machine guns, torpedo boats–continued the industrialisation of warfare, with predictable results to the human body and concomitant developments both in battlefield medicine and in the perception of courage and honour."[1]

John Reed has conscientiously examined these poetic representations in "historical, mythological, and imagined wars", and argued that, since most of the conflicts involving the British armed forces in the nineteenth century occurred outside Britain and even Europe, war literature involving actual combat often has an "exotic" sense while some other poets turned to such long-past war topic as the medieval, chivalric motifs and ethics for expression. "Towards the end of the nineteenth century, though loyalty to the Empire remained strong, a note of melancholy and even doubt appeared," as he concluded in such words: "While the fate of the common soldier touched many Victorian hearts, belief in war as politically necessary, commercially advantageous, and morally improving was slow to die. War was geographically distant from Victorian Britons, but the public had unprecedented access to the facts of the conflict, a situation that resulted in an uneasy tension between glorifying individual heroics and recognising war's cost. At the turn of the century, invasion fears, long laid to rest by Waterloo, were current again. The elegiac mood of fin-de-siècle war literature has in it a note of warning."[2]

There had been too many wars in which the British were involved across the globe, and poets often addressed several wars currently taking place sometimes with heavy allusions to the past in a single poem. It is thus impossible to collect a certain war poem under a single category. The anthology of British war poetry in the 19th century makes its arrangements according to the poets' year of birth, but respectively classified with "Anti-war Voices" and "Apology for Wars".

1. Anti-war Voices in Victorian Verse

The Anti-war voices had made up of the overwhelming majority of war poems during the period concerned, with their respective specificities of themes ranging from corruption of humanity, the tragedy of human suffering, the endless slaughter of lives, and so on, which may have been "full of sound and fury" but "signifies nothing." These poets include Alfred Tennyson, William Makepeace Thackeray, Robert Browning, and others, all of whom write in the vein of T. W. H. Crosland's "Slain 'Dulce et decorum est pro patria mori'," constantly revaluating the Horatian slogan that "it is sweet and fitting to die for one's country."

---

1 Kate Mcloughlin, ed., *The Cambridge Companion to War Writing*. Cambridge, New York: Cambridge University Press, 2009, pp. 135-136.
2 Kate Mcloughlin, ed., *The Cambridge Companion to War Writing*. Cambridge, New York: Cambridge University Press, 2009, p. 145.

Alfred Tennyson (1809–1892)

Alfred Tennyson, in full "Alfred Tennyson, the 1st Baron Tennyson of Aldworth and Freshwater," is a British poet and dramatist, generally considered to be the most representative of the Victorian age in poetry. As a poet laureate, he emphatically wrote verses about public events, making himself the embodiment of his age both to his contemporaries and to modern readers. He published his first volume of poetry of *Poems by Two Brothers* in 1827 when he was only in his teens. Three years later in 1830, he turned out another collection *Poems, Chiefly Lyrical*. The two volumes of *Poems* (1842) have witnessed his rise of huge popularity, and *The Princess* (1847) is his first attempt at a long narrative poem, with three other major long works of the same genre followed: *In Memoriam* (1859)*, Maud, and Other Poems* (1859), and *Idylls of the King* (1859), among which *In Memoriam* is considered the greatest. In his later years, he tried dramas but also published *Ballads and Other Poems* (1880).

Tennyson wrote a number of war poems with historical materials, such as King Arthur in his *Idylls of the King* and Constantinus or King of the Scots in his *The Battle of Brunanburh*. But different from the traditional poetic representation of nobility and heroism, grim battle-play, breaking of the shield-wall of the enemy, the day-long pursuit and terrible slaughter, and presence of the beasts of battle feasting on the bodies, he questions those confident, patriotic, victorious with "eternal glory" of the Anglo-Saxons, for instance in "English War Song", "Maud" and others. The great heroic "Ode on the Death of the Duke of Wellington" (1854) pays tribute to the "Iron Duke", and "The Charge of the Light Brigade", said to be written after reading an account of the battle in *The Times*, is a narrative poem written in 1854 about the tragic charge of the Light Brigade of British cavalry toward Russian artillery at the Battle of Balaclava during the Crimean War.[3]

"English War Song"[4]

Who fears to die? Who fears to die?

Is there any here who fears to die

He shall find what he fears, and none shall grieve

---

3 The Crimean War (1853–1856) involved the British and French (with assistance) fighting against the Russians, supposedly in defense of the Ottoman Empire, but really to prevent Russian expansionism. Part of what the British significantly termed "The Great Game" (the ongoing competition for land and power between the British Empire and Russia)

4 "English War Song" is the twentieth poem collected in *Poems, Chiefly Lyrical* (1830). According to J. C. Thomson's *The Suppressed Poems of Alfred Lord Tennyson, 1830–1868*, these poems are "written and published during Tennyson's active literary career, but ultimately rejected as unsatisfactory. Of this considerable body of verse, a great part was written, not in youth or old age, but while Tennyson's powers were at their greatest. Whatever reasons may once have existed for suppressing the poems that follow, the student of English literature is entitled to demand that the whole body of Tennyson's work should now be open, without restriction or impediment, to the critical study to which the works of his compeers are subjected." (http://www.gutenberg.org/files/14094/14094-h/14094-h.htm#Page_8)

For the man who fears to die:
But the withering scorn of the many shall cleave
To the man who fears to die.

Chorus.—Shout for England!
Ho! for England!
George for England!
Merry England!
England for aye!

The hollow at heart shall crouch forlorn,
He shall eat the bread of common scorn;
It shall be steeped in the salt, salt tear,
Shall be steeped in his own salt tear:
Far better, far better he never were born
Than to shame merry England here.

Chorus.—Shout for England! *etc.*

There standeth our ancient enemy;
Hark! he shouteth—the ancient enemy!
On the ridge of the hill his banners rise;
They stream like fire in the skies;
Hold up the Lion of England on high
Till it dazzle and blind his eyes.

Chorus.—Shout for England! *etc.*

Come along! we alone of the earth are free;
The child in our cradles is bolder than he;
For where is the heart and strength of slaves?
Oh! where is the strength of slaves?
He is weak! we are strong; he a slave, we are free;
Come along! we will dig their graves.

Chorus.—Shout for England! *etc.*

There standeth our ancient enemy;
Will he dare to battle with the free?

Spur along! spur amain! charge to the fight:
Charge! charge to the fight!
Hold up the Lion of England on high!
Shout for God and our right!

Chorus.—Shout for England! *etc*.

"The Charge of the Light Brigade"

I

Half a league, half a league,
Half a league onward,
All in the valley of Death
  Rode the six hundred.
"Forward, the Light Brigade!
Charge for the guns!" he said.
Into the valley of Death
  Rode the six hundred.

II

"Forward, the Light Brigade!"
Was there a man dismayed?
Not though the soldier knew
  Someone had blundered.
Theirs not to make reply,
Theirs not to reason why,
Theirs but to do and die.
Into the valley of Death
Rode the six hundred.

III

Cannon to right of them,
Cannon to left of them,
Cannon in front of them
  Volleyed and thundered;
Stormed at with shot and shell,
Boldly they rode and well,
Into the jaws of Death,
Into the mouth of hell
  Rode the six hundred.

IV

Flashed all their sabres bare,

Flashed as they turned in air

Sabring the gunners there,

Charging an army, while

All the world wondered.

Plunged in the battery-smoke

Right through the line they broke;

Cossack and Russian

Reeled from the sabre stroke

Shattered and sundered.

Then they rode back, but not

    Not the six hundred.

V

Cannon to right of them,

Cannon to left of them,

Cannon behind them

    Volleyed and thundered;

Stormed at with shot and shell,

While horse and hero fell.

They that had fought so well

Came through the jaws of Death,

Back from the mouth of hell,

All that was left of them,

    Left of six hundred.

VI

When can their glory fade?

O the wild charge they made!

    All the world wondered.

Honour the charge they made!

Honour the Light Brigade,

    Noble six hundred!

"Ode on the Death of the Duke of Wellington"

I

BURY the Great Duke

With an empire's lamentation,

Let us bury the Great Duke

To the noise of the mourning of a mighty nation,

Mourning when their leaders fall,

Warriors carry the warrior's pall,

And sorrow darkens hamlet and hall.

II

Where shall we lay the man whom we deplore?

Here, in streaming London's central roar.

Let the sound of those he wrought for,

And the feet of those he fought for,

Echo round his bones for evermore.

III

Lead out the pageant: sad and slow,

As fits an universal woe,

Let the long long procession go,

And let the sorrowing crowd about it grow,

And let the mournful martial music blow;

The last great Englishman is low.

IV

Mourn, for to us he seems the last,

Remembering all his greatness in the Past.

No more in soldier fashion will he greet

With lifted hand the gazer in the street.

O friends, our chief state-oracle is mute:

Mourn for the man of long-enduring blood,

The statesman-warrior, moderate, resolute,

Whole in himself, a common good.

Mourn for the man of amplest influence,

Yet clearest of ambitious crime,

Our greatest yet with least pretence,

Great in council and great in war,

Foremost captain of his time,

Rich in saving common-sense,

And, as the greatest only are,

In his simplicity sublime.

O good gray head which all men knew,

O voice from which their omens all men drew,

O iron nerve to true occasion true,

O fall'n at length that tower of strength

Which stood four-square to all the winds that blew!

Such was he whom we deplore.

The long self-sacrifice of life is o'er.

The great World-victor's victor will be seen no more.

V

All is over and done:

Render thanks to the Giver,

England, for thy son.

Let the bell be toll'd.

Render thanks to the Giver,

And render him to the mould.

Under the cross of gold

That shines over city and river,

There he shall rest for ever

Among the wise and the bold.

Let the bell be toll'd:

And a reverent people behold

The towering car, the sable steeds:

Bright let it be with its blazon'd deeds,

Dark in its funeral fold.

Let the bell be toll'd:

And a deeper knell in the heart be knoll'd;

And the sound of the sorrowing anthem roll'd

Thro' the dome of the golden cross;

And the volleying cannon thunder his loss;

He knew their voices of old.

For many a time in many a clime

His captain's-ear has heard them boom

Bellowing victory, bellowing doom:

When he with those deep voices wrought,

Guarding realms and kings from shame;

With those deep voices our dead captain taught

The tyrant, and asserts his claim

In that dread sound to the great name,

Which he has worn so pure of blame,

In praise and in dispraise the same,

A man of well-attemper'd frame.

O civic muse, to such a name,

To such a name for ages long,

To such a name,

Preserve a broad approach of fame,

And ever-echoing avenues of song.

VI

Who is he that cometh, like an honor'd guest,

With banner and with music, with soldier and with priest,

With a nation weeping, and breaking on my rest?

Mighty Seaman, this is he

Was great by land as thou by sea.

Thine island loves thee well, thou famous man,

The greatest sailor since our world began.

Now, to the roll of muffled drums,

To thee the greatest soldier comes;

For this is he

Was great by land as thou by sea;

His foes were thine; he kept us free;

O give him welcome, this is he

Worthy of our gorgeous rites,

And worthy to be laid by thee;

For this is England's greatest son,

He that gain'd a hundred fights,

Nor ever lost an English gun;

This is he that far away

Against the myriads of Assaye

Clash'd with his fiery few and won;

And underneath another sun,

Warring on a later day,

Round affrighted Lisbon drew

The treble works, the vast designs

Of his labor'd rampart lines,

Where he greatly stood at bay,

Whence he issued forth anew,

And ever great and greater grew,

Beating from the wasted vines

Back to France her banded swarms,

Back to France with countless blows,

Till o'er the hills her eagles flew

Beyond the Pyrenean pines,

Follow'd up in valley and glen

With blare of bugle, clamor of men,

Roll of cannon and clash of arms,

And England pouring on her foes.

Such a war had such a close.

Again their ravening eagle rose

In anger, wheel'd on Europe-shadowing wings,

And barking for the thrones of kings;

Till one that sought but Duty's iron crown

On that loud sabbath shook the spoiler down;

A day of onsets of despair!

Dash'd on every rocky square

Their surging charges foam'd themselves away;

Last, the Prussian trumpet blew;

Thro' the long-tormented air

Heaven flash'd a sudden jubilant ray,

And down we swept and charged and over-threw.

So great a soldier taught us there,

What long-enduring hearts could do

In that world-earthquake, Waterloo!

Mighty Seaman, tender and true,

And pure as he from taint of craven guile,

O saviour of the silver-coasted isle,

O shaker of the Baltic and the Nile,

If aught of things that here befall

Touch a spirit among things divine,

If love of country move thee there at all,

Be glad, because his bones are laid by thine!

And thro' the centuries let a people's voice

In full acclaim,

A people's voice,

The proof and echo of all human fame,

A people's voice, when they rejoice

At civic revel and pomp and game,

Attest their great commander's claim

With honor, honor, honor, honor to him,

Eternal honor to his name.

> VII

A people's voice! we are a people yet.

Tho' all men else their nobler dreams forget,

Confus'd by brainless mobs and lawless Powers;

Thank Him who isl'd us here, and roughly set

His Briton in blown seas and storming showers,

We have a voice, with which to pay the debt

Of boundless love and reverence and regret

To those great men who fought, and kept it ours.

And keep it ours, O God, from brute control;

O Statesmen, guard us, guard the eye, the soul

Of Europe, keep our noble England whole,

And save the one true seed of freedom sown

Betwixt a people and their ancient throne,

That sober freedom out of which there springs

Our loyal passion for our temperate kings;

For, saving that, ye help to save mankind

Till public wrong be crumbled into dust,

And drill the raw world for the march of mind,

Till crowds at length be sane and crowns be just.

But wink no more in slothful overtrust.

Remember him who led your hosts;

He bade you guard the sacred coasts.

Your cannons moulder on the seaward wall;

His voice is silent in your council-hall

For ever; and whatever tempests lour

For ever silent; even if they broke

In thunder, silent; yet remember all

He spoke among you, and the Man who spoke;

Who never sold the truth to serve the hour,

Nor palter'd with Eternal God for power;

Who let the turbid streams of rumor flow

Thro' either babbling world of high and low;

Whose life was work, whose language rife

With rugged maxims hewn from life;

Who never spoke against a foe;

Whose eighty winters freeze with one rebuke

All great self-seekers trampling on the right:

Truth-teller was our England's Alfred nam'd;

Truth-lover was our English Duke;

Whatever record leap to light

He never shall be sham'd.

VIII

Lo, the leader in these glorious wars
Now to glorious burial slowly borne,
Follow'd by the brave of other lands,
He, on whom from both her open hands
Lavish Honor shower'd all her stars,
And affluent Fortune emptied all her horn.
Yea, let all good things await
Him who cares not to be great,
But as he saves or serves the state.
Not once or twice in our rough island-story,
The path of duty was the way to glory:
He that walks it, only thirsting
For the right, and learns to deaden
Love of self, before his journey closes,
He shall find the stubborn thistle bursting
Into glossy purples, which outredden
All voluptuous garden-roses.
Not once or twice in our fair island-story,
The path of duty was the way to glory:
He, that ever following her commands,
On with toil of heart and knees and hands,
Thro' the long gorge to the far light has won
His path upward, and prevail'd,
Shall find the toppling crags of Duty scal'd
Are close upon the shining table-lands
To which our God Himself is moon and sun.
Such was he: his work is done.
But while the races of mankind endure,
Let his great example stand
Colossal, seen of every land,
And keep the soldier firm, the statesman pure:
Till in all lands and thro' all human story
The path of duty be the way to glory:
And let the land whose hearths he sav'd from shame
For many and many an age proclaim
At civic revel and pomp and game,
And when the long-illumin'd cities flame,
Their ever-loyal iron leader's fame,

With honor, honor, honor, honor to him,
Eternal honor to his name.

IX

Peace, his triumph will be sung
By some yet unmoulded tongue
Far on in summers that we shall not see:
Peace, it is a day of pain
For one about whose patriarchal knee
Late the little children clung:
O peace, it is a day of pain
For one, upon whose hand and heart and brain
Once the weight and fate of Europe hung.
Ours the pain, be his the gain!
More than is of man's degree
Must be with us, watching here
At this, our great solemnity.
Whom we see not we revere;
We revere, and we refrain
From talk of battles loud and vain,
And brawling memories all too free
For such a wise humility
As befits a solemn fane:
We revere, and while we hear
The tides of Music's golden sea
Setting toward eternity,
Uplifted high in heart and hope are we,
Until we doubt not that for one so true
There must be other nobler work to do
Than when he fought at Waterloo,
And victor he must ever be.
For tho' the Giant Ages heave the hill
And break the shore, and evermore
Make and break, and work their will;
Tho' world on world in myriad myriads roll
Round us, each with different powers,
And other forms of life than ours,
What know we greater than the soul?
On God and Godlike men we build our trust.
Hush, the Dead March wails in the people's ears:

The dark crowd moves, and there are sobs and tears:

The black earth yawns: the mortal disappears;

Ashes to ashes, dust to dust;

He is gone who seem'd so great.—

Gone; but nothing can bereave him

Of the force he made his own

Being here, and we believe him

Something far advanced in State,

And that he wears a truer crown

Than any wreath that man can weave him.

Speak no more of his renown,

Lay your earthly fancies down,

And in the vast cathedral leave him,

God accept him, Christ receive him.

William Makepeace Thackeray (1811–1863)

William Makepeace Thackeray is mainly known as a novelist for his great novels such as *The History of Henry Esmond, Esq.* (1852), *Vanity Fair* (1847–1848), *The Rose and the Ring* (1855), and *The Virginians* (1857–1859), but he also wrote poems, especially in his youth. The excerpted "The Due of the Dead" (1854) is an anti-war writing that alludes to the Allied British and French forces entering the Crimea in September 1854, engaging in a year-long series of debilitating battles in the area of the Alma River before finally capturing Sevastopol.

"The Due of the Dead"

I sit beside my peaceful hearth,

    With curtains drawn and lamp trimmed bright

I watch my children's noisy mirth;

    I drink in home, and its delight.

I sip my tea, and criticise

    The war, from flying rumours caught;

Trace on the map, to curious eyes,

    How here they marched, and there they fought.

In intervals of household chat,

    I lay down strategetic laws;

Why this manœuvre, and why that;

    Shape the event, or show the cause.

Or, in smooth dinner-table phrase,
  'Twixt soup and fish, discuss the fight;
Give to each chief his blame or praise;
  Say who was wrong and who was right.

Meanwhile o'er Alma's bloody plain
  The scathe of battle has rolled by—
The wounded writhe and groan—the slain
  Lie naked staring to the sky.

The out-worn surgeon plies his knife,
  Nor pauses with the closing day;
While those who have escaped with life
  Find food and fuel as they may.

And when their eyes in sleep they close,
  After scant rations duly shared,
Plague picks his victims out, from those
  Whom chance of battle may have spared.

Still when the bugle sounds the march,
  He tracks his prey through steppe and dell;
Hangs fruit to tempt the throats that parch,
  And poisons every stream and well.

All this with gallant hearts is done;
  All this with patient hearts is borne:
And they by whom the laurel's won
  Are seldom they by whom 'tis worn.

No deed, no suffering of the war,
  But wins us fame, or spares us ill;
Those noble swords, though drawn afar,
  Are guarding English homesteads still.

Owe we a debt to these brave men,
  Unpaid by aught that's said or sung;
By leaders from a ready pen,
  Or phrases from a flippant tongue.

The living, England's hand may crown
    With recognition, frank and free;
With titles, medals, and renown;
    The wounded shall our pensioners be.

But they, who meet a soldier's doom—
    Think you, it is enough, good friend,
To plant the laurel at their tomb,
    And carve their names—and there an end?

No. They are gone: but there are left
    Those they loved best while they were here—
Parents made childless, babes bereft,
    Desolate widows, sisters dear.

All these let grateful England take;
    And, with a large and liberal heart,
Cherish, for her slain soldiers' sake,
    And of her fullness give them part.

Fold them within her sheltering breast;
    Their parent, husband, brother, prove.
That so the dead may be at rest,
    Knowing those cared for whom they love.

Robert Browning (1812–1889)

Robert Browning is one of the most important English poets of the Victorian period. In 1833, he anonymously published his first major work, *Pauline: A Fragment of a Confession*. In 1835, he published *Paracelsus*, in 1840, *Sordello, and in 1850, Christmas-Eve and Easter-Day*. His other works include his poetic collection *Men and Women* (1855) and his most noted work of dramatic monologues and the psycho-historical epic *is The Ring and the Book* (1868–1869), a story of a Roman murder trial in 12 books, which established him with his mastery of dramatic monologue and psychological portraiture.

Works of his last years, such as *Prince Hohenstiel-Schwangau* (1871), *Fifine at the Fair* (1872), *Red Cotton Night-Cap Country* (1873), *The Inn Album* (1875), and the two series of *Dramatic Idyls* (1879; 1880), are long narrative or dramatic poems dealing with contemporary themes. His final volume of verse, *Asolando: Fancies and Facts*, was published in the year of his death. The two excerpted poems are "Incident of the French Camp" (1842), which writes the "Battle of Ratisbon" between Napoleon and the Archduke Charles of Bavaria on April 22,

1809; and "Childe Roland to the Dark Tower Came" (1855), in which the combatant cannot be said merely to be projecting suicidal, pathological symptoms onto the landscape, since it is the landscape's central defining feature, the Dark Tower.

"Incident of the French Camp"

I

You know, we French stormed Ratisbon:
      A mile or so away,
On a little mound, Napoleon
      Stood on our storming-day;
With neck out-thrust, you fancy how,
      Legs wide, arms locked behind,
As if to balance the prone brow
      Oppressive with its mind.

II

Just as perhaps he mused 'My plans
      That soar, to earth may fall,
Let once my army-leader Lannes
      Waver at yonder wall,'—
Out 'twixt the battery-smokes there flew
      A rider, bound on bound
Full-galloping; nor bridle drew
      Until he reached the mound.

III

Then off there flung in smiling joy,
      And held himself erect
By just his horse's mane, a boy:
      You hardly could suspect—
(So tight he kept his lips compressed,
      Scarce any blood came through)
You looked twice ere you saw his breast
      Was all but shot in two.

IV

'Well,' cried he, 'Emperor, by God's grace
      We've got you Ratisbon!
The Marshal's in the market-place,
      And you'll be there anon
To see your flag-bird flap his vans

Where I, to heart's desire,
Perched him!' The chief's eye flashed; his plans
Soared up again like fire.
V
The chief's eye flashed; but presently
Softened itself, as sheathes
A film the mother-eagle's eye
When her bruised eaglet breathes;
'You're wounded!' 'Nay,' the soldier's pride
Touched to the quick, he said:
'I'm killed, Sire!' And his chief beside,
Smiling the boy fell dead.

"Childe Roland to the Dark Tower Came"

MY first thought was, he lied in every word,
That hoary cripple, with malicious eye
Askance to watch the working of his lie
On mine, and mouth scarce able to afford
Suppression of the glee, that purs'd and scor'd
Its edge, at one more victim gain'd thereby.

What else should he be set for, with his staff?
What, save to waylay with his lies, ensnare
All travellers who might find him posted there,
And ask the road? I guess'd what skull-like laugh
Would break, what crutch 'gin write my epitaph
For pastime in the dusty thoroughfare,

If at his counsel I should turn aside
Into that ominous tract which, all agree,
Hides the Dark Tower. Yet acquiescingly
I did turn as he pointed: neither pride
Nor hope rekindling at the end descried,
So much as gladness that some end might be.

For, what with my whole world-wide wandering,
What with my search drawn out thro' years, my hope
Dwindled into a ghost not fit to cope

With that obstreperous joy success would bring,—
I hardly tried now to rebuke the spring
My heart made, finding failure in its scope.

As when a sick man very near to death
Seems dead indeed, and feels begin and end
The tears and takes the farewell of each friend,
And hears one bid the other go, draw breath
Freelier outside, ("since all is o'er," he saith,
"And the blow fallen no grieving can amend;")

While some discuss if near the other graves
Be room enough for this, and when a day
Suits best for carrying the corpse away,
With care about the banners, scarves and staves,
And still the man hears all, and only craves
He may not shame such tender love and stay.

Thus, I had so long suffer'd, in this quest,
Heard failure prophesied so oft, been writ
So many times among "The Band"—to wit,
The knights who to the Dark Tower's search address'd
Their steps—that just to fail as they, seem'd best.
And all the doubt was now—should I be fit?

So, quiet as despair, I turn'd from him,
That hateful cripple, out of his highway
Into the path the pointed. All the day
Had been a dreary one at best, and dim
Was settling to its close, yet shot one grim
Red leer to see the plain catch its estray.

For mark! no sooner was I fairly found
Pledged to the plain, after a pace or two,
Than, pausing to throw backward a last view
O'er the safe road, 't was gone; gray plain all round:
Nothing but plain to the horizon's bound.
I might go on; nought else remain'd to do.

So, on I went. I think I never saw

Such starv'd ignoble nature; nothing throve:

For flowers—as well expect a cedar grove!

But cockle, spurge, according to their law

Might propagate their kind, with none to awe,

You 'd think; a burr had been a treasure trove.

No! penury, inertness and grimace,

In the strange sort, were the land's portion. "See

Or shut your eyes," said Nature peevishly,

"It nothing skills: I cannot help my case:

'T is the Last Judgment's fire must cure this place,

Calcine its clods and set my prisoners free."

If there push'd any ragged thistle—stalk

Above its mates, the head was chopp'd; the bents

Were jealous else. What made those holes and rents

In the dock's harsh swarth leaves, bruis'd as to baulk

All hope of greenness? 'T is a brute must walk

Pashing their life out, with a brute's intents.

As for the grass, it grew as scant as hair

In leprosy; thin dry blades prick'd the mud

Which underneath look'd kneaded up with blood.

One stiff blind horse, his every bone a-stare,

Stood stupefied, however he came there:

Thrust out past service from the devil's stud!

Alive? he might be dead for aught I know,

With that red, gaunt and collop'd neck a-strain,

And shut eyes underneath the rusty mane;

Seldom went such grotesqueness with such woe;

I never saw a brute I hated so;

He must be wicked to deserve such pain.

I shut my eyes and turn'd them on my heart.

As a man calls for wine before he fights,

I ask'd one draught of earlier, happier sights,

Ere fitly I could hope to play my part.

Think first, fight afterwards—the soldier's art:
One taste of the old time sets all to rights.

Not it! I fancied Cuthbert's reddening face
Beneath its garniture of curly gold,
Dear fellow, till I almost felt him fold
An arm in mine to fix me to the place,
That way he us'd. Alas, one night's disgrace!
Out went my heart's new fire and left it cold.

Giles then, the soul of honor—there he stands
Frank as ten years ago when knighted first.
What honest man should dare (he said) he durst.
Good—but the scene shifts—faugh! what hangman hands
Pin to his breast a parchment? His own bands
Read it. Poor traitor, spit upon and curst!

Better this present than a past like that;
Back therefore to my darkening path again!
No sound, no sight as far as eye could strain.
Will the night send a howlet of a bat?
I asked: when something on the dismal flat
Came to arrest my thoughts and change their train.

A sudden little river cross'd my path
As unexpected as a serpent comes.
No sluggish tide congenial to the glooms;
This, as it froth'd by, might have been a bath
For the fiend's glowing hoof—to see the wrath
Of its black eddy bespate with flakes and spumes.

So petty yet so spiteful All along,
Low scrubby alders kneel'd down over it;
Drench'd willows flung them headlong in a fit
Of mute despair, a suicidal throng:
The river which had done them all the wrong,
Whate'er that was, roll'd by, deterr'd no whit.

Which, while I forded,—good saints, how I fear'd

To set my foot upon a dead man's cheek,
Each step, or feel the spear I thrust to seek
For hollows, tangled in his hair or beard!
—It may have been a water-rat I spear'd,
But, ugh! it sounded like a baby's shriek.

Glad was I when I reach'd the other bank.
Now for a better country. Vain presage!
Who were the strugglers, what war did they wage
Whose savage trample thus could pad the dank
Soil to a plash? Toads in a poison'd tank,
Or wild cats in a red-hot iron cage—

The fight must so have seem'd in that fell cirque.
What penn'd them there, with all the plain to choose?
No foot-print leading to that horrid mews,
None out of it. Mad brewage set to work
Their brains, no doubt, like galley-slaves the Turk
Pits for his pastime, Christians against Jews.

And more than that—a furlong on—why, there!
What bad use was that engine for, that wheel,
Or brake, not wheel—that harrow fit to reel
Men's bodies out like silk? with all the air
Of Tophet's tool, on earth left unaware,
Or brought to sharpen its rusty teeth of steel.

Then came a bit of stubb'd ground, once a wood,
Next a marsh, it would seem, and now mere earth
Desperate and done with; (so a fool finds mirth,
Makes a thing and then mars it, till his mood
Changes and off he goes!) within a rood—
Bog, clay, and rubble, sand and stark black dearth.

Now blotches rankling, color'd gay and grim,
Now patches where some leanness of the soil's
Broke into moss or substances like thus;
Then came some palsied oak, a cleft in him
Like a distorted mouth that splits its rim

Gaping at death, and dies while it recoils.

And just as far as ever from the end,
Nought in the distance but the evening, nought
To point my footstep further! At the thought,
A great black bird, Apollyon's bosom-friend,
Sail'd past, nor beat his wide wing dragon-penn'd
That brush'd my cap—perchance the guide I sought.

For, looking up, aware I somehow grew,
Spite of the dusk, the plain had given place
All round to mountains—with such name to grace
Mere ugly heights and heaps now stolen in view.
How thus they had surpris'd me,—solve it, you!
How to get from them was no clearer case.

Yet half I seem'd to recognize some trick
Of mischief happen'd to me, God knows when—
In a bad perhaps. Here ended, then,
Progress this way. When, in the very nick
Of giving up, one time more, came a click
As when a trap shuts—you 're inside the den.

Burningly it came on me all at once,
This was the place! those two hills on the right,
Couch'd like two bulls lock'd horn in horn in fight,
While, to the left, a tall scalp'd mountain … Dunce,
Dotard, a-dozing at the very nonce,
After a life spent training for the sight!

What in the midst lay but the Tower itself?
The round squat turret, blind as the fool's heart,
Built of brown stone, without a counter-part
In the whole world. The tempest's mocking elf
Points to the shipman thus the unseen shelf
He strikes on, only when the timbers start.

Not see? because of night perhaps?—Why, day
Came back again for that! before it left,

The dying sunset kindled through a cleft:
The hills, like giants at a hunting, lay,
Chin upon hand, to see the game at bay,—
"Now stab and end the creature—to the heft!"

Not hear? when noise was everywhere! it toll'd
Increasing like a bell. Names in my ears
Of all the lost adventurers my peers,—
How such a one was strong, and such was bold,
And such was fortunate, yet each of old
Lost, lost! one moment knell'd the woe of years.

There they stood, ranged along the hill-sides, met
To view the last of me, a living frame
For one more picture! in a sheet of flame
I saw them and I knew them all. And yet
Dauntless the slug-horn to my lips I set,
And blew "Childe Roland to the Dark Tower came."

William Edmonstoune Aytoun (1813–1865)

William Edmonstoune Aytoun is a Scottish poet, prose writer, and professor of rhetoric and belles lettres at the University of Edinburgh, and his distinctive legacy as a professor has made himself "first modern professor of English Literature". His poetic collection includes *Lays of the Scottish Cavaliers* (1848) and *Firmilian, a Spasmodic Tragedy* (1854), the latter of which is considered his best-known dramatic verse. He has made a great contribution to *Collection of the Ballads of Scotland* (1858). The poem "Edinburgh after Flodden" is from *Lays of the Scottish Cavaliers*": On September 9 of 1513 at Flodden in Northumberland just over the Scottish border, the English under the Earl of Surrey defeated the Scots under James IV, who was killed together with many of his nobles in their unsuccessful invasion of England. The "Battle of Flodden" was the most devastating clash, and the Scots ended up as losers with a crushing body blow which lasted for a long time.

"Edinburgh after Flodden"

NEWS of battle!—news of battle!
        Hark! 'tis ringing down the street:
And the archways and the pavement
        Bear the clang of hurrying feet.
News of battle? Who hath brought it?

News of triumph? Who should bring
Tidings from our noble army,
    Greetings from our gallant King?
All last night we watched the beacons
    Blazing on the hills afar,
Each one bearing, as it kindled,
    Message of the opened war.
All night long the northern streamers
    Shot across the trembling sky:
Fearful lights, that never beckon
    Save when kings or heroes die.

News of battle! Who hath brought it?
    All are thronging to the gate;
"Warder—warder! open quickly!
    Man—is this a time to wait?"
And the heavy gates are opened:
    Then a murmur long and loud,
And a cry of fear and wonder
    Bursts from out the bending crowd.
For they see in battered harness
    Only one hard-stricken man,
And his weary steed is wounded,
    And his cheek is pale and wan.
Spearless hangs a bloody banner
    In his weak and drooping hand—
God! can that be Randolph Murray,
    Captain of the city band?
Round him crush the people, crying,
    "Tell us all—oh, tell us true!
Where are they who went to battle,
    Randolph Murray, sworn to you?
Where are they, our brothers—children?
    Have they met the English foe?
Why art thou alone, unfollowed?
    Is it weal, or is it woe?"
Like a corpse the grisly warrior
    Looks from out his helm of steel;
But no word he speaks in answer,

Only with his armèd heel
Chides his weary steed, and onward
      Up the city streets they ride;
Through the streets the death-word rushes,
      Spreading terror, sweeping on—
"Jesus Christ! our King has fallen—
      O great God, King James is gone!
Holy Mother Mary, shield us,
      Thou who erst did lose thy Son!
O the blackest day for Scotland
      That she ever knew before!
O our King—the good, the noble,
      Shall we see him never more?
Woe to us and woe to Scotland,
      O our sons, our sons and men!
Surely some have 'scaped the Southron
      Surely some will come again!"
Till the oak that fell last winter
      Shall uprear its shattered stem—
Wives and mothers of Dunedin—
      Ye may look in vain for them!

But within the Council Chamber
      All was silent as the grave,
Whilst the tempest of their sorrow
      Shook the bosoms of the brave.
Well indeed might they be shaken
      With the weight of such a blow:
He was gone—their prince, their idol,
      Whom they loved and worshipped so!
Like a knell of death and judgment
      Rung from heaven by angel hand,
Fell the words of desolation
      On the elders of the land.
Hoary heads were bowed and trembling,
      Withered hands were clasped and wrung:
God had left the old and feeble,
      He had ta'en away the young.

Then the Provost he uprose,
    And his lip was ashen white,
But a flush was on his brow,
    And his eye was full of light.
"Thou hast spoken, Randolph Murray,
    Like a soldier stout and true;
Thou hast done a deed of daring
    Had been perilled but by few.
For thou hast not shamed to face us,
    Nor to speak thy ghastly tale,
Standing—thou, a knight and captain—
    Here, alive within thy mail!
Now, as my God shall judge me,
    I hold it braver done,
Than hadst thou tarried in thy place,
    And died above my son!
Thou needst not tell it: he is dead.
    God help us all this day!
But speak—how fought the citizens
    Within the furious fray?
For, by the might of Mary,
    'Twere something still to tell
That no Scottish foot went backward
    When the Royal Lion fell!"

"No one failed him! He is keeping
    Royal state and semblance still;
Knight and noble lie around him,
    Cold on Flodden's fatal hill.
Of the brave and gallant-hearted,
    Whom ye sent with prayers away,
Not a single man departed
    From his monarch yesterday.
Had you seen them, O my masters!
    When the night began to fall,
And the English spearmen gathered
    Round a grim and ghastly wall!
As the wolves in winter circle
    Round the leaguer on the heath,

So the greedy foe glared upward,

    Panting still for blood and death.

But a rampart rose before them,

    Which the boldest dared not scale;

Every stone a Scottish body,

    Every step a corpse in mail!

And behind it lay our monarch

    Clenching still his shivered sword:

By his side Montrose and Athole,

    At his feet a Southern lord.

All so thick they lay together,

    When the stars lit up the sky,

That I knew not who were stricken,

    Or who yet remained to die,

Few there were when Surrey halted,

    And his wearied host withdrew;

None but dying men around me,

    When the English trumpet blew.

Then I stooped, and took the banner,

    As ye see it, from his breast,

And I closed our hero's eyelids,

    And I left him to his rest.

In the mountains growled the thunder,

    As I leaped the woeful wall,

And the heavy clouds were settling

    Over Flodden, like a pall."

Matthew Arnold (1822–1888)

Matthew Arnold is a British poet and literary and social critic. He is best remembered for his elegantly argued critical essays, such as *Essays in Criticism* (1865; 1888) and *Culture and Anarchy* (1869), in which he launches constant waves of classical attacks on the contemporary tastes and manners of the aristocratic "Barbarians", the commercial middle class "Philistines" and the mundane "Populace." In spite of being an apostle of "culture" and contemporary "cultural studies", he began his career as a poet. His poetic collection includes *The Strayed Reveller, and Other Poems* (1849), *Empedocles on Etna and Other Poems* (1852), *Poems* (1853), and *New Poems* (1869). The excerpt is from his *Sohrab and Rustum, and Other Poems* (1853). It is a great epic or narrative poem, which narrates the exploits of Persia's kings and champions over a space of thirty-six centuries, bears the same relation to Persian literature as the *Iliad* and *Odyssey* to the Greek, though in structure resembles *Morte D'Arthur*.

Excerpts from *Sohrab and Rustum: An Episode*

Then Sohrab with his sword smote Rustum's helm,
Nor clove its steel quite through; but all the crest
He shore away, and that proud horsehair plume,
Never till now defiled, sank to the dust;
And Rustum bowed his head; but then the gloom
Grew blacker, thunder rumbled in the air,
And lightnings rent the cloud; and Ruksh, the horse,
Who stood at hand, uttered a dreadful cry;
No horse's cry was that, most like the roar
Of some pained desert-lion, who all day
Hath trailed the hunter's javelin in his side,
And comes at night to die upon the sand.
The two hosts heard that cry, and quaked for fear,
And Oxus curdled as it crossed his stream.
But Sohrab heard, and quailed not, but rushed on,
And struck again; and again Rustum bowed
His head; but this time all the blade, like glass,
Sprang in a thousand shivers on the helm,
And in the hand the hilt remained alone.
Then Rustum raised his head; his dreadful eyes
Glared, and he shook on high his menacing spear,
And shouted: *Rustum!* —Sohrab heard that shout,
And shrank amazed; back he recoiled one step,
And scanned with blinking eyes the advancing form;
And then he stood bewildered; and he dropped
His covering shield, and the spear pierced his side.
He reeled, and staggering back, sank to the ground;
And then the gloom dispersed, and the wind fell ,
And the bright sun broke forth, and melted all
The cloud; and the two armies saw the pair—
Saw Rustum standing, safe upon his feet,
And Sohrab, wounded, on the bloody sand.
         Then, with a bitter smile, Rustum began:—
'Sohrab, thou thoughtest in thy mind to kill
A Persian lord this day, and strip his corpse,
And bear thy trophies to Afrasiab's tent.
Or else that the great Rustum would come down

Himself to fight, and that thy wiles would move

His heart to take a gift, and let thee go.

And then that all the Tartar host would praise

Thy courage or thy craft, and spread thy fame,

To glad thy father in his weak old age.

Fool, thou art slain, and by an unknown man!

Dearer to the red jackals shalt thou be

Than to thy friends, and to thy father old.'

.   .   .

Then, at the point of death, Sohrab replied:—

'A life of blood indeed, thou dreadful man!

But thou shalt yet have peace; only not now,

Not yet! but thou shalt have it on that day,

When thou shalt sail in a high-masted ship,

Thou and the other peers of Kai Khosroo,

Returning home over the salt blue sea,

From laying thy dear master in his grave.'

And Rustum gazed in Sohrab's face, and said:—

'Soon be that day, my son, and deep that sea!

Till then, if fate so wills, let me endure.'

He spoke; and Sohrab smiled on him, and took

The spear, and drew it from his side, and eased

His wound's imperious anguish; but the blood

Came welling from the open gash, and life

Flowed with the stream; all down his cold white side

The crimson torrent ran, dim now and soiled,

Like the soiled tissue of white violets

Left, freshly gathered, on their native bank,

By children whom their nurses call with haste

Indoors from the sun's eye; his head drooped low,

His limbs grew slack; motionless, white, he lay—

White, with eyes closed; only when heavy gasps,

Deep heavy gasps quivering through all his frame,

Convulsed him back to life, he opened them,

And fixed them feebly on his father's face;

Till now all strength was ebbed, and from his limbs

Unwillingly the spirit fled away,

Regretting the warm mansion which it left,

And youth, and bloom, and this delightful world.

So, on the bloody sand, Sohrab lay dead;

And the great Rustum drew his horseman's cloak

Down o'er his face, and sate by his dead son.

As those black granite pillars, once high-reared

By Jemshid in Persepolis, to bear

His house, now 'mid their broken flights of steps

Lie prone, enormous, down the mountain side—

So in the sand lay Rustum by his son.

        And night came down over the solemn waste,

And the two gazing hosts, and that sole pair,

And darkened all; and a cold fog, with night,

Crept from the Oxus. Soon a hum arose,

As of a great assembly loosed, and fires

Began to twinkle through the fog; for now

Both armies moved to camp, and took their meal;

The Persians took it on the open sands

Southward, the Tartars by the river marge;

And Rustum and his son were left alone.

        But the majestic river floated on,

Out of the mist and hum of that low land,

Into the frosty starlight, and there moved,

Rejoicing, through the hushed Chorasmian waste,

Under the solitary moon; he flowed

Right for the polar star, past Orgunjè,

Brimming, and bright, and large; then sands begin

To hem his watery march, and dam his streams,

And split his currents; that for many a league

The shorn and parcelled Oxus strains along

Through beds of sand and matted rushy isles—

Oxus, forgetting the bright speed he had

In his high mountain-cradle in Pamere,

A foiled circuitous wanderer—till at last

The longed-for dash of waves is heard, and wide

His luminous home of waters opens, bright

And tranquil, from whose floor the new-bathed stars

Emerge, and shine upon the Aral Sea.

Thomas Hardy (1840–1928)

Thomas Hardy is best known as an English novelist for his classics such *The Return of the Native* (1878), *The Mayor of Casterbridge* (1886), *Tess of the D'Urbervilles* (1891) and *Jude the Obscure* (1895), but his reputation as a striking and versatile modernist poet of lyrics, ballads, sonnets, dramatic monologues and love verses has grown steadily from the mid-20th century. His *Wessex Poems* (1898) brings together his poetry from over thirty years, exploring a fatalist outlook against the dark, rugged landscape of his native Dorset. He wrote of the First Afghan War in "The Casterbridge Captains" (1898), which begins with the familiar trope of the discrepancy between the numbers of those going out to fight and those safely returning. The section in his *Poems of the Past and the Present* (1901) entitled "War Poems" includes a number of poems referring to the Boer Wars. His verse epic about the Napoleonic Wars, *The Dynasts,* was published in three parts between 1904 and 1908. In later years he also published *Time's Laughingstocks* (1909) and *Satires of Circumstance* (1914), both of which offer a sardonic lament on the bleakness of the human condition. The first excerpt is from Scene VIII, Act Six of *The Dynasts*, which is sub-titled "An Epic-Drama of the War with Napoleon, in Three Parts, Nineteen Acts, and One Hundred and Thirty Scenes"[5], with the overall beginning lines:

And I heard sounds of insult, shame, and wrong,

And trumpets blown for wars.

By the way, *The Dynasts* is intended simply for mental performance, and not for the stage. It is a kind of writing in play-shape but not to be played.

Excerpts from *The Dynasts*

[By and by the English army also lies down, the men huddling together on the ploughed mud in their wet blankets, while some sleep sitting round the dying fires.]

CHORUS OF THE YEARS [aerial music]

The eyelids of eve fall together at last,
And the forms so foreign to field and tree
Lie down as though native, and slumber fast!

CHORUS OF THE PITIES

Sore are the thrills of misgiving we see

---

5 The French defeat at the Battle of Waterloo, on 18 June 1815, concluded the Napoleonic Wars. British and Prussian forces under the Duke of Wellington and Field Marshal Blücher routed Napoleon's army; on 22 June Napoleon left the field and signed his abdication. French casualties totaled over 32,000, British and Prussian 23,000.

In the artless champaign at this harlequinade,
Distracting a vigil where calm should be!

The green seems opprest, and the Plain afraid
Of a Something to come, whereof these are the proofs,—
Neither earthquake, nor storm, nor eclipses's shade!

CHORUS OF THE YEARS

Yea, the coneys are scared by the thud of hoofs,
And their white scuts flash at their vanishing heels,
And swallows abandon the hamlet-roofs.

The mole's tunnelled chambers are crushed by wheels,
The lark's eggs scattered, their owners fled;
And the hedgehog's household the sapper unseals.

The snail draws in at the terrible tread,
But in vain; he is crushed by the felloe-rim
The worm asks what can be overhead,

And wriggles deep from a scene so grim,
And guesses him safe; for he does not know
What a foul red flood will be soaking him!

Beaten about by the heel and toe
Are butterflies, sick of the day's long rheum,
To die of a worse than the weather-foe.

Trodden and bruised to a miry tomb
Are ears that have greened but will never be gold,
And flowers in the bud that will never bloom.

CHORUS OF THE PITIES

So the season's intent, ere its fruit unfold,
Is frustrate, and mangled, and made succumb,
Like a youth of promise struck stark and cold!...

And what of these who to-night have come?

CHORUS OF THE YEARS

The young sleep sound; but the weather awakes
In the veterans, pains from the past that numb;

Old stabs of Ind, old Peninsular aches,
Old Friedland chills, haunt their moist mud bed,
Cramps from Austerlitz; till their slumber breaks.

CHORUS OF SINISTER SPIRITS

And each soul shivers as sinks his head
On the loam he's to lease with the other dead
From to-morrow's mist-fall till Time be sped!

[The fires of the English go out, and silence prevails, save for the soft hiss of the
rain that falls impartially on both the sleeping armies.]

"The Casterbridge Captains"

THREE captains went to Indian wars,
    And only one returned:
Their mate of yore, he singly wore
    The laurels all had earned.

At home he sought the ancient aisle
    Wherein, untrumped of fame,
The three had sat in pupilage,
    And each had carved his name.

The names, rough-hewn, of equal size,
    Stood on the panel still;
Unequal since.—"'Twas theirs to aim,
    Mine was it to fulfil!"

—"Who saves his life shall lose it, friends!"
    Outspake the preacher then,

Unweeting he his listener, who
    Looked at the names again.

That he had come and they'd been stayed,
    'Twas but the chance of war:
Another chance, and they'd sat here,
    And he had lain afar.

Yet saw he something in the lives
    Of those who'd ceased to live
That sphered them with a majesty
    Which living failed to give.

Transcendent triumph in return
    No longer lit his brain;
Transcendence rayed the distant urn
    Where slept the fallen twain.

"Embarcation"[6]

HERE, where Vespasian's legions struck the sands,
And Cerdic with his Saxons entered in,
And Henry's army leapt afloat to win
Convincing triumphs over neighbour lands,

Vaster battalions press for further strands,
To argue in the self-same bloody mode
Which this late age of thought, and pact, and code,
Still fails to mend.—Now deckward tramp the bands,
Yellow as autumn leaves, alive as spring;
And as each host draws out upon the sea
Beyond which lies the tragical To-be,
None dubious of the cause, none murmuring,

Wives, sisters, parents, wave white hands and smile,

---

6 The poem is also entitled with place and time of witing: Southampton Docks: October, 1899. On 12 October 1899, following the dispatch of British troops into their territory, Dutch settlers (Boers) in the Transvaal and the Orange Free State of South Africa declared war on Great Britain. Despite ill health, Thomas Hardy bicycled 50 miles and back to the pier in Southampton to watch the British soldiers embark.

As if they knew not that they weep the while.

"The Dead Drummer"[7]

I

THEY throw in Drummer Hodge, to rest
Uncoffined—just as found:
His landmark is a kopje-crest
    That breaks the veldt around;
And foreign constellations west
    Each night above his mound.

II

Young Hodge the Drummer never knew—
    Fresh from his Wessex home—
The meaning of the broad Karoo,
    The Bush, the dusty loam,
And why uprose to nightly view
    Strange stars amid the gloam.

III

Yet portion of that unknown plain
    Will Hodge for ever be;
His homely Northern breast and brain
    Grow up a Southern tree.
And strange-eyed constellations reign
    His stars eternally.

"The Sick God"

I

IN days when men had joy of war,
A God of Battles sped each mortal jar;
The peoples pledged him heart and hand,
From Israel's land to isles afar.

II

His crimson form, with clang and chime,
Flashed on each murk and murderous meeting-time,
And kings invoked, for rape and raid,

---

7 A poem about the Boer Wars.

His fearsome aid in rune and rhyme.

III

On bruise and blood-hole, scar and seam,

On blade and bolt, he flung his fulgid beam:

His haloes rayed the very gore,

And corpses wore his glory-gleam.

IV

Often an early King or Queen,

And storied hero onward, knew his sheen;

'Twas glimpsed by Wolfe, by Ney anon,

And Nelson on his blue demesne.

V

But new light spread. That god's gold nimb

And blazon have waned dimmer and more dim;

Even his flushed form begins to fade,

Till but a shade is left of him.

VI

That modern meditation broke

His spell, that penmen's pleadings dealt a stroke,

Say some; and some that crimes too dire

Did much to mire his crimson cloak.

VII

Yea, seeds of crescive sympathy

Were sown by those more excellent than he,

Long known, though long contemned till then—

The gods of men in amity.

VIII

Souls have grown seers, and thought out-brings

The mournful many-sidedness of things

With foes as friends, enfeebling ires

And fury-fires by gaingivings!

IX

He scarce impassions champions now;

They do and dare, but tensely—pale of brow;

And would they fain uplift the arm

Of that faint form they know not how.

X

Yet wars arise, though zest grows cold;

Wherefore, at whiles, as 'twere in ancient mould

He looms, bepatched with paint and lath;
But never hath he seemed the old!

            XI

Let men rejoice, let men deplore.
The lurid Deity of heretofore
Succumbs to one of saner nod;
The Battle-god is god no more.

"The Man He Killed"

"HAD he and I but met
By some old ancient inn,
We should have sat us down to wet
Right many a nipperkin!

"But ranged as infantry,
And staring face to face,
I shot at him as he at me,
And killed him in his place.

"I shot him dead because—
Because he was my foe,
Just so: my foe of course he was;
That's clear enough; although

"He thought he'd 'list, perhaps,
Off-hand like—just as I—
Was out of work—had sold his traps—
No other reason why.

"Yes; quaint and curious war is!
You shoot a fellow down
You'd treat if met where any bar is,
Or help to half-a-crown."

"Drummer Hodge"

            I

They throw in Drummer Hodge, to rest

Uncoffined—just as found:
His landmark is a kopje-crest
    That breaks the veldt around;
And foreign constellations west
    Each night above his mound.

II

Young Hodge the Drummer never knew—
    Fresh from his Wessex home—
The meaning of the broad Karoo,
    The Bush, the dusty loam,
And why uprose to nightly view
    Strange stars amid the gloam.

III

Yet portion of that unknown plain
    Will Hodge for ever be;
His homely Northern breast and brain
    Grow to some Southern tree,
And strange-eyed constellations reign
    His stars eternally.

"Men Who March Away"[8]

What of the faith and fire within us
    Men who march away
    Ere the barn-cocks say
    Night is growing gray,
Leaving all that here can win us;
What of the faith and fire within us
    Men who march away?

Is it a purblind prank, O think you,
    Friend with the musing eye,
    Who watch us stepping by
    With doubt and dolorous sigh?
Can much pondering so hoodwink you!
Is it a purblind prank, O think you,
    Friend with the musing eye?

---

8 The poem was marked with the date: 5 September 1914.

Nay. We well see what we are doing,
    Though some may not see—
    Dalliers as they be—
    England's need are we;
Her distress would leave us rueing:
Nay. We well see what we are doing,
    Though some may not see!

In our heart of hearts believing
    Victory crowns the just,
    And that braggarts must
    Surely bite the dust,
Press we to the field ungrieving,
In our heart of hearts believing
    Victory crowns the just.

Hence the faith and fire within us
    Men who march away
    Ere the barn-cocks say
    Night is growing gray,
Leaving all that here can win us;
Hence the faith and fire within us
    Men who march away.

T. W. H. Crosland (1865–1924)

Thomas William Hodgson Crosland is a minor English poet, satirist, and writer, very little known in any English literary history and anthology. He compiled poetic collections such as *English Songs and Ballads* (1902) and wrote a great number of prose books while inspiring strong reactions from his wide-reaching social and professional networks: some calls him "rasping satirist" while others "true poet, a master of prose, an acute, fearless and sane critic, a great satirist ... and one of the most original and remarkable literary men that ever lived." The excerpt is his satire upon wars, written in 1899.

"Slain 'Dulce et decorum est pro patria mori'[9]"

You who are still and white
    And cold like stone;

---

9 Latin quotation from Horace: "it is sweet and proper to die for one's country."

For whom the unfailing light
Is spent and done;

For whom no more the breath
Of dawn, nor evenfall,
Nor Spring nor love nor death
Matter at all;

Who were so strong and young,
And brave and wise,
And on the dark are flung
With darkened eyes;

Who roystered and caroused
But yesterday,
And now are dumbly housed
In stranger clay;

Who valiantly led,
Who followed valiantly,
Who knew no touch of dread
Of that which was to be;

Children that were as nought
Ere ye were tried,
How have ye dared and fought,
Triumphed and died!

.   .   .

Yea, it is very sweet
And decorous
The omnipotent Shade to meet
And flatter thus.

Edgar Wallace (1875–1932)

Richard Horatio Edgar Wallace is an English crime writer, journalist, novelist, screenwriter, playwright, and poet. He wrote 175 novels, 24 plays, and numerous articles in newspapers and journals. It is said that more than 160 films have been made of his novels, and some even claims that a quarter of all books read in England were written by him. The excerpt is an anti-war poem of his written in 1900. In 1969, The Edgar Wallace Society was formed by his youngest daughter Penelope Wallace.

"War"

I

A tent that is pitched at the base:

  A wagon that comes from the night:

A stretcher—and on it a Case:

  A surgeon, who's holding a light.

The Infantry's bearing the brunt—

  O hark to the wind-carried cheer!

A mutter of guns at the front:

  A whimper of sobs at the rear.

And it's *War* ! 'Orderly, hold the light.

  You can lay him down on the table: so.

Easily—gently! Thanks—you may go.'

  And it's *War* ! but the part that is not for show.

II

A tent, with a table athwart,

  A table that's laid out for one;

A waterproof cover—and nought

  But the limp, mangled work of a gun.

A bottle that's stuck by the pole,

  A guttering dip in its neck;

The flickering light of a soul

  On the wondering eyes of The Wreck,

And it's *War* ! 'Orderly, hold his hand.

  I'm not going to hurt you, so don't be afraid.

A richochet! God! what a mess it has made!'

  And it's *War* ! and a very unhealthy trade.

III

The clink of a stopper and glass:

  A sigh as the chloroform drips:

A trickle of—what? on the grass,

  And bluer and bluer the lips.

The lashes have hidden the stare …

  A rent, and the clothes fall away…

A touch, and the wound is laid bare…

  A cut, and the face has turned grey…

And it's *War* ! 'Orderly, take It out.

It's hard for his child, and it's rough on his wife,

There might have been—sooner—a chance for his life.

But it's *War*! And—Orderly, clean this knife!'

2. Apology for Wars in Victorian Verse

Although the mainstream Victorian attitude toward wars is negative, there were many who lauded war efforts. These poets urged their country to fight for "a patriotic nature" as in Algernon Charles Swinburne, Sir Henry Newbolt, and especially Rudyard Kipling, the warmonger and apologist for British imperialism.

Algernon Charles Swinburne (1837–1909)

Algernon Charles Swinburne is a British poet, dramatist and critic. His dramatic production includes *The Queen-Mother and Rosamond* (1860), *Atlanta in Calydon* (1865) and *Chasteland* in 1866, the same year that he began to publish a series of books of poetry: *Poems and Ballads* (1866). The collection had a notable impact on Victorian poetry with its groundbreaking portrayal of sexuality and taboo, serving as a preeminent symbol of rebellion against the conservative values of his time, so are the political meditative verse *Songs Before Sunrise* (1871) and the French-influenced *Poems and Ballads, Second Series* (1878). Swinburne also published poems of a patriotic nature about war and the preparation for war near the end of his career, such as "A Word for the Navy" (1896) that cautions about the growing sea strength of Germany and others, "The Transvaal" (1899) that urges England to strike back at the Boers, and "The Turning of the Tide" (1900) that applauds British success against the Boers in highly figurative language.

"A Word for the Navy"

I

Queen born of the sea, that hast borne her

The mightiest of seamen on earth,

Bright England, whose glories adorn her

And bid her rejoice in thy birth

As others made mothers

Rejoice in births sublime,

She names thee, she claims thee,

The lordliest child of time.

II

All hers is the praise of thy story,

All thine is the love of her choice

The light of her waves is thy glory,

      The sound of thy soul is her voice.

      They fear it who hear it

      And love not truth nor thee:

      They sicken, heart-stricken,

      Who see and would not see.

        III

The lords of thy fate, and thy keepers

      Whose charge is the strength of thy ships,

If now they be dreamers and sleepers,

      Or sluggards with lies at their lips,

      Thy haters and traitors,

      False friends or foes descried,

      Might scatter and shatter

      Too soon thy princely pride.

        IV

Dark Muscovy, reptile in rancour,

      Base Germany, blatant in guile,

Lay wait for thee riding at anchor

      On waters that whisper and smile.

      They deem thee or dream thee

      Less living now than dead,

      Deep sunken and drunken

      With sleep whence fear has fled.

        V

And what though thy song as thine action

      Wax faint, and thy place be not known,

While faction is grappling with faction,

      Twin curs with thy corpse for a bone?

      They care not, who spare not

      The noise of pens or throats;

      Who bluster and muster

      Blind ranks and bellowing votes.

        VI

Let populace jangle with peerage

      And ministers shuffle their mobs;

Mad pilots who reck not of steerage

      Though tempest ahead of them throbs.

That throbbing and sobbing
    Of wind and gradual wave
They hear not and fear not
    Who guide thee toward thy grave.

        VII

No clamour of cries or of parties
    Is worth but a whisper from thee,
While only the trust of thy heart is
    At one with the soul of the sea.
    In justice her trust is
    Whose time her tidestreams keep;
    They sink not, they shrink not,
    Time casts them not on sleep.

        VIII

Sleep thou: for thy past was so royal,
    Love hardly would bid thee take heed
Were Russia not faithful and loyal
    Nor Germany guiltless of greed.
    No nation, in station
    Of story less than thou,
    Re-risen from prison,
    Can stand against thee now.

        IX

Sleep on: is the time not a season
    For strong men to slumber and sleep,
And wise men to palter with treason?
    And that they sow tares, shall they reap?
    The wages of ages
    Wherein men smiled and slept,
    Fame fails them, shame veils them,
    Their record is not kept.

        X

Nay, whence is it then that we know it,
    What wages were theirs, and what fame?
Deep voices of prophet and poet
    Bear record against them of shame.
    Death, starker and darker
    Than seals the graveyard grate,
    Entombs them and dooms them

To darkness deep as fate.

XI

But thou, though the world should misdoubt thee,

Be strong as the seas at thy side;

Bind on but thine armour about thee,

That girds thee with power and with pride.

Where Drake stood, where Blake stood,

Where fame sees Nelson stand,

Stand thou too, and now too

Take thou thy fate in hand.

XII

At the gate of the sea, in the gateway,

They stood as the guards of thy gate;

Take now but thy strengths to thee straightway,

Though late, we will deem it not late.

Thy story, thy glory,

The very soul of thee,

It rose not, it grows not,

It comes not save by sea.

"The Transvaal"

Patience, long sick to death, is dead. Too long

Have sloth and doubt and treason bidden us be

What Cromwell's England was not, when the sea

To him bore witness given of Blake how strong

She stood, a commonweal that brooked no wrong

From foes less vile than men like wolves set free

Whose war is waged where none may fight or flee—

With women and with weanlings. Speech and song

Lack utterance now for loathing. Scarce we hear

Foul tongues that blacken God's dishonoured name

With prayers turned curses and with praise found shame

Defy the truth whose witness now draws near

To scourge these dogs, agape with jaws afoam,

Down out of life. Strike, England, and strike home.

"The Turning of the Tide"

Storm, strong with all the bitter heart of hate,
    Smote England, now nineteen dark years ago,
    As when the tide's full wrath in seaward flow
Smites and bears back the swimmer. Fraud and fate
Were leagued against her: fear was fain to prate
    Of honour in dishonour, pride brought low,
    And humbleness whence holiness must grow,
And greatness born of shame to be so great.

The winter day that withered hope and pride
    Shines now triumphal on the turning tide
That sets once more our trust in freedom free,
That leaves a ruthless and a truthless foe
    And all base hopes that hailed his cause laid low,
And England's name a light on land and sea.

Sir Henry Newbolt (1862–1938)

Sir Henry Newbolt is a British poet, novelist, lawyer, playwright and magazine editor. His poetry champions the virtues of chivalry and sportsmanship but in the service of the British Empire. His first slim volume, *Admirals All* (1897), is an instant success, and his second book of poems, *The Island Race* (1898), suggested a fine and chivalrous calling for the courage of soldiers and sailors. At the beginning of the First World War, he was recruited by Britain's War Propaganda Bureau (WPB) to help shape and maintain public opinion in favour of the war effort, later took charge of the British warring telecommunications, and was knighted in 1915. He was thus regarded as a warmonger and a blimp. The excerpt comes from his 1897 poetic collection.

"He Fell among Thieves"

'Ye have robbed,' said he, 'ye have slaughtered and made an end,
    Take your ill-got plunder, and bury the dead:
What will ye more of your guest and sometime friend?'
    'Blood for our blood,' they said.

He laughed: 'If one may settle the score for five,
    I am ready; but let the reckoning stand till day:
I have loved the sunlight as dearly as any alive.'

'You shall die at dawn,' said they.

He flung his empty revolver down the slope,
    He climbed alone to the Eastward edge of the trees;
All night long in a dream untroubled of hope
    He brooded, clasping his knees.

He did not hear the monotonous roar that fills
    The ravine where the Yassîn river sullenly flows;
He did not see the starlight on the Laspur hills,
    Or the far Afghan snows.

He saw the April noon on his books aglow,
    The wisteria trailing in at the window wide;
He heard his father's voice from the terrace below
    Calling him down to ride.

He saw the grey little church across the park,
    The mounds that hid the loved and honoured dead;
The Norman arch, the chancel softly dark,
    The brasses black and red.

He saw the School Close, sunny and green,
    The runner beside him, the stand by the parapet wall,
The distant tape, and the crowd roaring between,
    His own name over all.

He saw the dark wainscot and timbered roof,
    The long tables, and the faces merry and keen;
The College Eight and their trainer dining aloof,
    The Dons on the daïs serene.

He watched the liner's stem ploughing the foam,
    He felt her trembling speed and the thrash of her screw;
He heard her passengers' voices talking of home,
    He saw the flag she flew.

And now it was dawn. He rose strong on his feet,
    And strode to his ruined camp below the wood;

He drank the breath of the morning cool and sweet:
  His murderers round him stood.

Light on the Laspur hills was broadening fast,
  The blood-red snow-peaks chilled to a dazzling white:
He turned, and saw the golden circle at last,
  Cut by the Eastern height.

'O glorious Life, Who dwellest in earth and sun,
  I have lived, I praise and adore Thee.'
                                    A sword swept.
Over the pass the voices one by one
  Faded, and the hill slept.

Rudyard Kipling (1865–1936)

Rudyard Kipling was born in Bombay, India, the son of John Lockwood Kipling, a museum director, author and illustrator. He is a British novelist and poet, notoriously remembered for his celebration of British imperialism: labelled by some scholar as "a colonialist, a jingoist, a racist, an anti-Semite, a misogynist, a right-wing imperialist warmonger" and thus has always remained "politically toxic". He was awarded the Nobel Prize for literature in 1907, mainly for his fiction such as *Captains Courageous* (1897), *Just-So Stories* (1902), *Kim* (1902), *Plain Tales from the Hills* (1888), *The Jungle Book* (1894), *and The Light That Failed* (1891), as the Prize motivation has dictated: "In consideration of the power of observation, originality of imagination, virility of ideas and remarkable talent for narration which characterise the creations of this world-famous author."

Kipling's collection of poems includes *Departmental Ditties and Other Verses* (1886), *Barrack-Room Ballads* (1892), and *The Five Nations* (1903). The imperial hymn "The White Man's Burden" (1899) is propaganda for the Empire, and in fact, he assisted with a variety of propaganda in his tales and poems, but "Recessional" (1897) expresses anxiety about simplistic national triumphalism, so is his "Epitaphs of the War" (1919), in which he writes that the son's death is simply due to his father who keenly supported the war: "If any question why we died, / Tell them, because our fathers lied". The poem "Lichtenberg" writes about a combatant's death in a foreign land, but in support of the British cause in the Boer Wars in South Africa. "The Last of the Light Brigade" (1890) echoes Alfred Tennyson's "The Charge of the Light Brigade" some forty years ago, exposing the terrible hardship faced in old age by veterans of the Crimean War.

"The White Man's Burden"[10]

Take up the White Man's burden—
Send forth the best ye breed—
Go bind your sons to exile
To serve your captives' need;
To wait in heavy harness
On fluttered folk and wild—
Your new-caught sullen peoples,
Half devil and half child.

Take up the White Man's burden—
In patience to abide
To veil the threat of terror
And check the show of pride;
By open speech and simple,
An hundred times made plain,
To seek another's profit,
And work another's gain.

Take up the White Man's burden—
The savage wars of peace—
Fill full the mouth of famine
And bid the sickness cease;
And when your goal is nearest
The end for others sought,
Watch Sloth and heathen Folly
Bring all your hopes to nought.

Take up the White Man's burden—

---

10 In February 1899, Rudyard Kipling wrote a poem entitled "The White Man's Burden: The United States and The Philippine Islands." In this poem, Kipling urged the U.S. to take up the "burden" of empire, as had Britain and other European nations. Published in the February, 1899 issue of *McClure's Magazine*, the poem coincided with the beginning of the Philippine-American War and U.S. Senate ratification of the treaty that placed Puerto Rico, Guam, Cuba, and the Philippines under American control. Theodore Roosevelt, soon to become vice-president and then president, copied the poem and sent it to his friend, Senator Henry Cabot Lodge, commenting that it was "rather poor poetry, but good sense from the expansion point of view." Not everyone was as favorably impressed as Roosevelt. The racialized notion of the "White Man's burden" became a euphemism for imperialism, and many anti-imperialists couched their opposition in reaction to the phrase. (http://historymatters.gmu.edu/d/5478/)

No tawdry rule of kings,
But toil of serf and sweeper—
The tale of common things.
The ports ye shall not enter,
The roads ye shall not tread,
Go make them with your living,
And mark them with your dead!

Take up the White Man's burden—
And reap his old reward,
The blame of those ye better,
The hate of those ye guard—
The cry of hosts ye humour
(Ah slowly!) towards the light: —
"Why brought ye us from bondage,"
"Our loved Egyptian night?"

Take up the White Man's burden—
Ye dare not stoop to less—
Nor call too loud on Freedom
To cloak your weariness;
By all ye cry or whisper,
By all ye leave or do,
The silent sullen peoples
Shall weigh your Gods and you.

Take up the White Man's burden—
Have done with childish days—
The lightly proffered laurel,
The easy, ungrudged praise.
Comes now, to search your manhood
Through all the thankless years,
Cold-edged with dear-bought wisdom,
The judgement of your peers.

"Lichtenberg"

Smells are surer than sounds or sights
To make your heart-strings crack—

They start those awful voices o' nights
That whisper, "Old man, come back!"
That must be why the big things pass
And the little things remain,
Like the smell of the wattle by Lichtenberg,
Riding in, in the rain.

There was some silly fire on the flank
And the small wet drizzling down—
There were the sold-out shops and the bank
And the wet, wide-open town;
And we were doing escort-duty
To somebody's baggage-train,
And I smelt wattle by Lichtenberg—
Riding in, in the rain.

It was all Australia to me—
All I had found or missed:
Every face I was crazy to see,
And every woman I'd kissed:
All that I should n't ha' done, God knows!
(As He knows I'll do it again),
That smell of the wattle round Lichtenberg,
Riding in, in the rain!

And I saw Sydney the same as ever,
The picnics and brass-bands;
And my little homestead on Hunter River
And my new vines joining hands.
It all came over me in one act
Quick as a shot through the brain—
With the smell of the wattle round Lichtenberg,
Riding in, in the rain.

I have forgotten a hundred fights,
But one I shall not forget—
With the raindrops bunging up my sights
And my eyes bunged up with wet;
And through the crack and the stink of the cordite

(Ah Christ! My country again!)

The smell of the wattle by Lichtenberg,

Riding in, in the rain!

"The Revenge: A Ballad of the Fleet"

I

At Flores in the Azores Sir Richard Grenville lay,

And a pinnace, like a fluttered bird, came flying from far away:

'Spanish ships of war at sea! we have sighted fifty-three!'

Then sware Lord Thomas Howard: ''Fore God I am no coward;

But I cannot meet them here, for my ships are out of gear,

And the half my men are sick. I must fly, but follow quick.

We are six ships of the line; can we fight with fifty-three?'

II

Then spake Sir Richard Grenville: 'I know you are no coward;

You fly them for a moment to fight with them again.

But I've ninety men and more that are lying sick ashore.

I should count myself the coward if I left them, my Lord Howard,

To these Inquisition dogs and the devildoms of Spain.'

III

So Lord Howard past away with five ships of war that day,

Till he melted like a cloud in the silent summer heaven;

But Sir Richard bore in hand all his sick men from the land

Very carefully and slow,

Men of Bideford in Devon,

And we laid them on the ballast down below;

For we brought them all aboard,

And they blest him in their pain, that they were not left to Spain,

To the thumbscrew and the stake, for the glory of the Lord.

IV

He had only a hundred seamen to work the ship and to fight,

And he sailed away from Flores till the Spaniard came in sight,

With his huge sea-castles heaving upon the weather bow.

'Shall we fight or shall we fly?

Good Sir Richard, tell us now,

For to fight is but to die!

There'll be little of us left by the time this sun be set.'

And Sir Richard said again: 'We be all good English men.

213

Let us bang these dogs of Seville, the children of the devil,

For I never turned my back upon Don or devil yet.'

V

Sir Richard spoke and he laughed, and we roared a hurrah, and so

The little *Revenge* ran on sheer into the heart of the foe,

With her hundred fighters on deck, and her ninety sick below;

For half of their fleet to the right and half to the left were seen,

And the little *Revenge* ran on through the long sea-lane between.

VI

Thousands of their soldiers looked down from their decks and laughed,

Thousands of their seamen made mock at the mad little craft

Running on and on, till delayed

By their mountain-like San Philip that, of fifteen hundred tons,

And up-shadowing high above us with her yawning tiers of guns,

Took the breath from our sails, and we stayed.

VII

And while now the great San Philip hung above us like a cloud

Whence the thunderbolt will fall

Long and loud,

Four galleons drew away

From the Spanish fleet that day,

And two upon the larboard and two upon the starboard lay,

And the battle-thunder broke from them all.

VIII

But anon the great San Philip, she bethought herself and went

Having that within her womb that had left her ill content;

And the rest they came aboard us, and they fought us hand to hand,

For a dozen times they came with their pikes and musqueteers,

And a dozen times we shook 'em off as a dog that shakes his ears

When he leaps from the water to the land.

IX

And the sun went down, and the stars came out far over the summer sea,

But never a moment ceased the fight of the one and the fifty-three.

Ship after ship, the whole night long, their high-built galleons came,

Ship after ship, the whole night long, with her battle-thunder and flame;

Ship after ship, the whole night long, drew back with her dead and her shame.

For some were sunk and many were shattered, and so could fight us no more—

God of battles, was ever a battle like this in the world before?

214

X

For he said 'Fight on! fight on!'

Though his vessel was all but a wreck;

And it chanced that, when half of the short summer night was gone,

With a grisly wound to be dressed he had left the deck,

But a bullet struck him that was dressing it suddenly dead,

And himself he was wounded again in the side and the head,

And he said 'Fight on! fight on!'

XI

And the night went down, and the sun smiled out far over the summer sea,

And the Spanish fleet with broken sides lay round us all in a ring;

But they dared not touch us again, for they feared that we still could sting,

So they watched what the end would be.

And we had not fought them in vain,

But in perilous plight were we,

Seeing forty of our poor hundred were slain,

And half of the rest of us maimed for life

In the crash of the cannonades and the desperate strife;

And the sick men down in the hold were most of them stark and cold,

And the pikes were all broken or bent, and the powder was all of it spent;

And the masts and the rigging were lying over the side;

But Sir Richard cried in his English pride,

'We have fought such a fight for a day and a night

As may never be fought again!

We have won great glory, my men!

And a day less or more

At sea or ashore,

We die—does it matter when?

Sink me the ship, Master Gunner—sink her, split her in twain!

Fall into the hands of God, not into the hands of Spain!'

XII

And the gunner said 'Ay, ay,' but the seamen made reply:

'We have children, we have wives,

And the Lord hath spared our lives.

We will make the Spaniard promise, if we yield, to let us go;

We shall live to fight again and to strike another blow.'

And the lion there lay dying, and they yielded to the foe.

XIII

And the stately Spanish men to their flagship bore him then,

215

Where they laid him by the mast, old Sir Richard caught at last,

And they praised him to his face with their courtly foreign grace;

But he rose upon their decks, and he cried:

'I have fought for Queen and Faith like a valiant man and true;

I have only done my duty as a man is bound to do:

With a joyful spirit I Sir Richard Grenville die!'

And he fell upon their decks, and he died.

XIV

And they stared at the dead that had been so valiant and true,

And had holden the power and glory of Spain so cheap

That he dared her with one little ship and his English few;

Was he devil or man? He was devil for aught they knew,

But they sank his body with honour down into the deep,

And they manned the *Revenge* with a swarthier alien crew,

And away she sailed with her loss and longed for her own;

When a wind from the lands they had ruined awoke from sleep,

And the water began to heave and the weather to moan,

And or ever that evening ended a great gale blew,

And a wave like the wave that is raised by an earthquake grew,

Till it smote on their hulls and their sails and their masts and their flags ,

And the whole sea plunged and fell on the shot-shattered navy of Spain,

And the little *Revenge* herself went down by the island crags

To be lost evermore in the main.

"The Last of the Light Brigade"

THERE were thirty million English who talked of England's might,

There were twenty broken troopers who lacked a bed for the night.

They had neither food nor money, they had neither service nor trade;

They were only shiftless soldiers, the last of the Light Brigade.

They felt that life was fleeting; they knew not that art was long,

That though they were dying of famine, they lived in deathless song.

They asked for a little money to keep the wolf from the door;

And the thirty million English sent twenty pounds and four!

They laid their heads together that were scarred and lined and gray;

Keen were the Russian sabres, but want was keener than they;

And an old troop sergeant muttered, "Let us go to the man who writes

216

The things on Balaclava the kiddies at school recites."

They went without bands or colours, a regiment ten-file strong,
To look for the Master-singer who had crowned them all in his song;
And, waiting his servant's order, by the garden gate they stayed,
A desolate little cluster, the last of the Light Brigade.

They strove to stand to attention, to straighten the toil-bowed back;
They drilled on an empty stomach, the loose-knit files fell slack;
With stooping of weary shoulders, in garments tattered and frayed,
They shambled into his presence, the last of the Light Brigade.

The old troop sergeant was spokesman, and "Beggin' your pardon," he said,
"You wrote o' the Light Brigade, sir. Here's all that isn't dead.
An' it's all come true what you wrote, sir, regardin' the mouth of hell;
For we're all of us nigh to the workhouse, an' we thought we'd call an' tell.

"No, thank you, we don't want food, sir; but couldn't you take an' write
A sort of 'to be continued' and 'see next page' o' the fight?
We think that someone has blundered, an' couldn't you tell 'em how?
You wrote we were heroes once, sir. Please, write we are starving now."

The poor little army departed, limping and lean and forlorn.
And the heart of the Master-singer grew hot with "the scorn of scorn."
And he wrote for them wonderful verses that swept the land like flame,
Till the fatted souls of the English were scourged with the thing called Shame.

O thirty million English that babble of England's might,
Behold there are twenty heroes who lack their food to-night;
Our children's children are lisping to "honour the charge they made—"
And we leave to the streets and the workhouse the charge of the Light Brigade!

"The Dykes"

We have no heart for the fishing—we have no hand for the oar—
All that our fathers taught us of old pleases us now no more.
All that our own hearts bid us believe we doubt where we do not deny—
There is no proof in the bread we eat nor rest in the toil we ply.

Look you, our foreshore stretches far through sea-gate, dyke, and groin—
Made land all, that our fathers made, where the flats and the fairway join.
They forced the sea a sea-league back. They died, and their work stood fast.
We were born to peace in the lee of the dykes, but the time of our peace is past.

Far off, the full tide clambers and slips, mouthing and testing all,
Nipping the flanks of the water-gates, baying along the wall;
Turning the shingle, returning the shingle, changing the set of the sand...
We are too far from the beach, men say, to know how the outworks stand.

So we come down, uneasy, to look; uneasily pacing the beach.
These are the dykes our fathers made: we have never known a breach.
Time and again has the gale blown by and we were not afraid;
Now we come only to look at the dykes—at the dykes our fathers made.

O'er the marsh where the homesteads cower apart the harried sunlight flies,
Shifts and considers, wanes and recovers, scatters and sickens and dies—
An evil ember bedded in ash—a spark blown west by the wind...
We are surrendered to night and the sea—the gale and the tide behind!

At the bridge of the lower saltings the cattle gather and blare,
Roused by the feet of running men, dazed by the lantern-glare.
Unbar and let them away for their lives—the levels drown as they stand,
Where the flood-wash forces the sluices aback and the ditches deliver inland.

Ninefold deep to the top of the dykes the galloping breakers stride,
And their overcarried spray is a sea—a sea on the landward side.
Coming, like stallions they paw with their hooves, going they snatch with their teeth,
Till the bents and the furze and the sand are dragged out, and the old-time hurdles beneath.

Bid men gather fuel for fire, the tar, the oil, and the tow—
Flame we shall need, not smoke, in the dark if the riddled sea-banks go.
Bid the ringers watch in the tower (who knows how the dawn shall prove?)
Each with his rope between his feet and the trembling bells above.

Now we can only wait till the day, wait and apportion our shame.
These are the dykes our fathers left, but we would not look to the same.
Time and again were we warned of the dykes, time and again we delayed:
Now, it may fall, we have slain our sons, as our fathers we have betrayed.

"Recessional"

God of our fathers, known of old,
    Lord of our far-flung battle-line,
Beneath whose awful Hand we hold
    Dominion over palm and pine—
Lord God of Hosts, be with us yet,
Lest we forget—lest we forget!

The tumult and the shouting dies;
    The Captains and the Kings depart:
Still stands Thine ancient sacrifice,
    A humble and a contrite heart.
Lord God of Hosts, be with us yet,
Lest we forget—lest we forget!

Far-called, our navies melt away;
    On dune and headland sinks the fire:
Lo, all our pomp of yesterday
    Is one with Nineveh and Tyre!
Judge of the Nations, spare us yet,
Lest we forget—lest we forget!

If, drunk with sight of power, we loose
    Wild tongues that have not Thee in awe,
Such boastings as the Gentiles use,
    Or lesser breeds without the Law—
Lord God of Hosts, be with us yet,
Lest we forget—lest we forget!

For heathen heart that puts her trust
    In reeking tube and iron shard,
All valiant dust that builds on dust,
    And guarding, calls not Thee to guard,
For frantic boast and foolish word—
Thy mercy on Thy People, Lord!

Chapter V

American War Poetry from Monroe Doctrine to the First World War (1832–1918)

Besides the American Civil War that was fought between the Union and the Confederacy, Americans, from the 1830s, had involved themselves in constant waves of wars of territorial expansion, until the looming denouement of the First World War that was fought between the Triple Alliance of Germany, Italy and Austria-Hungary, and the Triple Entente of Britain, France and Russia, and in which it joined on the side of the Triple Entente in 1917. The first as such witnessed the War of Texas Independence from 1836: Mexico controlled the territory until 1836 when Texas won its independence, becoming an independent republic; in 1845, Texas joined the union as the 28th state; and the state's annexation set off a chain of events that led to the Mexican-American War (1846–1848), the U.S. Army's first experience waging extended conflicts in foreign land. Toward the end of the 19th century, the Spanish-American War broke out: The 1898 conflict between the United States and Spain ended the Spanish colonial rule in the Americas and resulted in the U.S. acquisition of territories in the western Pacific and Latin America.

Relatively speaking, the United States remained politically isolated throughout the 19th century and the beginning of the 20th century. In 1823, President James Monroe gave voice to what would later be termed the Monroe Doctrine ("In the wars of the European powers, in matters relating to themselves, we have never taken part, nor does it comport with our policy, so to do"). Only when German and Japanese imperialism began to expand did Americans snuff out their contented aloofness. During the Spanish-American War, its occupation of the Philippines thrust U.S. interests into the far western Pacific Ocean. Moreover, in World War

I, Germans provoked the U.S. into abandoning the neutrality it had upheld for so many years, so its resultant participation in World War I against the Central Powers marked its first major departure from the isolationist policy.

War writing of this period leaned heavily on the American Civil War, but other wars also had considerable poetic production, especially the First World War. The anthology has selected three representative poets who wrote about the Mexico-American War, three representative poets who wrote about the Spanish-American War, several poets who addressed the general topics of wars, and finally, a variety of poets who wrote about the First World War, leaving poetry of the American Civil War to be anthologised in the next chapter.

1. The Mexico-American War

The Mexico-American War came from the avaricious American greed for expanding territories. The Americans took the offensive, invaded Mexico, annexed Texas and other Mexican territories, including large patches of land in California from 1846 to 1848. The War was in many ways a precursor to the Civil War for most important Civil War generals also fought in the Mexican-American War, and the massive territories gained make up a large percentage of present-day United States. American poets usually wrote the war with a victorious tone as a bonanza, while Mexicans regarded Americans as "aggressors" and "thieves" who stole so much of their land.

Charles Fenno Hoffman (1806–1884)

Charles Fenno Hoffman is an American poet and service man. The excerpt "Monterey" is from his collection *Poems* (1873): On September 19–24, 1846, the assaulting American army at the attack on Monterey numbered 6625; the defeated Mexicans were about 10,000.

"Monterey"

We were not many—we who stood
    Before the iron sleet that day;
Yet many a gallant spirit would
Give half his years if but he could
    Have with us been at Monterey.

Now here, now there, the shot it hailed
    In deadly drifts of fiery spray,
Yet not a single soldier quailed
When wounded comrades round them wailed
    Their dying shout at Monterey.

And on—still on our column kept,

    Through walls of flame, its withering way

Where fell the dead, the living stept,

Still charging on the guns which swept

    The slippery streets of Monterey.

The foe himself recoiled aghast,

    When, striking where he strongest lay,

We swooped his flanking batteries past,

And, braving full their murderous blast,

    Stormed home the towers of Monterey.

Our banners on those turrets wave,

    And there our evening bugles play;

Where orange-boughs above their grave

Keep green the memory of the brave

    Who fought and fell at Monterey.

We are not many—we who pressed

    Beside the brave who fell that day;

But who of us has not confessed

He'd rather share their warrior rest

    Than not have been at Monterey?

Albert Pike (1809–1891)

Albert Pike is an American writer, poet, attorney, journalist, military leader, and member of the Freemasons. He participated in two major wars in US history, the Mexican-American War and the Civil War, while in the later war, he served as an officer in the Confederate States Army, and was appointed a brigadier general and assigned the command of the Indian Territory in 1861. He is also a legendary historical Masonic figure, a 33rd degree Freemason Occultist Grand Master and creator of the Southern Jurisdiction of the Masonic Scottish Rite Order. It is widely rumoured that speculation claimed that Albert Pike wrote to Giuseppe Mazzini in 1871 regarding a conspiracy involving three world wars that were planned in an attempt to take over the world: "The First World War" must be brought about in order to permit the Illuminati to overthrow the power of the Czars in Russia and of making that country a fortress of atheistic Communism; "The Second World War" must be fomented by taking advantage of the differences between the Fascists and the political Zionists; and "The Third World War" must be fomented by taking advantage of the differences caused by the political Zionists and the leaders of Islamic World, in which the war must be conducted in such a way that Islam (the Moslem Arabic World) and political Zionism (the State of Israel) mutually destroy each other. But till today, no hard proof exists to show that this letter was ever written. The excerpt "Buena Vista" appears in one of the popular collections written by General Pike, dated February 28, 1847.

"Buena Vista"

From the Rio Grande's waters to the icy lakes of Maine,
Let all exult! for we have met the enemy again;
Beneath their stern old mountains we have met them in their pride,
And rolled from BUENA VISTA back the battle's bloody tide;
Where the enemy came surging swift, like the Mississippi's flood,
And the reaper, Death, with strong arms swung his sickle red with blood.

SANTANA boasted loudly that, before two hours were past,
His Lancers through Saltillo should pursue us fierce and fast:—
On comes his solid infantry, line marching after line;
Lo! their great standards in the sun like sheets of silver shine:
With thousands upon thousands,—yea, with more than three to one,—
Their forests of bright bayonets fierce-flashing in the sun.

Lo! Guanajuato's regiment; Morelos' boasted corps,
And Guadalajara's chosen troops!—all veterans tried before.
Lo! galloping upon the right four thousand lances gleam,
Where, floating in the morning-wind, their blood-red pennons stream;
And here his stern artillery climbs up the broad plateau:
To-day he means to strike at us an overwhelming blow.

Now, WOOL, hold strongly to the heights! for, lo! the mighty tide
Comes, thundering like an avalanche, deep, terrible and wide.
Now, ILLINOIS stand steady! Now, KENTUCKY, to their aid!
For a portion of our line, alas! is broken and dismayed:
Great bands of shameless fugitives are fleeing from the field,
And the day is lost, if Illinois and brave Kentucky yield.

One of O'Brien's guns is gone!—On, on their masses drift,
Till their cavalry and infantry outflank us on the left;
Our light troops, driven from the hills, retreat in wild dismay,
And round us gather, thick and dark, the Mexican array.

SANTANA thinks the day is gained; for, now approaching near,
MIÑON'S dark cloud of Lancers sternly menaces our rear.

Now, LINCOLN, gallant gentleman, lies dead upon the field,
Who strove to stay those cravens, when before the storm they reeled.
Fire, WASHINGTON, fire fast and true! Fire, SHERMAN, fast and far!
Lo! BRAGG comes thundering to the front, to breast the adverse war!
SANTANA thinks the day is gained! On, on his masses crowd,
And the roar of battle swells again more terrible and loud.

NOT YET! Our brave old General comes to regain the day;
KENTUCKY, to the rescue! MISSISSIPPI, to the fray!
Again our line advances! Gallant DAVIS fronts the foe,
And back before his rifles, in red waves the Lancers flow.
Upon them yet once more, ye brave! The avalanche is stayed!
Back roll the Aztec multitudes, all broken and dismayed.

Ride! MAY!—To Buena Vista! for the Lancers gain our rear,
And we have few troops there to check their vehement career.
Charge, ARKANSAS! KENTUCKY, charge! YELL, PORTER, VAUGHAN, are slain,
But the shattered troops cling desperately unto that crimsoned plain;
Till, with the Lancers intermixed, pursuing and pursued,
Westward, in combat hot and close, drifts off the multitude.

And May comes charging from the hills with his ranks of flaming steel,
While shattered with a sudden fire, the foe already reel:
They flee amain!—Now to the left, to stay the torrent there,
Or else the day is surely lost, in horror and despair!
For their hosts pour swiftly onward, like a river in the spring,
Our flank is turned, and on our left their cannon thundering.

Now, good Artillery! bold Dragoons! Steady, brave hearts, be calm!
Through rain, cold hail, and thunder, now nerve each gallant arm!
What though their shot fall round us here, yet thicker than the hail?
We'll stand against them, as the rock stands firm against the gale.
Lo! their battery is silenced! but our iron sleet still showers:
They falter, halt, retreat!—Hurrah! the glorious day is ours!

In front, too, has the fight gone well, where upon gallant LANE,

And on stout Mississippi, the thick Lancers charged in vain:
Ah! brave Third Indiana! you have nobly wiped away
The reproach that through another corps befell your State to-day;
For back, all broken and dismayed, before your storm of fire,
SANTANA's boasted chivalry, a shattered wreck, retire.

Now charge again, SANTANA! or the day is surely lost—
For back, like broken waves, along our left your hordes are tossed.
Still faster roar his batteries,—his whole reserve moves on;
More work remains for us to do, ere the good fight is won.
Now for your wives and children men! Stand steady yet once more!
Fight for your lives and honors! Fight as you never fought before!

Ho! HARDIN breasts it bravely! and heroic BISSELL there
Stands firm before the storm of balls that fill the astonished air:
The Lancers dash upon them too! The foe swarm ten to one:
HARDIN is slain; McKEE and CLAY the last time see the sun:
And many another gallant heart, in that last desperate fray,
Grew cold, its last thought turning to its loved ones far away.

Speed, speed, Artillery! to the front!—for the hurricane of fire
Crushes those noble regiments, reluctant to retire!
Speed swiftly! Gallop! Ah! they come! Again BRAGG climbs the ridge,
And his grape sweeps down the swarming foe, as a strong man moweth sedge:
Thus baffled in their last attack, compelled perforce to yield,
Still menacing in firm array, their columns leave the field.

The guns still roared at intervals; but silence fell at last,
And on the dead and dying came the evening shadows fast.
And then above the mountains rose the cold moon's silver shield,
And patiently and pitying she looked upon the field.
While careless of his wounded, and neglectful of his dead,
Despairingly and sullenly by night SANTANA fled.

And thus on BUENA VISTA's heights a long day's work was done,
And thus our brave old General another battle won.
Still, still our glorious banner waves, unstained by flight or shame,
And the Mexicans among their hills still tremble at our name.
SO, HONOR UNTO THOSE THAT STOOD! DISGRACE TO THOSE THAT FLED!

AND EVERLASTING GLORY UNTO BUENA VISTA'S DEAD!

Theodore O'Hara (1820–1867)

Theodore O'Hara is an American poet and an officer. He served in the Mexican War, Cuban rebellion, and the American Civil War. The excerpt "The Bivouac of the Dead" was written to commemorate the burial of Kentucky soldiers who fell at the Battle of Buena Vista, which was also called the "Battle of Angostura" (1847), a battle fought near Monterrey of Mexico during the Mexican-American War.

"The Bivouac of the Dead"

THE muffled drum's sad roll has beat
    The soldier's last tattoo;
No more on Life's parade shall meet
    That brave and fallen few.
On Fame's eternal camping-ground
    Their silent tents are spread,
And Glory guards, with solemn round,
    The bivouac of the dead.

No rumor of the foe's advance
    Now swells upon the wind;
No troubled thought at midnight haunts
    Of loved ones left behind;
No vision of the morrow's strife
    The warrior's dream alarms;
No braying horn nor screaming fife
    At dawn shall call to arms.

Their shivered swords are red with rust;
    Their plumèd heads are bowed;
Their haughty banner, trailed in dust,
    Is now their martial shroud.
And plenteous funeral tears have washed
    The red stains from each brow,
And the proud forms, by battle gashed,
    Are free from anguish now.

The neighing troop, the flashing blade,

The bugle's stirring blast,
The charge, the dreadful cannonade,
The din and shout are past;
Nor war's wild note, nor glory's peal,
Shall thrill with fierce delight
Those breasts that nevermore may feel
The rapture of the fight.

Like the fierce northern hurricane
That sweeps his great plateau,
Flushed with the triumph yet to gain,
Came down the serried foe.
Who heard the thunder of the fray
Break o'er the field beneath,
Knew well the watchword of that day
Was "Victory or Death."

Long had the doubtful conflict raged
O'er all that stricken plain,
For never fiercer fight had waged
The vengeful blood of Spain;
And still the storm of battle blew,
Still swelled the gory tide;
Not long our stout old chieftain knew,
Such odds his strength could bide.

'Twas in that hour his stern command
Called to a martyr's grave
The flower of his belovèd land,
The nation's flag to save.
By rivers of their fathers' gore
His first-born laurels grew
And well he deemed the sons would pour
There lives for glory too.

Full many a norther's breath has swept,
O'er Angostura's plain—And long the pitying sky has wept
Above its mouldered slain.
The raven's scream or eagle's flight

228

Or shepherd's pensive lay,
    Alone awakes each sullen height
That frowned o'er that dread fray.

Sons of the Dark and Bloody ground,
    Ye must not slumber there,
Where stranger steps and tongues resound
    Along the heedless air.
Your own proud land's heroic soil
    Shall be your fitter grave;
She claims from war his richest spoil—
    The ashes of her brave.

Thus 'neath their parent turf they rest,
    Far from the gory field,
Borne to a Spartan mother's breast
    On many a bloody shield;
The sunshine of their native sky
    Smiles sadly on them here,
And kindred eyes and hearts watch by
    The heroes' sepulchre.

Rest on, embalmed and sainted dead!
    Dear as the blood ye gave,
No impious footstep here shall tread
    The herbage of your grave;
Nor shall your story be forgot,
    While Fame her record keeps,
Or Honor points the hallowed spot
    Where Valor proudly sleeps.

Yon marble minstrel's voiceless stone
    In deathless song shall tell
When many a vanished age hath flown,
    The story how ye fell;
Nor wreck, nor change, nor winter's blight,
    Nor Time's remorseless doom,
Shall dim one ray of glory's light
    That gilds your deathless tomb.

2. The Spanish-American War

After the Civil War, America has experienced a relative period of stability and prosperity for its comprehensive reconstruction of the South, but when the Reconstruction was accomplished, it began to have an imperialist expansion. Towards the end of the 19th century, the US government hoped to capitalise on its trade opportunities and continued to challenge (with an even greater power) the European influence in the Western Hemisphere. The Spanish rule in Cuba had been exempted from the Monroe Doctrine. When the Cuban economy took a drastic shutdown, the opportunity came for the Americans, who launched the War in 1898. In his *War-Time Echoes: Patriotic Poems, Heroic and Pathetic, Humorous and Dialectic, of the Spanish-American War* (1989), James Henry Brownlee wrote: "THE WAR between the United States of America and Spain, which will be known in history as the War for Humanity, lasted only one hundred and thirteen days. Though brief, it was glorious. At the call of the President for volunteers, a million men responded, of whom only one-fourth was required. Such unanimity of patriotic sentiment had never before been exhibited in our history. Party spirit was hushed; men remembered only that they were Americans. Those who wore the blue and those who wore the grey during the great Civil War, now touched fraternal elbows as they fell into rank under the beautiful banner of their common country..."[1] As can be seen in the following selection, the major topic of such war poetry is "Freedom", and the sole object of focus is "Cuba".

Guy Wetmore Carryl (1873–1904)

Guy Wetmore Carryl was an American humorist and poet. He has three collections of parody poems: *Fables for the Frivolous* (1898), *Mother Goose for Grown-Ups* (1900), *Grimm Tales Made Gay* (1902). The excerpted poem "Ad Finem Fideles" (1898) was written just after the end of the war with Spain for the freeing of Cuba.

"Ad Finem Fideles"

Far out, far out they lie. Like stricken women weeping,
    Eternal vigil keeping with slow and silent tread—
Soft-shod as are the fairies, the winds patrol the prairies,
    The sentinels of God about the pale and patient dead!
Above them, as they slumber in graves that none may number,
    Dawns grow to day, days dim to dusk, and dusks in darkness pass;
Unheeded springs are born, unheeded summers brighten,
    And winters wait to whiten the wilderness of grass.

---

1 James Henry Brownlee, *War-Time Echoes: Patriotic Poems, Heroic and Pathetic, Humorous and Dialectic, of the Spanish-American War*. New York and Chicago: The Werner Company, 1989.

Slow stride appointed years across their bivouac places,

  With stern, devoted faces they lie, as when they lay,

In long battalions dreaming, till dawn, to eastward gleaming,

  Awoke the clarion greeting of the bugles to the day.

The still and stealthy speeding of the pilgrim days unheeding,

  At rest upon the roadway that their feet unfaltering trod,

The faithful unto death abide, with trust unshaken,

  The morn when they shall waken to the reveille of God.

The faithful unto death! Their sleeping-places over

  The torn and trampled clover to braver beauty blows;

Of all their grim campaigning no sight or sound remaining,

  The memory of them mutely to greater glory grows.

Through waning ages winding, new inspiration finding,

  Their creed of consecration like a silver ribbon runs,

Sole relic of the strife that woke the world to wonder

  With riot and the thunder of a sundered people's guns.

What matters now the cause? As little children resting,

  No more the battle breasting to the rumble of the drums,

Enlinked by duty's tether, the blue and gray together,

  They wait the great hereafter when the last assembly comes.

Where'er the summons found them, whate'er the tie that bound them,

  'Tis this alone the record of the sleeping army saith:—

They knew no creed but this, in duty not to falter,

  With strength that naught could alter to be faithful unto death.

Joaquin Miller (1837–1913)

 Joaquin Miller is an American poet of rare gifts. He was unexcelled in his field as the interpreter of the Western life and landscape for his weird adventures and fabulous imagination. The excerpt is about the freedom of Cuba.

"Cuba Libre: A Prophecy Made Eighteen Years Ago"

COMES a cry from Cuban water,

  From the warm, dusk Antilles,

From the lost Atlanta's daughter,

  Drowned in blood as drowned in seas;

Comes a cry of purpled anguish—
    See her struggles, hear her cries!
Shall she live, or shall she languish?
    Shall she sink or shall she rise?

Shall she rise by all that's holy!
    Shall she live and shall she last;
Rise as we, when crushed and lonely,
    From the blackness of the past?
Bid her strike! Lo! It is written
    Blood for blood and life for life.
Bid her smite as she is smitten;
    Stars and stripes were born for strife.

Once we flashed her lights of freedom,
    Lights that dazzled her dark eyes
Till she could but yearning heed them,
    Reach her hands and try to rise.
Then they stabbed her, choked her, drowned her;
    Ah! these rustling chains that bound her!
    Oh! these robbers at her throat!

And the land that forged these fetters?
    Ask five hundred years of news.
Stake and thumbscrew for their betters?
    Inquisitions! Banished Jews!
Chains and slavery! What reminder
    Of one red man in that land?
Why, these very chains that bind her
    Bound Columbus, foot and han!

She shall rise as rose Columbus,
    From his chains, from shame and wrong—
Rise as morning, matchless, wondrous—
    Rise as some rich morning song—
Rise a ringing song and story, Valor,
    Love personified?
Stars and stripes espouse her glory,
    Love and Liberty allied.

Lloyd Mifflin (1846–1921):

Lloyd Mifflin is an American poet, but his background information is little known. The excerpted poem was written in 1998, serving as a tribute to the fighters in Cuban wars.

"Half Mast!"

ON every school-house, ship, and staff,
  From Golden Gate to Marblehead,
Let droop the Starry Banner now,
  In sorrow for our sailors dead:
Half-mast! Half-mast! O'er all the land!
  The verdict wait; your wrath restrain!
Half-mast for all that gallant band—
  The sailors of the *Maine*!

Not till a treachery is proved
  His sword the patriot soldier draws;
War is the last alternative—
Be patient till ye know the cause:
Meanwhile —Half-mast o'er all the land!
  The verdict wait; your wrath restrain!
Half-mast! for all that gallant band—
  The Martyrs of the *Maine*!

3. The First World War

When the First World War broke out, Americans were caught not only off guard, but also innocently kept an attitude of neutrality, having no interests in interfering with those "corruptions" of Old Europe, but American newspapers reported the conflict as a conflict between the democratic Allies and the autocratic Central Powers. Before its final entry to the War, there were reportedly 2 million American volunteers, fighting for the Allies in France. Kate Mcloughlin's edited *The Cambridge Companion to War Writing* (2009) had summarised as follows: "Once the United States entered the war, the cause had to be made worthy of the sacrifice. The propaganda machine found two particularly rich themes to exploit. The first was that this was a war to save democracy; the second was that the conflict would serve as a purging agent for the crass materialism and slackness that had fallen over Americans since the country's founding."[2]

---

2 Kate Mcloughlin, ed., *The Cambridge Companion to War Writing*. Cambridge: Cambridge University Press, 2009, p. 179.

Marie Van Vorst (1867–1936)

Marie Van Vorst is an American social activist and writer, whose works such as *The Woman Who Toils: Being the Experiences of Two Gentlewomen as Factory Girls* (1903) and *Amanda of the Mill* are well-known social propaganda tools. The excerpted poem "The American Volunteers" wrote those many Americans who took service under the flag of France in the long months before the United States entered the war in 1917.

"The American Volunteers"

NEUTRAL! America, you cannot give
    To your sons' souls neutrality. Your powers
Are sovereign, Mother, but past histories live
    In hearts as young as ours.

We who are free disdain oppression, lust
    And infamous raid. We have been pioneers
For freedom and our code of honor must
    Dry and not startle tears.

We've read of Lafayette, who came to give
    His youth, with his companions and their powers,
To help the Colonies—and heroes live
    In hearts as young as ours!

Neutral! We who go forth with sword and lance,
    A little band to swell the battle's flow,
Go willingly, to pay again to France
    Some of the debt we owe.

Henry Van Dyke (1852–1933)

Henry Van Dyke is an American playwright, scholar, diplomat and poet, whose output included short stories, poems, and essays. He was extremely popular in the early decades of the 20th century. His short story collection includes *The Ruling Passion* (1901), *The Blue Flower* (1902), *The Unknown Quantity* (1912), *The Valley of Vision* (1919), and *The Golden Key* (1926), and his popularity extended to his verse, as had been collected in *Poems* (1920). He wrote about the First World War in his poetic production. He was a professor of English literature at Princeton from 1899 to 1913 and from 1919 to 1923, while in 1913–1916, he served as U.S. minister to The Netherlands and Luxembourg. When the fighting ceased on November 11, 1918, there were two million American soldiers in France. The excerpt experienced such a scene.

"America's Welcome Home"

Oh, gallantly they fared forth in khaki and in blue,
America's crusading host of warriors bold and true;
They battled for the rights of man beside our brave Allies,
And now they're coming home to us with glory in their eyes.

Oh, it's home again, and home again, America for me!
Our hearts are turning home again and there we long to be,
In our beautiful big country beyond the ocean bars,
Where the air is full of sunlight and the flag is full of stars.

Our boys have seen the Old World as none have seen before.
They know the grisly horror of the German gods of war:
The noble faith of Britain and the hero-heart of France,
The soul of Belgium's fortitude and Italy's romance.

They bore our country's great word across the rolling sea,
"America swears brotherhood with all the just and free."
They wrote that word victorious on fields of mortal strife,
And many a valiant lad was proud to seal it with his life.

Oh, welcome home in Heaven's peace, dear spirits of the dead!
And welcome home ye living sons America hath bred!
The lords of war are beaten down, your glorious task is done;
You fought to make the whole world free, and the victory is won.

Now it's home again, and home again, our hearts are turning west,
Of all the lands beneath the sun America is best.
We're going home to our own folks, beyond the ocean bars,
Where the air is full of sunlight and the flag is full of stars.

Corinne Roosevelt Robinson (1861–1933)

Corinne Roosevelt Robinson is an American social activist and writer. She is the younger sister of American president Theodore Roosevelt and wife of Douglas Robinson, also a poet and active member of the Republican Party. The excerpt "To Peace, With Victory" was written on November 11, 1918, to celebrate the termination of the war.

"To Peace, With Victory"

I could not welcome you, oh! longed-for peace,
Unless your coming had been heralded
By victory. The legions who have bled
Had elsewise died in vain for our release.

But now that you come sternly, let me kneel
And pay my tribute to the myriad dead,
Who counted not the blood that they have shed
Against the goal their valor shall reveal.

Ah! what had been the shame, had all the stars
And stripes of our brave flag drooped still unfurled,
When the fair freedom of the weary world
Hung in the balance. Welcome then the scars!

Welcome the sacrifice! With lifted head
Our nation greets dear Peace as honor's right;
And ye the Brave, the Fallen in the fight,
Had ye not perished, then were honor dead!

You cannot march away! However far,
Farther and faster still I shall have fled
Before you; and that moment when you land,
Voiceless, invisible, close at your hand
My heart shall smile, hearing the steady tread
    Of your faith-keeping feet.

First at the trenches I shall be to greet;
There's not a watch I shall not share with you;
But more—but most—there where for you the red,
Drenched, dreadful, splendid, sacrificial field lifts up
Inflexible demand,
    I will be there!

My hands shall hold the cup.
My hands beneath your head
Shall bear you—not the stretcher bearer's—through

All anguish of the dying and the dead;

With all your wounds I shall have ached and bled,

Waked, thirsted, starved, been fevered, gasped for breath,

Felt the death dew;

And you shall live, because my heart has said

To Death

That Death itself shall have no part in you!

Grace Ellery Channing (1862–1937)

Grace Ellery Channing is an American social activist and writer. Her grandfather was William Ellery Channing, the founder of the American Unitarian Church, and her father was an inventor who patented a portable electro-magnetic telegraph (1877), an electric fire alarm, and other inventions. She began her career as a writer by editing her grandfather's memoirs, *Dr. Channing's Notebook* (1887). Later, she travelled extensively in Europe and praised for wars. *The Sister of a Saint* (1895) and *The Fortune of a Day* (1900) were collections of short stories concerning heroines who suffered beautiful martyrdoms. She published a collection of poems, *Sea Drift*, in 1899. As a war correspondent, she wrote about the Italian front and Italy's part in the war. Her stories and poems criticised exemption from military service, encouraging the war effort and idealising the sacrifice of wives and mothers who encouraged their menfolk to enlist. Her poetry idealising war and war heroism won much praise. The excerpted poem "Any Woman to a Soldier" was possibly written in 1917 or 1918.

"Any Woman to a Soldier"

The day you march away—let the sun shine,

Let everything be blue and gold and fair,

Triumph of trumpets calling through bright air,

Flags slanting, flowers flaunting—not a sign

That the unbearable is now to bear,

The day you march away.

The day you march away—this I have sworn,

No matter what comes after, that shall be

Hid secretly between my soul and me

As women hide the unborn—

You shall see brows like banners, lips that frame

Smiles, for the pride those lips have in your name.

You shall see soldiers in my eyes that day—

That day, O soldier, when you march away.

237

The day you march away—cannot I guess?
There will be ranks and ranks, all leading on
To one white face, and then—the white face gone,
And nothing left but a gray emptiness—
Blurred moving masses, faceless, featureless—
　　The day you march away.

Edith Wharton (1862–1937)

Edith Wharton is an American writer, best known for her stories and novels about upper-class society. Coming from a distinguished and long-established New York family, she made her debut in society in 1879 and married Edward Wharton, a wealthy Boston banker, in 1885. Later they divorced, and she came to live in Europe mainly. Her works of narrative achievement include *The House of Mirth* (1905), *Ethan Frome* (1911), *The Reef* (1912), *The Custom of the Country* (1913), *Summer* (1917), and *The Age of Innocence* (1920). Among her later novels are *Twilight Sleep* (1927), *Hudson River Bracketed* (1929), and its sequel, *The Gods Arrive* (1932). In all, Wharton published more than 50 books, including fiction, short stories, travel books, historical novels, and criticism. She published a variety of poems about the "Great War", collected as the following.

"Battle Sleep"[3]

SOMEWHERE, O sun, some corner there must be
Thou visitest, where down the strand
Quietly, still, the waves go out to sea
From the green fringes of a pastoral land.

Deep in the orchard-bloom the roof-trees stand,
The brown sheep graze along the bay,
And through the apple-boughs above the sand
The bees' hum sounds no fainter than the spray.

There through uncounted hours declines the day
To the low arch of twilight's close,
And, just as night about the moon grows gray,
One sail leans westward to the fading rose.

Giver of dreams, O thou with scatheless wing

---

3 "Battle Sleep" was published in *Century Magazine* 90: 736 (Sept. 1915)

Forever moving through the fiery hail,

To flame-seared lids the cooling vision bring,

And let some soul go seaward with that sail!

"On Active Service"[4]

HE is dead that was alive.

How shall friendship understand?

Lavish heart and tireless hand

Bidden not to give or strive,

Eager brain and questing eye

Like a broken lens laid by.

He, with so much left to do,

Such a gallant race to run,

What concern had he with you,

Silent Keeper of things done?

Tell us not that, wise and young,

Elsewhere he lives out his plan.

Our speech was sweetest to his tongue,

And his great gift was to be man.

Long and long shall we remember,

In our breasts his grave be made.

It shall never be December

Where so warm a heart is laid,

But in our saddest selves a sweet voice sing,

Recalling him, and Spring.

"You and You; to the American private in the Great War"[5]

EVERY one of you won the war—

You and you and you—

---

4 "On Active Service" was published about American Expeditionary Force in *Scribner's Magazine* 64: 619. (Nov. 1918); On November 11, The Armistice between Germany and the Allied and Associated Powers was signed in a railway coach near Compiègne, ending World War I.

5 "You and You; to the American private in the Great War" was published in *Scribner's Magazine* 65 (Feb. 1919).

Each one knowing what it was for,
And what was his job to do.

Every one of you won the war,
Obedient, unwearied, unknown,
Dung in the trenches, drift on the shore,
Dust to the world's end blown;
Every one of you, steady and true,
You and you and you—
Down in the pit or up in the blue,
Whether you crawled or sailed or flew,
Whether your closest comrade knew
Or you bore the brunt alone—

All of you, all of you, name after name,
Jones and Robinson, Smith and Brown,
You from the piping prairie town,
You from the Fundy fogs that came,
You from the city's roaring blocks,
You from the bleak New England rocks
With the shingled roof in the apple boughs,
You from the brown adobe house—
You from the Rockies, you from the Coast,
You from the burning frontier-post
And you from the Klondyke's frozen flanks,
You from the cedar-swamps, you from the pine,
You from the cotton and you from the vine,
You from the rice and the sugar-brakes,
You from the Rivers and you from the Lakes,
You from the Creeks and you from the Licks
And you from the brown bayou—
You and you and you—
You from the pulpit, you from the mine,
You from the factories, you from the banks,
Closer and closer, ranks on ranks,
Airplanes and cannon, and rifles and tanks,
Smith and Robinson, Brown and Jones,
Ruddy faces or bleaching bones,
After the turmoil and blood and pain

Swinging home to the folks again

Or sleeping along in the fine French rain—

Every one of you won the war.

Every one of you won the war—

You and you and you—

Pressing and pouring forth, more and more,

Toiling and straining from shore to shore

To reach the flaming edge of the dark

Where man in his millions went up like a spark,

You, in your thousands and millions coming,

All the sea ploughed with you, all the air humming,

All the land loud with you,

All our hearts proud with you,

All our souls bowed with the awe of your coming!

Where's the Arch high enough,

Lads, to receive you,

Where's the eye dry enough,

Dears, to perceive you,

When at last and at last in your glory you come,

Tramping home?

Every one of you won the war,

You and you and you—

You that carry an unscathed head,

You that halt with a broken tread,

And oh, most of all, you Dead, you Dead!

Lift up the Gates for these that are last,

That are last in the great Procession.

Let the living pour in, take possession,

Flood back to the city, the ranch, the farm,

The church and the college and mill,

Back to the office, the store, the exchange,

Back to the wife with the babe on her arm,

Back to the mother that waits on the sill,

And the supper that's hot on the range.

And now, when the last of them all are by,

Be the Gates lifted up on high

To let those Others in,

Those Others, their brothers, that softly tread,

That come so thick, yet take no ground,

That are so many, yet make no sound,

Our Dead, our Dead, our Dead!

O silent and secretly-moving throng,

In your fifty thousand strong,

Coming at dusk when the wreaths have dropt,

And streets are empty, and music stopt,

Silently coming to hearts that wait

Dumb in the door and dumb at the gate,

And hear your step and fly to your call—

Every one of you won the war,

But you, you Dead, most of all!

"With the Tide"[6]

SOMEWHERE I read, in an old book whose name

Is gone from me, I read that when the days

Of a man are counted, and his business done,

There comes up the shore at evening, with the tide,

To the place where he sits, a boat—

And in the boat, from the place where he sits, he sees,

Dim in the dusk, dim and yet so familiar,

The faces of his friends long dead; and knows

They come for him, brought in upon the tide,

To take him where men go at set of day.

Then rising, with his hands in theirs, he goes

Between them his last steps, that are the first

Of the new life—and with the ebb they pass,

Their shaken sail grown small upon the moon.

Often I thought of this, and pictured me

How many a man who lives with throngs about him,

---

6 "With the Tide" was published in *Saturday Evening Post* of 29 March, 1919. Theodore Roosevelt died, and Edith wrote the memorial poem.

Yet straining through the twilight for that boat
Shall scarce make out one figure in the stern,
And that so faint its features shall perplex him
With doubtful memories—and his heart hang back.
But others, rising as they see the sail
Increase upon the sunset, hasten down,
Hands out and eyes elated; for they see
Head over head, crowding from bow to stern,
Repeopling their long loneliness with smiles,
The faces of their friends; and such go forth
Content upon the ebb tide, with safe hearts.

But never
To worker summoned when his day was done
Did mounting tide bring in such freight of friends
As stole to you up the white wintry shingle
That night while they that watched you thought you slept.
Softly they came, and beached the boat, and gathered
In the still cove under the icy stars,
Your last-born, and the dear loves of your heart,
And all men that have loved right more than ease,
And honor above honors; all who gave
Free-handed of their best for other men,
And thought their giving taking: they who knew
Man's natural state is effort, up and up—
All these were there, so great a company
Perchance you marveled, wondering what great ship
Had brought that throng unnumbered to the cove
Where the boys used to beach their light canoe
After old happy picnics—

But these, your friends and children, to whose hands
Committed, in the silent night you rose
And took your last faint steps—
These led you down, O great American,
Down to the winter night and the white beach,
And there you saw that the huge hull that waited
Was not as are the boats of the other dead,
Frail craft for a brief passage; no, for this

243

Was first of a long line of towering transports,

Storm-worn and ocean-weary every one,

The ships you launched, the ships you manned, the ships

That now, returning from their sacred quest

With the thrice-sacred burden of their dead,

Lay waiting there to take you forth with them,

Out with the ebb tide, on some farther quest.

Angela Morgan (1875–1957)

Angela Morgan is an American poet and novelist. She is the author of numerous collections of poems while some with anti-war themes. She participated in the International Congress of Women at The Hague in 1915 and subsequent activities of the Women's International League for Peace and Freedom. Her career peaked in the era from 1914 to 1930, and she continued to write and publish poetry right down to her death in 1957. She lived during both of the World Wars. This excerpt "The Unknown Soldier" was read by the author over the casket of the Unknown Soldier, at the special memorial exercises held in the rotunda of the Capitol at Washington on November 10, 1921, while the other says that despite a devastating war raging on, everything in nature continued as if nothing was happening; the same can be true about our lives; life continues even when terrible things happen, so this poem encourages us to look at the beauty around us rather than focus on the negative aspects of our lives. This is also the theme of the excerpt "In Spite of War".

"The Unknown Solider"

He is known to the sun-white Majesties

Who stand at the gates of dawn.

He is known to the cloud-borne company

Whose souls but late have gone.

Like wind-flung stars through lattice bars

They throng to greet their own,

With voice of flame they sound his name

Who died to us unknown.

He is hailed by the time-crowned brotherhood,

By the Dauntless of Marathon,

By Raymond, Godfrey and Lion Heart

Whose dreams he carried on.

His name they call through the heavenly hall

Unheard by earthly ear,

He is claimed by the famed in Arcady
Who knew no title here.

Oh faint was the lamp of Sirius
And dim was the Milky Way.
Oh far was the floor of Paradise
From the soil where the soldier lay.
Oh chill and stark was the crimson dark
Where huddled men lay deep;
His comrades all denied his call—
Long had they lain in sleep.

Oh strange how the lamp of Sirius
Drops low to the dazzled eyes,
Oh strange how the steel-red battlefields
Are floors of Paradise.
Oh strange how the ground with never a sound
Swings open, tier on tier,
And standing there in the shining air
Are the friends he cherished here.
They are known to the sun-shod sentinels
Who circle the morning's door,
They are led by a cloud-bright company
Through paths unseen before.
Like blossoms blown, their souls have flown
Past war and reeking sod,
In the book unbound their names are found—
They are known in the courts of God!

"In Spite of War"

In spite of war, in spite of death,
In spite of all man's sufferings,
Something within me laughs and sings
And I must praise with all my breath.
In spite of war, in spite of hate
Lilacs are blooming at my gate,
Tulips are tripping down the path
In spite of war, in spite of wrath.

"Courage!" the morning-glory saith;
"Rejoice!" the daisy murmureth,
And just to live is so divine
When pansies lift their eyes to mine.

The clouds are romping with the sea,
And flashing waves call back to me
That naught is real but what is fair,
That everywhere and everywhere
A glory liveth through despair.
Though guns may roar and cannon boom,
Roses are born and gardens bloom;
My spirit still may light its flame
At that same torch whence poppies came.
Where morning's altar whitely burns
Lilies may lift their silver urns
In spite of war, in spite of shame.

And in my ear a whispering breath,
"Wake from the nightmare! Look and see
That life is naught but ecstasy
In spite of war, in spite of death!"

Joyce Kilmer (1886–1918)

Joyce Kilmer is an American journalist and poet. He enlisted in the New York National Guard in 1917 when the United States entered World War I and joined in the battle of Ourcq. He was killed by a sniper's bullet on July 30, 1918, and later was awarded by the French the prestigious Croix de Guerre (War Cross) for his bravery. As a poet, he published his first poetry collection, *A Summer of Love* (1911), followed by *Trees and Other Poems* (1914) and *Main Street and Other Poems* (1917), his last poetry collection. The three excerpts, "Prayer of a Soldier in France", "Rouge Bouquet" and "Memorial Day", seemed heroic, but touched with cynicism and sorrow.

"Prayer of a Soldier in France"

My shoulders ache beneath my pack
(Lie easier, Cross, upon His back).

I march with feet that burn and smart

(Tread, Holy Feet, upon my heart).

Men shout at me who may not speak
(They scourged Thy back and smote Thy cheek).

I may not lift a hand to clear
My eyes of salty drops that sear.

(Then shall my fickle soul forget
Thy agony of Bloody Sweat?)

My rifle hand is stiff and numb
(From Thy pierced palm red rivers come).

Lord, Thou didst suffer more for me
Than all the hosts of land and sea.

So let me render back again
This millionth of Thy gift. Amen.

"Rouge Bouquet"

In a wood they call the Rouge Bouquet
There is a new-made grave to-day,
Build by never a spade nor pick
Yet covered with earth ten metres thick.
There lie many fighting men,
     Dead in their youthful prime,
Never to laugh nor love again
     Nor taste the Summertime.
For Death came flying through the air
And stopped his flight at the dugout stair,
Touched his prey and left them there,
     Clay to clay.
He hid their bodies stealthily
In the soil of the land they fought to free
     And fled away.
Now over the grave abrupt and clear
     Three volleys ring;

And perhaps their brave young spirits hear
    The bugle sing:
"Go to sleep!
Go to sleep!
Slumber well where the shell screamed and fell.
Let your rifles rest on the muddy floor,
You will not need them any more.
Danger's past;
Now at last,
Go to sleep!"

There is on earth no worthier grave
To hold the bodies of the brave
Than this place of pain and pride
Where they nobly fought and nobly died.
Never fear but in the skies
Saints and angels stand
Smiling with their holy eyes
    On this new-come band.
St. Michael's sword darts through the air
And touches the aureole on his hair
As he sees them stand saluting there,
    His stalwart sons;
And Patrick, Brigid, Columkill
Rejoice that in veins of warriors still
    The Gael's blood runs.
And up to Heaven's doorway floats,
    From the wood called Rouge Bouquet,
A delicate cloud of buglenotes
    That softly say:
"Farewell!
Farewell!
Comrades true, born anew, peace to you!
And your memory shine like the morning-star.
Brave and dear,
Shield us here.
Farewell!"

"Memorial Day"

The bugle echoes shrill and sweet,
But not of war it sings to-day.
The road is rhythmic with the feet
Of men-at-arms who come to pray.

The roses blossom white and red
On tombs where weary soldiers lie;
Flags wave above the honored dead
And martial music cleaves the sky.

Above their wreath-strewn graves we kneel,
They kept the faith and fought the fight.
Through flying lead and crimson steel
They plunged for Freedom and the Right.

May we, their grateful children, learn
Their strength, who lie beneath this sod,
Who went through fire and death to earn
At last the accolade of God.

In shining rank on rank arrayed
They march, the legions of the Lord;
He is their Captain unafraid,
The Prince of Peace...Who brought a sword.

Alan Seeger (1888–1916)

Alan Seeger is an American soldier and poet. He joined the French Foreign Legion in 1914, but was killed in action in northern France on July 4, 1916. Known for his poetic representation of the First World War, he was the author of *Poems* (1916) and *Letters and Diary of Alan Seeger* (1917), both published posthumously.

"A Message to America"

You have the grit and the guts, I know;
You are ready to answer blow for blow
You are virile, combative, stubborn, hard,
But your honor ends with your own back-yard;

Each man intent on his private goal,
You have no feeling for the whole;
What singly none would tolerate
You let unpunished hit the state,
Unmindful that each man must share
The stain he lets his country wear,
And (what no traveller ignores)
That her good name is often yours.

You are proud in the pride that feels its might;
From your imaginary height
Men of another race or hue
Are men of a lesser breed to you:
The neighbor at your southern gate
You treat with the scorn that has bred his hate.
To lend a spice to your disrespect
You call him the "greaser". But reflect!
The greaser has spat on you more than once;
He has handed you multiple affronts;
He has robbed you, banished you, burned and killed;
He has gone untrounced for the blood he spilled;
He has jeering used for his bootblack's rag
The stars and stripes of the gringo's flag;
And you, in the depths of your easy-chair—
What did you do, what did you care?
Did you find the season too cold and damp
To change the counter for the camp?
Were you frightened by fevers in Mexico?
I can't imagine, but this I know—
You are impassioned vastly more
By the news of the daily baseball score
Than to hear that a dozen countrymen
Have perished somewhere in Darien,
That greasers have taken their innocent lives
And robbed their holdings and raped their wives.

Not by rough tongues and ready fists
Can you hope to jilt in the modern lists.
The armies of a littler folk

Shall pass you under the victor's yoke,
Sobeit a nation that trains her sons
To ride their horses and point their guns—
Sobeit a people that comprehends
The limit where private pleasure ends
And where their public dues begin,
A people made strong by discipline
Who are willing to give—what you've no mind to—
And understand—what you are blind to—
The things that the individual
Must sacrifice for the good of all.

You have a leader who knows—the man
Most fit to be called American,
A prophet that once in generations
Is given to point to erring nations
Brighter ideals toward which to press
And lead them out of the wilderness.
Will you turn your back on him once again?
Will you give the tiller once more to men
Who have made your country the laughing-stock
For the older peoples to scorn and mock,
Who would make you servile, despised, and weak,
A country that turns the other cheek,
Who care not how bravely your flag may float,
Who answer an insult with a note,
Whose way is the easy way in all,
And, seeing that polished arms appal
Their marrow of milk-fed pacifist,
Would tell you menace does not exist?
Are these, in the world's great parliament,
The men you would choose to represent
Your honor, your manhood, and your pride,
And the virtues your fathers dignified?
Oh, bury them deeper than the sea
In universal obloquy;
Forget the ground where they lie, or write
For epitaph: "Too proud to fight."

I have been too long from my country's shores

To reckon what state of mind is yours,

But as for myself I know right well

I would go through fire and shot and shell

And face new perils and make my bed

In new privations, if ROOSEVELT led;

But I have given my heart and hand

To serve, in serving another land,

Ideals kept bright that with you are dim;

Here men can thrill to their country's hymn,

For the passion that wells in the Marseillaise

Is the same that fires the French these days,

And, when the flag that they love goes by,

With swelling bosom and moistened eye

They can look, for they know that it floats there still

By the might of their hands and the strength of their will,

And through perils countless and trials unknown

Its honor each man has made his own.

They wanted the war no more than you,

But they saw how the certain menace grew,

And they gave two years of their youth or three

The more to insure their liberty

When the wrath of rifles and pennoned spears

Should roll like a flood on their wrecked frontiers.

They wanted the war no more than you,

But when the dreadful summons blew

And the time to settle the quarrel came

They sprang to their guns, each man was game;

And mark if they fight not to the last

For their hearths, their altars, and their past:

Yea, fight till their veins have been bled dry

For love of the country that WILL not die.

O friends, in your fortunate present ease

(Yet faced by the self-same facts as these),

If you would see how a race can soar

That has no love, but no fear, of war,

How each can turn from his private role

That all may act as a perfect whole,

How men can live up to the place they claim
And a nation, jealous of its good name,
Be true to its proud inheritance,
Oh, look over here and learn from FRANCE!

"I Have a Rendezvous with Death"

I have a rendezvous with Death
At some disputed barricade,
When Spring comes back with rustling shade
And apple-blossoms fill the air—
I have a rendezvous with Death
When Spring brings back blue days and fair.
It may be he shall take my hand
And lead me into his dark land
And close my eyes and quench my breath—
It may be I shall pass him still.
I have a rendezvous with Death
On some scarred slope of battered hill,
When Spring comes round again this year
And the first meadow-flowers appear.

God knows 'twere better to be deep
Pillowed in silk and scented down,
Where Love throbs out in blissful sleep,
Pulse nigh to pulse, and breath to breath,
Where hushed awakenings are dear…
But I've a rendezvous with Death
At midnight in some flaming town,
When Spring trips north again this year,
And I to my pledged word am true,
I shall not fail that rendezvous.

"At the Tomb of Napoleon"

I stood beside his sepulchre whose fame,
Hurled over Europe once on bolt and blast,
Now glows far off as storm-clouds overpast
Glow in the sunset flushed with glorious flame.

Has Nature marred his mould? Can Art acclaim

No hero now, no man with whom men side

As with their hearts' high needs personified?

There are will say, One such our lips could name;

Columbia gave him birth. Him Genius most

Gifted to rule. Against the world's great man

Lift their low calumny and sneering cries

The Pharisaic multitude, the host

Of piddling slanderers whose little eyes

Know not what greatness is and never can.

"Do You Remember Once"

I

Do you remember once, in Paris of glad faces,

The night we wandered off under the third moon's rays

And, leaving far behind bright streets and busy places,

Stood where the Seine flowed down between its quiet quais?

The city's voice was hushed; the placid, lustrous waters

Mirrored the walls across where orange windows burned.

Out of the starry south provoking rumors brought us

Far promise of the spring already northward turned.

And breast drew near to breast, and round its soft desire

My arm uncertain stole and clung there unrepelled.

I thought that nevermore my heart would hover nigher

To the last flower of bliss that Nature's garden held.

There, in your beauty's sweet abandonment to pleasure,

The mute, half-open lips and tender, wondering eyes,

I saw embodied first smile back on me the treasure

Long sought across the seas and back of summer skies.

Dear face, when courted Death shall claim my limbs and find them

Laid in some desert place, alone or where the tides

Of war's tumultuous waves on the wet sands behind them

Leave rifts of gasping life when their red flood subsides,

Out of the past's remote delirious abysses
Shine forth once more as then you shone, —beloved head,
Laid back in ecstasy between our blinding kisses,
Transfigured with the bliss of being so coveted.

And my sick arms will part, and though hot fever sear it,
My mouth will curve again with the old, tender flame.
And darkness will come down, still finding in my spirit
The dream of your brief love, and on my lips your name.

II

You loved me on that moonlit night long since.
You were my queen and I the charming prince
Elected from a world of mortal men.
You loved me once. . . . What pity was it, then,
You loved not Love. . . . Deep in the emerald west,
Like a returning caravel caressed
By breezes that load all the ambient airs
With clinging fragrance of the bales it bears
From harbors where the caravans come down,
I see over the roof-tops of the town
The new moon back again, but shall not see
The joy that once it had in store for me,
Nor know again the voice upon the stair,
The little studio in the candle-glare,
And all that makes in word and touch and glance
The bliss of the first nights of a romance
When will to love and be beloved casts out
The want to question or the will to doubt.
You loved me once. . . . Under the western seas
The pale moon settles and the Pleiades.
The firelight sinks; outside the night-winds moan—
The hour advances, and I sleep alone.

III

Farewell, dear heart, enough of vain despairing!
If I have erred I plead but one excuse—
The jewel were a lesser joy in wearing
That cost a lesser agony to lose.

I had not bid for beautifuller hours

255

Had I not found the door so near unsealed,

Nor hoped, had you not filled my arms with flowers,

For that one flower that bloomed too far afield.

If I have wept, it was because, forsaken,

I felt perhaps more poignantly than some

The blank eternity from which we waken

And all the blank eternity to come.

And I betrayed how sweet a thing and tender

(In the regret with which my lip was curled)

Seemed in its tragic, momentary splendor

My transit through the beauty of the world.

"On Returning to the Front after Leave"

Apart sweet women (for whom Heaven be blessed),

Comrades, you cannot think how thin and blue

Look the leftovers of mankind that rest,

Now that the cream has been skimmed off in you.

War has its horrors, but has this of good—

That its sure processes sort out and bind

Brave hearts in one intrepid brotherhood

And leave the shams and imbeciles behind.

Now turn we joyful to the great attacks,

Not only that we face in a fair field

Our valiant foe and all his deadly tools,

But also that we turn disdainful backs

On that poor world we scorn yet die to shield—

That world of cowards, hypocrites, and fools.

"Ode in Memory of the American Volunteers Fallen for France"

I

Ay, it is fitting on this holiday,

Commemorative of our soldier dead,

When—with sweet flowers of our New England May

Hiding the lichened stones by fifty years made gray—

Their graves in every town are garlanded,

That pious tribute should be given too

To our intrepid few

Obscurely fallen here beyond the seas.

Those to preserve their country's greatness died;

But by the death of these

Something that we can look upon with pride

Has been achieved, nor wholly unreplied

Can sneerers triumph in the charge they make

That from a war where Freedom was at stake

America withheld and, daunted, stood aside.

II

Be they remembered here with each reviving spring,

Not only that in May, when life is loveliest,

Around Neuville-Saint-Vaast and the disputed crest

Of Vimy, they, superb, unfaltering,

In that fine onslaught that no fire could halt,

Parted impetuous to their first assault;

But that they brought fresh hearts and springlike too

To that high mission, and 'tis meet to strew

With twigs of lilac and spring's earliest rose

The cenotaph of those

Who in the cause that history most endears

Fell in the sunny morn and flower of their young years.

III

Yet sought they neither recompense nor praise,

Nor to be mentioned in another breath

Than their blue coated comrades whose great days

It was their pride to share—ay, share even to the death!

Nay, rather, France, to you they rendered thanks

(Seeing they came for honor, not for gain),

Who, opening to them your glorious ranks,

Gave them that grand occasion to excel,

That chance to live the life most free from stain

And that rare privilege of dying well.

IV

O friends! I know not since that war began

From which no people nobly stands aloof

If in all moments we have given proof

Of virtues that were thought American.

257

I know not if in all things done and said

All has been well and good,

Or if each one of us can hold his head

As proudly as he should,

Or, from the pattern of those mighty dead

Whose shades our country venerates to-day,

If we've not somewhat fallen and somewhat gone astray.

But you to whom our land's good name is dear,

If there be any here

Who wonder if her manhood be decreased,

Relaxed its sinews and its blood less red

Than that at Shiloh and Antietam shed,

Be proud of these, have joy in this at least,

And cry: "Now heaven be praised

That in that hour that most imperilled her,

Menaced her liberty who foremost raised

Europe's bright flag of freedom, some there were

Who, not unmindful of the antique debt,

Came back the generous path of Lafayette;

And when of a most formidable foe

She checked each onset, arduous to stem—

Foiled and frustrated them—

On those red fields where blow with furious blow

Was countered, whether the gigantic fray

Rolled by the Meuse or at the Bois Sabot,

Accents of ours were in the fierce melee;

And on those furthest rims of hallowed ground

Where the forlorn, the gallant charge expires,

When the slain bugler has long ceased to sound,

And on the tangled wires

The last wild rally staggers, crumbles, stops,

Withered beneath the shrapnel's iron showers: —

Now heaven be thanked, we gave a few brave drops;

Now heaven be thanked, a few brave drops were ours."

V

There, holding still, in frozen steadfastness,

Their bayonets toward the beckoning frontiers,

They lie—our comrades—lie among their peers,

Clad in the glory of fallen warriors,

Grim clusters under thorny trellises,

Dry, furthest foam upon disastrous shores,

Leaves that made last year beautiful, still strewn

Even as they fell, unchanged, beneath the changing moon;

And earth in her divine indifference

Rolls on, and many paltry things and mean

Prate to be heard and caper to be seen.

But they are silent, calm; their eloquence

Is that incomparable attitude;

No human presences their witness are,

But summer clouds and sunset crimson-hued,

And showers and night winds and the northern star.

Nay, even our salutations seem profane,

Opposed to their Elysian quietude;

Our salutations calling from afar,

From our ignobler plane

And undistinction of our lesser parts:

Hail, brothers, and farewell; you are twice blest, brave hearts.

Double your glory is who perished thus,

For you have died for France and vindicated us.

John Peale Bishop (1892–1944)

John Peale Bishop is an American poet, critic, and the author of both a novel and a collection of short fiction. He was commissioned as a second lieutenant in the U.S. Army in 1917. He published his first poetry collection *Green Fruit* after graduation, and with later collections, he achieved an international reputation and moved into literary circles that included F. Scott Fitzgerald, Ernest Hemingway, John Dos Passos, and E. E. Cummings. The excerpted poem was written in 1933, reflecting the First World War with cynicism.

"In the Dordogne"

We stood up before day

And shaved by metal mirrors

In the faint flame of a faulty candle.

And we hurried down the wide stone stairs

With a clirr of spur chains

On stone. And we thought

When the cocks crew

That the ghosts of a dead dawn
Would rise and be off. But they stayed
Under the window, crouched on the staircase,
The windows now the color of morning.

The colonel slept in the bed of Sully
Slept on: but we descended
And saw in a niche in the white wall
A Virgin and Child, serene
Who were stone: we saw sycamores:
Three aged mages
Scattering gifts of gold.
But when the wind blew, there were autumn odors
And the shadowed trees
Had the dapplings of young fawns.

And each day one died or another
Died: each week we sent out thousands
That returned by hundreds
Wounded or gassed. And those that died
We buried close to the old wall
Within a stone's throw of Périgord
Under the tower of the troubadours.

And because we had courage;
Because there was courage and youth
Ready to be wasted; because we endured
And were prepared for all endurance;
We thought something must come of it:
That the Virgin would raise her Child and smile;
The trees gather up their gold and go;
That courage would avail something
And something we had never lost
Be regained through wastage, by dying,
By burying the others under the English tower.

The colonel slept on in the bed of Sully
Under the ravelling curtains; the leaves fell
And were blown away; the young men rotted

Under the shadow of the tower
In a land of small clear silent streams
Where the coming on of evening is
The letting down of blue and azure veils
Over the clear and silent streams
Delicately bordered by poplars.

4. General Reflections of War

As the last two decades of the 19th century and the beginning decades of the 20th century teemed with waves of wars on both banks of the Atlantic, there appeared a number of American poets who meditated on the social phenomenon of war. Wars in verses had become an important topic and instrument for modern poetic production, not only examining the decline of the West and but also looking for therapy of war as a cultural pathology. This is, of course, a dominant feature of literary modernity. A number of poets addressed wars generally without specifying any particular war, taking a sociological study of wars in terms of aesthetic reflections in verses. Due to the fact that a great number of modernist poetry had been related to wars, the anthology only selected the most related and representative of war reflections.

Stephen Crane (1871–1900)

Stephen Crane is one of the American foremost modernist writers. He marks the beginning of modern American literary Naturalism in his novella *Maggie: A Girl of the Streets* (1893) and Civil War novel *The Red Badge of Courage* (1895), the latter of which is a classic of American literature which depicts the psychological complexities of fear and courage on the battlefield. He once reported on the Greco-Turkish war in 1897. His poetic collections include *The Black Riders and Other Lines* (1895), and *War Is Kind* (1899). The excerpts are the beginning and end part of *War Is Kind*.

Excerpts from *War is Kind*

Do not weep, maiden, for war is kind.
Because your lover threw wild hands toward the sky
And the affrighted steed ran on alone,
Do not weep.
War is kind.

       Hoarse, booming drums of the regiment,
       Little souls who thirst for fight,
       These men were born to drill and die.

The unexplained glory flies above them,

Great is the Battle-God, great, and his Kingdom—

A field where a thousand corpses lie.

Do not weep, babe, for war is kind.

Because your father tumbled in the yellow trenches,

Raged at his breast, gulped and died,

Do not weep.

War is kind.

Swift blazing flag of the regiment,

Eagle with crest of red and gold,

These men were born to drill and die.

Point for them the virtue of slaughter,

Make plain to them the excellence of killing

And a field where a thousand corpses lie.

Mother whose heart hung humble as a button

On the bright splendid shroud of your son,

Do not weep.

War is kind.

　　　…

I wonder if sometimes in the dusk,

When the brave lights that gild thy evenings

Have not yet been touched with flame,

I wonder if sometimes in the dusk

Thou rememberest a time,

A time when thou loved me

And our love was to thee thy all?

Is the memory rubbish now?

An old gown

Worn in an age of other fashions?

Woe is me, oh, lost one,

For that love is now to me

A supernal dream,

White, white, white with many suns.

Love met me at noonday,

—Reckless imp,

To leave his shaded nights

And brave the glare,—

And I saw him then plainly

For a bungler,

A stupid, simpering, eyeless bungler,

Breaking the hearts of brave people

As the snivelling idiot-boy cracks his bowl,

And I cursed him,

Cursed him to and fro, back and forth,

Into all the silly mazes of his mind,

But in the end

He laughed and pointed to my breast,

Where a heart still beat for thee, beloved.

I have seen thy face aflame

For love of me,

Thy fair arms go mad,

Thy lips tremble and mutter and rave.

And—surely—

This should leave a man content?

Thou lovest not me now,

But thou didst love me,

And in loving me once

Thou gavest me an eternal privilege,

For I can think of thee.

Robert Frost (1874–1963)

Robert Frost is one of the most celebrated American poets. His depictions of the rural life of New England, his command of American colloquial speech, his realistic portrayal of ordinary people in everyday situations, and his philosophical meditations of commonplace matters have won him great popularity. He was invited in 1961 to read his poem "The Gift Outright" at the inauguration of President John F. Kennedy. His representative poetic collection includes *A Boy's Will* (1913), *North of Boston* (1914), *New Hampshire* (1923), *Collected Poems* (1930), *Steeple Bush* (1947), *In the Clearing* (1962). The excerpt "Range-Finding" (1916) is about the effects of war, showcasing the difference between innocence and violence.

"Range-Finding"

The battle rent a cobweb diamond-strung
And cut a flower beside a ground bird's nest
Before it stained a single human breast.
The stricken flower bent double and so hung.
And still the bird revisited her young.
A butterfly its fall had dispossessed
A moment sought in air his flower of rest,
Then lightly stooped to it and fluttering clung.

On the bare upland pasture there had spread
O'ernight 'twixt mullein stalks a wheel of thread
And straining cables wet with silver dew.
A sudden passing bullet shook it dry.
The indwelling spider ran to greet the fly,
But finding nothing, sullenly withdrew.

Carl Sandburg (1878–1967)

Carl Sandburg is an American poet, historian, novelist, folklorist, and especially one of the most popular American poets of the twentieth century for his poetic imagism and celebration of America with free verse. He has personally experienced the Spanish American War, understanding deeply that this war was evil, cruel and absurd. In 1904, he published his first volume of poetry called *Reckless Ecstasy*. His literary reputation steadily rose with the publication of his *Chicago Poems* (1916) and *Cornhuskers* (1918), for which he received the Pulitzer Prize in 1919. In 1920, he turned out *Smoke and Steel* (1920), witnessing his first prolonged attempt to portray industrial America and celebrate beauty in modern industrialism. His other collections include *The People, Yes* (1936), *The American Songbag* and *The New American Songbag* (1950). He received a second Pulitzer Prize for his *Complete Poems* in 1950. His final volumes of verse are *Harvest Poems, 1910–1960* (1960) and *Honey and Salt* (1963).

The brief poem "Grass" was published during World War I, which alludes to two of the most famous battles at Ypres and Verdun. With allusions of Napoleonic wars at Austerlitz and Waterloo and the American Civil War at Gettysburg, it explains all wars as "a waste", for people quickly forget fallen soldiers, as their corpses were soon covered by mud and grass that concealed the grim evidence of mass slaughter.

"Grass"

Pile the bodies high at Austerlitz and Waterloo.
Shovel them under and let me work—
        I am the grass; I cover all.

And pile them high at Gettysburg
And pile them high at Ypres and Verdun.
Shovel them under and let me work.
Two years, ten years, and passengers ask the conductor:
        What place is this?
        Where are we now?

        I am the grass.
        Let me work.

"Among the Red Guns"

Among the red guns,
In the hearts of soldiers
Running free blood
In the long, long campaign:
Dreams go on.

Among the leather saddles,
In the heads of soldiers
Heavy in the wracks and kills
Of all straight fighting:
Dreams go on.

Among the hot muzzles,
In the hands of soldiers
Brought from flesh-folds of women—
Soft amid the blood and crying—
In all your hearts and heads
Among the guns and saddles and muzzles:

Dreams,
Dreams go on,

265

Out of the dead on their backs,

Broken and no use any more:

Dreams of the way and the end go on.

Wallace Stevens (1879–1955)

Wallace Stevens is not only one of America's most respected 20th century poets writing in the veins of Imagism and French Symbolism, but also a master stylist employing an extraordinary vocabulary and a rigorous precision in poetic production, and in addition, a philosopher of aesthetics exploring the notion of poetry as the supreme fusion of the creative imagination and objective reality. His first poetic collection *Harmonium* was published in 1923, but only until his most evaluated *Collected Poems* (1954) was published did he win overwhelming public recognition. His other major works include *Ideas of Order* (1935), *The Man with the Blue Guitar* (1937), and *Notes towards a Supreme Fiction* (1942). The excerpt "The Death of a Soldier" was written in 1918.

"The Death of a Soldier"

Life contracts and death is expected,

As in a season of autumn.

The soldier falls.

He does not become a three-days personage,

Imposing his separation,

Calling for pomp.

Death is absolute and without memorial,

As in a season of autumn,

When the wind stops,

When the wind stops and, over the heavens,

The clouds go, nevertheless,

In their direction.

Sara Teasdale (1884–1933)

Sara Teasdale is an American poetess, best known for her poetry of simplicity and clarity, use of classical forms, and passionate and romantic subject matter. As an extraordinarily sensitive and almost reclusive woman, she ended her life by suicide at the age of 48. She published her first volume of verse *Sonnets to Duse, and Other Poems* in 1907, the second *Helen of Troy, and Other Poems* in 1911, and the third, *Rivers to the Sea*, in 1915. In the

1920s and toward the end of her life, she published three more volumes of poetry: *Flame and Shadow* (1920), *Dark of the Moon* (1926), and *Stars To-night* (1930), and *Strange Victory* (1933). In the excerpts, Teasdale assumes that if humans ever did disappear, the basic natural processes of sex and reproduction would go blissfully on without us, and war would leave no trace on earth.

"There Will Come Soft Rains"

There will come soft rains and the smell of the ground,
And swallows circling with their shimmering sound;

And frogs in the pools singing at night,
And wild plum trees in tremulous white;

Robins will wear their feathery fire,
Whistling their whims on a low fence-wire;

And not one will know of the war, not one
Will care at last when it is done.

Not one would mind, neither bird nor tree,
If mankind perished utterly;

And Spring herself, when she woke at dawn
Would scarcely know that we were gone.

Ezra Pound (1885–1972)

Ezra Pound has been considered the most important modernist poet for such three statuses: the most responsible for defining and promoting a modernist aesthetic for his promulgation of Imagism that stresses clarity, precision, and economy of language and foregoing traditional rhyme and meter; the most influential and in some ways the best critic in England or America during a crucial decade in the history of modern literature, approximately 1912–1922, having advanced the work of such major contemporaries as W. B. Yeats, Robert Frost, William Carlos Williams, Marianne Moore, H. D., James Joyce, Ernest Hemingway, and especially T. S. Eliot; and finally, his authoring of more than 70 books, with such most admired works, *Homage to Sextus Propertius* (1919) and *Hugh Selwyn Mauberley* and voluminous *The Cantos* that he began writing from 1920, which tackled a wide range of subjects, from the artist and society to the horrors of mass production and World War I and collapse of the Western civilisation.

Unfortunately, he served as the "Tokyo Rose" of Italy during WWII, making several hundred anti-American radio broadcasts in an effort to undermine the US war effort. After the defeat of the Axis powers, he was arrested and returned to the United States to face treason charges, but was examined by physicians and pronounced unfit for trial due to his insanity. Confined in a hospital for the criminally insane for 12 years, he was finally freed in 1958 from treason charges and returned to Italy where he continued writing poetry and translating ancient Chinese texts until his lonely death.

Excerpts from *Hugh Selwyn Mauberley*

These fought in any case,
and some believing,
            pro domo, in any case...
Some quick to arm,
some for adventure,
some from fear of weakness,
some from fear of censure,
some for love of slaughter, in imagination,
learning later...
some in fear, learning love of slaughter;
Died some, pro patria,
            non 'dulce' non 'et decor'...
walked eye-deep in hell
believing in old men's lies, then unbelieving
came home, home to a lie,
home to many deceits,
home to old lies and new infamy;
usury age-old and age-thick
and liars in public places.

Daring as never before, wastage as never before.
Young blood and high blood,
fair cheeks, and fine bodies;

fortitude as never before

frankness as never before,
disillusions as never told in the old days,
hysterias, trench confessions,
laughter out of dead bellies.

There died a myriad,
And of the best, among them,

For an old bitch gone in the teeth,
For a botched civilization,

Charm, smiling at the good mouth,
Quick eyes gone under earth's lid,

For two gross of broken statues,
For a few thousand battered books.

E. E. Cummings (1894–1962)

E. E. Cummings is one of the most innovative American poets of the 20th century. In 1917, he left the United States for France as a volunteer ambulance driver in World War I, a proper job for a pacifist with his outspoken anti-war convictions. His first collection, *Eight Harvard Poets*, was published in the same year. His other collections include *Tulips and Chimneys* (1923), *No Thanks* (1935), *50 Poems* (1940), *95 Poems* (1958), *73 Poems* (1962) and so on. He experimented radically with form, punctuation, spelling, and syntax, abandoning traditional techniques and structures to create a new, highly idiosyncratic means of poetic expression, especially with his attention to subjects such as war and sex.

"I Sing of Olaf"[7]

i sing of Olaf glad and big
whose warmest heart recoiled at war:
a conscientious object-or

his wellbelovèd colonel (trig
westpointer most succinctly bred)
took erring Olaf soon in hand;
but—though an host of overjoyed
noncoms (first knocking on the head
him) do through icy waters roll
that helplessness which others stroke

---

7 Olaf is written here as the most courageous and virtuous character, symbolizing all war resisters. In the United States, harsh laws were passed to penalize overt resistance to the war, and those who abuse Olaf are not disobedient renegades. Instead, they indicate the larger power structure—it is ultimately the president who seems responsible for Olaf's death.

with brushes recently employed
anent this muddy toiletbowl,
while kindred intellects evoke
allegiance per blunt instruments—
Olaf (being to all intents
a corpse and wanting any rag
upon what God unto him gave)
responds, without getting annoyed
"I will not kiss your fling flag"
straightway the silver bird looked grave
(departing hurriedly to shave)

but—though all kinds of officers
(a yearning nation's blueeyed pride)
their passive prey did kick and curse
until for wear their clarion
voices and boots were much the worse,
and egged the firstclassprivates on
his rectum wickedly to tease
by means of skilfully applied
bayonets roasted hot with heat—
Olaf(upon what were once knees)
does almost ceaselessly repeat
"there is some s. I will not eat"

our president,being of which
assertions duly notified
threw the yellowsonofabitch
into a dungeon,where he died

Christ(of His mercy infinite)
i pray to see; and Olaf, too

preponderatingly because
unless statistics lie he was
more brave than me: more blond than you.

Chapter VI

Poetry of the American Civil War (1861–1865)

The American Civil War, also called "War Between States" or "War between Brothers", is a four-year military conflict (1861–1865) between the Northern states (called the Union) and 11 Southern states that seceded from the Union and formed the Confederacy. When Abraham Lincoln, the candidate of the explicitly anti-slavery Republican Party, won the 1860 presidential election, seven Southern states (South Carolina, Mississippi, Florida, Alabama, Georgia, Louisiana, and Texas) carried out their threats and seceded, organising as the Confederate States of America. Later on, eleven southern states declared their Ordinances of Secession from the United States and formed the Confederate States of America, also known as "the Confederacy", and twenty-two mostly-Northern states formed the Union. The Border States (Maryland, Kentucky, Missouri) began with both Union and Confederate Governments till near the end of the war. In the early morning hours of April 12, 1861, rebels opened fire on Fort Sumter, at the entrance to the harbour of Charleston, South Carolina. Curiously, this first encounter of what would be the bloodiest war in the history of the United States claimed no victims.

The Civil War was the greatest war in American history. Three million fought, and 600,000 paid the ultimate price for freedom. The desire for freedom travelled deeper than the colour of skin and farther than the borders of any state. The American Revolution, which occurred from 1776 to 1783, was responsible for the formation of the country. However, it was the American Civil War that really set the course for how the nation would be run. It was the Civil War that determined whether or not the United States would truly become its own indivisible nation. It

271

also determined whether or not the United States would continue being the country with the largest number of slaves, which was ironic, since the country was founded on the idea that all men are created equal and entitled to be free. In short, the Civil War had defined the American nation.

Some critics say that the Civil War poetry is an independent poetic genre since the similarities between Northern and Southern poems far outweigh the differences: both sides are arguing and announcing that God is on their side; both sides are claiming that they're fighting for independence, although obviously, they're using that word quite differently with quite different meanings. When Edmund Wilson dismissed the poetry of the Civil War as a "versified journalism" in 1962, he summed up a common set of critiques: American poetry of the era is mostly nationalist doggerel, with little in the way of formal innovation. Competing political ideas are therefore apparent in many of these poems. More compelling, however, is an immediacy of emotion that can be felt only in poems by writers for whom the war was a lived experience. So in her Words for the Hour: A New Anthology of American Civil War Poetry (2006), Barrett argued: "In reading nineteenth-century poetry from a twenty-first-century standpoint, we must bear in mind that in this era, poetry was seen as serving a vital political function. A nineteenth-century reader of poetry would not have considered a politically engaged stance to be an artistic liability; indeed, both during and after the Civil War, poetry was seen as playing a central role in defining new versions of American identity."[1]

Different anthologies of Civil War poetry were rather common in the later decades of the nineteenth century, for instance *War Poetry of the South* (1866) edited by William Gilmore Simms, *Bugle-Echoes: A Collection of Poems of the Civil War Northern and Southern* (1886) edited by Francis Fisher Browne, and so on. The recent major anthology that comes to mind is Richard Marius's *The Columbia Book of Civil War Poetry* (1994). This anthology of "the American civil war in verse" serves two important purposes: first as a significant contribution to the latest scholarship that examines, and in certain cases re-examines, the literary representation of the world war in general and the war with Anglo-American involvement in particular, and second as to supply primary material for students and scholars since the anthology focuses on poetry that is especially noteworthy from writers North and South, male and female, white and black—that deepens our understanding of how ordinary people thought about the war.[2]

---

1 Faith Barrett, and Cristanne Miller, eds, Words for the Hour: A New Anthology of American Civil War Poetry. Amherst: University of Massachusetts Press, 2006, p. 3.
2 Other good studies include Edmund Wilson's *Patriotic Gore: Studies in the Literature of the American Civil War* (New York: Oxford University Press, 1962), Daniel Aaron' *The Unwritten War: American Writers and the Civil War* (New York: Knopf, 1973), Kathleen Diffley's *Where My Heart Is Turning Ever: Civil War Stories and Constitutional Reform, 1861–1876* (Athens: University of Georgia Press, 1992), Elizabeth Young's *Disarming the Nation: Women's Writing and the American Civil War* (Chicago: University of Chicago Press, 1999), Alice Fahs' *The Imagined Civil War: Popular Literature of the North and South, 1861–1865* (Chapel Hill: University of North Carolina Press, 2001), and et al.

1. Singing for the Union

As said above, those poets living in the "North" often wrote for the Union, and those living in the "South" spoke for the South: both are writing for freedom and justice. But strangely enough, a number of poets had shown quite an ambivalent attitude toward the War even they wrote for their sides, which has been an interesting phenomenon in American literary history. What should be noticed in this new anthology is that attention is to be paid to those who have personal experiences during the War though they are poets of little known reputation.

Walt Whitman (1819–1892)

Walt Whitman is one of the best American poets, journalists, and essayists. His verse collection *Leaves of Grass*, first published in 1855, is a landmark in the history of American literature for its celebration of democracy, nature, love, friendship, and singing praises to the body as well as to the soul and finding beauty and reassurance even in death. The 1855 edition consists of twelve untitled poems and a preface. The second appears in 1856, containing thirty-two poems, a letter from Emerson and a long open letter by himself in response, and with the constant addition of poems, he creates his deathbed edition in 1891–1892 while preparing his final volume of poems and prose, *Good-Bye My Fancy* (1891).

Whitman supported the Civil War, at the outbreak of which he vowed to live a "purged" and "cleansed" life. He wrote his poem "Beat! Beat! Drums!" (1861) as a patriotic rally call for the North. He worked as a freelance journalist, visited the wounded at various hospitals, and even volunteered for a time as a nurse in the army hospitals. He travelled to Washington, D. C. in December 1862 to care for his brother, who had been wounded in the war. His collection *Drum-Taps* (1865) deals with his experiences during the War.

"Beat! Beat! Drums!"

Beat! beat! drums!—blow! bugles! blow!
Through the windows—through doors—burst like a ruthless force,
Into the solemn church, and scatter the congregation,
Into the school where the scholar is studying;
Leave not the bridegroom quiet—no happiness must he have now with his bride,
Nor the peaceful farmer any peace, ploughing his field or gathering his grain,
So fierce you whirr and pound you drums—so shrill you bugles blow.

Beat! beat! drums!—blow! bugles! blow!
Over the traffic of cities—over the rumble of wheels in the streets;
Are beds prepared for sleepers at night in the houses? no sleepers must sleep in those beds,
No bargainers' bargains by day—no brokers or speculators—would they continue?

Would the talkers be talking? would the singer attempt to sing?

Would the lawyer rise in the court to state his case before the judge?

Then rattle quicker, heavier drums—you bugles wilder blow.

Beat! beat! drums!—blow! bugles! blow!

Make no parley—stop for no expostulation,

Mind not the timid—mind not the weeper or prayer,

Mind not the old man beseeching the young man,

Let not the child's voice be heard, nor the mother's entreaties,

Make even the trestles to shake the dead where they lie awaiting the hearses,

So strong you thump O terrible drums—so loud you bugles blow.

"Come up from the Fields Father"

Come up from the fields father, here's a letter from our Pete,

And come to the front door mother, here's a letter from thy dear son.

Lo, 'tis autumn,

Lo, where the trees, deeper green, yellower and redder,

Cool and sweeten Ohio's villages with leaves fluttering in the moderate wind,

Where apples ripe in the orchards hang and grapes on the trellised vines,

(Smell you the smell of the grapes on the vines?

Smell you the buckwheat where the bees were lately buzzing?)

Above all, lo, the sky so calm, so transparent after the rain, and with wondrous clouds,

Below too, all calm, all vital and beautiful, and the farm prospers well.

Down in the fields all prospers well,

But now from the fields come father, come at the daughter's call,

And come to the entry mother, to the front door come right away.

Fast as she can she hurries, something ominous, her steps trembling,

She does not tarry to smooth her hair nor adjust her cap.

Open the envelope quickly,

O this is not our son's writing, yet his name is signed,

O a strange hand writes for our dear son, O stricken mother's soul!

All swims before her eyes, flashes with black, she catches the main words only,

Sentences broken, *gunshot wound in the breast, cavalry skirmish, taken to hospital,*

At present low, but will soon be better.

Ah now the single figure to me,

Amid all teeming and wealthy Ohio with all its cities and farms,

Sickly white in the face and dull in the head, very faint,

By the jamb of a door leans.

Grieve not so, dear mother , (the just-grown daughter speaks through her sobs,

The little sisters huddle around speechless and dismayed,)

See, dearest mother, the letter says Pete will soon be better.

Alas poor boy, he will never be better, (nor may-be needs to be better, that brave and
   simple soul,)

While they stand at home at the door he is dead already,

The only son is dead.

But the mother needs to be better,

She with thin form presently dressed in black,

By day her meals untouched, then at night fitfully sleeping, often waking,

In the midnight waking, weeping, longing with one deep longing,

O that she might withdraw unnoticed, silent from life escape and withdraw,

To follow, to seek, to be with her dear dead son.

"Vigil Strange I Kept on the Field one Night"

Vigil strange I kept on the field one night;

When you my son and my comrade dropped at my side that day,

One look I but gave which your dear eyes returned with a look I shall never forget,

One touch of your hand to mine O boy, reached up as you lay on the ground,

Then onward I sped in the battle, the even-contested battle,

Till late in the night relieved to the place at last again I made my way,

Found you in death so cold dear comrade, found your body son of responding
   kisses, (never again on earth responding,)

Bared your face in the starlight, curious the scene, cool blew the moderate night-
   wind,

Long there and then in vigil I stood, dimly around me the battlefield spreading,

Vigil wondrous and vigil sweet there in the fragrant silent night,

But not a tear fell, not even a long-drawn sigh, long, long I gazed,

Then on the earth partially reclining sat by your side leaning my chin in my hands,

Passing sweet hours, immortal and mystic hours with you dearest comrade—not a
   tear, not a word,

Vigil of silence, love and death, vigil for you my son and my soldier,

As onward silently stars aloft, eastward new ones upward stole,

Vigil final for you brave boy, (I could not save you, swift was your death,

I faithfully loved you and cared for you living, I think we shall surely meet again,)

Till at latest lingering of the night, indeed just as the dawn appeared,

My comrade I wrapped in his blanket, enveloped well his form,

Folded the blanket well tucking it carefully over head and carefully under feet,

And there and then and bathed by the rising sun, my son in his grave, in his rude-
    dug grave I deposited,

Ending my vigil strange with that, vigil of night and battlefield dim,

Vigil for boy of responding kisses, (never again on earth responding,)

Vigil for comrade swiftly slain, vigil I never forget, how as day brightened,

I rose from the chill ground and folded my soldier well in his blanket,

And buried him where he fell.

"When Lilacs Last in the Dooryard Bloom'd"

1

When lilacs last in the dooryard bloom'd,

And the great star early droop'd in the western sky in the night,

I mourn'd, and yet shall mourn with ever-returning spring.

Ever-returning spring, trinity sure to me you bring,

Lilac blooming perennial and drooping star in the west,

And thought of him I love.

2

O powerful western fallen star!

O shades of night—O moody, tearful night!

O great star disappear'd—O the black murk that hides the star!

O cruel hands that hold me powerless—O helpless soul of me!

O harsh surrounding cloud that will not free my soul.

3

In the dooryard fronting an old farm-house near the white-wash'd palings,

Stands the lilac-bush tall-growing with heart-shaped leaves of rich green,

With many a pointed blossom rising delicate, with the perfume strong I love,

With every leaf a miracle—and from this bush in the dooryard,

With delicate-color'd blossoms and heart-shaped leaves of rich green,

A sprig with its flower I break.

4

In the swamp in secluded recesses,

A shy and hidden bird is warbling a song.

Solitary the thrush,
The hermit withdrawn to himself, avoiding the settlements,
Sings by himself a song.

Song of the bleeding throat,
Death's outlet song of life, (for well dear brother I know,
If thou wast not granted to sing thou would'st surely die.)

5

Over the breast of the spring, the land, amid cities,
Amid lanes and through old woods, where lately the violets peep'd from the ground,
    spotting the gray debris,
Amid the grass in the fields each side of the lanes, passing the endless grass,
Passing the yellow-spear'd wheat, every grain from its shroud in the dark-brown
    fields uprisen,
Passing the apple-tree blows of white and pink in the orchards,
Carrying a corpse to where it shall rest in the grave,
Night and day journeys a coffin.

6

Coffin that passes through lanes and streets,
Through day and night with the great cloud darkening the land,
With the pomp of the inloop'd flags with the cities draped in black,
With the show of the States themselves as of crape-veil'd women standing,
With processions long and winding and the flambeaus of the night,
With the countless torches lit, with the silent sea of faces and the unbared heads,
With the waiting depot, the arriving coffin, and the sombre faces,
With dirges through the night, with the thousand voices rising strong and solemn,
With all the mournful voices of the dirges pour'd around the coffin,
The dim-lit churches and the shuddering organs—where amid these you journey,
With the tolling tolling bells' perpetual clang,
Here, coffin that slowly passes,
I give you my sprig of lilac.

7

(Nor for you, for one alone,
Blossoms and branches green to coffins all I bring,
For fresh as the morning, thus would I chant a song for you O sane and sacred
    death.

All over bouquets of roses,

O death, I cover you over with roses and early lilies,

But mostly and now the lilac that blooms the first,

Copious I break, I break the sprigs from the bushes,

With loaded arms I come, pouring for you,

For you and the coffins all of you O death.)

8

O western orb sailing the heaven,

Now I know what you must have meant as a month since I walk'd,

As I walk'd in silence the transparent shadowy night,

As I saw you had something to tell as you bent to me night after night,

As you droop'd from the sky low down as if to my side, (while the other stars all look'd on,)

As we wander'd together the solemn night, (for something I know not what kept me from sleep,)

As the night advanced, and I saw on the rim of the west how full you were of woe,

As I stood on the rising ground in the breeze in the cool transparent night,

As I watch'd where you pass'd and was lost in the netherward black of the night,

As my soul in its trouble dissatisfied sank, as where you sad orb,

Concluded, dropt in the night, and was gone.

9

Sing on there in the swamp,

O singer bashful and tender, I hear your notes, I hear your call,

I hear, I come presently, I understand you,

But a moment I linger, for the lustrous star has detain'd me,

The star my departing comrade holds and detains me.

10

O how shall I warble myself for the dead one there I loved?

And how shall I deck my song for the large sweet soul that has gone?

And what shall my perfume be for the grave of him I love?

Sea-winds blown from east and west,

Blown from the Eastern sea and blown from the Western sea, till there on the prairies meeting,

These and with these and the breath of my chant,

I'll perfume the grave of him I love.

11

O what shall I hang on the chamber walls?

And what shall the pictures be that I hang on the walls,

278

To adorn the burial-house of him I love?

Pictures of growing spring and farms and homes,
With the Fourth-month eve at sundown, and the gray smoke lucid and bright,
With floods of the yellow gold of the gorgeous, indolent, sinking sun, burning,
    expanding the air,
With the fresh sweet herbage under foot, and the pale green leaves of the trees
    prolific,
In the distance the flowing glaze, the breast of the river, with a wind-dapple here
    and there,
With ranging hills on the banks, with many a line against the sky, and shadows,
And the city at hand with dwellings so dense, and stacks of chimneys,
And all the scenes of life and the workshops, and the workmen homeward returning.

12

Lo, body and soul—this land,
My own Manhattan with spires, and the sparkling and hurrying tides, and the ships,
The varied and ample land, the South and the North in the light, Ohio's shores and
    flashing Missouri,
And ever the far-spreading prairies cover'd with grass and corn.

Lo, the most excellent sun so calm and haughty,
The violet and purple morn with just-felt breezes,
The gentle soft-born measureless light,
The miracle spreading bathing all, the fulfill'd noon,
The coming eve delicious, the welcome night and the stars,
Over my cities shining all, enveloping man and land.

13

Sing on, sing on you gray-brown bird,
Sing from the swamps, the recesses, pour your chant from the bushes,
Limitless out of the dusk, out of the cedars and pines.

Sing on dearest brother, warble your reedy song,
Loud human song, with voice of uttermost woe.

O liquid and free and tender!
O wild and loose to my soul—O wondrous singer!
You only I hear—yet the star holds me, (but will soon depart,)
Yet the lilac with mastering odor holds me.

14

Now while I sat in the day and look'd forth,

In the close of the day with its light and the fields of spring, and the farmers preparing their crops,

In the large unconscious scenery of my land with its lakes and forests,

In the heavenly aerial beauty, (after the perturb'd winds and the storms,)

Under the arching heavens of the afternoon swift passing, and the voices of children and women,

The many-moving sea-tides, and I saw the ships how they sail'd,

And the summer approaching with richness, and the fields all busy with labor,

And the infinite separate houses, how they all went on, each with its meals and minutia of daily usages,

And the streets how their throbbings throbb'd, and the cities pent—lo, then and there,

Falling upon them all and among them all, enveloping me with the rest,

Appear'd the cloud, appear'd the long black trail,

And I knew death, its thought, and the sacred knowledge of death.

Then with the knowledge of death as walking one side of me,

And the thought of death close-walking the other side of me,

And I in the middle as with companions, and as holding the hands of companions,

I fled forth to the hiding receiving night that talks not,

Down to the shores of the water, the path by the swamp in the dimness,

To the solemn shadowy cedars and ghostly pines so still.

And the singer so shy to the rest receiv'd me,

The gray-brown bird I know receiv'd us comrades three,

And he sang the carol of death, and a verse for him I love.

From deep secluded recesses,

From the fragrant cedars and the ghostly pines so still,

Came the carol of the bird.

And the charm of the carol rapt me,

As I held as if by their hands my comrades in the night,

And the voice of my spirit tallied the song of the bird.

Come lovely and soothing death,

Undulate round the world, serenely arriving, arriving,

In the day, in the night, to all, to each,
Sooner or later delicate death.

Prais'd be the fathomless universe,
For life and joy, and for objects and knowledge curious,
And for love, sweet love—but praise! praise! praise!
For the sure-enwinding arms of cool-enfolding death.

Dark mother always gliding near with soft feet,
Have none chanted for thee a chant of fullest welcome?
Then I chant it for thee, I glorify thee above all,
I bring thee a song that when thou must indeed come, come unfalteringly.

Approach strong deliveress,
When it is so, when thou hast taken them I joyously sing the dead,
Lost in the loving floating ocean of thee,
Laved in the flood of thy bliss O death.

From me to thee glad serenades,
Dances for thee I propose saluting thee, adornments and feastings for thee,
And the sights of the open landscape and the high-spread sky are fitting,
And life and the fields, and the huge and thoughtful night.

The night in silence under many a star,
The ocean shore and the husky whispering wave whose voice I know,
And the soul turning to thee O vast and well-veil'd death,
And the body gratefully nestling close to thee.

Over the tree-tops I float thee a song,
Over the rising and sinking waves, over the myriad fields and the prairies wide,
Over the dense-pack'd cities all and the teeming wharves and ways,
I float this carol with joy, with joy to thee O death.

15

To the tally of my soul,
Loud and strong kept up the gray-brown bird,
With pure deliberate notes spreading filling the night.

Loud in the pines and cedars dim,
Clear in the freshness moist and the swamp-perfume,

And I with my comrades there in the night.

While my sight that was bound in my eyes unclosed,
As to long panoramas of visions.

And I saw askant the armies,
I saw as in noiseless dreams hundreds of battle-flags,
Borne through the smoke of the battles and pierc'd with missiles I saw them,
And carried hither and yon through the smoke, and torn and bloody,
And at last but a few shreds left on the staffs, (and all in silence,)
And the staffs all splinter'd and broken.

I saw battle-corpses, myriads of them,
And the white skeletons of young men, I saw them,
I saw the debris and debris of all the slain soldiers of the war,
But I saw they were not as was thought,
They themselves were fully at rest, they suffer'd not,
The living remain'd and suffer'd, the mother suffer'd,
And the wife and the child and the musing comrade suffer'd,
And the armies that remain'd suffer'd.

16

Passing the visions, passing the night,
Passing, unloosing the hold of my comrades' hands,
Passing the song of the hermit bird and the tallying song of my soul,
Victorious song, death's outlet song, yet varying ever-altering song,
As low and wailing, yet clear the notes, rising and falling, flooding the night,
Sadly sinking and fainting, as warning and warning, and yet again bursting with joy,
Covering the earth and filling the spread of the heaven,
As that powerful psalm in the night I heard from recesses,
Passing, I leave thee lilac with heart-shaped leaves,
I leave thee there in the door-yard, blooming, returning with spring.

I cease from my song for thee,
From my gaze on thee in the west, fronting the west, communing with thee,
O comrade lustrous with silver face in the night.

Yet each to keep and all, retrievements out of the night,
The song, the wondrous chant of the gray-brown bird,
And the tallying chant, the echo arous'd in my soul,

With the lustrous and drooping star with the countenance full of woe,

With the holders holding my hand nearing the call of the bird,

Comrades mine and I in the midst, and their memory ever to keep, for the dead I
    loved so well,

For the sweetest, wisest soul of all my days and lands—and this for his dear sake,

Lilac and star and bird twined with the chant of my soul,

There in the fragrant pines and the cedars dusk and dim.

"The Wound-Dresser"

An old man bending I come among new faces,

Years looking backward resuming in answer to children,

Come tell us old man, as from young men and maidens that love me,

(Aroused and angry, I'd thought to beat the alarum, and urge relentless war,

But soon my fingers failed me, my face drooped and I resigned myself,

To sit by the wounded and soothe them, or silently watch the dead;)

Years hence of these scenes, of these furious passions, these chances,

Of unsurpassed heroes, (was one side so brave? the other was equally brave;)

Now be witness again, paint the mightiest armies of earth,

Of those armies so rapid so wondrous what saw you to tell us?

What stays with you latest and deepest? of curious panics,

Of hard-fought engagements or sieges tremendous what deepest remains?

O maidens and young men I love and that love me,

What you ask of my days those the strangest and sudden your talking recalls,

Soldier alert I arrive after a long march covered with sweat and dust,

In the nick of time I come, plunge in the fight, loudly shout in the rush of successful
    charge,

Enter the captured works—yet lo, like a swift-running river they fade,

Pass and are gone they fade—I dwell not on soldiers' perils or soldiers' joys,

(Both I remember well—many the hardships, few the joys, yet I was content.)

But in silence, in dreams' projections,

While the world of gain and appearance and mirth goes on,

So soon what is over forgotten, and waves wash the imprints off the sand,

With hinged knees returning I enter the doors, (while for you up there,

Whoever you are, follow without noise and be of strong heart.)

Bearing the bandages, water and sponge,

Straight and swift to my wounded I go,

Where they lie on the ground after the battle brought in,
Where their priceless blood reddens the grass the ground,

Or to the rows of the hospital tent, or under the roofed hospital,
To the long rows of cots up and down each side I return,
To each and all one after another I draw near, not one do I miss,
An attendant follows holding a tray, he carries a refuse pail,
Soon to be filled with clotted rags and blood, emptied, and filled again.

I onward go, I stop,
With hinged knees and steady hand to dress wounds,
I am firm with each, the pangs are sharp yet unavoidable,
One turns to me his appealing eyes—poor boy! I never knew you,
Yet I think I could not refuse this moment to die for you, if that would save you.

On, on I go, (open doors of time! open hospital doors!)
The crushed head I dress, (poor crazed hand tear not the bandage away,)
The neck of the cavalry-man with the bullet through and through I examine,
Hard the breathing rattles, quite glazed already the eye, yet life struggles hard,
(Come sweet death! be persuaded O beautiful death!
In mercy come quickly.)

From the stump of the arm, the amputated hand,
I undo the clotted lint, remove the slough, wash off the matter and blood,
Back on his pillow the soldier bends with curved neck and side-falling head,
His eyes are closed, his face is pale, he dares not look on the bloody stump,
And has not yet looked on it.

I dress a wound in the side, deep, deep,
But a day or two more, for see the frame all wasted and sinking,
And the yellow-blue countenance see.

I dress the perforated shoulder, the foot with the bullet-wound,
Cleanse the one with a gnawing and putrid gangrene, so sickening, so offensive,
While the attendant stands behind aside me holding the tray and pail.

I am faithful, I do not give out,
The fractured thigh, the knee, the wound in the abdomen,
These and more I dress with impassive hand, (yet deep in my breast a fire, a burning

flame.)

Thus in silence in dreams' projections,
Returning, resuming, I thread my way through the hospitals,
The hurt and wounded I pacify with soothing hand,
I sit by the restless all the dark night, some are so young,
Some suffer so much, I recall the experience sweet and sad,
(Many a soldier's loving arms about this neck have crossed and rested,
Many a soldier's kiss dwells on these bearded lips.)

"An Army Corps on the March"

With its cloud of skirmishers in advance,
With now the sound of a single shot snapping like a whip, and now an irregular
    volley,
The swarming ranks press on and on, the dense brigades press on,
Glittering dimly, toiling under the sun—the dust-cover'd men,
In columns rise and fall to the undulations of the ground,
With artillery interspers'd—the wheels rumble, the horses sweat,
As the army corps advances.

"Adieu to a Soldier"

Adieu O soldier,
You of the rude campaigning, (which we shared,)
The rapid march, the life of the camp,
The hot contention of opposing fronts, the long manoeuvre,
Bed battles with their slaughter, the stimulus, the strong, terrific game,
Spell of all brave and manly hearts, the trains of time through you and like of you
    all fill'd,
With war and war's expression.

Adieu dear comrade,
Your mission is fulfill'd—but I, more warlike,
Myself and this contentious soul of mine,
Still on our own campaigning bound,
Through untried roads with ambushes opponents lined,
Through many a sharp defeat and many a crisis, often baffled,
Here marching, ever marching on, a war fight out—aye here,

To fiercer, weightier battles give expression.

"O Captain! My Captain!"[3]

O Captain! my Captain! our fearful trip is done,
The ship has weather'd every rack, the prize we sought is won;
The port is near, the bells I hear, the people all exulting,
While follow eyes the steady keel, the vessel grim and daring:
      But O heart! heart! heart!
        O the bleeding drops of red,
           Where on the deck my Captain lies,
             Fallen cold and dead!

O Captain! my Captain! rise up and hear the bells;
Rise up—for you the flag is flung—for you the bugle trills;
For you bouquets and ribbon'd wreaths—for you the shores a-crowding;
For you they call, the swaying mass, their eager faces turning;
      Here, Captain! dear father!
        This arm beneath your head;
           It is some dream that on the deck
             You've fallen cold and dead.

My Captain does not answer, his lips are pale and still;
My father does not feel my arm, he has no pulse nor will:
The ship is anchor'd safe and sound, its voyage closed and done;
From fearful trip the victor ship comes in with object won:
      Exult, O shores, and ring, O bells!
        But I, with mournful tread,
           Walk the deck my Captain lies,
             Fallen cold and dead.

Herman Melville (1819–1891)

Herman Melville is a novelist, short story writer and poet, but is best known as a novelist for his novels such as *Typee* (1846), *Omoo* (1847), *White-Jacket* (1850), *Pierre; or the Ambiguities* (1852), *The Confidence Man* (1857). In 1851, he completed his masterpiece, *Moby-Dick, or The Whale*, which is considered by modern scholars to be one of the greatest American novels. He observed the Senate's debating secession of the American Civil War

---

3 On April 15, 1865, Abraham Lincoln was killed by John Wilkes Booth, almost exactly four years after the first shot was fired at Fort Sumter.

during a visit to Washington D.C. in 1861, and made a trip to the front with his brother in 1864. The War witnesses a transition in his writing from fiction to poetry, and becomes the principal subject of his later verse. His first published book of poems is *Battle-Pieces and Aspects of the War: Civil War Poems* (1866), subtitled with: "The Battle-Pieces in this volume are dedicated to the memory of the THREE HUNDRED THOUSAND who in the war for the maintenance of the Union fell devotedly under the flag of their fathers." He went on to write three more volumes of poetry, including *Clarel: A Poem and Pilgrimage in the Holy Land* (1876), *John Marr and Other Sailors* (1888), and *Timoleon* (1891). His poetry is historically significant, thematically complex, but one of the major themes among other themes is that he criticised the War vehemently.

"Ball's Bluff: A Reverie"[4]

One noonday, at my window in the town,
      I saw a sight—saddest that eyes can see—
      Young soldiers marching lustily
          Unto the wars,
With fifes, and flags in mottoed pageantry;
      While all the porches, walks, and doors
Were rich with ladies cheering royally.

They moved like Juny morning on the wave,
      Their hearts were fresh as clover in its prime
      (It was the breezy summer time),
          Life throbbed so strong,
How should they dream that Death in a rosy clime
      Would come to thin their shining throng?
Youth feels immortal, like the gods sublime.

Weeks passed; and at my window, leaving bed,
      By night I mused, of easeful sleep bereft,
      On those brave boys (Ah War! thy theft);
          Some marching feet
Found pause at last by cliffs Potomac cleft;
      Wakeful I mused, while in the street
Far footfalls died away till none were left.

---

4 The poem was written in October 1861. On 21 October 1861, four regiments of Union troops packed into boats on the Potomac River faced Confederate attack at Ball's Bluff, where they were pinned against a hundred-foot cliff. More than 1,000 Union soldiers were killed in the massacre that ensued.

"The College Colonel"

He rides at their head;
    A crutch by his saddle just slants in view,
One slung arm is in splints, you see,
    Yet he guides his strong steed—how coldly too.

He brings his regiment home—
    Not as they filed two years before,
But a remnant half-tattered, and battered, and worn,
Like castaway sailors, who—stunned
        By the surf's loud roar,
    Their mates dragged back and seen no more—
Again and again breast the surge,
    And at last crawl, spent, to shore.

A still rigidity and pale—
    An Indian aloofness lones his brow;
He has lived a thousand years
Compressed in battle's pains and prayers,
    Marches and watches slow.

There are welcoming shouts, and flags;
    Old men off hat to the Boy,
Wreaths from gay balconies fall at his feet,
    But to *him* —there comes alloy.

It is not that a leg is lost,
    It is not that an arm is maimed,
It is not that the fever has racked—
    Self he has long disclaimed.

But all through the Seven Days' Fight,
    And deep in the Wilderness grim,
And in the field-hospital tent,
    And Petersburg crater, and dim
Lean brooding in Libby, there came—
    Ah heaven!—what *truth* to him.

"Shiloh: A Requiem"[5]

Skimming lightly, wheeling still,
    The swallows fly low
Over the field in clouded days,
    The forest-field of Shiloh—
Over the field where April rain
Solaced the parched ones stretched in pain
Through the pause of night
That followed the Sunday fight
    Around the church of Shiloh—
The church so lone, the log-built one,
That echoed to many a parting groan
    And natural prayer
Of dying foemen mingled there—
Foemen at morn, but friends at eve—
    Fame or country least their care:
(What like a bullet can undeceive!)
    But now they lie low,
While over them the swallows skim,
    And all is hushed at Shiloh.

"The March into Virginia, Ending in the First Manassas"

Did all the lets and bars appear
    To every just or larger end,
Whence should come the trust and cheer?
    Youth must its ignorant impulse lend—
Age finds place in the rear.
    All wars are boyish, and are fought by boys,
The champions and enthusiasts of the state:
    Turbid ardors and vain joys
    Not barrenly abate—
Stimulants to the power mature,
    Preparatives of fate.

---

5 The poem was written in April 1862. One of the bloodiest battles of the American Civil War was fought around the Shiloh Baptist Church in Tennessee on 6 and 7 April 1862. The Union losses totaled more than 13,000 men, the Confederates losses more than 10,000.

Who here forecasteth the event?
What heart but spurns at precedent
And warnings of the wise,
Contemned foreclosures of surprise?

The banners play, the bugles call,
The air is blue and prodigal.
    No berrying party, pleasure-wooed,
No picnic party in the May,
Ever went less loth than they
    Into that leafy neighborhood.
In Bacchic glee they file toward Fate,
Moloch's uninitiate;
Expectancy, and glad surmise
Of battle's unknown mysteries.
All they feel is this: 'tis glory,
A rapture sharp, though transitory,
Yet lasting in belaureled story.
So they gayly go to fight,
Chatting left and laughing right.

But some who this blithe mood present,
    As on in lightsome files they fare,
Shall die experienced ere three days are spent—
    Perish, enlightened by the vollied glare;
Or shame survive, and, like to adamant,
    The throe of Second Manassas share.

"The Eagle of the Blue"[6]

Aloft he guards the starry folds
    Who is the brother of the star;
The bird whose joy is in the wind
    Exultleth in the war.

---

6 Among the Northwestern regiments there would seem to have been more than one which carried a living eagle as an added ensign. The bird commemorated here was, according to the account, borne aloft on a perch beside the standard; went through successive battles and campaigns; was more than once under the surgeon's hands; and at the close of the contest found honorable repose in the capital of Wisconsin, from which state he had gone to the wars.

No painted plume—a sober hue,
  His beauty is his power;
That eager calm of gaze intent
  Foresees the Sibyl's hour.
Austere, he crowns the swaying perch,
  Flapped by the angry flag;
The hurricane from the battery sings,
  But his claw has known the crag.
Amid the scream of shells, his scream
  Runs shrilling; and the glare
Of eyes that brave the blinding sun
  The vollied flame can bear.
The pride of quenchless strength is his—
  Strength which, though chained, avails;
The very rebel looks and thrills—
  The anchored Emblem hails.
Though scarred in many a furious fray,
  No deadly hurt he knew;
Well may we think his years are charmed—
  The Eagle of the Blue.

"The Surrender at Appomattox"

As billows upon billows roll,
  On victory victory breaks;
Ere yet seven days from Richmond's fall
  And crowning triumph wakes
The loud joy-gun, whose thunders run
  By sea-shore, streams, and lakes.
    The hope and great event agree
    In the sword that Grant received from Lee.

The warring eagles fold the wing,
  But not in Cæsar's sway;
Not Rome o'ercome by Roman arms we sing,
  As on Pharsalia's day,
But Treason thrown, though a giant grown,
  And Freedom's larger play.
    All human tribes glad token see

In the close of the wars of Grant and Lee.

"The Martyr: Indicative of the passion of the people on the 15th of April, 1865"

Good Friday was the day
  Of the prodigy and crime,
When they killed him in his pity,
  When they killed him in his prime
Of clemency and calm—
  When with yearning he was filled
  To redeem the evil-willed,
And, though conqueror, be kind;
  But they killed him in his kindness,
  In their madness and their blindness,
And they killed him from behind.

There is sobbing of the strong,
  And a pall upon the land;
But the People in their weeping
  Bare the iron hand:
Beware the People weeping
  When they bare the iron hand.

He lieth in his blood—
  The father in his face;
They have killed him, the Forgiver—
  The Avenger takes his place,
The Avenger wisely stern,
  Who in righteousness shall do
  What the heavens call him to,
And the parricides remand;
  For they killed him in his kindness,
  In their madness and their blindness,
And his blood is on their hand.

There is sobbing of the strong,
  And a pall upon the land;
But the People in their weeping
  Bare the iron hand:

> Beware the People weeping
>> When they bare the iron hand.

James Russell Lowell (1819–1891)

James Russell Lowell is an American Romantic poet, critic, editor, and diplomat, associated with the Fireside Poets, a group of New England writers who were among the first American poets who rivaled the popularity of British poets. His numerous poetic collections include *A Year's Life, and Other Poems* (1841), *The Biglow Papers, First Series* (1848), and *The Biglow Papers, Second Series* (1867), which employs a humorous and original New England dialect to express his opposition to the Mexican War as an attempt to extend the area of slavery. After the Civil War, he expressed his devotion to the Union cause in four memorial odes, the best of which is *Ode Recited at the Harvard Commemoration* (1865).

"The Washers of the Shroud"

Along a riverside, I know not where,
I walked one night in mystery of dream;
A chill creeps curdling yet beneath my hair,
To think what chanced me by the pallid gleam
Of a moon-wraith that waned through haunted air.

Pale fireflies pulsed within the meadow-mist
Their halos, wavering thistledowns of light;
The loon, that seemed to mock some goblin tryst,
Laughed; and the echoes, huddling in affright,
Like Odin's hounds, fled baying down the night.

Then all was silent, till there smote my ear
A movement in the stream that checked my breath:
Was it the slow plash of a wading deer?
But something said, "This water is of Death!
The Sisters wash a shroud,—ill thing to hear!"

I, looking then, beheld the ancient Three
Known to the Greek's and to the Northman's creed,
That sit in shadow of the mystic Tree,
Still crooning, as they weave their endless brede,
One song: "Time was, Time is, and Time shall be."

No wrinkled crones were they, as I had deemed,
But fair as yesterday, to-day, to-morrow,
To mourner, lover, poet, ever seemed;
Something too high for joy, too deep for sorrow,
Thrilled in their tones, and from their faces gleamed.

"Still men and nations reap as they have strawn,"
So sang they, working at their task the while;
The fatal raiment must be cleansed ere dawn;
For Austria? Italy? the Sea-Queen's isle?
O'er what quenched grandeur must our shroud be drawn?

Or is it for a younger, fairer corse,
That gathered States for children round his knees,
That tamed the wave to be his posting-horse,
Feller of forests, linker of the seas,
Bridge-builder, hammerer, youngest son of Thor's?

"What make we, murmur'st thou? and what are we?
When empires must be wound, we bring the shroud,
The time-old web of the implacable Three:
Is it too coarse for him, the young and proud?
Earth's mightiest deigned to wear it,—why not he?"

"Is there no hope?" I moaned, "so strong, so fair!
Our Fowler whose proud bird would brook erewhile
No rival's swoop in all our western air!
Gather the ravens, then, in funeral file
For him, life's morn yet golden in his hair?"

"Leave me not hopeless, ye unpitying dames!
I see, half seeing. Tell me, ye who scanned
The stars, Earth's elders, still must noblest aims
Be traced upon oblivious ocean-sands?
Must Hesper join the wailing ghosts of names?"

"When grass-blades stiffen with red battle-dew
Ye deem we choose the victor and the slain:
Say, choose we them that shall be leal and true

To the heart's longing, the high faith of brain?
Yet there the victory lies, if ye but knew."

"Three roots bear up Dominion: Knowledge, Will,—
These twain are strong, but stronger yet the third,—
Obedience,—'t is the great tap-root that still,
Knit round the rock of Duty, is not stirred,
Though Heaven-loosed tempests spend their utmost skill."

"Is the doom sealed for Hesper? 'T is not we
Denounce it, but the Law before all time:
The brave makes danger opportunity;
The waverer, paltering with the chance sublime,
Dwarfs it to peril: which shall Hesper be?"

"Hath he let vultures climb his eagle's seat
To make Jove's bolts purveyors of their maw?
Hath he the Many's plaudits found more sweet
Than Wisdom? held Opinion's wind for Law?
Then let him hearken for the doomster's feet."

"Rough are the steps, slow-hewn in flintiest rock,
States climb to power by; slippery those with gold
Down which they stumble to eternal mock:
No chafferer's hand shall long the sceptre hold,
Who, given a Fate to shape, would sell the block."

"We sing old Sagas, songs of weal and woe,
Mystic because too cheaply understood;
Dark sayings are not ours; men hear and know,
See Evil weak, see strength alone in Good,
Yet hope to stem God's fire with walls of tow."

"Time Was unlocks the riddle of Time Is,
That offers choice of glory or of gloom;
The solver makes Time Shall Be surely his.
But hasten, Sisters! for even now the tomb
Grates its slow hinge and calls from the abyss."

"But not for him," I cried, "not yet for him,
Whose large horizon, westering, star by star
Wins from the void to where on Ocean's rim
The sunset shuts the world with golden bar,
Not yet his thews shall fail, his eye grow dim!"

"His shall be larger manhood, saved for those
That walk unblenching through the trial-fires;
Not suffering, but faint heart, is worst of woes,
And he no base-born son of craven sires,
Whose eye need blench confronted with his foes."

"Tears may be ours, but proud, for those who win
Death's royal purple in the foeman's lines;
Peace, too, brings tears; and 'mid the battle-din,
The wiser ear some text of God divines,
For the sheathed blade may rust with darker sin."

"God, give us peace! not such as lulls to sleep,
But sword on thigh, and brow with purpose knit!
And let our Ship of State to harbor sweep,
Her ports all up, her battle-lanterns lit,
And her leashed thunders gathering for their leap!"

So cried I with clenched hands and passionate pain,
Thinking of dear ones by Potomac's side;
Again the loon laughed mocking, and again
The echoes bayed far down the night and died,
While waking I recalled my wandering brain.

Excerpts from *Ode Recited at the Harvard Commemoration*

I

Weak-winged is song,
Nor aims at that clear-ethered height
Whither the brave deed climbs for light:
    We seem to do them wrong,
Bringing our robin's-leaf to deck their hearse
Who in warm life-blood wrote their nobler verse,

Our trivial song to honor those who come
With ears attuned to strenuous trump and drum,
And shaped in squadron-strophes their desire,
Live battle-odes whose lines were steel and fire:
    Yet sometimes feathered words are strong,
A gracious memory to buoy up and save
From Lethe's dreamless ooze, the common grave
    Of the unventurous throng.

.   .   .

XI

    Not in anger, not in pride,
    Pure from passion's mixture rude
    Ever to base earth allied,
    But with far-heard gratitude,
    Still with heart and voice renewed,
To heroes living and dear martyrs dead,
The strain should close that consecrates our brave.
    Lift the heart and lift the head!
    Lofty be its mood and grave,
    Not without a martial ring,
    Not without a prouder tread
    And a peal of exultation:
    Little right has he to sing
    Through whose heart in such an hour
    Beats no march of conscious power,
    Sweeps no tumult of elation!
    'Tis no Man we celebrate,
    By his country's victories great ,
    A hero half, and half the whim of Fate,
But the pith and marrow of a Nation
    Drawing force from all her men,
    Highest, humblest, weakest, all,
    For her time of need, and then
    Pulsing it again through them,
Till the basest can no longer cower,
Feeling his soul spring up divinely tall,
Touched but in passing by her mantle-hem.
Come back, then, noble pride, for 'tis her dower!
    How could poet ever tower,

If his passions, hopes, and fears,

If his triumphs and his tears,

Kept not measure with his people?

Boom, cannon, boom to all the winds and waves!

Clash out, glad bells, from every rocking steeple!

Banners, adance with triumph, bend your staves!

And from every mountain-peak

Let beacon-fire to answering beacon speak,

Katahdin tell Monadnock, Whiteface he,

And so leap on in light from sea to sea,

Till the glad news be sent

Across a kindling continent,

Making earth feel more firm and air breathe braver:

'Be proud! for she is saved, and all have helped to save her!

She that lifts up the manhood of the poor,

She of the open soul and open door,

With room about her hearth for all mankind!

The fire is dreadful in her eyes no more;

From her bold front the helm she doth unbind,

Sends all her handmaid armies back to spin,

And bids her navies, that so lately hurled

Their crashing battle, hold their thunders in,

Swimming like birds of calm along the unharmful shore.

No challenge sends she to the elder world,

That looked askance and hated; a light scorn

Plays o'er her mouth, as round her mighty knees

She calls her children back, and waits the morn

Of nobler day, enthroned between her subject seas.'

Julia Ward Howe (1819–1910)

Julia Ward Howe is best remembered as a constructive reformer rather than a poet, but her "The Battle Hymn of the Republic", written on November 19, 1861, was tremendously popular. This war song was written to the tune of "John Brown's Body"—a tune to which thousands of volunteers were marching to the front. She was the first woman elected to the American Academy of Arts and Letters.

"The Battle Hymn of the Republic"

Mine eyes have seen the glory of the coming of the Lord:

He is trampling out the vintage where the grapes of wrath are stored;
He hath loosed the fatal lightning of His terrible swift sword:
　　His truth is marching on.

I have seen Him in the watch-fires of a hundred circling camps,
They have builded Him an altar in the evening dews and damps;
I can read His righteous sentence by the dim and flaring lamps:
　　His day is marching on.

I have read a fiery gospel writ in burnished rows of steel:
'As ye deal with my contemners, so with you my grace shall deal;
Let the Hero, born of woman, crush the serpent with his heel,
　　Since God is marching on.'

He has sounded forth the trumpet that shall never call retreat;
He is sifting out the hearts of men before his judgement seat:
Oh, be swift, my soul, to answer Him! Be jubilant, my feet!
　　Our God is marching on.

In the beauty of the lilies Christ was born across the sea,
With a glory in his bosom that transfigures you and me:
As he died to make men holy, let us die to make men free,
　　While God is marching on.

Thomas Buchanan Read (1822–1872)

Thomas Buchanan Read is an American poet and painter. He lived in Boston from 1840 to 1845, busy with pen and brush, winning recognition as an artist. He contributed poems to *Graham's Magazine* and other newspapers. During the Civil War, he worked for the Union as a lecturer and propagandist. His poems were patriotic celebrations of America, extremely popular during the Civil War. His volumes of poetry include *Lays and Ballads* (1848), *Poems* (1852), *The New Pastoral* (1855), *A Summer Story, Sheridan's Ride, and Other Poems* (1865), and *Good Samaritans* (1867). The excerpts were respectively published in 1864 and 1865.

"Sheridan's Ride"[7]

Up from the South at break of day,
Bringing to Winchester fresh dismay,

---

7 General Early surprised and routed the Union troops during General Sheridan's absence in Washington. Sheridan hastened to the front, rallied his men, and won a complete victory.

The affrighted air with a shudder bore,
Like a herald in haste, to the chieftain's door,
The terrible grumble, and rumble, and roar,
Telling the battle was on once more,
And Sheridan twenty miles away.

And wider still those billows of war
Thundered along the horizon's bar;
And louder yet into Winchester rolled
The roar of that red sea uncontrolled,
Making the blood of the listener cold,
As he thought of the stake in that fiery fray,
And Sheridan twenty miles away.

But there is a road from Winchester town,
A good, broad highway leading down;
And there, through the flush of the morning light,
A steed as black as the steeds of night,
Was seen to pass, as with eagle flight,
As if he knew the terrible need;
He stretched away with his utmost speed;
Hills rose and fell; but his heart was gay,
With Sheridan fifteen miles away.

Still sprung from those swift hoofs, thundering South,
The dust, like smoke from the cannon's mouth;
Or the trail of a comet, sweeping faster and faster,
Foreboding to traitors the doom of disaster.
The heart of the steed and the heart of the master
Were beating like prisoners assaulting their walls,
Impatient to be where the battle-field calls;
Every nerve of the charger was strained to full play,
With Sheridan only ten miles away.

Under his spurning feet the road
Like an arrowy Alpine river flowed,
And the landscape sped away behind
Like an ocean flying before the wind,
And the steed, like a bark fed with furnace fire,

Swept on, with his wild eye full of ire.

But lo! he is nearing his heart's desire;

He is snuffing the smoke of the roaring fray,

With Sheridan only five miles away.

The first that the general saw were the groups

Of stragglers, and then the retreating troops,

What was done? what to do? a glance told him both,

Then striking his spurs, with a terrible oath,

He dashed down the line, mid a storm of huzzas,

And the wave of retreat checked its course there, because

The sight of the master compelled it to pause.

With foam and with dust, the black charger was gray

By the flash of his eye, and the red nostril's play,

He seemed to the whole great army to say,

"I have brought you Sheridan all the way

From Winchester, down to save the day!"

Hurrah! hurrah for Sheridan!

Hurrah! hurrah for horse and man!

And when their statues are placed on high,

Under the dome of the Union sky,

The American soldiers' Temple of Fame,

There with the glorious general's name

Be it said, in letters both bold and bright,

"Here is the steed that saved the day,

By carrying Sheridan into the fight,

From Winchester, twenty miles away!"

"The Attack"

IN Hampton Roads the airs of March were bland,

    Peace on the deck, and in the fortress sleeping,

Till, in the lookout of the Cumberland,

The sailor, with his well-poised glass in hand,

    Descried the iron island downward creeping.

A sudden wonder seized on land and bay,

    And Tumult, with her train, was there to follow;

For still the stranger kept its seaward way,
Looking a great leviathan blowing spray,
     Seeking with steady course his ocean wallow.

And still it came, and largened on the sight;
     A floating monster, ugly and gigantic;
In shape, a wave, with long and shelving height,
As if a mighty billow, heaved at night,
     Should turn to iron in the mid-Atlantic.

Then ship and fortress gazed with anxious stare,
     Until the Cumberland's cannon, silence breaking,
Thundered its guardian challenge, "Who comes there?"
But, like a rock-flung echo in the air,
     The shot rebounded, no impression making.

Then roared a broadside; though directed well,
     On, like a nightmare, moved the shape defiant;
The tempest of our pounding shot and shell,
Crumbled to harmless nothing, thickly fell
     From off the sounding armor of the giant!

Unchecked, still onward through the storm it broke,
     With beak directed at the vessel's centre;
Then through the constant cloud of sulphurous smoke
Drove, till it struck the warrior's wall of oak,
     Making a gateway for the waves to enter.

Struck, and to note the mischief done, withdrew,
     And then, with all a murderer's impatience,
Rushed on again, crushing her ribs anew,
Cleaving the noble hull wellnigh in two,
     And on it sped its fiery imprecations.

Swift through the vessel swept the drowning swell,
With splash, and rush, and guilty rise appalling;
While sinking cannon rung their own loud knell.
Then cried the traitor, from his sulphurous cell,
     "Do you surrender?" Oh, those words were galling!

How spake our captain to his comrades then?

    It was a shout from out a soul of splendor,

Echoed from lofty maintop, and again

Between-decks, from the lips of dying men,

    "Sink! sink, boys, sink! but never say surrender!"

Down went the ship! Down, down; but never down

    Her sacred flag to insolent dictator.

Weep for the patriot heroes, doomed to drown;

Pledge to the sunken Cumberland's renown.

    She sank, thank God! unsoiled by foot of traitor!

George H. Boker (1823–1890)

George H. Boker is an American journalist, dramatist, author, diplomat, and poet. He was born into a wealthy banker's family, and was brought up in an atmosphere of ease and refinement. He had his first volume of verse, *The Lessons of Life, and other Poems*, published in 1848. The Civil War turned his pen to the Union Cause, and changed him politically from a Democrat to a staunch Republican. Another of his collection is named *Königsmark, The Legend of the Hounds and other Poems* in 1869. The two excerpts are about his reflections about the War, respectively published in 1862 and 1863.

"Dirge for a Soldier"[8]

Close his eyes; his work is done!

What to him is friend or foeman,

Rise of moon, or set of sun,

Hand of man, or kiss of woman?

Lay him low, lay him low,

In the clover or the snow!

What cares he? he can not know:

Lay him low!

As man may, he fought his fight,

Proved his truth by his endeavor;

Let him sleep in solemn night,

Sleep forever and forever.

Lay him low, lay him low,

---

8 It is written in memory of General Philip Kearny, killed at Chantilly after he had ridden out in advance of his men to reconnoitre.

In the clover or the snow!

What cares he? he can not know:

Lay him low!

Fold him in his country's stars,

Roll the drum and fire the volley!

What to him are all our wars,

What but death bemocking folly?

Lay him low, lay him low,

In the clover or the snow!

What cares he? he can not know:

Lay him low!

Leave him to God's watching eye,

Trust him to the hand that made him.

Mortal love weeps idly by:

God alone has power to aid him,

Lay him low, lay him low,

In the clover or the snow!

What cares he? he can not know:

Lay him low!

"The Black Regiment"[9]

Dark as the clouds of even,

Ranked in the western heaven,

Waiting the breath that lifts

All the dread mass, and drifts

Tempest and falling brand

Over a ruined land;—

So still and orderly,

Arm to arm, knee to knee,

Waiting the great event,

Stands the black regiment.

Down the long dusky line

Teeth gleam and eyeballs shine;

---

9 "The colored troops fought nobly" was a frequent phrase in war bulletins; never did they better deserve this praise than at Port Hudson.

And the bright bayonet,
Bristling and firmly set,
Flashed with a purpose grand,
Long ere the sharp command
Of the fierce rolling drum
Told them their time had come,
Told them what work was sent
For the black regiment.

"Now," the flag-sergeant cried,
"Though death and hell betide,
Let the whole nation see
If we are fit to be
Free in this land; or bound
Down, like the whining hound,—
Bound with red stripes of pain
In our old chains again!"
O, what a shout there went
From the black regiment!

"Charge!" Trump and drum awoke,
Onward the bondmen broke;
Bayonet and sabre-stroke
Vainly opposed their rush.
Through the wild battle's crush.
With but one thought aflush,
Driving their lords like chaff,
In the guns' mouths they laugh;
Or at the slippery brands
Leaping with open hands,
Down they tear man and horse,
Down in their awful course;
Trampling with bloody heel
Over the crashing steel,
All their eyes forward bent,
Rushed the black regiment.

"Freedom!" their battle-cry,—
"Freedom! or leave to die!"

Ah! and they meant the word,
Not as with us 'tis heard,
Not a mere party shout:
They gave their spirits out;
Trusted the end to God,
And on the gory sod
Rolled in triumphant blood.

Glad to strike one free blow,
Whether for weal or woe;
Glad to breathe one free breath,
Though on the lips of death.
Praying—alas! in vain!—
That they might fall again,
So they could once more see
That burst to liberty!
This was what "freedom" lent
To the black regiment.

Hundreds on hundreds fell;
But they are resting well;
Scourges and shackles strong
Never shall do them wrong.
O, to the living few,
Soldiers, be just and true!
Hail them as comrades tried;
Fight with them side by side;
Never, in field or tent,
Scorn the black regiment.

Phoebe Cary (1824–1871)

Phoebe Cary is an American poetess. She was quite active in the early days of the women's rights movement. Her volumes of poetry include *Poems of Alice and Phoebe Cary* (1850), *Poems and Parodies* (1854), and *Poems of Faith, Hope and Love* (1868). The excerpt was written when the war broke out in 1861.

"Ready"

Loaded with gallant soldiers,

A boat shot in to the land,
And lay at the right of Rodman's Point
With her keel upon the sand.

Lightly, gayly, they came to shore,
And never a man afraid;
When sudden the enemy opened fire
From his deadly ambuscade.

Each man fell flat on the bottom
Of the boat; and the captain said:
"If we lie here, we all are captured,
And the first who moves is dead!"

Then out spoke a negro sailor,
No slavish soul had he;
"Somebody's got to die, boys,
And it might as well be me!"

Firmly he rose, and fearlessly
Stepped out into the tide;
He pushed the vessel safely off,
Then fell across her side:

Fell, pierced by a dozen bullets,
As the boat swung clear and free;—
But there wasn't a man of them that day
Who was fitter to die than he!

Charles G. Halpine (1829–1868)

Charles Graham Halpine is an American journalist, poet, reformer, and Union soldier in the Civil War. He immigrated to the United States in 1851 from Ireland, and enlisted in Company D of the 69th New York State Militia on April 20, 1861. During the Civil War, he penned poetry and prose for periodicals and eventually books under the pseudonym of "Miles O'Reilly". He was later promoted to brigadier general for his merit.

"Song of the Soldiers"

Comrades known in marches many,

Comrades, tried in dangers many,
Comrades, bound by memories many,
  Brothers let us be.
Wounds or sickness may divide us,
Marching orders may divide us,
But whatever fate betide us,
  Brothers of the heart are we.

Comrades, known by faith the clearest,
Tried when death was near and nearest,
Bound we are by ties the dearest,
  Brothers evermore to be.
And, if spared, and growing older,
Shoulder still in line with shoulder,
And with hearts no thrill the colder,
  Brothers ever we shall be.

By communion of the banner,—
Crimson, white, and starry banner,—
By the baptism of the banner,
  Children of one Church are we.
Creed nor faction can divide us,
Race nor language can divide us
Still, whatever fate betide us,
  Children of the flag are we.

Bret Harte (1836–1902)

Bret Harte is an American editor, short-story writer, literary celebrity, and diplomat. He helped create the local-colour school in American fiction, and his well-anthologized collection of stories is *The Luck of Roaring Camp, and Other Sketches* (1870). He also wrote poetry. The excerpted poem was written on July 1, 1863.

"John Burns of Gettysburg"

Have you heard the story that gossips tell
Of Burns of Gettysburg?—No? Ah, well,
Brief is the glory that hero earns,
Briefer the story of poor John Burns:
He was the fellow who won renown,—

The only man who didn't back down
When the rebels rode through his native town;
But held his own in the fight next day,
When all his townsfolk ran away.
That was in July, Sixty-three,
The very day that General Lee,
Flower of Southern chivalry,
Baffled and beaten, backward reeled
From a stubborn Meade and a barren field.
I might tell how but the day before
John Burns stood at his cottage door,
Looking down the village street,
Where, in the shade of his peaceful vine,
He heard the low of his gathered kine,
And felt their breath with incense sweet
Or I might say, when the sunset burned
The old farm gable, he thought it turned
The milk that fell like a babbling flood
Into the milk-pail red as blood!
Or how he fancied the hum of bees
Were bullets buzzing among the trees.
But all such fanciful thoughts as these
Were strange to a practical man like Burns,
Who minded only his own concerns,
Troubled no more by fancies fine
Than one of his calm-eyed, long-tailed kine,—
Quite old-fashioned and matter-of-fact,
Slow to argue, but quick to act.
That was the reason, as some folks say,
He fought so well on that terrible day.

And it was terrible. On the right
Raged for hours the heady fight,
Thundered the battery's double bass,—
Difficult music for men to face;
While on the left—where now the graves
Undulate like the living waves
That all that day unceasing swept
Up to the pits the Rebels kept—

Round shot ploughed the upland glades,
Sown with bullets, reaped with blades;
Shattered fences here and there
Tossed their splinters in the air;
The very trees were stripped and bare;
The barns that once held yellow grain
Were heaped with harvests of the slain;
The cattle bellowed on the plain,
The turkeys screamed with might and main,
And brooding barn-fowl left their rest
With strange shells bursting in each nest.

Just where the tide of battle turns,
Erect and lonely stood old John Burns.
How do you think the man was dressed?
He wore an ancient long buff vest,
Yellow as saffron,—but his best,
And, buttoned over his manly breast,
Was a bright blue coat, with a rolling collar,
And large gilt buttons,—size of a dollar,—
With tails that the country-folk called "swaller."
He wore a broad-brimmed, bell-crowned hat,
White as the locks on which it sat.
Never had such a sight been seen
For forty years on the village green,
Since old John Burns was a country beau,
And went to the "quiltings" long ago.

Close at his elbows all that day,
Veterans of the Peninsula,
Sunburnt and bearded, charged away;
And striplings, downy of lip and chin,—
Clerks that the Home Guard mustered in,—
Glanced, as they passed, at the hat he wore,
Then at the rifle his right hand bore;
And hailed him, from out their youthful lore,
With scraps of a slangy *repertoire*:
"How are you, White Hat? Put her through!"
"Your head's level!" and "Bully for you!"

Called him "Daddy,"—begged he'd disclose
The name of the tailor who made his clothes,
And what was the value he set on those;
While Burns, unmindful of jeer and scoff,
Stood there picking the rebels off,—
With his long brown rifle and bell-crown hat,
And the swallow-tails they were laughing at.

'Twas but a moment, for that respect
Which clothes all courage their voices checked:
And something the wildest could understand
Spake in the old man's strong right hand,
And his corded throat, and the lurking frown
Of his eyebrows under his old bell-crown;
Until, as they gazed, there crept an awe
Through the ranks in whispers, and some men saw,
In the antique vestments and long white hair,
The Past of the Nation in battle there;
And some of the soldiers since declare
That the gleam of his old white hat afar,
Like the crested plume of the brave Navarre,
That day was their oriflamme of war.

So raged the battle. You know the rest:
How the rebels, beaten and backward pressed,
Broke at the final charge, and ran.
At which John Burns—a practical man—
Shouldered his rifle, unbent his brows,
And then went back to his bees and cows.

That is the story of old John Burns;
This is the moral the reader learns:
In fighting the battle, the question's whether
You'll show a hat that's white, or a feather!

George Parsons Lathrop (1851–1898)

George Parsons Lathrop is an American poet and story-writer. His poetic volumes include *Dreams and Days* (1892) and *Rose and Roof-Tree* (James R. Osgood, 1875). The excerpt was published on the *Century Magazine* in June, 1881.

"Keenan's Charge"[10]

By the shrouded gleam of the western skies,
Brave Keenan looked in Pleasonton's eyes
For an instant—clear, and cool, and still;
Then, with a smile, he said: "I will."

"Cavalry, charge!" Not a man of them shrank.
Their sharp, full cheer, from rank on rank,
Rose joyously, with a willing breath—
Rose like a greeting hail to death.
Then forward they sprang, and spurred and clashed;
Shouted the officers, crimson-sash'd;
Rode well the men, each brave as his fellow,
In their faded coats of the blue and yellow;
And above in the air, with an instinct true,
Like a bird of war their pennon flew.
With clank of scabbards and thunder of steeds,
And blades that shine like sunlit reeds,
And strong brown faces bravely pale
For fear their proud attempt shall fail,
Three hundred Pennsylvanians close
On twice ten thousand gallant foes.

Line after line the troopers came
To the edge of the wood that was ring'd with flame;
Rode in and sabred and shot—and fell;
Nor came one back his wounds to tell.
And full in the midst rose Keenan, tall
In the gloom, like a martyr awaiting his fall,
While the circle-stroke of his sabre, swung
'Round his head, like a halo there, luminous hung.

Line after line; ay, whole platoons,
Struck dead in their saddles, of brave dragoons

---

10 During the second day of the battle of Chancellorsville, General Pleasonton was trying to get twenty-two guns into a vital position as Stonewall Jackson made a sudden advance. Time had to be bought, so Pleasanton ordered Major Peter Keenan, commanding the Eighth Pennsylvania Cavalry (four hundred strong), to charge the advancing ten thousand of the enemy. All took place on May 2, 1863.

By the maddened horses were onward borne
And into the vortex flung, trampled and torn;
As Keenan fought with his men, side by side.
So they rode, till there were no more to ride.

But over them, lying there, shattered and mute,
What deep echo rolls?—'Tis a death salute
From the cannon in place; for, heroes, you braved
Your fate not in vain: the army was saved!

Over them now—year following year—
Over their graves, the pine-cones fall,
And the whip-poor-will chants his spectre-call;
But they stir not again: they raise no cheer:
They have ceased. But their glory shall never cease,
Nor their light be quenched in the light of peace.
The rush of their charge is resounding still
That saved the army at Chancellorsville.

2. Singing for the Confederacy

In his timely edition *War Poetry of the South* (1866), William Gilmore Simms illustrated the significance of his anthology in the following words: "these poems will be recognized, not only as highly creditable to the Southern mind, but as truly illustrative, if not justificatory of, that sentiment and opinion with which they have been written; which sentiment and opinion have sustained their people through a war unexampled in its horrors in modern times, and which has fully tested their powers of endurance, as well as their ability in creating their own resources, under all reverses, and amidst every form of privation." Poetry of the Civil War South is creditable to the genius and culture of the Southern people, and honorable, as in accordance with their convictions, as it is derived from all the States of the late Southern Confederacy, and will be found truthfully to exhibit the sentiment and opinion prevailing more or less generally throughout the period.

Anonymous: "The Valiant Conscript"

The "war song" of the Civil War South is an important category of war poetry. Some critics say that the tone of the Southern songs was not only a good deal more ferocious and savage than that of those of the North, but there were fewer indications of that spirit of humor which pervaded the Northern camps, and found expression in the soldiers' songs. There is, however,

313

one Southern piece of verse, descriptive of the emotions of the newly drafted conscript, which has an original flavor of comicality, although evidently inspired by the spirit of Yankee Doodle, in such poems as "The Valiant Conscript" and others.

"The Valiant Conscript"

How are you, boys? I'm just from camp,
    And feel as brave as Cæsar;
The sound of bugle, drum, and fife
    Has raised my Ebenezer.
I'm full of fight, odds shot and shell,
    I'll leap into the saddle,
And when the Yankees see me come,
    Lord, how they will skedaddle!

Hold up your head, up, Shanghai, Shanks,
    Don't shake your knees and blink so,
It is no time to dodge the act;
    Brave comrades, don't you think so?

I was a ploughboy in the field,
    A gawky, lazy dodger,
When came the conscript officer
    And took me for a sodger.
He put a musket in my hand,
    And showed me how to fire it;
I marched and countermarched all day;
    Lord, how I did admire it!

With corn and hog fat for my food,
    And digging, guarding, drilling,
I got as thin as twice-skimmed milk,
    And was scarcely worth the killing.
And now I'm used to homely fare,
    My skin as tough as leather,
I do guard duty cheerfully
    In every kind of weather.

I'm brimful of fight, my boys,

I would not give a "thank ye"
For all the smiles the girls can give
    Until I've killed a Yankee.
High private is a glorious rank,
    There's wide room for promotion;
I'll get a corporal's stripes some day,
    When fortune's in the notion.

'Tis true I have not seen a fight,
    Nor have I smelt gunpowder,
But then the way I'll pepper 'em
    Will be a sin to chowder.
A sergeant's stripes I now will sport,
    Perhaps be color-bearer,
And then a captain—good for me—
    I'll be a regular tearer.

I'll then begin to wear the stars,
    And then the wreaths of glory,
Until the army I command,
    And poets sing my story.
Our Congress will pass votes of thanks
    To him who rose from zero,
The people in a mass will shout,
    Hurrah, behold the hero!
(Fires his gun by accident.)

What's that? oh dear! a boiler's burst,
    A gaspipe has exploded,
Maybe the Yankees are hard by
    With muskets ready loaded.
On, gallant soldiers, beat'em back,
    I'll join you in the frolic,
But I 've a chill from head to foot,
    And symptoms of the colic.

"Battle Hymn"

Lord of Hosts, that beholds us in battle, defending

The homes of our sires 'gainst the hosts of the foe,
     Send us help on the wings of thy angels descending,
          And shield from his terrors, and baffle his blow.
Warm the faith of our sons, till they flame as the iron,
          Red-glowing from the fire-forge, kindled by zeal;
Make them forward to grapple the hordes that environ,
          In the storm-rush of battle, through forests of steel!

Teach them, Lord, that the cause of their country makes glorious
          The martyr who falls in the front of the fight;—
That the faith which is steadfast makes ever victorious
          The arm which strikes boldly defending the right;—
That the zeal, which is roused by the wrongs of a nation,
          Is a war-horse that sweeps o'er the field as his own;
And the Faith, which is winged by the soul's approbation,
          Is a warrior, in proof, that can ne'er be o'erthrown.

"Our Confederate Dead, or What the Heart of a Young Girl Said to the Dead Soldier"

Unknown to me, brave boy, but still I wreathe
          For you the tenderest of wildwood flowers;
And o'er your tomb a virgin's prayer I breathe,
          To greet the pure moon and the April showers.

I only know, I only care to know,
          You died for me—for me and country bled;
A thousand Springs and wild December snow
          Will weep for one of all the SOUTHERN DEAD.

Perchance, some mother gazes up the skies,
          Wailing, like Rachel, for her martyred brave—
Oh, for her darling sake, my dewy eyes
          Moisten the turf above your lowly grave.

The cause is sacred, when our maidens stand
          Linked with sad matrons and heroic sires,
Above the relics of a vanquished land
          And light the torch of sanctifying fires.

Your bed of honor has a rosy cope
    To shimmer back the tributary stars;
And every petal glistens with a hope
    Where Love hath blossomed in the disk of Mars.

Sleep! On your couch of glory slumber comes
    Bosomed amid the archangelic choir;
Not with the grumble of impetuous drums
    Deepening the chorus of embattled ire.

Above you shall the oak and cedar fling
    Their giant plumage and protecting shade;
For you the song-bird pause upon his wing
    And warble requiems ever undismayed.

Farewell! And if your spirit wander near
    To kiss this plant of unaspiring art—
Translate it, even in the heavenly sphere,
    As the libretto of a maiden's heart.

William Gilmore Simms (1806–1870)

William Gilmore Simms is the most successful and prolific writer of the antebellum South. His best known novels include *The Yemassee* (1835), *The Partisan* (1835), and *The Golden Christmas* (1852), all of which trace the development of the region from the colonial era through the Revolution and into the antebellum period. He also published border and mountain romances like *Richard Hurdis* (1838) and *Voltmeier* (1869). His fiction is written in the Gothic genre. As a literary scholar and critic, he also edited a version of *War Poetry of the South* (1866), in which a number of war poets writing for the South were anthologised. The excerpt is of his own.

"Sumter in Ruins"

I

Ye batter down the lion's den,
    But yet the lordly beast g'oes free;
And ye shall hear his roar again,
From mountain height, from lowland glen,
From sandy shore and reedy fen—
Where'er a band of freeborn men

Rears sacred shrines to liberty.

II

The serpent scales the eagle's nest,

    And yet the royal bird, in air,

Triumphant wins the mountain's crest,

And sworn for strife, yet takes his rest,

And plumes, to calm, his ruffled breast,

Till, like a storm-bolt from the west,

    He strikes the invader in his lair.

III

What's loss of den, or nest, or home,

    If, like the lion, free to go;—

If, like the eagle, wing'd to roam,

We span the rock and breast the foam,

Still watchful for the hour of doom,

When, with the knell of thunder-boom,

    We bound upon the serpent foe!

IV

Oh! noble sons of lion heart!

    Oh! gallant hearts of eagle wing!

What though your batter'd bulwarks part,

Your nest be spoiled by reptile art—

Your souls, on wings of hate, shall start

For vengeance, and with lightning-dart,

    Rend the foul serpent ere he sting!

V

Your battered den, your shattered nest,

    Was but the lion's crouching-place;—

It heard his roar, and bore his crest,

His, or the eagle's place of rest;—

But not the soul in either breast!

This arms the twain, by freedom bless'd,

    To save and to avenge their race!

"In Memoriam of Our Right-Revered Father in God, Leonidas Polk, Lieutenant-General Confederate States Army"

Peace, troubled soul! The strife is done,

    This life's fierce conflicts and its woes are ended:

There is no more—eternity begun,

    Faith merged in sight—hope with fruition blended.

    Peace, troubled soul!

The Warrior rests upon his bier,

    Within his coffin calmly sleeping.

His requiem the cannon peals,

And heroes of a hundred fields

    Their last sad watch are round him keeping.

Joy, sainted soul! Within the vale

    Of Heaven's great temple, is thy blissful dwelling;

Bathed in a light, to which the sun is pale,

    Archangels' hymns in endless transports swelling.

        Joy, sainted soul!

Back to her altar which he served,

    The Holy Church her child is bringing.

The organ's wail then dies away,

And kneeling priests around him pray,

    As *De Profundis* they are singing.

Bring all the trophies, that are owed

    To him at once so great, so good.

His Bible and his well-used sword—

    His snowy lawn not "stained with blood!"

No! pure as when before his God,

    He laid its spotless folds aside,

War's path of awful duty trod,

    And on his country's altar died!

Oh! Warrior-bishop, Church and State

    Sustain in thee an equal loss;

But who would call thee from thy weight

    Of glory, back to bear life's cross!

The Faith was kept—thy course was run,

    Thy good fight finished; hence the word,

"Well done, oh! faithful child, well done,

Taste thou the mercies of thy Lord!"

No dull decay nor lingering pain,

    By slow degrees, consumed thy health,

A glowing messenger of flame

    Translated thee by fiery death!

And we who in one common grief

    Are bending now beneath the rod,

In this sweet thought may find relief,

    "Our holy father walked with God,

And is not—God has taken him!"

S. Teackle Wallis (1816–1894)

Severn Teackle Wallis is an American lawyer, a poet and a writer. He was one of the founders of the Maryland Historical Society. As a Confederate sympathizer, he had not advocated secession, and had argued against the doctrine of military necessity. He was imprisoned at Fort Lafayette for 14 months beginning in September 1861, spending more than a year imprisoned in several Union forts because of his alleged transgressions. He was released in 1862 without ever knowing the reason for his arrest. Today, he is immortalised in his statue on Baltimore's Mount Vernon square.

"A Prayer for Peace"

Peace! Peace! God of our fathers, grant us Peace!

Unto our cry of anguish and despair

Give ear and pity! From the lonely homes,

Where widowed beggary and orphaned woe

Fill their poor urns with tears; from trampled plains,

Where the bright harvest Thou has sent us rots—

The blood of them who should have garnered it

Calling to Thee—from fields of carnage, where

The foul-beaked vultures, sated, flap their wings

O'er crowded corpses, that but yesterday

Bore hearts of brothers, beating high with love

And common hopes and pride, all blasted now—

Father of Mercies! not alone from these

Our prayer and wail are lifted. Not alone

Upon the battle's seared and desolate track,

Nor with the sword and flame, is it, O God,

That Thou hast smitten us. Around our hearths,

And in the crowded streets and busy marts,

Where echo whispers not the far-off strife
That slays our loved ones; in the solemn halls
Of safe and quiet counsel—nay, beneath
The temple-roofs that we have reared to Thee,
And 'mid their rising incense—God of Peace!
The curse of war is on us. Greed and hate
Hungering for gold and blood; Ambition, bred
Of passionate vanity and sordid lusts,
Mad with the base desire of tyrannous sway
Over men's souls and thoughts, have set their price
On human hecatombs, and sell and buy
Their sons and brothers for the shambles. Priests,
With white, anointed, supplicating hands,
From Sabbath unto Sabbath clasped to Thee,
Burn, in their tingling pulses, to fling down
Thy censers and Thy cross, to clutch the throats
Of kinsmen, by whose cradles they were born,
Or grasp the brand of Herod, and go forth
Till Rachel hath no children left to slay.
The very name of Jesus, writ upon
Thy shrines beneath the spotless, outstretched wings,
Of Thine Almighty Dove, is wrapt and hid
With bloody battle-flags, and from the spires
That rise above them angry banners flout
The skies to which they point, amid the clang
Of rolling war-songs tuned to mock Thy praise.

All things once prized and honored are forgot:
The freedom that we worshipped next to Thee;
The manhood that was freedom's spear and shield;
The proud, true heart; the brave, outspoken word,
Which might be stifled, but could never wear
The guise, whate'er the profit, of a lie;
All these are gone, and in their stead have come
The vices of the miser and the slave—
Scorning no shame that bringeth gold or power,
Knowing no love, or faith, or reverence,
Or sympathy, or tie, or aim, or hope,
Save as begun in self, and ending there.

With vipers like to these, oh! blessed God!
Scourge us no longer! Send us down, once more,
Some shining seraph in Thy glory glad,
To wake the midnight of our sorrowing
With tidings of good-will and peace to men;
And if the star, that through the darkness led
Earth's wisdom then, guide not our folly now,
Oh, be the lightning Thine Evangelist,
With all its fiery, forked tongues, to speak
The unanswerable message of Thy will.

Peace! Peace! God of our fathers, grant us peace!
Peace in our hearts, and at Thine altars; Peace
On the red waters and their blighted shores;
Peace for the leaguered cities, and the hosts
That watch and bleed around them and within,
Peace for the homeless and the fatherless;
Peace for the captive on his weary way,
And the mad crowds who jeer his helplessness;
For them that suffer, them that do the wrong
Sinning and sinned against.—O God! for all;
For a distracted, torn, and bleeding land—
Speed the glad tidings! Give us, give us Peace!

"The Guerillas: A Southern War-Song"

"Awake!" and to horse, my brothers!
  For the dawn is glimmering gray;
And hark! in the crackling brushwood
  There are feet that tread this way.

"Who cometh?" "A friend." "What tidings?"
  O God! I sicken to tell,
For the earth seems earth no longer,
  And its sights are sights of hell!

There's rapine and fire and slaughter,
  From the mountain down to the shore;
There's blood on the trampled harvest—

There's blood on the homestead floor.

From the far-off conquered cities
          Comes the voice of a stifled wail;
And the shrieks and moans of the houseless
          Ring out, like a dirge, on the gale.

I've seen, from the smoking village
          Our mothers and daughters fly;
I've seen where the little children
          Sank down, in the furrows, to die.

On the banks of the battle-stained river
          I stood, as the moonlight shone,
And it glared on the face of my brother,
          As the sad wave swept him on.

Where my home was glad, are ashes,
          And horror and shame had been there—
For I found, on the fallen lintel,
          This tress of my wife's torn hair.

They are turning the slave upon us,
          And, with more than the fiend's worst art,
Have uncovered the fires of the savage
          That slept in his untaught heart.

The ties to our hearths that bound him,
          They have rent, with curses, away,
And maddened him, with their madness,
          To be almost as brutal as they.

With halter and torch and Bible,
          And hymns to the sound of the drum,
They preach the gospel of Murder,
          And pray for Lust's kingdom to come.

To saddle! to saddle! my brothers!
          Look up to the rising sun,

And ask of the God who shines there,
    Whether deeds like these shall be done!

Wherever the vandal cometh,
    Press home to his heart with your steel,
And when at his bosom you cannot,
    Like the serpent, go strike at his heel!

Through thicket and wood go hunt him,
    Creep up to his camp fireside,
And let ten of his corpses blacken
    Where one of our brothers hath died.

In his fainting, foot-sore marches,
    In his flight from the stricken fray,
In the snare of the lonely ambush,
    The debts that we owe him pay,

In God's hand, alone, is judgment;
    But He strikes with the hands of men,
And His blight would wither our manhood
    If we smote not the smiter again.

By the graves where our fathers slumber,
    By the shrines where our mothers prayed,
By our homes and hopes and freedom.
    Let every man swear on his blade.—

That he will not sheath nor stay it,
    Till from point to heft it glow
With the flush of Almighty vengeance,
    In the blood of the felon foe.

They swore—and the answering sunlight
    Leapt red from their lifted swords,
And the hate in their hearts made echo
    To the wrath in their burning words.

There's weeping in all New England,

And by Schuylkill's banks a knell,
And the widows there, and the orphans,
How the oath was kept can tell.

Frank Ticknor (1822–1874)

As the compiler of this critical anthology has examined academically, Frank Ticknor is called Francis Orrery Ticknor. He is a well-known American soldier and writer. The two excerpts are combined and revised from several anthologies.

"The Old Rifleman"

Now bring me out my buckskin suit!
My pouch and powder, too!
We'll see if seventy-six can shoot
As sixteen used to do.

Old Bess! we've kept our barrels bright!
Our trigger quick and true!
As far, if not as *fine* a sight,
As long ago we drew!

And pick me out a trusty flint!
A real white and blue,
Perhaps 'twill win the *other* tint
Before the hunt is through!

Give boys your brass percussion caps!
Old "shut-pan" suits as well!
There's something in the *sparks:* perhaps
There's something in the smell!

We've seen the red-coat Briton bleed!
The red-skin Indian, too!
We've never thought to draw a bead
On Yanke-doodle-doo!

But, Bessie! bless your dear old heart!
Those days are mostly done;
And now we must revive the art

Of shooting on the run!

If Doodle must be meddling, why,
  There's only this to do—
Select the black spot in his eye,
  And let the daylight through!

And if he doesn't like the way
  That Bess presents the view,
He'll maybe change his mind, and stay
  Where the good Doodles do!

Where Lincoln lives. The man, you know,
  Who kissed the Testament;
To keep the Constitution? No!
  To keep the Government!

We'll hunt for Lincoln, Bess! old tool,
  And take him half and half;
We'll aim to *hit* him, if a fool,
  And *miss* him, if a calf!

We'll teach these shot-gun boys the tricks
  By which a war is won;
Especially how Seventy-six
  Took Tories on the run.

"The Virginians of the Shenandoah Valley"

The knightliest of the knightly race
  Who, since the clays of old,
Have kept the lamp of chivalry
  Alight in hearts of gold;
The kindliest of the kindly band
  Who rarely hated ease,
Yet rode with Smith around the land,
  And Raleigh o'er the seas;
Who climbed the blue Virginia hills,
  Amid embattled foes,

And planted there, in valleys fair,
　　The lily and the rose;
Whose fragrance lives in many lands,
　　Whose beauty stars the earth,
And lights the hearths of thousand homes
　　With loveliness and worth,—
We feared they slept!—the sons who kept
　　The names of noblest sires,
And waked not, though the darkness crept
　　Around their vigil fires;
But still the Golden Horse-shoe Knights
　　Their "Old Dominion" keep:
The foe has found the enchanted ground,
　　But not a knight asleep.

George H. Miles (1824–1871)

George Henry Miles is an American novelist and dramatist, but his background is little known, and only his ballads or songs of the South have been well quoted, of which the excerpt serves as such.

"God Save the South"

God save the South!
God save the South!
Her altars and firesides—
　　God save the South!
Now that the war is nigh—
Now that we am to die—
Chanting—our battle-cry,
　　Freedom or Death!

God be our shield!
At home or a-field,
Stretch Thine arm over us,
　　Strengthen and save!
What though they're five to one,
Forward each sire and son,
Strike till the war is done,
　　Strike to the grave.

God make the right
Stronger than might!
Millions would trample us
    Down in their pride.
Lay, thou, their legions low;
Roll back the ruthless foe;
Let the proud spoiler know
    God's on our side!

Hark! honor's call,
Summoning all—
Summoning all of us
    Up to the strife.
Sons of the South, awake!
Strike till the brand shall break!
Strike for dear honor's sake,
    Freedom and Life!

Rebels before
Were our fathers of yore;
Rebel, the glorious name
    Washington bore,
Why, then, be ours the same
Title he snatched from shame;
Making it first in fame,
    Odious no more.

War to the hilt!
Theirs be the guilt,
Who fetter the freeman
    To ransom the slave.
Up, then, and undismayed,
Sheathe not the battle-blade?
Till the last foe is laid
    Low in the grave.

God save the South!
God save the South!
Dry the dim eyes that now

Follow our path.
Still let the light feet rove
Safe through the orange grove;
Still keep the land we love
Safe from all wrath.

God save the South!
God save the South!
Her altars and firesides—
God save the South!
For the rude war is nigh,
And we must win or die;
Chanting our battle-cry
Freedom or Death!

Esther Blythe Cheesborough (1825–1905): "Charleston"

Proudly she stands by the crystal sea,
With the fires of hate around her,
But a cordon of love as strong as fate,
With adamant links surround her.
Let them hurl their bolts through the azure sky,
And death-bearing missiles send her,
She finds in our God a mighty shield,
And in heaven a sure defender.

Her past is a page of glory bright,
Her present a blaze of splendor,
You may turn o'er the leaves of the jewell'd tome,
You'll not find the word *surrender*;
For sooner than lay down her trusty arms,
She'd build her own funeral pyre,
And the flames that give her a martyr's fate
Will kindle her glory higher.

How the demons glare as they see her stand
In majestic pride serenely,
And gnash with the impotent rage of hate,
Creeping up slowly, meanly;

While she cries, "Come forth from your covered dens,
    All your hireling legions send me,
I'll bare my breast to a million swords,
    Whilst God and my sons defend me."

Oh, brave old town, o'er thy sacred form
    Whilst the fiery rain is sweeping,
May He whose love is an armor strong
    Embrace thee in tender keeping;
And when the red war-cloud has rolled away,
    Anoint thee with holy chrism,
And sanctified, chastened, regenerate, true,
    Thou surviv'st this fierce baptism.

Henry Timrod (1828–1867)

    Henry Timrod is the Poet Laureate of the Confederacy. He lived a short life, served only a few months in the Confederate Army and had to leave the service because of his poor health. He had been writing and publishing poems in *The Southern Literary Messenger* since 1848, and his first and only volume of poems published in his lifetime was printed in Boston in 1860. He cherished poetic creation as once he said that "A true poet is one of the most precious gifts that can be bestowed on a generation." In Gutenburg's Digital Project of *Poems of Henry Timrod*, there were the following assessments of his poetry: "his song is the voice of the Southland…his life cast in the seething torrent of civil war, his voice was also the voice of Carolina, and through her of the South, in all the rich glad life poured out in patriotic pride into that fatal struggle, in all the valor and endurance of that dark conflict, in all the gloom of its disaster, and in all the sacred tenderness that clings about its memories. He was the poet of the Lost Cause, the finest interpreter of the feelings and traditions of the splendid heroism of a brave people. Moreover, by his catholic spirit, his wide range, and world-wide sympathies, he is a true American poet."

"A Cry to Arms"

Ho! woodsmen of the mountain-side!
    Ho! dwellers in the vales!
Ho! ye who by the chafing tide
    Have roughened in the gales!
Leave barn and byre, leave kin and cot,
    Lay by the bloodless spade;
Let desk, and case, and counter rot,

And burn your books of trade.

The despot roves your fairest lands;
      And till he flies or fears,
Your fields must grow but armed bands,
      Your sheaves be sheaves of spears!
Give up to mildew and to rust
      The useless tools of gain;
And feed your country's sacred dust
      With floods of crimson rain!

Come, with the weapons at your call—
      With musket, pike, or knife;
He wields the deadliest blade of all
      Who lightest holds his life.
The arm that drives its unbought blows
      With all a patriot's scorn,
Might brain a tyrant with a rose,
      Or stab him with a thorn.

Does any falter? let him turn
      To some brave maiden's eyes,
And catch the holy fires that burn
      In those sublunar skies.
Oh! could you like your women feel,
      And in their spirit march,
A day might see your lines of steel
      Beneath the victor's arch.

What hope, O God! would not grow warm
      When thoughts like these give cheer?
The lily calmly braves the storm,
      And shall the palm-tree fear?
No! rather let its branches court
      The rack that sweeps the plain;
And from the lily's regal port
      Learn how to breast the strain!

Ho! woodsmen of the mountain-side!

Ho! dwellers in the vales!
Ho! ye who by the roaring tide
    Have roughened in the gales!

Come! flocking gayly to the fight
    From forest, hill, and lake;
We battle for our country's right,
    And for the lily's sake!

"The Fire of Freedom"

The holy fire that nerved the Greek
    To make his stand at Marathon,
Until the last red foeman's shriek
    Proclaimed that freedom's fight was won,
Still lives unquenched—unquenchable:
    Through every age its fires will burn—
Lives in the hermit's lonely cell,
    And springs from every storied urn.

The hearthstone embers hold the spark
    Where fell oppression's foot hath trod;
Through superstition's shadow dark
    It flashes to the living God!
From Moscow's ashes springs the Russ;
    In Warsaw, Poland lives again:
Schamyl, on frosty Caucasus,
    Strikes liberty's electric chain!

Tell's freedom-beacon lights the Swiss;
    Vainly the invader ever strives;
He finds *Sic Semper Tyrannis*
    In San Jacinto's bowie-knives!
Than these—than all—a holier fire
    Now burns thy soul, Virginia's son!
Strike then for wife, babe, gray-haired sire,
    Strike for the grave of Washington!

The Northern rabble arms for greed;

The hireling parson goads the train—
In that foul crop from, bigot seed,
    Old "Praise God Barebones" howls again!
We welcome them to "Southern lands,"
    We welcome them to "Southern slaves,"
We welcome them "with bloody hands
    To hospitable Southern graves!"

"Address"[11]

A FAIRY ring
Drawn in the crimson of a battle-plain—
From whose weird circle every loathsome thing
    And sight and sound of pain
Are banished, while about it in the air,
And from the ground, and from the low-hung skies,
    Throng, in a vision fair
As ever lit a prophet's dying eyes,
    Gleams of that unseen world
That lies about us, rainbow-tinted shapes
    With starry wings unfurled,
Poised for a moment on such airy capes
    As pierce the golden foam
    Of sunset's silent main—
Would image what in this enchanted dome,
    Amid the night of war and death
In which the armed city draws its breath,
    We have built up!
For though no wizard wand or magic cup
    The spell hath wrought,
Within this charmed fane we ope the gates
    Of that divinest fairy-land
    Where, under loftier fates
Than rule the vulgar earth on which we stand,
Move the bright creatures of the realm of thought.

Shut for one happy evening from the flood

---

11 The poetic address was delivered at the opening of the new theatre at Richmond.

That roars around us, here you may behold—
    As if a desert way
    Could blossom and unfold
    A garden fresh with May—
Substantialized in breathing flesh and blood,
    Souls that upon the poet's page
    Have lived from age to age,
And yet have never donned this mortal clay.
    A golden strand
Shall sometimes spread before you like the isle
    Where fair Miranda's smile
Met the sweet stranger whom the father's art
    Had led unto her heart,
Which, like a bud that waited for the light,
    Burst into bloom at sight!
Love shall grow softer in each maiden's eyes
As Juliet leans her cheek upon her hand,
    And prattles to the night.
    Anon, a reverend form
    With tattered robe and forehead bare,
That challenge all the torments of the air,
    Goes by!
And the pent feelings choke in one long sigh,
While, as the mimic thunder rolls, you hear
    The noble wreck of Lear
Reproach like things of life the ancient skies,
    And commune with the storm!
Lo! next a dim and silent chamber, where
Wrapt in glad dreams, in which, perchance, the Moor
    Tells his strange story o'er,
The gentle Desdemona chastely lies,
Unconscious of the loving murderer nigh.
    Then through a hush like death
    Stalks Denmark's mailed ghost!
And Hamlet enters with that thoughtful breath
Which is the trumpet to a countless host
Of reasons, but which wakes no deed from sleep;
    For while it calls to strife,
He pauses on the very brink of fact

To toy as with the shadow of an act,
And utter those wise saws that cut so deep
        Into the core of life!

Nor shall be wanting many a scene
        Where forms of more familiar mien,
Moving through lowlier pathways, shall present
        The world of every day,
Such as it whirls along the busy quay,
Or sits beneath a rustic orchard wall,
Or floats about a fashion-freighted hall,
Or toils in attics dark the night away.
Love, hate, grief, joy, gain, glory, shame, shall meet,
As in the round wherein our lives are pent;
        Chance for a while shall seem to reign,
While goodness roves like guilt about the street,
        And guilt looks innocent.

But all at last shall vindicate the right.
Crime shall be meted with its proper pain,
Motes shall be taken from the doubter's sight,
And fortune's general justice rendered plain.
Of honest laughter there shall be no dearth,
Wit shall shake hands with humor grave and sweet,
Our wisdom shall not be too wise for mirth,
Nor kindred follies want a fool to greet.
As sometimes from the meanest spot of earth
A sudden beauty unexpected starts,
So you shall find some germs of hidden worth
        Within the vilest hearts;
And now and then, when in those moods that turn
To the cold Muse that whips a fault with sneers,
You shall, perchance, be strangely touched to learn
        You've struck a spring of tears!

But while we lead you thus from change to change,
Shall we not find within our ample range
Some type to elevate a people's heart—
Some haro who shall teach a hero's part

In this distracted time?
Rise from thy sleep of ages, noble Tell!
And, with the Alpine thunders of thy voice,
As if across the billows unenthralled,
Thy Alps unto the Alleghanies called,
      Bid liberty rejoice!
Proclaim upon this trans-Atlantic strand
The deeds which, more than their own awful mien,
Make every crag of Switzerland sublime!
And say to those whose feeble souls would lean
Not on themselves, but on some outstretched hand,
That once a single mind sufficed to quell
The malice of a tyrant; let them know
That each may crowd in every well-aimed blow,
Not the poor strength alone of arm and brand,
But the whole spirit of a mighty land!

Bid liberty rejoice! Aye, though its day
Be far or near, these clouds shall yet be red
With the large promise of the coming ray.
Meanwhile, with that calm courage which can smile
Amid the terrors of the wildest fray,
Let us among the charms of art awhile
      Fleet the deep gloom away;
Nor yet forget that on each hand and head
Rest the dear rights for which we fight and pray.

"Charleston"

Calm as that second summer which precedes
      The first fall of the snow,
In the broad sunlight of heroic deeds,
      The city bides the foe.

As yet, behind their ramparts, stern and proud,
      Her bolted thunders sleep—
Dark Sumter, like a battlemented cloud,
      Looms o'er the solemn deep.

No Calpe frowns from lofty cliff or scaur
    To guard the holy strand;
But Moultrie holds in leash her dogs of war,
    Above the level sand.

And down the dunes a thousand guns lie couched.
    Unseen, beside the flood—
Like tigers in some Orient jungle crouched,
    That wait and watch for blood.

Meanwhile, through streets still echoing with trade,
    Walk grave and thoughtful men,
Whose hands may one day wield the patriot's blade
    As lightly as the pen.

And maidens, with such eyes as would grow dim
    Over a bleeding hound,
Seem each one to have caught the strength of him
    Whose sword she sadly bound.

Thus girt without and garrisoned at home,
    Day patient following day,
Old Charleston looks from roof, and spire, and dome,
    Across her tranquil bay.

Ships, through a hundred foes, from Saxon lands
    And spicy Indian ports,
Bring Saxon steel and iron to her hands,
    And summer to her courts.

But still, along yon dim Atlantic line,
    The only hostile smoke
Creeps like a harmless mist above the brine,
    From some frail, floating oak.

Shall the spring dawn, and she still clad in smiles,
    And with an unscathed brow,
Rest in the strong arms of her palm-crowned isles,
    As fair and free as now?

We know not; in the temple of the Fates
    God has inscribed her doom;
And, all untroubled in her faith, she waits
    The triumph or the tomb.

"The Two Armies"

Two armies stand enrolled beneath
The banner with the starry wreath:
One, facing battle, blight, and blast,
Through twice a hundred fields has passed;
Its deeds against a ruffian foe,
Stream, valley, hill, and mountain know,
Till every wind that sweeps the land
Goes, glory-laden, from the strand.

The other, with a narrower scope,
Yet led by not less grand a hope,
Hath won, perhaps, as proud a place,
And wears its fame with meeker grace.
Wives march beneath its glittering sign,
Fond mothers swell the lovely line:
And many a sweetheart hides her blush
In the young patriot's generous flush.

No breeze of battle ever fanned
The colors of that tender band;
Its office is beside the bed,
Where throbs some sick or wounded head.
It does not court the soldier's tomb,
But plies the needle and the loom;
And, by a thousand peaceful deeds,
Supplies a struggling nation's needs.

Nor is that army's gentle might
Unfelt amid the deadly fight;
It nerves the son's, the husband's hand,
It points the lover's fearless brand;
It thrills the languid, warms the cold,

Gives even new courage to the bold;

And sometimes lifts the veriest clod

To its own lofty trust in God.

When Heaven shall blow the trump of peace,

And bid this weary warfare cease,

Their several missions nobly done,

The triumph grasped, and freedom won,

Both armies, from their toils at rest,

Alike may claim the victor's crest,

But each shall see its dearest prize

Gleam softly from the other's eyes.

"The Unknown Dead"

The rain is plashing on my sill,

But all the winds of Heaven are still;

And so, it falls with that dull sound

Which thrills us in the churchyard ground,

When the first spadeful drops like lead

Upon the coffin of the dead.

Beyond my streaming window-pane,

I cannot see the neighboring vane,

Yet from its old familiar tower

The bell comes, muffled, through the shower.

What strange and unsuspected link

Of feeling touched has made me think—

While with a vacant soul and eye

I watch that gray and stony sky—

Of nameless graves on battle plains,

Washed by a single winter's rains,

Where, some beneath Virginian hills,

And some by green Atlantic rills,

Some by the waters of the West,

A myriad unknown heroes rest?

Ah! not the chiefs who, dying, see

Their flags in front of victory,

Or, at their life-blood's noblest cost

Pay for a battle nobly lost,

Claim from their monumental beds

The bitterest tears a nation sheds.

Beneath yon lonely mound—the spot,

By all save some fond few forgot—

Lie the true martyrs of the fight,

Which strikes for freedom and for right.

Of them, their patriot zeal and pride,

The lofty faith that with them died,

No grateful page shall further tell

Than that so many bravely fell;

And we can only dimly guess

What worlds of all this world's distress,

What utter woe, despair, and dearth,

Their fate has brought to many a hearth.

Just such a sky as this should weep

Above them, always, where they sleep;

Yet, haply, at this very hour,

Their graves are like a lover's bower;

And Nature's self, with eyes unwet,

Oblivious of the crimson debt

To which she owes her April grace,

Laughs gayly o'er their burial place.

John R. Thompson (1823–1873)

John R. Thompson is an American editor, critic, journalist, and Civil War poet. His well anthologized poems about the Civil War include "Music in Camp" (1862), "Obsequies of Stuart" (1864), and other poems.

"Music in Camp"

Two armies covered hill and plain
    Where Rappahannock's waters
Ran deeply crimsoned with the stain
    Of battle's recent slaughters.

The summer clouds lay pitched like tents
    In meads of heavenly azure;
And each dread gun of the elements
    Slept in its hid embrasure.

The breeze so softly blew, it made
    No forest leaf to quiver,
And the smoke of the random cannonade
    Rolled slowly from the river.

And now where circling hills looked down
    With cannon grimly planted,
O'er listless camp and silent town
    The golden sunset slanted;

When on the fervid air there came
    A strain, now rich, now tender,
The music seemed itself aflame
    With day's departing splendor.

A Federal band, which eve and morn
    Played measures brave and nimble,
Had just struck up with flute and horn
    And lively clash of cymbal.

Down flocked the soldiers to the bank;
    Till margined by its pebbles,
One wooded shore was blue with "Yanks,"
    And one was gray with "Rebels."

Then all was still; and then the band
    With movements light and tricksy,
Made stream and forest, hill and strand,
    Reverberate with "Dixie."

The conscious stream, with burnished glow,
    Went proudly o'er its pebbles,
But thrilled throughout its deepest flow
    With yelling of the Rebels.

Again a pause, and then again
    The trumpet pealed sonorous,
And Yankee Doodle was the strain
    To which the shore gave chorus.

The laughing ripple shoreward flew
    To kiss the shining pebbles—
Loud shrieked the crowding Boys in Blue
    Defiance to the Rebels.

And yet once more the bugle sang
    Above the stormy riot;
No shout upon the evening rang
    There reigned a holy quiet.

The sad, lone stream its noiseless tread
    Spread o'er the glistening pebbles:
All silent now the Yankees stood;
    All silent stood the Rebels:

For each responsive soul had heard
    That plaintive note's appealing,
So deeply "Home, Sweet Home" had stirred
    The hidden founts of feeling.

Or blue or gray, the soldier sees,
    As by the wand of fairy,
The cottage neath the live-oak trees,
    The cottage by the prairie.

Or cold or warm, his native skies
    Bend in their beauty o'er him:
Sending the tear-mist in his eyes—
    The dear ones stand before him.

As fades the iris after rain
    In April's tearful weather,
The vision vanished as the strain
    And daylight died together.

But memory, waked by music's art
    Expressed in simplest numbers,
Subdued the sternest Yankee's heart,
    Made light the Rebel's slumbers.

And fair the form of Music shines,
    That bright, celestial creature,
Who still 'mid war's embattled lines
    Gave this one touch of nature.

"Obsequies of Stuart"[12]

WE could not pause, while yet the noontide air
    Shook with the cannonade's incessant pealing,
The funeral pageant fitly to prepare—
    A nation's grief revealing.

The smoke, above the glimmering woodland wide
    That skirts our southward border in its beauty,
Marked where our heroes stood and fought and died
    For love and faith and duty.

And still, what time the doubtful strife went on,
    We might not find expression for our sorrow;
We could but lay our dear dumb warrior down,
    And gird us for the morrow.

One weary year agone, when came a lull
    With victory in the conflict's stormy closes,
When the glad Spring, all flushed and beautiful,
    First mocked us with her roses,

With dirge and bell and minute-gun, we paid
    Some few poor rites—an inexpressive token
Of a great people's pain—to Jackson's shade,
    In agony unspoken.

No wailing trumpet and no tolling bell,
    No cannon, save the battle's boom receding,
When Stuart to the grave we bore, might tell,
With hearts all crushed and bleeding.

---

12 On May 12, 1864, General J. E. B. Stuart, the famous chief of the Confederate cavalry, fell in an engagement with General Sheridan's forces, at Yellow Tavern, Virginia.

The crisis suited not with pomp, and she
    Whose anguish bears the seal of consecration
Had wished his Christian obsequies should be
    Thus void of ostentation.

Only the maidens came, sweet flowers to twine
    Above his form so still and cold and painless,
Whose deeds upon our brightest records shine,
    Whose life and sword were stainless.

They well remembered how he loved to dash
    Into the fight, festooned from summer bowers;
How like a fountain's spray his sabre's flash
    Leaped from a mass of flowers.

And so we carried to his place of rest
    All that of our great Paladin was mortal:
The cross, and not the sabre, on his breast,
    That opes the heavenly portal.

No more of tribute might to us remain;
    But there will still come a time when Freedom's martyrs
A richer guerdon of renown shall gain
    Than gleams in stars and garters.

I hear from out that sunlit land which lies
    Beyond these clouds that gather darkly o'er us,
The happy sounds of industry arise
    In swelling peaceful chorus.

And mingling with these sounds, the glad acclaim
    Of millions undisturbed by war's afflictions,
Crowning each martyr's never dying name
    With grateful benedictions.

In some fair future garden of delights,
    Where flowers shall bloom and song-birds sweetly warble,
Art shall erect the statues of our knights
    In living bronze and marble.

And none of all that bright heroic throng
> Shall wear to far-off time a semblance grander,
Shall still be decked with fresher wreaths of song,
> Than this beloved commander.

The Spanish legend tells us of the Cid,
> That after death he rode, erect, sedately,
Along his lines, even as in life he did,
> In presence yet more stately;

And thus our Stuart, at this moment, seems
> To ride out of our dark and troubled story
Into the region of romance and dreams,
> A realm of light and glory;

And sometimes, when the silver bugles blow,
> That ghostly form, in battle reappearing,
Shall lead his horsemen headlong on the foe,
> In victory careering!

"The Battle Rainbow"[13]

The warm, weary day, was departing—the smile
> Of the sunset gave token the tempest had ceased;
And the lightning yet fitfully gleamed for a while
> On the cloud that sank sullen and dark in the east.

There our army—awaiting the terrible fight
> Of the morrow—lay hopeful, and watching, and still;
Where their tents all the region had sprinkled with white,
> From river to river, o'er meadow and hill.

While above them the fierce cannonade of the sky
> Blazed and burst from the vapors that muffled the sun,
Their "counterfeit clamors" gave forth no reply;

---

13 Written just after the Seven Days of Battle near Richmond in 1862, the poem was suggested by the appearance of a rainbow, the evening before the grand trial of strength between the contending armies. This rainbow overspread the eastern sky, and exactly defined the position of the Confederate army, as seen from the Capitol at Richmond.

345

And slept till the battle, the charge in each gun.

When lo! on the cloud, a miraculous thing!
　　Broke in beauty the rainbow our host to enfold!
The centre o'erspread by its arch, and each wing
　　Suffused with its azure and crimson and gold.

Blest omen of victory, symbol divine
　　Of peace after tumult, repose after pain;
How sweet and how glowing with promise the sign,
　　To eyes that should never behold it again!

For the fierce flame of war on the morrow flashed out,
　　And its thunder-peals filled all the tremulous air:
Over slippery intrenchment and reddened redoubt,
　　Rang the wild cheer of triumph, the cry of despair.

Then a long week of glory and agony came—
　　Of mute supplication, and yearning, and dread;
When day unto day gave the record of fame,
　　And night unto night gave the list of its dead.

We had triumphed—the foe had fled back to his ships—
　　His standard in rags and his legions a wreck—
But alas! the stark faces and colorless lips
　　Of our loved ones, gave triumph's rejoicing a check.

Not yet, oh not yet, as a sign of release,
　　Had the Lord set in mercy his bow in the cloud;
Not yet had the Comforter whispered of peace
　　To the hearts that around us lay bleeding and bowed.

But the promise was given—the beautiful arc,
　　With its brilliant profusion of colors, that spanned
The sky on that exquisite eve, was the mark
　　Of the Infinite Love overarching the land:

And that Love, shining richly and full as the day,
　　Through the tear-drops that moisten each martyr's proud pall,

On the gloom of the past the bright bow shall display

Of Freedom, Peace, Victory, bent over all.

Paul Hamilton Hayne (1830–1886)

Paul Hamilton Hayne is well-known nineteenth-century Southern American poet, critic, and editor, and was even appreciated throughout the country as the unofficial poet laureate of the South. He served in the Confederate army in 1861, and once served as aide-de-camp to South Carolina Governor Francis Pickens. Hayne was instrumental with William Gilmore Simms in the founding of *Russell's Magazine*, for which Hayne served as the editor. His friendship with fellow Southern poet Henry Timrod was also notorious, and as an emerging poet, he published various collections of poems, including a complete edition in 1882. His poetry emphasizes romantic verse, long narrative poems, and ballads, of which the excerpts are of good examples.

"Our Martyrs"

I am sitting lone and weary

On the hearth of my darkened room,

And the low wind's *miserere*

Makes sadder the midnight gloom;

There's a terror that's nameless nigh me—

There's a phantom spell in the air,

And methinks that the dead glide by me,

And the breath of the grave's in my hair!

'Tis a vision of ghastly faces,

All pallid, and worn with pain,

Where the splendor of manhood's graces

Give place to a gory stain;

In a wild and weird procession

They sweep by my startled eyes,

And stern with their fate's fruition,

Seem melting in blood-red skies.

Have they come from the shores supernal,

Have they passed from the spirit's goal,

'Neath the veil of the life eternal,

To dawn on my shrinking soul?

Have they turned from the choiring angels,

Aghast at the woe and dearth
That war, with his dark evangels,
　　　Hath wrought in the loved of earth?

Vain dream! 'mid the far-off mountains
　　　They lie, where the dew-mists weep,
And the murmur of mournful fountains
　　　Breaks over their painful sleep;
On the breast of the lonely meadows,
　　　Safe, safe from the despot's will,
They rest in the star-lit shadows,
　　　And their brows are white and still!

Alas! for the martyred heroes
　　　Cut down at their golden prime,
In a strife with the brutal Neroes,
　　　Who blacken the path of Time!
For them is the voice of wailing,
　　　And the sweet blush-rose departs
From the cheeks of the maidens, paling
　　　O'er the wreck of their broken hearts!

And alas! for the vanished glory
　　　Of a thousand household spells!
And alas! for the tearful story
　　　Of the spirit's fond farewells!
By the flood, on the field, in the forest,
　　　Our bravest have yielded breath,
But the shafts that have smitten sorest,
　　　Were launched by a viewless death!

Oh, Thou, that hast charms of healing,
　　　Descend on a widowed land,
And bind o'er the wounds of feeling
　　　The balms of Thy mystic hand!
Till the hearts that lament and languish,
　　　Renewed by the touch divine,
From the depths of a mortal anguish
　　　May rise to the calm of Thine!

"The Battle of Charleston Harbor"

I

Two hours, or more, beyond the prime of a blithe April day,
The Northman's mailed "Invincibles" steamed up fair Charleston Bay;
They came in sullen file, and slow, low-breasted on the wave,
Black as a midnight front of storm, and silent as the grave.

II

A thousand warrior-hearts beat high as those dread monsters drew
More closely to the game of death across the breezeless blue,
And twice ten thousand hearts of those who watched the scene afar,
Thrill in the awful hush that bides the battle's broadening Star!

III

Each gunner, moveless by his gun, with rigid aspect stands,
The ready linstocks firmly grasped in bold, untrembling hands,
So moveless in their marbled calm, their stern heroic guise,
They looked like forms of statued stone with burning human eyes!

IV

Our banners on the outmost walls, with stately rustling fold,
Flash back from arch and parapet the sunlight's ruddy gold—
They mount to the deep roll of drums, and widely-echoing cheers,
And then—once more, dark, breathless, hushed, wait the grim cannoneers.

V

Onward—in sullen file, and slow, low glooming on the wave,
Near, nearer still, the haughty fleet glides silent as the grave,
When sudden, shivering up the calm, o'er startled flood and shore,
Burst from the sacred Island Fort the thunder-wrath of yore!

VI

Ha! brutal Corsairs! tho' ye come thrice-cased in iron mail,
Beware the storm that's opening now, God's vengeance guides the hail!
Ye strive the ruffian types of Might 'gainst law, and truth, and Right,
Now quail beneath a sturdier Power, and own a mightier Might!

VII

No empty boast! I for while we speak, more furious, wilder, higher,
Dart from the circling batteries a hundred tongues of fire.
The waves gleam red, the lurid vault of heaven seems rent above.
Fight on! oh! knightly Gentlemen! for faith, and home, and love!

VIII

There's not in all that line of flame, one soul that would not rise,

To seize the Victor's wreath of blood, tho' Death must give the prize—
There's not in all this anxious crowd that throngs the ancient Town,
A maid who does not yearn for power to strike one despot down.

IX

The strife grows fiercer! ship by ship the proud Armada sweeps,
Where hot from Sumter's raging breast the volleyed lightning leaps;
And ship by ship, raked, overborne, 'ere burned the sunset bloom,
Crawls seaward, like a hangman's hearse bound to his felon tomb!

X

Oh! glorious Empress of the Main! from out thy storied spires,
Thou well mayst peal thy bells of joy, and light thy festal fires—
Since Heaven this day hath striven for thee, hath nerved thy dauntless sons,
And thou, in clear-eyed faith hast seen God's Angels near the guns!

J. Augustine Signaigo (1835–1876)

"If You Love Me"

You have told me that you love me,
    That you worship at my shrine;
That no purity above me
    Can on earth be more divine.
Though the kind words you have spoken.
    Sound to me most sweetly strange,
Will your pledges ne'er be broken?
    Will there be in you no change?

If you love me half so wildly—
    Half so madly as you say,
Listen to me, darling, mildly—
    Would you do aught I would pray?
If you would, then hear the thunder
    Of our country's cannon speak!
While by war she's rent asunder,
    Do not come my love to seek.

If you love me, do not ponder,
    Do not breathe what you would say,
Do not look at me with wonder,

Join your country in the fray.
Go! your aid and right hand lend her,
    Breast the tyrant's angry blast:
Be her own and my defender—
    Strike for freedom to the last,

Then I'll vow to love none other,
    While you nobly dare and do;
As you're faithful to our mother,
    So I'll faithful prove to you.
But return not while the thunder
    Lives in one invading sword;
Strike the despot's hirelings under—
    Own no master but the Lord.

"Battle of Belmont"

I
Now glory to our Southern cause, and praises be to God,
That He hath met the Southron's foe, and scourged him with his rod:
On the tented plains of Belmont, in their might the Vandals came,
And they gave unto destruction all they found, with sword and flame;
But they met a stout resistance from a little band that day,
Who swore nobly they would conquer, or return to mother clay.

II
But the Vandals with presumption—for they came in all their might—
Gave free vent unto their feelings, for they thought to win the fight;
And they forced our little cohorts to the very river's brink,
With a breath between destruction and of life's remaining link:
When the cannon of McCown, belching fire from out its mouth,
Brought destruction to the Vandals and protection to the South.

III
There was Pillow, Polk and Cheatham, who had sworn that day on high
That field should see them conquer, or that field should see them die;
And amid the groan of dying and amid the battle's din,
Came the echo back from heaven, that they should that battle win:
And amid the boom of cannons, and amid the clash of swords,
Came destruction to the foeman—and the vengeance was the Lord's!

IV

When the fight was raging hottest, came the wild and cheering cry,

That brought terror to the foeman, and that raised our spirits high!

It was "Cheatham!" "Cheatham!" "Cheatham!" that the Vandals' ears did sting,

And our boys caught up the echo till it made the welkin ring;

And the moment that the Hessians thought the fight was surely won,

From the crackling of our rifles—bravely then they had to run!

V

Then they ran unto their transports in deep terror and dismay,

And their great grandchildren's children will be shamed to name that day;

For the woe they came to bring to the people of the South

Was returned tenfold to them at the cannon's booming mouth:

And the proud old Mississippi ran that day a horrid flood,

For its banks were deeply crimsoned with the hireling Northman's blood.

VI

Let us think of those who fell there, fighting foremost with the foe,

And who nobly struck for Freedom, dealing Tyranny a blow:

Like the ocean beating wildly 'gainst a prow of adamant,

Or the storm that keeps on bursting, but cannot destroy the plant;

Brave Lieutenant Walker, wounded, still fought on the bloody field,

Cheering on his noble comrades, ne'er unto the foe to yield!

VII

None e'er knew him but to love him, the brave martyr to his clime—

Now his name belongs to Freedom, to the very end of Time:

And the last words that he uttered will forgotten be by few:

"I have bravely fought them, mother—I have bravely fought for you!"

Let his memory be green in the hearts who love the South,

And his noble deeds the theme that shall dwell in every mouth.

VIII

In the hottest of the battle stood a Vandal bunting rag,

Proudly to the breeze 'twas floating in defiance to our flag;

And our Southern boys knew well that, to bring that bunting down,

They would meet the angel death in his sternest, maddest frown;

But it could not gallant Armstrong, dauntless Vollmer, or brave Lynch,

Though ten thousand deaths confronted, from the task of honor flinch!

IX

And they charged upon that bunting, guarded by grim-visaged Death,

Who had withered all around it with the blister of his breath;

But they plucked it from his grasp, and brave Vollmner waved it high,

On the gory field of battle, where the three were doomed to die;

But before their spirits fled came the death-shout of the three,

Cheering for the sunny South and beloved old Tennessee!

X

Let the horrors of this day to the foe a warning be,

That the Lord is with the South, that His arm is with the free;

That her soil is pure and spotless, as her clear and sunny sky.

And that he who dare pollute it on her soil shall basely die;

For His fiat hath gone forth, e'en among the Hessian horde,

That the South has got His blessing, for the South is of the Lord.

XI

Then glory to our Southern cause, and praises give to God,

That He hath met the Southron's foe and scourged him with His rod;

That He hath been upon our side, with all His strength and might,

And battled for the Southern cause in every bloody fight;

Let us, in meek humility, to all the world proclaim,

We bless and glorify the Lord, and battle in His name.

"The Heights of Mission Ridge"

When the foes, in conflict heated,

    Battled over road and bridge,

While Bragg sullenly retreated

    From the heights of Mission Ridge—

There, amid the pines and wildwood,

    Two opposing colonels fell,

Who had schoolmates been in childhood,

    And had loved each other well.

There, amid the roar and rattle,

    Facing Havoc's fiery breath,

Met the wounded two in battle,

    In the agonies of death.

But they saw each other reeling

    On the dead and dying men,

And the old time, full of feeling,

    Came upon them once again.

When that night the moon came creeping,

    With its gold streaks, o'er the slain,

She beheld two soldiers, sleeping,

Free from every earthly pain.
Close beside the mountain heather,
Where the rocks obscure the sand,
They had died, it seems, together,
As they clasped each other's hand.

James R. Randall (1839–1908)

James Ryder Randall is an American serviceman and poet. He wrote a number of war songs that were vibrant in style, function, and feeling, many of which become marching songs and hymns, still recognized today for their impact on American music and poetic tradition.

"The Battle-Cry of the South"[14]

Brothers! the thunder-cloud is black,
And the wail of the South wings forth;
Will ye cringe to the hot tornado's rack,
And the vampires of the North?
Strike! ye can win a martyr's goal,
Strike! with a ruthless hand—
Strike! with the vengeance of the soul,
For your bright, beleaguered land!
To arms! to arms! for the South needs help,
And a craven is he who flees—
For ye have the sword of the Lion's Whelp,
And the God of the Maccabees!

Arise! though the stars have a rugged glare,
And the moon has a wrath-blurred crown—
Brothers! a blessing is ambushed there
In the cliffs of the Father's frown:
Arise! ye are worthy the wondrous light
Which the Sun of Justice gives—
In the caves and sepulchres of night
Jehovah the Lord King lives!
To arms! to arms! for the South needs help,

---

14 At the beginning of the poem, there is a quotation from *Maccabees I*, which says: "Arm yourselves and be valiant men, and see that ye be in readiness against the morning, that ye may fight with these nations that are assembled against us, to destroy us and our sanctuary. For it is better for us to die in battle than to behold the calamities of our people and our sanctuary."

And a craven is he who flees—
For ye have the sword of the Lion's Whelp,
And the God of the Maccabees!

Think of the dead by the Tennessee,
In their frozen shrouds of gore—
Think of the mothers who shall see
Those darling eyes no more!
But better are they in a hero grave
Than the serfs of time and breath,
For they are the children of the brave,
And the cherubim of death!
To arms! to arms! for the South needs help,
And a craven is he who flees—
For ye have the sword of the Lion's Whelp,
And the God of the Maccabees!

Better the charnels of the West,
And a hecatomb of lives,
Than the foul invader as a guest
'Mid your sisters and your wives—
But a spirit lurketh in every maid,
Though, brothers, ye should quail,
To sharpen a Judith's lurid blade,
And the livid spike of Jael!
To arms! to arms! for the South needs help,
And a craven is he who flees—
For ye have the sword of the Lion's Whelp,
And the God of the Maccabees!

Brothers! I see you tramping by,
With the gladiator gaze,
And your shout is the Macedonian cry
Of the old, heroic days!
March on! with trumpet and with drum,
With rifle, pike, and dart,
And die—if even death must come—
Upon your country's heart!
To arms! to arms! for the South needs help,

And a craven is he who flees—
For ye have the sword of the Lion's Whelp,
And the God of the Maccabees!

Brothers! the thunder-cloud is black,
And the wail of the South wings forth;
Will ye cringe to the hot tornado's rack,
And the vampires of the North?
Strike! ye can win a martyr's goal,
Strike! with a ruthless hand—
Strike! with the vengeance of the soul
For your bright, beleaguered land!
To arms! to arms! for the South needs help,
And a craven is he who flees—
For ye have the sword of the Lion's Whelp,
And the God of the Maccabees!

"The Cameo Bracelet"

Eva sits on the ottoman there,
Sits by a Psyche carved in stone,
With just such a face, and just such an air,
As Esther upon her throne.

She's sifting lint for the brave who bleed,
And I watch her fingers float and flow
Over the linen, as, thread by thread,
It flakes to her lap like snow.

A bracelet clinks on her delicate wrist,
Wrought, as Cellini's were at Rome,
Out of the tears of the amethyst,
And the wan Vesuvian foam.

And full on the bauble-crest alway—
A cameo image keen and fine—
Glares thy impetuous knife, Corday,
And the lava-locks are thine!

I thought of the war-wolves on our trail,
      Their gaunt fangs sluiced with gouts of blood;
Till the Past, in a dead, mesmeric veil,
      Drooped with a wizard flood.

Till the surly blaze through the iron bars
      Shot to the hearth with a pang and cry—
And a lank howl plunged from the Champ de Mars
      To the Column of July—

Till Corday sprang from the gem, I swear,
      And the dove-eyed damsel I knew had flown—
For Eva was not on the ottoman there,
      By the Psyche carved in stone.

She grew like a Pythoness flushed with fate,
      With the incantation in her gaze,
A lip of scorn—an arm of hate—
      And a dirge of the "Marseillaise!"

Eva, the vision was not wild,
      When wreaked on the tyrants of the land—
For you were transfigured to Nemesis, child,
      With the dagger in your hand!

"John Pelham"

Just as the spring came laughing through the strife,
      With all its gorgeous cheer;
In the bright April of historic life
      Fell the great cannoneer.

The wondrous lulling of a hero's breath
      His bleeding country weeps—
Hushed in the alabaster arms of death,
      Our young Marcellus sleeps.

Nobler and grander than the Child of Rome,
      Curbing his chariot steeds;

The knightly scion of a Southern home
    Dazzled the land with deeds.

Gentlest and bravest in the battle brunt,
    The champion of the truth,
He bore his banner to the very front
    Of our immortal youth.

A clang of sabres 'mid Virginian snow,
    The fiery pang of shells—
And there's a wail of immemorial woe
    In Alabama dells.

The pennon drops that led the sacred band
    Along the crimson field;
The meteor blade sinks from the nerveless hand
    Over the spotless shield.

We gazed and gazed upon that beauteous face
    While 'round the lips and eyes,
Couched in the marble slumber, flashed the grace
    Of a divine surprise.

Oh, mother of a blessed soul on high!
    Thy tears may soon be shed—
Think of thy boy with princes of the sky,
    Among the Southern dead.

How must he smile on this dull world beneath,
    Fevered with swift renown—
He—with the martyr's amaranthine wreath
    Twining the victor's crown!

W. Gordon McCabe (1841–1920)

W. Gordon McCabe is the former Captain of A.P. Hill's Corps, Army of Northern Virginia. He was also a member of the official Virginia State Committee in charge of commissioning the statue of Robert E. Lee at Gettysburg. The two excerpts were written when he was young, possibly reflecting his experiences in the Army of Northern Virginia.

"Christmas Night of '62"

THE WINTRY blast goes wailing by,
    The snow is falling overhead;
    I hear the lonely sentry's tread,
And distant watch-fires light the sky.

Dim forms go flitting through the gloom;
    The soldiers cluster round the blaze,
    To talk of other Christmas days,
And softly speak of home and home.

My sabre swinging overhead
    Gleams in the watch-fire's fitful glow,
    While fiercely drives the blinding snow,
And memory leads me to the dead.

My thoughts go wandering to and fro,
    Vibrating 'twixt the Now and Then;
    I see the low-browed home again,
The old hall wreathed with mistletoe.

And sweetly from the far-off years
    Comes borne the laughter faint and low,
    The voices of the Long Ago!
My eyes are wet with tender tears.

I feel again the mother-kiss,
    I see again the glad surprise
    That lightened up the tranquil eyes
And brimmed them o'er with tears of bliss,

As, rushing from the old hall-door,
    She fondly clasped her wayward boy—
    Her face all radiant with the joy
She felt to see him home once more.

My sabre swinging on the bough
    Gleams in the watch-fire's fitful glow,

While fiercely drives the blinding snow
Aslant upon my saddened brow.

Those cherished faces all are gone!
  Asleep within the quiet graves
  Where lies the snow in drifting waves,—
And I am sitting here alone.

There's not a comrade here to-night
  But knows that loved ones far away
  On bended knees this night will pray:
"God bring our darling from the fight."

But there are none to wish me back,
  For me no yearning prayers arise.
  The lips are mute and closed the eyes—
My home is in the bivouac.

"Captives Going Home"

No flaunting banners o'er them wave,
  No arms flash back the sun's bright ray,
No shouting crowds around them throng,
  No music cheers them on their way:
They're going home. By adverse fate
  Compelled their trusty swords to sheathe;
True soldiers they, even though disarmed—
  Heroes, though robbed of victory's wreath.

Brave Southrons! 'Tis with sorrowing hearts
  We gaze upon them through our tears,
And sadly feel how vain were all
  Their heroic deeds through weary years;
Yet 'mid their enemies they move
  With firm, bold step and dauntless mien:
Oh, Liberty! in every age,
  Such have thy chosen heroes been.

Going home! Alas, to them the words

Bring visions fraught with gloom and woe:
Since last they saw those cherished homes
　　The legions of the invading foe
Have swept them, simoon-like, along,
　　Spreading destruction with the wind!
"They found a garden, but they left
　　A howling wilderness behind."

Ah! in those desolated homes
　　To which the "fate of war has come,"
Sad is the welcome—poor the feast—
　　That waits the soldier's coming home;
Yet loving ones will round him throng,
　　With smiles more tender, if less gay,
And joy will brighten pallid cheeks
　　At sight of the dear boys in gray.

Aye, give them welcome home, fair South,
　　For you they've made a deathless name;
Bright through all after-time will glow
　　The glorious record of their fame.
They made a nation. What, though soon
　　Its radiant sun has seemed to set;
The past has shown what they can do,
　　The future holds bright promise yet.

3. "The Brotherly War" and its Reflections

Although there were conflicting poetic voices respectively for the North and South, there were also a number of poets who stood on the higher principle of humanity to reflect the War itself, for instance, John Greenleaf Whittier's "pacifism" that opposed such a war by the Union to prevent secession, Francis Miles Finch's humanitarian attitude that "treated the dead of both Confederate and Union soldiers as equals despite the lingering rancor of the war," Allen Tate's ideological remembrance of the Confederate soldiers without regarding whether they fought for the North and South, and other similar voices.

John Greenleaf Whittier (1807–1892)

John Greenleaf Whittier is an American poet and abolitionist, a household name in both England and the United States at his time. He is best remembered both as a staunch abolitionist with a Quaker's pacifism and as a poet whose best known works were nostalgic tributes to a bucolic vision of early 19th century New England. True to his Quaker beliefs, he did not support a war by the Union to prevent secession, a position which put him at odds with the more radical proponents of abolitionism in Boston. Introduced to poetry by a teacher, he wrote his first poem, "The Exile's Departure", in 1826. Later, he published a series of stirring lyrics and moral denunciations whose titles can tell their own story: *Voices of Freedom* (1841), *The Panorama, and Other Poems* (1856), *In War-Time* (1863). After the Civil War, he wrote the beauty of New England's scenery, the sober charm of her rural life in his masterpiece *Snow-Bound* (1865), *The Tent on the Beach* (1867), and a number of other slight poems. The excerpt is a war poem in terms of its anti-slavery stand.

"Barbara Frietchie"[15]

Up from the meadows rich with corn,
Clear in the cool September morn.

The clustered spires of Frederick stand
Green-walled by the hills of Maryland.

Round about them orchards sweep,
Apple and peach tree fruited deep,

Fair as the garden of the Lord
To the eyes of the famished rebel horde,

On that pleasant morn of the early fall
When Lee marched over the mountain-wall;

Over the mountains winding down,
Horse and foot, into Frederick town.

---

15 John Greenleaf Whittier explained the writing of this poem in his original collection *In War-Time* (1863): "This poem was written in strict conformity to the account of the incident as I had it from respectable and trustworthy sources. It has since been the subject of a good deal of conflicting testimony, and the story was probably incorrect in some of its details. It is admitted by all that Barbara Frietchie was no myth, but a worthy and highly esteemed gentlewoman, intensely loyal and a hater of the Slavery Rebellion, holding her Union flag sacred and keeping it with her Bible; that when the Confederates halted before her house, and entered her dooryard, she denounced them in vigorous language, shook her cane in their faces, and drove them out; and when General Burnside's troops followed close upon Jackson's, she waved her flag and cheered them. It is stated that May Qnantrell, a brave and loyal lady in another part of the city, did wave her flag in sight of the Confederates. It is possible that there has been a blending of the two incidents."

Forty flags with their silver stars,
Forty flags with their crimson bars,

Flapped in the morning wind: the sun
Of noon looked down, and saw not one.

Up rose old Barbara Frietchie then,
Bowed with her fourscore years and ten;

Bravest of all in Frederick town,
She took up the flag the men hauled down;

In her attic window the staff she set,
To show that one heart was loyal yet.

Up the street came the rebel tread,
Stonewall Jackson riding ahead.

Under his slouched hat left and right
He glanced; the old flag met his sight.

"Halt!"—the dust-brown ranks stood fast.
"Fire!"—out blazed the rifle-blast.

It shivered the window, pane and sash;
It rent the banner with seam and gash.

Quick, as it fell, from the broken staff
Dame Barbara snatched the silken scarf.

She leaned far out on the window-sill,
And shook it forth with a royal will.

"Shoot, if you must, this old gray head,
But spare your country's flag," she said.

A shade of sadness, a blush of shame,
Over the face of the leader came;

The nobler nature within him stirred
To life at that woman's deed and word.

"Who touches a hair of yon gray head
Dies like a dog! March on!" he said.

All day long through Frederick street
Sounded the tread of marching feet.

All day long that free flag tost
Over the heads of the rebel host.

Ever its torn folds rose and fell
On the loyal winds that loved it well;

And through the hill-gaps sunset light
Shone over it with a warm good-night.

Barbara Frietchie's work is o'er,
And the Rebel rides on his raids no more.

Honor to her! and let a tear
Fall, for her sake, on Stonewall's bier.

Over Barbara Frietchie's grave,
Flag of Freedom and Union, wave!

Peace and order and beauty draw
Round thy symbol of light and law;

And ever the stars above look down
On thy stars below in Frederick town!

Francis Miles Finch (1827–1907)

Francis Miles Finch was an American judge, poet, and academic, associated with the early years of Cornell University. He wrote poetry throughout his life, but declined a chair in rhetoric literature at Cornell. His best known poem, "The Blue and the Gray", written in remembrance of the dead of the American Civil War, treated the dead of both Confederate and

Union soldiers as equals despite the lingering rancor of the war.[16]

"The Blue and the Gray"

By the flow of the inland river,
    Whence the fleets of iron have fled,
Where the blades of the grave-grass quiver,
    Asleep are the ranks of the dead:
        Under the sod and the dew,
            Waiting the judgment-day;
        Under the one, the Blue,
            Under the other, the Gray

These in the robings of glory,
    Those in the gloom of defeat,
All with the battle-blood gory,
    In the dusk of eternity meet:
        Under the sod and the dew,
            Waiting the judgement-day
        Under the laurel, the Blue,
            Under the willow, the Gray.

From the silence of sorrowful hours
    The desolate mourners go,
Lovingly laden with flowers
    Alike for the friend and the foe;
        Under the sod and the dew,
            Waiting the judgement-day;
        Under the roses, the Blue,
            Under the lilies, the Gray.

So with an equal splendor,
    The morning sun-rays fall,
With a touch impartially tender,

---

16 On April 25th, 1866, the women of Columbus, Mississippi, placed flowers of remembrance on the graves of soldiers who died in the Civil War. They laid the flowers impartially on the graves of both Union and Confederate soldiers. The city of Columbus was the first place where the dead of both sides were commemorated and this act of respect and forgiveness was important in the establishment of the Memorial Day holiday in the United States.

On the blossoms blooming for all:
Under the sod and the dew,
Waiting the judgment-day;
Broidered with gold, the Blue,
Mellowed with gold, the Gray.

So, when the summer calleth,
On forest and field of grain,
With an equal murmur falleth
The cooling drip of the rain:
Under the sod and the dew,
Waiting the judgment-day,
Wet with the rain, the Blue
Wet with the rain, the Gray.

Sadly, but not with upbraiding,
The generous deed was done,
In the storm of the years that are fading
No braver battle was won:
Under the sod adn the dew,
Waiting the judgment-day;
Under the blossoms, the Blue,
Under the garlands, the Gray

No more shall the war cry sever,
Or the winding rivers be red;
They banish our anger forever
When they laurel the graves of our dead!
Under the sod and the dew,
Waiting the judgment-day,
Love and tears for the Blue,
Tears and love for the Gray.

Chapter VII

British Poetry of the First World War (1914–1918)

The First World War, or the Great War, was a global war originating in Europe that lasted from 28 July 1914 to 11 November 1918, contemporaneously described as "the war to end all wars". The research anthology is sceptical of those "grand narratives" that glorify nation, religion and ideological status, having offered comprehensive explanations of an immensely complicated or even chaotic reality. For us, World War I was a war among capitalists; it benefited capitalism and imperialism; promoted the interests of the powerful and encouraged victims of war to accept their pain rather than opposing the exploitative economic system that promoted such suffering, and finally, anything that sustained the war and discouraged workers from turning against their oppressors was a useful tool of the ruling class, including employment of the War as an excuse and buffer zone for alleviating class tensions.

Any war involves an almost inevitable blurring of the opposition between love and hate (of course, politically), since soldiers are usually expected to love their countries, families, and comrades, but feel murderous hate for the enemy that had been identified and constructed by the dominants. The clear distinction between love and hate must be "deconstructed," for instance, to clarify the good term "England" or "Britain". It has been known that soldiers are devoted to "England," but a Marxist might regard "England" either as a mere abstraction, or as the seat of a gigantic exploitative empire, or as a conventional name for the current bourgeois power structure, devoted to nationalism, capitalism, and ruling-class interests. Similarly, workers from England, France, Germany, Austria, Russia, and all other nations should be united together and not allow themselves to be turned into enemies by the "big men of the world".

The First World War I was supposedly fought to promote and defend such "higher" objectives, whether "liberty" or "kultur" for which soldiers had much more to fear from enemy combatants, motivated by supposedly lofty human ideals: Germans took pride in a self-proclaimed "Kultur" which they considered superior to England's, and accordingly the English considered their culture much better than the Germans'. All these ideas are pathological. Perhaps, the true heroes about the war are those pacifists and conscientious objectors, but they have been often at great peril: War resisters were often imprisoned; many such people were forced to join the army where those who disobeyed orders were imprisoned; opponents of the war were denounced as cowards or even traitors.

We can imagine that if enough people in all the countries involved had followed the conscientious objectors' lead, the war would have been impossible to begin or sustain. Pacifism believes that violence, even in self-defence, is unjustifiable under any conditions and that negotiation is preferable to war as a means of solving disputes. Known as conscientious objectors, they refused to fight though some were willing to help the country by working in non-combat roles such as medical orderlies, stretcher-bearers, ambulance drivers, cooks or labourers.[1]

This critical anthology believes that Anglo-American Cultural Materialism or New Historicism has similarly instructed that power circulates in cultures and marginalised groups had to be focused for such groups as those disabled, are particularly powerless. During the War, so many soldiers—both officers and enlisted men alike—were fairly well educated and thus able to produce so many literate, potentially publishable reactions to their service. "Dulce et Decorum Est" alludes to a famous line by Horace, often translated as "It is sweet and appropriate to die for one's country." While some evoke an entire cultural ethos that stresses such ideals as patriotism, selfless service, and self-sacrifice, millions of others dissented from them more than we can imagine. The only persons who benefited from the war were war profiteers, and therefore it is not surprising that this war led to the rise of the first Marxist government in history.

This section divides "British Poetry of the First World War" into five categories: Anonymous "Trench Songs" to mark the general atmosphere of the War, Abner Cosens' collection of "War Rhymes" to define the very nature of the War, "Reflective Voices" to address the various topics initiated by the War, "Patriotic Voices" to praise those virtues in the War, and finally, "Anti-war Voices" to anatomise the pathology of the War or all wars.

---

1 In Great Britain, the No-Conscription Fellowship mounted a vigorous campaign against the punishment and imprisonment of conscientious objectors. In April 1939 Neville Chamberlain announced a return to conscription. However, lessons had been learned from the First World War. Tribunals were set up to deal with claims for exemption on conscience grounds, but this time there were no military representatives acting as prosecutors. In 1940, with the British government expecting a German invasion at any time, public opinion turned against Conscientious Objectors.

1. Trench Songs

The War was strikingly typified by its lack of movement and the years of stalemate exemplified on the Western Front from autumn 1914 to the spring of 1918. Consequently, life in the trenches was horrible, as had been described: deaths were daily, rats in their millions infested trenches, lice were never-ending, breeding in the seams of filthy clothing and causing men to itch unceasingly, frogs were found in shell holes covered in water, and slugs and horned beetles crowded the sides of the trench. Given that each side's front line was constantly under watch by snipers and look-outs during daylight, the movement was logically restricted until night fell. Thus, once men had concluded their assigned tasks, they were free to attend to more personal matters, among which reading, letter-writing, and singing were the daily killings of time. Thus came trench songs, slow, moving and sentimental.

Anonymous: "Oh! It's a Lovely War"

Up to your waist in water, up to your eyes in slush,

using the kind of language that makes the sergeant blush;

who wouldn't join the army, that's what we all enquire,

don't we pity the poor civilians sitting beside the fire?

CHORUS

Oh! Oh! Oh! It's a lovely war,

who wouldn't be a soldier eh!

Oh! it's a shame to take the pay.

As soon as 'reveille' has gone, we feel just as heavy as lead,

we never get up till the sergeant brings our breakfast up to bed.

Oh! Oh! Oh! It's a lovely war,

what do we want with eggs and ham

when we've got plum and apple jam?

Form fours! Right turn!

How shall we spend the money we earn?

Oh! Oh! Oh! It's a lovely war.

When does a soldier grumble?

When does he make a fuss?

No one is more contented in all the world than us:

Oh! it's a 'cushy' life, boys really we love it so,

once a fellow was sent on leave and simply refus'd to go.

CHORUS

Oh! Oh! It's a lovely war, (etc.)

Come to the Cookhouse door boys, sniff at the lovely stew.

Who is it says the Col'nel gets better grub than you?

Any complaints this morning? Do we complain? Not we,

what's the matter with lumps of onion floating around the tea?

CHORUS

Oh! Oh! Oh! It's a lovely war, (etc.)

"Bombed Last Night"

('Drunk Last Night and Drunk the Night Before')

Bombed last night and bombed the night before,

Going to get bombed tonight if we never get bombed anymore.

When we're bombed, we are scared as we can be.

Can't stop the bombing from old Higher Germany.

CHORUS

They're warning us, they're warning us

One shell hole for the four of us

Thank your lucky stars there is no more of us

'Cos one of us can fill it all alone.

Gassed last night and gassed the night before,

Going to get gassed tonight if we never get gassed anymore.

When we're gassed we're sick as we can be.

For Phosgene and Mustard Gas is much too much for me.

CHORUS

They're killing us, they're killing us

One respirator for the four of us.

Thank your lucky stars there is no more of us

So one of us can take it all alone.

"I Want to Go Home"

I want to go home, I want to go home.

I don't want to go to the trenches no more,

Where whizzbangs and shrapnel they whistle and roar.

Take me over the sea where the Alleyman can't get at me.

Oh my, I don't want to die, I want go home.

I want to go home, I want to go home,

I don't want to visit *la Belle France* no more,

For oh the Jack Johnsons they make such a roar.

Take me over the sea where the snipers they can't snipe at me.

Oh my, I don't want to die, I want to go home.

2. War Rhymes

Abner Cosens is little known today with his pseudonym as "Wayfarer". In his collected booklet *War Rhymes* (The Project Gutenberg EBook #19358), Abner Cosens wrote the themes of all these war rhymes: "The outbreak of hostilities, the invasion of Belgium, the Old Land in it and the rush of the British born to enlist, the early indifference of the majority of Canadians, the unemployment and distress of the winter of 1914–1915, the heartlessness of Germany, Canada stirred by the valor of her first battalions, recruiting general throughout the country, the slackness of the United States, financial and political profiteering in all countries, smaller European nations playing for position, Italy joining the Allies, the debacle of Russia, the awful casualty lists, the return of disabled soldiers, the ceaseless war work of our women, the United States at last declaring war on Germany, the final line up and defeat of the Hun, and the horror and apparent uselessness of it all." The excerpts "Modern Diplomacy, or How the War Started", "The Allied Forces" and "A Call to the Colors" were written from August 1914 to November 1915.

Anonymous: "Modern Diplomacy, or How the War Started"

Said Austria,—"You murderous Serb,

You the peace of all Europe disturb;

    Get down on your knees,

    And apologize, please,

Or I'll kick you right off my front curb."

Said Serbia,—"Don't venture too far,

Or I'll call in my uncle, the Czar;
    He won't see me licked,
    Nor insulted, nor kicked,
So you better leave things as they are."

Said the Kaiser,—"That Serb's a disgrace.
We must teach him to stay in his place,
    If Russia says boo,
    I'm in the game, too,
And right quickly we'll settle the case."

The Czar said,—"My cousin the Kaiser,
Was always a good advertiser;
    He's determined to fight,
    And insists he is right,
But soon he'll be older and wiser."

"For forty-four summers," said France,
"I have waited and watched for a chance
    To wrest Alsace-Lorraine
    From the Germans again,
And now is the time to advance."

Said Belgium,—"When armies immense
Pour over my boundary fence,
    I'll awake from my nap,
    And put up a scrap
They'll remember a hundred years hence."

Said John Bull,—"This 'ere Kaiser's a slob,
And 'is word isn't worth 'arf a bob,
    (If I lets Belgium suffer,
    I'm a blank bloomin' duffer)
So 'ere goes for a crack at 'is nob."

Said Italy,—"I think I'll stay out,
Till I know what this row is about;
    It's a far better plan,
    Just to sell my banan',

Till the issue is plain beyond doubt."

Said our good uncle Samuel, "I swaow
I had better keep aout of this raow,
    For with Mormons, and Niggers,
    And Greasers, I figgers
I have all I kin handle just naow."

"The Allied Forces"

When Johnnie Bull pledges his word,
To keep it he'll gird on his sword,
    While allies and sons
    Will shoulder their guns;
The prince, and the peasant, and lord.

First there's bold Tommy Aitkins himself,
For a shilling a day of poor pelf,
    And for love of his King,
    And the fun of the thing,
He fights till he's laid on the shelf.

Brave Taffy is ready to go
As soon as the war bugles blow;
    He fights like the diel,
    When it comes to cold steel,
And dies with his face to the foe.

And Donald from North Inverness,
Who fights in a ballet girl's dress;
    He likes a free limb,
    No tight skirts for him,
Impending his march to success.

The gun runner, stern, from Belfast,
Now stands at the head of the mast;
    If a tempest should come,
    Or a mine or a bomb,
He will stick to his post to the last.

And Hogan, that broth of a lad,
Home Ruler from Bally-na-fad,
    Writes—"I'm now in the trench
    With the English and French,
And we're licking the Germans, be dad!"

The Cockney Canuck from Toronto,
Whom Maple leaves hardly stick on to,
    Made haste to enlist,
    To fight the mailed fist,
When Canadian born didn't want to.

From where the wide-winged albatross
Floats white 'neath the Southern Cross,
    There came the swift cruisers,
    And Germans are losers;
Australians want no Kaiser boss.

From sheep run, pine forest and fern,
The stalwart New Zealanders turn
    To the land of their sires,
    For with ancestral fires
Their bosoms in ardor still burn.

The tall, turbanned, heathen Hindoo
Is proud to be in the game too,
    For the joy of his life,
    Is to help in the strife
Of the sahibs, and see the war through.

The Frenchman who made wooden shoes,
While airing his Socialist views,
    Deserted his bench
    For the horrible trench,
As soon as he heard the war news.

The wild, woolly, grinning, Turco,
From where the fierce desert winds blow,
    Will give up his life

In the thick of the strife,
And go where the good niggers go.

The versatile Jap's in the game,
Because of a treaty he came,
For old Johnnie Bull,
Will have his hands full,
The bellicose Germans to tame.

The hard riding Cossack and Russ,
At the very first sign of a fuss,
Cried—"Long live the white Czar,
We are off to the war,
No more Nihilist nonsense for us."

The bold Belgian burgher from Brussels,
Has fought in a hundred hard tussles,
And is still going strong,
Nor will it be long,
Ere the foe back to Berlin he hustles.

The hardy cantankerous Serb,
Whom even the Turk couldn't curb,
In having a go
With Emperor Joe,
Will the plans of the Kaiser disturb.

The fierce mountaineers of King Nick
Got into the ring good and quick,
They are never afraid,
For to fight is their trade,
While their wives have the living to pick.

"A Call to the Colors"

Ye strong young men of Huron,
Ye sons of Britons true,
Your fathers fought for freedom,
And now it's up to you;

Your brother's blood is calling,
    For you they fought and died,
Brave boys with souls unconquered,
    By Huns are crucified.

Ten million Hunnish outlaws,
    The Kaiser's tools and slaves,
Have strewn the sea with corpses,
    And scarred the earth with graves;
They know no god but mammon;
    No law but sword and flame,
They crush the weaker peoples,
    With deeds we dare not name.

See Belgium rent and bleeding,
    The Kaiser's hellish work,
Armenia vainly pleading
    For mercy from the Turk.
The Poles and Serbs are dying
    The victims of the Huns,
With anguished voices crying,
    "O send us men and guns!"

Think of the Lusitania,
    Of martyred Nurse Cavell,
Then say, "Can these be human
    Who act like fiends of hell."
The Empire's in the conflict,
    And bound to see it through;
Each man the old flag shelters,
    Must share the burden too.

Then rise, ye sons of Huron,
    All hell has broken loose,
The Kaiser's strafe is on us,
    With him we make no truce.
Come, rally to the colors
    Till victory is won,
Your King and country need you,

And duty must be done.

3. Reflective Voices

Just before, during, and after the war, a number of poets took the looming tragedy into serious consideration, and were greatly afraid that the world would collapse or terminate itself with modern advanced technology in weaponry. "Reflective Voices" thus refer to those conscientious evaluation, revaluation, meditation, and re-examination of preceding social context, the War itself, and its unexpected consequences. These poets have not joined the fighting in the war, but they wrote the war as those participating in, representatives of whom include Thomas Hardy, who, for instance, had a rational prophecy of the War; A. E. Housman, who thought over the inherent contradiction between pastoral peacefulness and wars, especially the looming "Great War", W. B. Yeats, who had been afraid that "the centre cannot hold" and "things fall apart", so are poets with similar lines. In addition, the section concludes with Philip Larkin and G. K. Chesterton's war poems as remembrance or commemoration.

Thomas Hardy (1840–1928)

"Channel Firing"[2]

That night your great guns, unawares,
Shook all our coffins as we lay,
And broke the chancel window-squares,
We thought it was the Judgment-day

And sat upright. While drearisome
Arose the howl of wakened hounds:
The mouse let fall the altar-crumb,
The worms drew back into the mounds,

The glebe cow drooled. Till God called, "No;
It's gunnery practice out at sea
Just as before you went below;
The world is as it used to be:

---

2 Published several months before the actual start of World War I, the poem imagines that some dead folks buried in a country churchyard are likely to hear gunnery practice in the English Channel meditating the booming noise of the Final Judgment at hand. Written with a humorous and macabre tone, it implies that humans have not changed much over the centuries, a rational prophecy that another war–The First World War is looming large, which shows its cultural pathology to its extremes.

"All nations striving strong to make
Red war yet redder. Mad as hatters
They do no more for Christés sake
Than you who are helpless in such matters.

"That this is not the judgment-hour
For some of them's a blessed thing,
For if it were they'd have to scour
Hell's floor for so much threatening. . . .

"Ha, ha. It will be warmer when
I blow the trumpet (if indeed
I ever do; for you are men,
And rest eternal sorely need)."

So down we lay again. "I wonder,
Will the world ever saner be,"
Said one, "than when He sent us under
In our indifferent century!"

And many a skeleton shook his head.
"Instead of preaching forty year,"
My neighbour Parson Thirdly said,
"I wish I had stuck to pipes and beer."

Again the guns disturbed the hour,
Roaring their readiness to avenge,
As far inland as Stourton Tower,
And Camelot, and starlit Stonehenge.

"England to Germany in 1914"[3]

'O England, may God punish thee!'
—Is it that Teuton genius flowers!
Only to breathe malignity
Upon its friend of earlier hours?
We have eaten your bread, you have eaten ours,

---

3 The poem was written in the 1914 Autumn.

We have loved your burgs, your pines' green moan,

Fair Rhine-stream, and its storied towers;

Your shining souls of deathless dowers

Have won us as they were our own:

We have nursed no dreams to shed your blood,

We have matched your might not rancorously

Save a flushed few whose blatant mood

You heard and marked as well as we

To tongue not in their country's key;

But yet you cry with face aflame,

'O England, may God punish thee!'

And foul in outward history,

And present sight, your ancient name.

"In Time of 'The Breaking of Nations'"[4]

Only a man harrowing clods

In a slow silent walk

With an old horse that stumbles and nods

Half asleep as they stalk.

Only thin smoke without flame

From the heaps of couch-grass;

Yet this will go onward the same

Though Dynasties pass.

Yonder a maid and her wight

Come whispering by:

War's annals will cloud into night

Ere their story die.

A. E. Housman (1859–1936)

Alfred Edward Housman is a British classical scholar and a poet. He was appointed professor of Latin at University College in 1892, and he became professor of Latin at Trinity

---

4 First published in 1916, the poem alludes in its title to Jeremiah 51.20: "Thou art my battle axe and weapon of war: for with thee will I break in pieces the nations, and with thee I will destroy kingdoms." The poem celebrates the peasant class with three vignettes of rural life, proposing that wars are merely temporary and comparatively insignificant contrasted with the basic, persistent activities of human life.

College in 1911. During his lifetime, he mainly lived as a recluse, rejecting honours and avoiding the public eye, but published two volumes of poetry: *A Shropshire Lad* (1896), lyrics of pastoral beauty, unrequited love, fleeting youth, grief, death, and the patriotism of the common soldier, and *Last Poems* (1922), meditative reflections of nature and nostalgia. The excerpted poems are from the two collections. The poem "On the Idle Hill of Summer" (1896) sings highly of pastoral peacefulness over destructive war, but the pastoral peacefulness might paradoxically provoke war, or a nation devoted to pastoral peacefulness might be most vulnerable to attack, while other excerpted are respectively from 1917 to 1922.

"On the Idle Hill of Summer"

On the idle hill of summer,
　　　Sleepy with the flow of streams,
Far I hear the steady drummer
　　　Drumming like a noise in dreams.

Far and near and low and louder
　　　On the roads of earth go by,
Dear to friends and food for powder,
　　　Soldiers marching, all to die.

East and west on fields forgotten
　　　Bleach the bones of comrades slain,
Lovely lads and dead and rotten;
　　　None that go return again.

Far the calling bugles hollo,
　　　High the screaming fife replies,
Gay the files of scarlet follow:
　　　Woman bore me, I will rise.

"Soldier from the Wars Returning"

Soldier from the wars returning,
　　　Spoiler of the taken town,
Here is ease that asks not earning;
　　　Turn you in and sit you down.

Peace is come and wars are over,
 Welcome you and welcome all,
While the charger crops the clover
 And his bridle hangs in stall.

Now no more of winters biting,
 Filth in trench from fall to spring,
Summers full of sweat and fighting
 For the Kesar or the King.

Rest you, charger, rust you, bridle;
 Kings and kesars, keep your pay;
Soldier, sit you down and idle
 At the inn of night for aye.

"Grenadier"

The Queen she sent to look for me,
 The sergeant he did say,
'Young man, a soldier will you be
 For thirteen pence a day?'

For thirteen pence a day did I
 Take off the things I wore,
And I have marched to where I lie,
 And I shall march no more .

My mouth is dry, my shirt is wet,
 My blood runs all away,
So now I shall not die in debt
 For thirteen pence a day.

Tomorrow after new young men
 The sergeant he must see,
For things will all be over then
 Between the Queen and me.

And I shall have to bate my price,
 For in the grave, they say,

Is neither knowledge nor device
    Nor thirteen pence a day.

"Lancer"

I 'listed at home for a lancer,
    Oh who would not sleep with the brave?
I 'listed at home for a lancer
    To ride on a horse to my grave.

And over the seas we were bidden
    A country to take and to keep;
And far with the brave I have ridden,
    And now with the brave I shall sleep.

For round me the men will be lying
    That learned me the way to behave,
And showed me my business of dying:
    Oh who would not sleep with the brave?

They ask and there is not an answer;
    That learned me the way to behave,
Says I, I will 'list for a lancer,
    Oh who would not sleep with the brave?

And I with the brave shall be sleeping
    At ease on my mattress of loam,
When back from their taking and keeping
    The squadron is riding at home.

The wind with the plumes will be playing,
    The girls will stand watching them wave,
And eyeing my comrades and saying
    Oh who would not sleep with the brave?

"Epitaph on an Army of Mercenaries"

These, in the day when heaven was falling,
    The hour when earth's foundations fled,

Followed their mercenary calling
    And took their wages and are dead.

Their shoulders held the sky suspended;
    They stood, and earth's foundations stay;
What God abandoned, these defended,
    And saved the sum of things for pay.

W. B. Yeats (1865–1939)

W. B. Yeats is the greatest Irish poet in history or the 20th century for his Symbolism and literary Modernist Movement. He is also an influential cultural leader and a major playwright of his century. He was, as one critic says, deeply involved in politics in Ireland, and in the twenties, despite Irish independence from England, his verse reflected a pessimism about the political situation in his country and the rest of Europe, paralleling with the increasing conservativism of his American counterparts in London, T. S. Eliot and Ezra Pound. During his lifetime, his poems are collected in his *The Poetical Works of William B. Yeats* (1906) and *The Collected Poems of W. B. Yeats* (1933). The five excerpts, "On Being Asked for a War Poem" (1915), "Sixteen Dead Men"(1916–1917), *"An Irish Airman Foresees His Death"* (1918), "Reprisals" (1920), and "The Second Coming" (1919), respectively reflected the War taking place before and after.

"On Being Asked for a War Poem"

I think it better that in times like these
A poet's mouth be silent, for in truth
We have no gift to set a statesman right;
He has had enough of meddling who can please
A young girl in the indolence of her youth,
Or an old man upon a winter's night.

"Sixteen Dead Men"

O but we talked at large before
The sixteen men were shot,
But who can talk of give and take,
What should be and what not
While those dead men are loitering there
To stir the boiling pot?

You say that we should still the land
Till Germany's overcome ;
But who is there to argue that
Now Pearse is deaf and dumb?
And is their logic to outweigh
MacDonagh's bony thumb?

How could you dream they'd listen
That have an ear alone
For those new comrades they have found,
Lord Edward and Wolfe Tone,
Or meddle with our give and take
That converse bone to bone?

"An Irish Airman Foresees His Death"[5]

I know that I shall meet my fate
Somewhere among the clouds above;
Those that I fight I do not hate,
Those that I guard I do not love;
My country is Kiltartan Cross,
My countrymen Kiltartan's poor,
No likely end could bring them loss
Or leave them happier than before.
Nor law, nor duty bade me fight,
Nor public men, nor cheering crowds,
A lonely impulse of delight
Drove to this tumult in the clouds;
I balanced all, brought all to mind,
The years to come seemed waste of breath,
A waste of breath the years behind
In balance with this life, this death.

"Reprisals"

Some nineteen German planes, they say,
You had brought down before you died.

---

5 Major Robert Gregory, recipient of the Military Cross and the Légion d'Honneur, was killed in action when his plane was shot down on the Italian front on 23 January 1918.

We called it a good death. Today
Can ghost or man be satisfied?
Although your last exciting year
Outweighed all other years, you said,
Though battle joy may be so dear
A memory, even to the dead,
It chases other thought away,
Yet rise from your Italian tomb,
Flit to Kiltartan Cross and stay
Till certain second thoughts have come
Upon the cause you served, that we
Imagined such a fine affair:
Half-drunk or whole-mad soldiery
Are murdering your tenants there.
Men that revere your father yet
Are shot at on the open plain.
Where may new-married women sit
And suckle children now? Armed men
May murder them in passing by
Nor law nor parliament take heed.
Then close your ears with dust and lie
Among the other cheated dead.

"The Second Coming"

Turning and turning in the widening gyre
The falcon cannot hear the falconer;
Things fall apart; the centre cannot hold;
Mere anarchy is loosed upon the world,
The blood-dimmed tide is loosed, and everywhere
The ceremony of innocence is drowned;
The best lack all conviction, while the worst
Are full of passionate intensity.
Surely some revelation is at hand;
Surely the Second Coming is at hand.
The Second Coming! Hardly are those words out
When a vast image out of *Spiritus Mundi*
Troubles my sight: somewhere in sands of the desert
A shape with lion body and the head of a man,

A gaze blank and pitiless as the sun,

Is moving its slow thighs, while all about it

Reel shadows of the indignant desert birds.

The darkness drops again; but now I know

That twenty centuries of stony sleep

Were vexed to nightmare by a rocking cradle,

And what rough beast, its hour come round at last,

Slouches towards Bethlehem to be born?

G. K. Chesterton (1874–1936)

G. K. Chesterton is a British poet and author, chiefly known for his nonfiction but best remembered for his fictional work—a mystery series about Father Brown, a Catholic priest and amateur detective. He also gained attention as a journalist and social philosopher writing in style characterised by enormous wit, paradox, humility and wonder. He advocates what is called "Distributism", a social philosophy that divided property holders into small communities to foster neighbourliness, regarding it as a counter to Socialism and Capitalism. The excerpt, borrowing a poetic title from Thomas Gray, was written to commemorate the dead of the First World War.

"Elegy in a Country Churchyard"

The men that worked for England

They have their graves at home:

And bees and birds of England

About the cross can roam.

But they that fought for England,

Following a falling star,

Alas, alas for England

They have their graves afar.

And they that rule in England,

In stately conclave met,

Alas, alas for England

They have no graves as yet.

4. Patriotic Voices

As war poetry in any historical period has shown, the two terms "War" and "Patriotism" have been "Twins", that is, war is always a social space where patriotism is not only closely interconnected, but also most vividly and most strikingly represented. "Patriotic Voices" of the First World poetry are loud, but much weaker than those similar voices in the preceding periods. The "Voices" may range from love of their work, volunteers to serve the country or army, or other actions that had favoured the national victory during the war.

May Sinclair (1863–1946)

May Sinclair is a British novelist, feminist, and poetess. She joined a voluntary ambulance corps and arrived in Flanders towards the end of September 1914. She felt a profound sense of betrayal when it became clear that she was no longer wanted by her ambulance corps.

"Field Ambulance in Retreat"
Via Dolorosa, Via Sacra

I

A straight flagged road, laid on the rough earth,

A causeway of stone from beautiful city to city,

Between the tall trees, the slender, delicate trees,

Through the flat green land, by plots of flowers, by black canals thick with heat.

II

The road-makers made it well

Of fine stone, strong for the feet of the oxen and of the great Flemish horses,

And for the high waggons piled with corn from the harvest.

But the labourers are few;

They and their quiet oxen stand aside and wait

By the long road loud with the passing of the guns, the rush of armoured cars and
    the tramp of an army on the march forward to battle;

And, where the piled corn-wagons went, our dripping Ambulance carries home

Its red and white harvest from the fields.

III

The straight flagged road breaks into dust, into a thin white cloud,

About the feet of a regiment driven back league by league,

Rifles at trail, and standards wrapped in black funeral cloths.

Unhasting, proud in retreat,

They smile as the Red Cross Ambulance rushes by.

(You know nothing of beauty and of desolation who have not seen

That smile of an army in retreat.)

They go: and our shining, beckoning danger goes with them,

And our joy in the harvests that we gathered in at nightfall in the fields;

And like an unloved hand laid on a beating heart
Our safety weighs us down.
Safety hard and strange; stranger and yet more hard
As, league after dying league, the beautiful, desolate Land
Falls back from the intolerable speed of an Ambulance in retreat
On the sacred, dolorous Way.

Alys Fane Trotter (1863–1961)

Alys Fane Trotter is a British poet. The excerpted poem "The Hospital Visitor", consisting of two 14-line sonnets, explores various important ideas, such as patriotism, bravery, and stoicism, and especially the idea that soldiers' sacrifice should be respected, implying the importance of optimism when facing adversity and maintaining one's spirit and sense of humour despite the pain.

"The Hospital Visitor"

When yesterday I went to see friends—
(Watching their patient faces in a row
I want to give each boy a D.S.O.)
When yesterday I went to see my friends
With cigarettes and foolish odds and ends,
(Knowing they understand how well I know
That nothing I can do will make amends,
But that I must not grieve, or tell them so),
A pale-faced Iniskilling, just eighteen,
Who'd fought two years, with eyes a little dim
Smiled up and showed me, there behind the screen
On the humped bandage that replaced a limb,
How someone left him, where the leg had been
A tiny green glass pig to comfort him.

Here are men who've learned to laugh at pain.
And if their lips have quivered when they spoke,
They've said brave words, or tried to make a joke,
Said it's not worse than trenches in the rain,
Or pools of water on a chalky plain,
Or bitter cold from which you stiffly woke,
Or deep wet mud that left you hardly sane,
Or the tense wait for "Fritz's master stroke."

You seldom hear them talk of their "bad luck."

And suffering has not spoiled their ready wit,

And oh! You'd hardly doubt their fighting pluck

When each new generation shows their grit,

Who never brag of blows for England struck,

But only yearn to "get about a bit."

Rudyard Kipling (1865–1936)

Rudyard Kipling has been constantly attacked as a warmonger and a jingoist, but he knew what happened in Europe and thus foresaw a greater war of "Armageddon" that would likely take place soon–The First World War. When the war of "Armageddon" broke out in 1914, he went on with his literary commissions on behalf of the War Propaganda Bureau and the navy. He promoted the recruitment drives, travelled to France (1915) and Italy (1917) as a war reporter, and encouraged correspondents such as Theodore Roosevelt to bring an end to American neutrality. He served on the Commonwealth War Graves Commission until he died in 1936. For other information, see what has been introduced about the poet in the preceding chapters.

"The Children"

These were our children who died for our lands: they were dear in our sight.

We have only the memory left of their home-treasured sayings and laughter.

The price of our loss shall be paid to our hands, not another's hereafter.

Neither the Alien nor Priest shall decide on it. That is our right.

But who shall return us the children?

At the hour the Barbarian chose to disclose his pretences,

And raged against Man, they engaged, on the breasts that they bared for us,

The first felon-stroke of the sword he had long-time prepared for us—

Their bodies were all our defence while we wrought our defences.

They bought us anew with their blood, forbearing to blame us,

Those hours which we had not made good when the Judgment o'ercame us.

They believed us and perished for it. Our statecraft, our learning

Delivered them bound to the Pit and alive to the burning

Whither they mirthfully hastened as jostling for honour.

Not since her birth has our Earth seen such worth loosed upon her.

Nor was their agony brief, or once only imposed on them.

The wounded, the war-spent, the sick received no exemption:
Being cured they returned and endured and achieved our redemption,
Hopeless themselves of relief, till Death, marvelling, closed on them

That flesh we had nursed from the first in all cleanness was given
To corruption unveiled and assailed by the malice of Heaven—
By the heart-shaking jests of Decay where it lolled on the wires—
To be blanched or gay-painted by fumes—to be cindered by fires—
To be senselessly tossed and retossed in stale mutilation
From crater to crater. For this we shall take expiation.
            But who shall return us our children?

"The Verdicts"
(Jutland)

Not in the thick of the fight,
        Not in the press of the odds,
Do the heroes come to their height,
        Or we know the demi-gods.

That stands over till peace.
        We can only perceive
Men returned from the seas,
        Very grateful for leave.

They grant us sudden days
        Snatched from their business of war;
But we are too close to appraise
        What manner of men they are.

And, whether their names go down
        With age-kept victories,
Or whether they battle and drown
        Unreckoned, is hid from our eyes.

They are too near to be great,
        But our children shall understand
When and how our fate
        Was changed, and by whose hand.

Our children shall measure their worth.
  We are content to be blind . . .
But we know that we walk on a new-born earth
  With the saviours of mankind.

"Mesopotamia"

They shall not return to us, the resolute, the young,
  The eager and whole-hearted whom we gave:
But the men who left them thriftily to die in their own dung,
  Shall they come with years and honour to the grave?

They shall not return to us, the strong men coldly slain
  In sight of help denied from day to day:
But the men who edged their agonies and chid them in their pain,
  Are they too strong and wise to put away?

Our dead shall not return to us while Day and Night divide—
  Never while the bars of sunset hold.
But the idle-minded overlings who quibbled while they died,
  Shall they thrust for high employments as of old?

Shall we only threaten and be angry for an hour?
  When the storm is ended shall we find
How softly but how swiftly they have sidled back to power
  By the favour and contrivance of their kind?

Even while they soothe us, while they promise large amends,
  Even while they make a show of fear,
Do they call upon their debtors, and take counsel with their friends,
  To confirm and re-establish each career?

Their lives cannot repay us—their death could not undo—
  The shame that they have laid upon our race.
But the slothfulness that wasted and the arrogance that slew,
  Shall we leave it unabated in its place?

"Justice"[6]

Across a world where all men grieve
  And grieving strive the more,
The great days range like tides and leave
  Our dead on every shore.
Heavy the load we undergo,
  And our own hands prepare,
If we have parley with the foe,
  The load our sons must bear.

Before we loose the word
  That bids new worlds to birth,
Needs must we loosen first the sword
  Of Justice upon earth;
Or else all else is vain
  Since life on earth began,
And the spent world sinks back again
  Hopeless of God and Man.

A people and their King
  Through ancient sin grown strong,
Because they feared no reckoning
  Would set no bound to wrong;
But now their hour is past,
  And we who bore it find
Evil Incarnate held at last
  To answer to mankind.

For agony and spoil
  Of nations beat to dust,
For poisoned air and tortured soil
  And cold, commanded lust,
And every secret woe
  The shuddering waters saw—
Willed and fulfilled by high and low—
  Let them relearn the Law.

---

6 The poem is subtitld with the date "October 1918".

That when the dooms are read,
      Not high nor low shall say:—
'My haughty or my humble head
      Has saved me in this day.'
That, till the end of time,
      Their remnant shall recall
Their fathers' old, confederate crime
      Availed them not at all.

That neither schools nor priests,
      Nor Kings may build again
A people with the heart of beasts
      Made wise concerning men.
Whereby our dead shall sleep
      In honour, unbetrayed,
And we in faith and honour keep
      That peace for which they paid.

"A Death-Bed"

'This is the State above the Law.
      The State exists for the State alone.'
[*This is a gland at the back of the jaw,
      And an answering lump by the collar-bone.*]

Some die shouting in gas or fire;
      Some die silent, by shell and shot.
Some die desperate, caught on the wire;
      Some die suddenly. This will not.

'Regis suprema Voluntas lex'
[*It will follow the regular course of—throats.*]
      Some die pinned by the broken decks,
Some die sobbing between the boats.

Some die eloquent, pressed to death
      By the sliding trench, as theirfriends can hear.
Some die wholly in half a breath.
      Some—give trouble for half a year.

'There is neither Evil nor Good in life
    Except as the needs of the State ordain.'
[*Since it is rather too late for the knife,*
    All we can do is to mask the pain.]

Some die saintly in faith and hope—
    One died thus in a prison-yard—
Some die broken by rape or the rope;
    Some die easily. This dies hard.

'I will dash to pieces who bar my way.
    Woe to the traitor! Woe to the weak!'
[*Let him write what he wishes to say.*
    It tires him out if he tries to speak.]

Some die quietly. Some abound
    In loud self-pity. Others spread
Bad morale through the cots around . . .
    This is a type that is better dead.

'The war was forced on me by my foes.
    All that I sought was the right to live.'
[*Don't be afraid of a triple dose;*
    The pain will neutralize half we give.

Here are the needles. See that he dies
    While the effects of the drug endure...
What is the question he asks with his eyes?—
    Yes, All-Highest, to God, be sure.]

Eva Dobell (1876–1963)

Eva Dobell is a British poetess. She worked as a nurse during the War. It may be difficult to read Dobell's poem as either simply pro-war or anti-war, and thus have always undermined many readers' commitment to the war. Opponents of the war could read the poem as graphic evidence of the waste and tragic suffering caused by armed conflict. Defenders of the war, conversely, could point to the young wounded soldier as the kind of hero that nations needed urgently.

"Advent, 1916"

I dreamt last night Christ came to earth again
To bless His own. My soul from place to place
On her dream-quest sped, seeking for His face
Through temple and town and lovely land, in vain.
Then came I to a place where death and pain
Had made of God's sweet world a waste forlorn,
With shattered trees and meadows gashed and torn,
Where the grim trenches scarred the shell-sheared plain.
And through that Golgotha of blood and clay,
Where watchers cursed the sick dawn, heavy-eyed,
There (in my dream) Christ passed upon His way,
Where His cross marks their nameless graves who died
Slain for the world's salvation where all day
For others' sake strong men are crucified.

"In a Soldier's Hospital I: Pluck"

Crippled for life at seventeen,
    His great eyes seem to question why:
With both legs smashed it might have been
    Better in that grim trench to die
    Than drag maimed years out helplessly.

A child—so wasted and so white,
    He told a lie to get his way,
To march, a man with men, and fight
    While other boys are still at play.
    A gallant lie your heart will say.

So broke with pain, he shrinks in dread
    To see the "dresser" drawing near;
And winds the clothes about his head
    That none may see his heart-sick fear.
    His shaking, strangled sobs you hear.

But when the dreaded moment's there
    He'll face us all, a soldier yet,

Watch his bared wounds with unmoved air,
(Though tell-tale lashes still are wet),
And smoke his Woodbine cigarette.

"In a Soldier's Hospital II: Gramophone Tunes"

Through the long ward the gramophone
Grinds out its nasal melodies:
"Where did you get that girl?" it shrills.
The patients listen at their ease,
Through clouds of strong tobacco smoke:
The gramophone can always please.

The Welsh boy has it by his bed,
(He's lame—one leg was blown away).
He'll lie propped up with pillows there,
And wind the handle half the day.
His neighbour, with the shattered arm,
Picks out the records he must play.

Jock with his crutches beats the time;
The gunner, with his head close-bound,
Listens with puzzled, patient smile:
(Shell shocked—he cannot hear a sound).
The others join in from their beds,
And send the chorus rolling round.

Somehow for me these common tunes
Can never sound the same again:
They've magic now to thrill my heart
And bring before me, clear and plain,
Man that is master of his flesh,
And has the laugh of death and pain.

Laurence Binyon (1869–1943)

Laurence Binyon is a British poet and art historian. He was too old to enlist in the military forces, but he went to work for the Red Cross as a medical orderly in 1916, during which several close friends and his brother-in-law were lost in the war. His major volumes of poetry include *Lyric Poems* (1894) and *Odes* (1901). He wrote and translated verse drama and worked as an art historian, and was appointed Norton professor of poetry at Harvard in 1933. He is best known for his poem "For the Fallen", written in mid-September 1914, a few weeks after the outbreak of the First World War. The poem has later been adopted by the Royal British Legion as an Exhortation for ceremonies of remembrance to commemorate fallen servicemen and women.

"For the Fallen"

With proud thanksgiving, a mother for her children,
England mourns for her dead across the sea.
Flesh of her flesh they were, spirit of her spirit,
Fallen in the cause of the free.

Solemn the drums thrill: Death august and royal
Sings sorrow up into immortal spheres.
There is music in the midst of desolation
And a glory that shines upon our tears.

They went with songs to the battle, they were young,
Straight of limb, true of eye, steady and aglow.
They were staunch to the end against odds uncounted,
They fell with their faces to the foe.

They shall grow not old, as we that are left grow old:
Age shall not weary them, nor the years condemn.
At the going down of the sun and in the morning
We will remember them.

They mingle not with their laughing comrades again;
They sit no more at familiar tables of home;
They have no lot in our labour of the day-time;
They sleep beyond England's foam.

But where our desires are and our hopes profound,
Felt as a well-spring that is hidden from sight,
To the innermost heart of their own land they are known
As the stars are known to the Night;

As the stars that shall be bright when we are dust,

Moving in marches upon the heavenly plain,

As the stars that are starry in the time of our darkness,

To the end, to the end, they remain.

Herbert Asquith (1881–1947)

Herbert Asquith is the second son of British Prime Minister H. H. Asquith. He married Lady Cynthia in 1910. He is a writer and soldier, greatly affected by his service with the Royal Artillery in World War I. The excerpts are his poems "The Volunteer" and "The Fallen Subaltern", respectively writing willingness of the service and tribute to fallen soldiers.

"The Volunteer"

Here lies a clerk who half his life had spent

Toiling at ledgers in a city grey,

Thinking that so his days would drift away

With no lance broken in life's tournament.

Yet ever 'twixt the books and his bright eyes

The gleaming eagles of the legions came,

And horsemen, charging under phantom skies,

Went thundering past beneath the oriflamme.

And now those waiting dreams are satisfied;

From twilight to the halls of dawn he went;

His lance is broken; but he lies content

With that high hour, in which he lived and died.

And falling thus he wants no recompense,

Who found his battle in the last resort;

Nor need he any hearse to bear him hence,

Who goes to join the men of Agincourt.

"The Fallen Subaltern"

The starshells float above, the bayonets glisten;

We bear our fallen friend without a sound;

Below the waiting legions lie and listen

To us, who march upon their burial-ground.

Wound in the flag of England, here we lay him;

The guns will flash and thunder o'er the grave;

What other winding sheet should now array him,
What other music should salute the brave?

As goes the Sun-god in his chariot glorious,
When all his golden banners are unfurled,
So goes the soldier, fallen but victorious,
And leaves behind a twilight in the world.

And those who come this way, in days hereafter,
Will know that here a boy for England fell,
Who looked at danger with the eyes of laughter,
And on the charge his days were ended well.

One last salute; the bayonets clash and glisten;
With arms reversed we go without a sound:
One more has joined the men who lie and listen
To us, who march upon their burial-ground.

Rupert Brooke (1887–1915)

Rupert Brooke is a British poet, not only known as one of the famous "War Poets of the First World War," but also as one receiving excessive praise and scornful condemnation for his unabashed patriotism and graceful lyricism. Often called "the most handsome man in England", he possessed a quiet personal charm and magnetism along with golden classical good looks. Before his death, he was popular in both literary and political circles, as he had befriended Winston Churchill, Henry James, and members of the Bloomsbury Group, including Virginia Woolf. In 1912 he compiled with others an anthology entitled *Georgian Poetry, 1911–12*. After experiencing a mental breakdown in 1913, he travelled extensively in America, Canada, and the South Seas for self-therapy. At the outbreak of the War, he came back to England and enlisted in the Royal Naval Division, but died of blood poisoning in April, 1915 while taking part in the Antwerp Expedition. His death witnesses a symbol in England of the tragic loss of talented youth during the war. His most famous collection, *1914 and Other Poems*, was published posthumously. All the following excerpts are from this well-known collection.

"The Soldier"

If I should die, think only this of me:
    That there's some corner of a foreign field
That is for ever England. There shall be

In that rich earth a richer dust concealed;
A dust whom England bore, shaped, made aware,
      Gave, once, her flowers to love, her ways to roam;
A body of England's, breathing English air,
      Washed by the rivers, blest by suns of home.

And think, this heart, all evil shed away,
      A pulse in the eternal mind, no less
          Gives somewhere back the thoughts by England given;
Her sights and sounds; dreams happy as her day;
      And laughter, learnt of friends; and gentleness,
          In hearts at peace, under an English heaven.

"The Dead (1) "

These hearts were woven of human joys and cares,
Washed marvelously with sorrow, swift to mirth.
The years had given them kindness. Dawn was theirs,
And sunset, and the colours of the earth.
These had seen movement, and heard music; known
Slumber and waking; loved; gone proudly friended;
Felt the quick stir of wonder; sat alone;
Touched flowers and furs and cheeks. All this is ended.

There are waters blown by changing winds to laughter
And lit by the rich skies, all day. And after,
Frost, with a gesture, stays the waves that dance
And wandering loveliness. He leaves a white
Unbroken glory, a gathered radiance,
A width, a shining peace, under the night.

"The Dead (2) "

Blow out, you bugles, over the rich Dead!
      There's none of these so lonely and poor of old,
But, dying, has made us rarer gifts than gold.
These laid the world away; poured out the red
Sweet wine of youth; gave up the years to be
      Of work and joy, and that unhoped serene,

That men call age; and those who would have been,
Their sons, they gave, their immortality.

Blow, bugles, blow! They brought us, for our dearth,
    Holiness, lacked so long, and Love, and Pain.
Honour has come back, as a king, to earth,
    And paid his subjects with a royal wage;
    And Nobleness walks in our ways again;
    And we have come into our heritage.

"Peace"

Now, God be thanked Who has matched us with His hour,
    And caught our youth, and wakened us from sleeping,
With hand made sure, clear eye, and sharpened power,
    To turn, as swimmers into cleanness leaping,
Glad from a world grown old and cold and weary,
    Leave the sick hearts that honour could not move,
And half-men, and their dirty songs and dreary,
    And all the little emptiness of love!

Oh! we, who have known shame, we have found release there,
    Where there's no ill, no grief, but sleep has mending.
Naught broken save this body, lost but breath;
    Nothing to shake the laughing heart's long peace there
But only agony, and that has ending;
    And the worst friend and enemy is but Death.

Julian Grenfell (1888–1915)

Julian Grenfell is a British patriotic poet. He joined the Royal Dragoons in 1910, and served in France after the outbreak of World War I. He obtained a reputation for bravery by stalking German snipers and then shooting them from close range. He was badly wounded when he was hit by shrapnel during action near Ypres, and died on 26th May 1915. A few days later, his poem, "Into Battle", was published in *The Times*, which later became one of the most popular poems of the War. The poem is patriotic and even idealistic in sharp contrast to those anti-war poets.

"Into Battle"

The naked earth is warm with Spring,
    And with green grass and bursting trees
Leans to the sun's gaze glorying,
    And quivers in the sunny breeze;

And life is colour and warmth and light,
    And a striving evermore for these;
And he is dead who will not fight;
    And who dies fighting has increase.

The fighting man shall from the sun
    Take warmth, and life from the glowing earth;
Speed with the light-foot winds to run,
    And with the trees to newer birth;
And find, when fighting shall be done,
    Great rest, and fullness after dearth.

All the bright company of Heaven
    Hold him in their high comradeship,
The Dog-Star, and the Sisters Seven,
    Orion's Belt and sworded hip.

The woodland trees that stand together,
    They stand to him each one a friend;
They gently speak in the windy weather;
    They guide to valley and ridge's end.

The kestrel hovering by day,
    And the little owls that call by night,
Bid him be swift and keen as they,
    As keen of ear, as swift of sight.

The blackbird sings to him, 'Brother, brother,
    If this be the last song you shall sing,
Sing well, for you may not sing another;
    Brother, sing.'

In dreary, doubtful waiting hours,
　　Before the brazen frenzy starts,
The horses show him nobler powers;
　　O patient eyes, courageous hearts!

And when the burning moment breaks,
　　And all things else are out of mind,
And only joy of battle takes
　　Him by the throat, and makes him blind,

Through joy and blindness he shall know,
　　Not caring much to know, that still
Nor lead nor steel shall reach him, so
　　That it be not the Destined Will.

The thundering line of battle stands,
　　And in the air Death moans and sings;
But Day shall clasp him with strong hands,
　　And Night shall fold him in soft wings.

George Orwell (1903–1950)

George Orwell is mainly a British novelist, essayist, and critic, famous for his novels *Animal Farm* (1945) and *Nineteen Eighty-four* (1949). His anti-utopian novels examine the dangers of totalitarian rule. During the 1930s, he began to consider himself a socialist and even a communist. He went to report on the Spanish Civil War and stayed to join the Republican militia. When World War II came, he was rejected for military service, and instead, he headed the Indian service of the BBC until 1943.

The excerpted poem was written when George Orwell was 11 years old. It is his first publication, which appeared in the local newspaper *Henley and South Oxfordshire Standard* on 2 October 1914, with his real name "Eric Blair". He only adopted the pseudonym George Orwell in the 1930s.

"Awake! Young Men of England"

OH! give me the strength of the Lion,
　　The wisdom of Reynard the Fox
And then I'll hurl troops at the Germans
　　And give them the hardest of knocks.

Oh! think of the War Lord's mailed fist,
　　That is striking at England today:
And think of the lives that our soldiers
　　Are fearlessly throwing away.

Awake! Oh you young men of England,
　　For if, when your Country's in need,
You do not enlist by the thousand,
　　You truly are cowards indeed.

5. Anti-War Voices

The overwhelming poetic voice of the First World War, among many voices, is its "Anti-War Voice", an antiwar voice with a multitude of diverse antiwar voices, though it is frequently called "a war to end all wars". Antiwar poetry of the concerned period proliferated in scale and impact, deploying figures such as the wounded soldiers or the grieving civilians. The antiwar sentiment demands that poets cease romanticising any conflict and violence. Owen's ironic "Dulce et Decorum Est" may be the most typical, for it not only subscribes to an anti-war manifesto or an explicit anti-war agenda, but also regards war as simply an execrable blot upon civilisation. The artistic exploitation of violence makes contemporary anti-war poetry seem sentimental and morally dubious, but it has always been clear that "to romanticise the war" or "to conceive a sense of patriotism" had indeed terminated. In his *Modern English War Poetry* (2006), Tim Kendall talks about "The Few to Profit: Poets Against War" in Chapter 12: "If truth is the first casualty of war, then the job of the war poet since Owen has been to keep the truth alive;" and it is "a lying war-profiteer who works the sufferings of others to his personal advantage."[7]

Charlotte Mew (1869–1928)

Charlotte Mew is a characteristically peculiar British poetess, who has insistently been haunted by unrequited passion and tormented by fears of madness, but produced poems of unique beauty and passion. She was greatly evaluated and esteemed by great poets of her time, such as Siegfried Sassoon, Ezra Pound and others, but committed suicide at the end of her life. Her poetic collection includes *Saturday Market* (1921) and the posthumously published *The Rambling Sailor* (1929). She has been all but forgotten today, but deserves attention again for her apprehensive voice and natural sense of foreboding. In the excerpted poem, Mew implies spring's superiority to winter, yet it was ironically in spring and summer that most deaths during World War I occurred.

7　Tim Kendall, *Modern English War Poetry*. Oxford: Oxford University Press, 2006, pp. 238-239.

"May, 1915"

Let us remember Spring will come again
    To the scorched, blackened woods, where the wounded trees
    Wait with their old wise patience for the heavenly rain,
Sure of the sky: sure of the sea to send its healing breeze,
    Sure of the sun. And even as to these
    Surely the Spring, when God shall please,
    Will come again like a divine surprise
To those who sit today with their great Dead, hands in their hands, eyes in their eyes,
At one with Love, at one with Grief: blind to the scattered things and changing skies.

John McCrae (1872–1918)

John McCrae is a British Common Wealth of Canadian poet, soldier, and physician. His poem included soldiers, soldiers' loved ones, survivors of dead soldiers, soldiers who had escaped death, and supporters of the war, who would have wanted to see battlefield deaths as events meaningful. The two excerpted poems are representative ones of the First World War.

"In Flanders Fields"

In Flanders fields the poppies blow
Between the crosses, row on row
That mark our place; and in the sky
The larks, still bravely singing, fly
Scarce heard amid the guns below.
We are the Dead. Short days ago
We lived, felt dawn, saw sunset glow,
Loved and were loved, and now we lie

In Flanders fields.
Take up our quarrel with the foe:
To you from failing hands we throw
The torch; be yours to hold it high.
If ye break faith with us who die
We shall not sleep, though poppies grow
In Flanders fields.

"The Anxious Dead"

O guns, fall silent till the dead men hear
  Above their heads the legions pressing on:
(These fought their fight in time of bitter fear,
  And died not knowing how the day had gone.)

O flashing muzzles, pause, and let them see
  The coming dawn that streaks the sky afar;
Then let your mighty chorus witness be
  To them, and Caesar, that we still make war.

Tell them, O guns, that we have heard their call,
  That we have sworn, and will not turn aside,
That we will onward till we win or fall,
  That we will keep the faith for which they died.

Bid them be patient, and some day, anon,
  They shall feel earth enwrapt in silence deep;
Shall greet, in wonderment, the quiet dawn,
  And in content may turn them to their sleep.

Robert W. Service (1874–1958)

Robert W. Service is a prolific British writer for his two autobiographies and six novels, and a poet regarded by some as "the people's poet". He served as an ambulance driver during World War I, after which he published *Rhymes of a Red Cross Man* (1916), a collection of mostly war poems. He also published numerous collections of poetry during his lifetime, including *Songs of a Sourdough or Spell of the Yukon and Other Verses* (1907), *Ballad of a Cheechako* (1909), *Rhymes of a Rolling Stone* (1913), and *Ballads of a Bohemian* (1921). The two excerpts are about his war experiences.

"Only a Boche"

We brought him in from between the lines: we'd better have let him lie;
For what's the use of risking one's skin for a TYKE that's going to die?
What's the use of tearing him loose under a gruelling fire,
When he's shot in the head, and worse than dead, and all messed up on the wire?

However, I say, we brought him in. DIABLE! The mud was bad;

The trench was crooked and greasy and high, and oh, what a time we had!
And often we slipped, and often we tripped, but never he made a moan;
And how we were wet with blood and with sweat! but we carried him in like our own.

Now there he lies in the dug-out dim, awaiting the ambulance,
And the doctor shrugs his shoulders at him, and remarks, "He hasn't a chance."
And we squat and smoke at our game of bridge on the glistening, straw-packed floor,
And above our oaths we can hear his breath deep-drawn in a kind of snore.

For the dressing station is long and low, and the candles gutter dim,
And the mean light falls on the cold clay walls and our faces bristly and grim;
And we flap our cards on the lousy straw, and we laugh and jibe as we play,
And you'd never know that the cursed foe was less than a mile away.
As we con our cards in the rancid gloom, oppressed by that snoring breath,
You'd never dream that our broad roof-beam was swept by the broom of death.

Heigh-ho! My turn for the dummy hand; I rise and I stretch a bit;
The fetid air is making me yawn, and my cigarette's unlit,
So I go to the nearest candle flame, and the man we brought is there,
And his face is white in the shabby light, and I stand at his feet and stare.
Stand for a while, and quietly stare: for strange though it seems to be,
The dying Boche on the stretcher there has a queer resemblance to me.

It gives one a kind of a turn, you know, to come on a thing like that.
It's just as if I were lying there, with a turban of blood for a hat,
Lying there in a coat grey-green instead of a coat grey-blue,
With one of my eyes all shot away, and my brain half tumbling through;
Lying there with a chest that heaves like a bellows up and down,
And a cheek as white as snow on a grave, and lips that are coffee brown.

And confound him, too! He wears, like me, on his finger a wedding ring,
And around his neck, as around my own, by a greasy bit of string,
A locket hangs with a woman's face, and I turn it about to see:
Just as I thought . . . on the other side the faces of children three;
Clustered together cherub-like, three little laughing girls,
With the usual tiny rosebud mouths and the usual silken curls.
"Zut!" I say. "He has beaten me; for me, I have only two,"
And I push the locket beneath his shirt, feeling a little blue.

Oh, it isn't cheerful to see a man, the marvellous work of God,

Crushed in the mutilation mill, crushed to a smeary clod;

Oh, it isn't cheerful to hear him moan; but it isn't that I mind,

It isn't the anguish that goes with him, it's the anguish he leaves behind.

For his going opens a tragic door that gives on a world of pain,

And the death he dies, those who live and love, will die again and again.

So here I am at my cards once more, but it's kind of spoiling my play,

Thinking of those three brats of his so many a mile away.

War is war, and he's only a Boche, and we all of us take our chance;

But all the same I'll be mighty glad when I'm hearing the ambulance.

One foe the less, but all the same I'm heartily glad I'm not

The man who gave him his broken head, the sniper who fired the shot.

No trumps you make it, I think you said?

    You'll pardon me if I err;

For a moment I thought of other things . . .

    MON DIEU! QUELLE VACHE DE GUERRE.

"The Song of the Soldier-born"

Give me the scorn of the stars and a peak defiant;

Wail of the pines and a wind with the shout of a giant;

Night and a trail unknown and a heart reliant.

Give me to live and love in the old, bold fashion;

A soldier's billet at night and a soldier's ration;

A heart that leaps to the fight with a soldier's passion.

For I hold as a simple faith there's no denying:

The trade of a soldier's the only trade worth plying;

The death of a soldier's the only death worth dying.

So let me go and leave your safety behind me;

Go to the spaces of hazard where nothing shall bind me;

Go till the word is War—and then you will find me.

Then you will call me and claim me because you will need me;

Cheer me and gird me and into the battle-wrath speed me. . . .

And when it's over, spurn me and no longer heed me.

For guile and a purse gold-greased are the arms you carry;
With deeds of paper you fight and with pens you parry;
You call on the hounds of the law your foes to harry.

You with your "Art for its own sake", posing and prinking;
You with your "Live and be merry", eating and drinking;
You with your "Peace at all hazard", from bright blood shrinking.

Fools! I will tell you now: though the red rain patters,
And a million of men go down, it's little it matters. . . .
There's the Flag upflung to the stars, though it streams in tatters.

There's a glory gold never can buy to yearn and to cry for;
There's a hope that's as old as the sky to suffer and sigh for;
There's a faith that out-dazzles the sun to martyr and die for.

Ah no! it's my dream that War will never be ended;
That men will perish like men, and valour be splendid;
That the Flag by the sword will be served, and honour defended.

That the tale of my fights will never be ancient story;
That though my eye may be dim and my beard be hoary,
I'll die as a soldier dies on the Field of Glory.

So give me a strong right arm for a wrong's swift righting;
Stave of a song on my lips as my sword is smiting;
Death in my boots may-be, but fighting, fighting.

Edward Thomas (1878–1917)

Edward Thomas is a Welsh poet, critic, and biographer. He joined the Artists' Rifles of the British Armed Forces in July 1915, served as a soldier during wartime. On April 9, 1917, he was killed... in action soon after he arrived in France at Arras. His poetic collection includes *Poems* (1917), *Last Poems* (1918), *Collected Poems* (1920), much of which blends his meditative recollections of his beloved countryside with his experiences in battle. He is best known for his careful depictions of rural England and his prescient understanding of modernity's tendency toward disconnection, alienation, and unsettledness as had been produced by the War.

"Tears"

It seems I have no tears left. They should have fallen—
Their ghosts, if tears have ghosts, did fall—that day
When twenty hounds streamed by me, not yet combed out
But still all equals in their rage of gladness
Upon the scent, made one, like a great dragon
In Blooming Meadow that bends towards the sun
And once bore hops: and on that other day
When I stepped out from the double-shadowed Tower
Into an April morning, stirring and sweet
And warm. Strange solitude was there and silence.
A mightier charm than any in the Tower
Possessed the courtyard. They were changing guard,
Soldiers in line, young English countrymen,
Fair-haired and ruddy, in white tunics. Drums
And fifes were playing "The British Grenadiers."
The men, the music piercing that solitude
And silence, told me truths I had not dreamed
And have forgotten since their beauty passed.

"Rain"

Rain, midnight rain, nothing but the wild rain
On this bleak hut, and solitude, and me
Remembering again that I shall die
And neither hear the rain nor give it thanks
For washing me cleaner than I have been
Since I was born into solitude.
Blessed are the dead that the rain rains upon:
But here I pray that none whom once I loved
Is dying tonight or lying still awake
Solitary, listening to the rain,
Either in pain or thus in sympathy
Helpless among the living and the dead,
Like a cold water among broken reeds,
Myriads of broken reeds all still and stiff,
Like me who have no love which this wild rain
Has not dissolved except the love of death,

If love it be towards what is perfect and
Cannot, the tempest tells me, disappoint.

"As the Team's Head Brass"

As the team's head brass flashed out on the turn
The lovers disappeared into the wood.
I sat among the boughs of the fallen elm
That strewed an angle of the fallow, and
Watched the plough narrowing a yellow square
Of charlock. Every time the horses turned
Instead of treading me down, the ploughman leaned
Upon the handles to say or ask a word,
About the weather, next about the war.
Scraping the share he faced towards the wood,
And screwed along the furrow till the brass flashed
Once more.

        The blizzard felled the elm whose crest
I sat in, by a woodpecker's round hole,
The ploughman said. 'When will they take it away?'
'When the war's over.' So the talk began—
One minute and an interval of ten,
A minute more and the same interval.
'Have you been out?' 'No.' 'And don't want to, perhaps?'
'If I could only come back again, I should.
I could spare an arm. I shouldn't want to lose
A leg. If I should lose my head, why, so,
I should want nothing more… Have many gone
From here?' 'Yes.' 'Many lost?' 'Yes, a good few.
Only two teams work on the farm this year.
One of my mates is dead. The second day
In France they killed him. It was back in March,
The very night of the blizzard, too. Now if
He had stayed here we should have moved the tree.'
'And I should not have sat here. Everything
Would have been different. For it would have been
Another world.' 'Ay, and a better, though
If we could see all might seem good.' Then

The lovers came out of the wood again:
The horses started and for the last time
I watched the clods crumble and topple over
After the ploughshare and the stumbling team.

Wilfrid Gibson (1878–1962)

Wilfrid Wilson Gibson is a British poet and playwright, best known as a leader of the Georgian movement of poetry. His earliest published poetry was *Mountain Lovers* (1902). He had several poems included in various volumes of *Georgian Poetry*. He had been denied entry into the army for several years due to his poor eyesight, but was finally allowed to become a soldier in 1917, so his wartime experience had greatly influenced his poetry. The most striking feature of his poetic production is an acute examination of the commonplace, characterised with the point of view of the ordinary foot soldier, poor industrial workers and village labourers, such as in his later collection *Collected Poems: 1905–1925* (1926), *The Island Stag* (1947), and *Within Four Walls* (1950). The two excerpts, "Breakfast" and "Flannan Isle", were respectively published in 1914 and 1917.

"Breakfast"

We ate our breakfast lying on our backs,
Because the shells were screeching overhead.
I bet a rasher to a loaf of bread
That Hull United would beat Halifax
When Jimmy Stainthorp played full-back instead
Of Billy Bradford. Ginger raised his head
And cursed, and took the bet; and dropt back dead.
We ate our breakfast lying on our backs,
Because the shells were screeching overhead.

"Flannan Isle"

THOUGH three men dwell on Flannan Isle
To keep the lamp alight,
As we steer'd under the lee, we caught
No glimmer through the night!

A passing ship at dawn had brought
The news; and quickly we set sail,
To find out what strange thing might all

The keepers of the deep-sea light.

The winter day broke blue and bright,
With glancing sun and glancing spray,
As o'er the swell our boat made way,
As gallant as a gull in flight.

But, as we near'd the lonely Isle;
And look'd up at the naked height;
And saw the lighthouse towering white,
With blinded lantern, that all night
Had never shot a spark
Of comfort through the dark,
So ghastly in the cold sunlight
It seem'd, that we were struck the while
With wonder all too dread for words.

And, as into the tiny creek
We stole beneath the hanging crag,
We saw three queer, black, ugly birds—
Too big, by far, in my belief,
For guillemot or shag—
Like seamen sitting bold upright
Upon a half-tide reef:
But, as we near'd, they plunged from sight,
Without a sound, or spurt of white.

And still too mazed to speak,
We landed; and made fast the boat;
And climb'd the track in single file,
Each wishing he was safe afloat,
On any sea, however far,
So it be far from Flannan Isle:
And still we seem'd to climb, and climb,
As though we'd lost all count of time,
And so must climb for evermore.
Yet, all too soon, we reached the door—
The black, sun-blister'd lighthouse door,
That gaped for us ajar.

As, on the threshold, for a spell,

We paused, we seem'd to breathe the smell

Of limewash and of tar,

Familiar as our daily breath,

As though 'twere some strange scent of death:

And so, yet wondering, side by side,

We stood a moment, still tongue-tied:

And each with black foreboding eyed

The door, ere we should fling it wide,

To leave the sunlight for the gloom:

Till, plucking courage up, at last,

Hard on each other's heels we pass'd

Into the living-room.

Yet, as we crowded through the door,

We only saw a table, spread

For dinner, meat and cheese and bread;

But all untouch'd; and no one there:

As though, when they sat down to eat,

Ere they could even taste,

Alarm had come; and they in haste

Had risen and left the bread and meat:

For on the table-head a chair

Lay tumbled on the floor.

We listen'd; but we only heard

The feeble cheeping of a bird

That starved upon its perch:

And, listening still, without a word,

We set about our hopeless search.

We hunted high, we hunted low,

And soon ransack'd the empty house;

Then o'er the Island, to and fro,

We ranged, to listen and to look

In every cranny, cleft or nook

That might have hid a bird or mouse:

But, though we searched from shore to shore,

We found no sign in any place:

And soon again stood face to face

Before the gaping door:
And stole into the room once more
As frighten'd children steal.

Aye: though we hunted high and low,
And hunted everywhere,
Of the three men's fate we found no trace
Of any kind in any place,
But a door ajar, and an untouch'd meal,
And an overtoppled chair.

And, as we listen'd in the gloom
Of that forsaken living-room—
O chill clutch on our breath—
We thought how ill-chance came to all
Who kept the Flannan Light:
And how the rock had been the death
Of many a likely lad:
How six had come to a sudden end
And three had gone stark mad:
And one whom we'd all known as friend
Had leapt from the lantern one still night,
And fallen dead by the lighthouse wall:
And long we thought
On the three we sought,
And of what might yet befall.

Like curs a glance has brought to heel,
We listen'd, flinching there:
And look'd, and look'd, on the untouch'd meal
And the overtoppled chair.

We seem'd to stand for an endless while,
Though still no word was said,
Three men alive on Flannan Isle,
Who thought on three men dead.

Margaret Sackville (1881–1963)

Margaret Sackville, also called Lady Margaret Sackville, is a British social activist and poetess, and some even say that she is a socialist and a pacifist. Her first book of poetry, *Floral Symphony*, was published in 1900, followed by her *Fairy Tales for the Old and Young* (1909), which has been highly praised for her gracious manner and classic beauty. On the outbreak of the First World War, she joined the anti-war organisation, the Union of Democratic Control. In 1916, she published a collection of poems called *The Pagent of War* (1916), and in 1919 *Selected Poems* (1919). Her final collection includes *Lyrical Woodlands* (1945) and *Miniatures* (1947). She has denounced women who betrayed their sons by not speaking out that "We mothers and we murderers of mankind" in the first excerpt "Nostra Culpa" (1916), and in the second, she emphasises upon civilian women casualties, focusing on groups usually "marginalised" or overlooked in the War.

"Nostra Culpa"

We knew the sword accursed, yet with the strong
Proclaimed the sword triumphant. Yea this wrong
Unto our children, unto those unborn
We did, blaspheming God. We feared the scorn
Of men; men worshipping pride, so where they led
We followed. Dare we now lament our dead?
Shadows and echoes, harlots! We betrayed
Our sons; because men laughed we were afraid.
That silent wisdom which was ours to kept
Deep buried; thousands perished; still we slept.
Children were slaughtered, women raped, the weak
Down-trodden. Very quiet was our sleep.

"A Memory"

There was no sound at all, no crying in the village,
    Nothing you would count as sound, that is, after the shells;
Only behind a wall the low sobbing of women,
    The creaking of a door, a lost dog—nothing else.

Silence which might be felt, no pity in the silence,
    Horrible, soft like blood, down all the blood-stained ways;
In the middle of the street two corpses lie unburied,
    And a bayoneted woman stares in the market-place.

Humble and ruined folk—for these no pride of conquest,

Their only prayer: "O Lord, give us our daily bread!"

Not by the battle fires, the shrapnel are we haunted;

Who shall deliver us from the memory of these dead?

Gilbert Frankau (1884–1952)

Gilbert Frankau is a British poet, novelist, and author mainly known for his work outside the field, most notably his Byronesque verse novel *One of Us* (1912) and its sequels. He joined the British army at the outbreak of World War I, and was commissioned as an officer. He was eventually posted to a field artillery unit in France, and fought in such major battles as Ypres, Loos and the Somme. He was in active service for almost the whole of World War I, registering some of its effects on him in his *The City of Fear and Other Poems*, until he was invalided out of the army in 1918.

According to his preface for *A Song of the Guns* (1916), the collection was "written under what are probably the most remarkable conditions in which a poem has ever been composed." It goes in such following words: "The author, who is now serving in Flanders, was present at the battle of Loos, and during a lull in the fighting—when the gunners, who had been sleepless for five nights, were resting like tired dogs under their guns—he jotted down the main theme of the poem. After the battle, the artillery brigade to which he was attached was ordered to Ypres, and it was during the long trench warfare in this district, within sight of the ruined tower of Ypres Cathedral, that the poem was finally completed. The last three stanzas were written at midnight in Brigade Headquarters with the German shells screaming over into the ruined town."[8] The excerpts, "A Song of the Guns", "Headquarters", and "The Voice of the Guns", are all from this collection.

"A Song of the Guns"

These are our masters, the slim
    Grim muzzles that irk in the pit;
That chafe for the rushing of wheels,
    For the teams plunging madly to bit
As the gunners wing down to unkey,
    For the trails sweeping half-circle-right,
For the six breech-blocks clashing as one
    To a target viewed clear on the sight—
Gray masses the shells search and tear
Into fragments that bunch as they run—
    For the hour of the red battle-harvest,

---

8 Gilbert Frankau, *A Song of the Guns (Gutenburg Digital, 1916.*

The dream of the slaves of the gun!

We have bartered our souls to the guns;
　　　Every fibre of body and brain
Have we trained to them, chained to them. Serfs?
　　　Aye! but proud of the weight of our chain,
Of our backs that are bowed to their workings,
　　　To hide them and guard and disguise,
Of our ears that are deafened with service,
　　　Of hands that are scarred, and of eyes
Grown hawklike with marking their prey,
　　　Of wings that are slashed as with swords
When we hover, the turn of a blade
　　　From the death that is sweet to our lords.

"Headquarters"

A league and a league from the trenches, from the traversed maze of the lines,—
Where daylong the sniper watches and daylong the bullet whines,
And the cratered earth is in travail with mines and with countermines,—

Here, where haply some woman dreamed, (are those her roses that bloom
In the garden beyond the windows of my littered working-room?)
We have decked the map for our masters as a bride is decked for the groom.

Here, on each numbered lettered square,—cross-road and mound and wire,
Loophole, redoubt, and emplacement, are the targets their mouths desire,—
Gay with purples and browns and blues, have we traced them their arcs of fire.

And ever the type-keys clatter; and ever our keen wires bring
Word from the watchers a-crouch below, word from the watchers a-wing;
And ever we hear the distant growl of our hid guns thundering;

Hear it hardly, and turn again to our maps, where the trench-lines crawl,
Red on the gray and each with a sign for the ranging shrapnel's fall—
Snakes that our masters shall scotch at dawn, as is written here on the wall.

For the weeks of our waiting draw to a close....
There is scarcely a leaf astir

In the garden beyond my windows where the twilight shadows blur
The blaze of some woman's roses...."Bombardment orders, sir."

"The Voice of the Guns"

We are the guns, and your masters! Saw ye our flashes?
Heard ye the scream of our shells in the night, and the shuddering crashes?
Saw ye our work by the roadside, the gray wounded lying,
Moaning to God that he made them—the maimed and the dying?
Husbands or sons, Fathers or lovers, we break them! We are the guns!

We are the guns and ye serve us! Dare ye grow weary,
Steadfast at nighttime, at noontime; or waking, when dawn winds blow dreary
Over the fields and the flats and the reeds of the barrier water,
To wait on the hour of our choosing, the minute decided for slaughter?
    Swift the clock runs;
Yes, to the ultimate second. Stand to your guns!

We are the guns and we need you! Here in the timbered
Pits that are screened by the crest and the copse where at dusk ye unlimbered,
Pits that one found us—and, finding, gave life (did he flinch from the giving?);
Laboured by moonlight when wraith of the dead brooded yet o'er the living,
    Ere with the sun's
Rising the sorrowful spirit abandoned its guns.

Who but the guns shall avenge him? Strip us for action!
Load us and lay to the centremost hair of the dial-sight's refraction.
    Set your quick hands to our levers to compass the sped soul's assoiling;
Brace your taut limbs to the shock when the thrust of the barrel recoiling
    Deafens and stuns!
Vengeance is ours for our servants. Trust ye the guns!

Least of our bond-slaves or greatest, grudge ye the burden?
Hard is this service of ours which has only our service for guerdon:
Grow the limbs lax, and unsteady the hands, which aforetime we trusted;
Flawed, the clear crystal of sight; and the clean steel of hardihood rusted?
    Dominant ones,
Are we not tried serfs and proven—true to our guns?

Ye are the guns! Are we worthy? Shall not these speak for us,

Out of the woods where the torn trees are slashed with the vain bolts that seek for us,

Thunder of batteries firing in unison, swish of shell flighting,

Hissing that rushes to silence and breaks to the thud of alighting?

      Death that outruns

Horseman and foot? Are we justified? Answer, O guns!

Yea! by your works are ye justified,—toil unrelieved;

Manifold labours, coördinate each to the sending achieved;

Discipline, not of the feet but the soul, unremitting, unfeigned;

Tortures unholy by flame and by maiming, known, faced, and disdained;

      Courage that shuns

Only foolhardiness;—even by these are ye worthy your guns!

Wherefore—and unto ye only—power has been given;

Yea! beyond man, over men, over desolate cities and riven;

Yea! beyond space, over earth and the seas and the sky's high dominions;

Yea! beyond time, over Hell and the fiends and the Death-Angel's pinions!

      Vigilant ones,

Loose them, and shatter, and spare not. We are the guns!

Geoffrey Bache Smith (1894–1916)

    Geoffrey Bache Smith is a soldier and poet. He joined the 19th Service Battalion of the Lancashire Fusiliers and participated in the Battle of the Somme. He was hit by shrapnel on November 29, 1916, and died four days later. His collection of poetry entitled *A Spring Harvest* was published in 1918. The excerpts are from the collection.

"April 1916"

Now spring is come upon the hills in France,

And all the trees are delicately fair,

As heeding not the great guns' voice, by chance

Brought down the valley on a wandering air:

Now day by day upon the uplands bare

Do gentle, toiling horses draw the plough,

And birds sing often in the orchards where

Spring wantons it with blossoms on her brow—

Aye! but there is no peace in England now.

O little isle amid unquiet seas,

Though grisly messengers knock on many doors,

Though there be many storms among your trees

And all your banners rent with ancient wars;

Yet such a grace and majesty are yours

There be still some, whose glad heart suffereth

All hate can bring from her misgotten stores,

Telling themselves, so England's self draw breath,

That's all the happiness on this side death.

"Anglia Valida in Senectute"
(On the Declaration of War)

Not like to those who find untrodden ways;

> But down the weary paths we know,

Through every change of sky and change of days

> Silent, processional we go.

Not unto us the soft, unlaboured breath

> Of children's hopes and children's fears:

We are not sworn to battle to the death

> With all the wrongs of all the years:

We are old, we are old, and worn and school'd with ills,

> Maybe our road is almost done,

Maybe we are drawn near unto the hills

> Where rest is and the setting sun:

But yet a pride is ours that will not brook

> The taunts of fools too saucy grown,

He that is rash to prove it, let him look

> He kindle not a fire unknown.

Since first we flung our gauntlet to the skies

> And dared the high Gods' will to bend,

A fire that still may burn deceit and lies

> Burn and consume them to the end.

"The Burial of Sophocles"
(The First Verses)[9]

GATHER great store of roses, crimson-red
    From ancient gardens under summer skies:
New opened buds, and some that soon must shed
    Their leaves to earth, that all expectant lies;
Some from the paths of poets' wandering,
    Some from the places where young lovers meet,
Some from the seats of dreamers pondering,
    And all most richly red, and honey-sweet.
For in the splendour of the afternoon,
    When sunshine lingers on the glittering town
And glorifies the temples wondrous-hewn
    All set about it like a deathless crown,
We will go mingle with the solemn throng,
    With neither eyes that weep, nor hearts that bleed,
That to his grave with slow, majestic song
    Bears down the latest of the godlike seed.
Many a singer lies on distant isle
    Beneath the canopy of changing sky:
Around them waves innumerable smile,
    And o'er their head the restless seabirds cry:
But we will lay him far from sound of seas,
    Far from the jutting crags' unhopeful gloom,
Where there blows never wind save summer breeze,
    And where the growing rose may clasp his tomb.
And thither in the splendid nights of spring,
    When stars in legions over heaven are flung,
Shall come the ancient gods, all wondering
    Why he sings not that had so richly sung:
There Heracles with peaceful foot shall press
    The springing herbage, and Hephæstus strong,
Hera and Aphrodite's loveliness,
    And the great giver of the choric song.
And thither, after weary pilgrimage,
    From unknown lands beyond the hoary wave,

9 "The Burial of Sophocles" was begun before the war and continued at odd times and in various circumstances afterwards; the final version was sent to the editor from the trenches.

Shall travellers through every coming age
    Approach to pluck a blossom from his grave:
Some in the flush of youth, or in the prime,
    Whose life is still as heapèd gold to spend,
And some who have drunk deep of grief and time,
    And who yet linger half-afraid the end.

"We who have Bowed Ourselves to Time"

WE who have bowed ourselves to time
Now arm an uneventful rime
    With panoply of flowers
    Through the long summer hours. . . .
But now our fierce and warlike Muse
Doth soft companionship refuse,
    And we must mount and ride
    Upon a steed untried. . . .
We who have led by gradual ways
Our placid life to sterner days
    And for old quiet things
    Have set the strife of kings,
Who battled have with bloody hands
Through evil times in barren lands,
    To whom the voice of guns
    Speaks and no longer stuns,
Calm, though with death encompassèd,
That watch the hours go overhead
    Knowing too well we must
    With all men come to dust. . . .
Crave of our masters' clemency
Silence a little space that we
    Upon their ear may force
    Tales of our trodden course.

"Dark is the World Our Fathers Left Us"

DARK is the world our fathers left us,
    Wearily, greyly the long years flow,
Almost the gloom has of hope bereft us,

Far is the high gods' song and low:

Sombre the crests of the mountains lonely,
  Leafless, wind-ridden, moan the trees:
Down in the valleys is twilight only,
  Twilight over the mourning seas:

Time was when earth was always golden,
  Time was when skies were always clear:
Spirits and souls of the heroes olden,
  Faint are cries from the darkness, hear!

Tear ye the veil of time asunder
  Tear the veil, 'tis the gods' command,
Hear we the sun-stricken breakers thunder
  Over the shore where the heroes stand.

Dark is the world our fathers left us,
  Heavily, greyly the long years flow,
Almost the gloom has of hope bereft us
  Far is the high gods' song and low.

Siegfried Sassoon (1886–1967)

Siegfried Sassoon is a British poet, novelist and writer, best known for his antiwar poetry and fictionalised autobiographies, being regarded as one of the most representative war poets of the First World War. He enlisted at the beginning of the War in 1914, and in May 1915 he was commissioned to the Royal Welch Fusiliers and soon left to fight in France. After the War, he became a pacifist and social activist, writing and speaking in public, protesting the war. His prose works include *Memoirs of a Fox-Hunting Man* (1928), *Memoirs of an Infantry Officer* (1930), *Sherston's Progress* (1936), *The Weald of Youth* (1942), and *Siegfried's Journey* (1945). His remarkable war poems were inspired by his war experiences, which were originally published in three volumes: *Picture-Show* (1919), *Counter-Attack and Other Poems* (1918), and *The Old Huntsman* (1917), while others include *The War Poems of Siegfried Sassoon* (1919), *Picture-Show* (1919), *Sequences* (1956), and *The Path to Peace* (1960). In 1957, he was awarded the Queen's Medal for Poetry. In his antiwar poetry, he questions every aspect of war machines of the state, church and military, such as the poem "They", which is a tribute to his fellow soldiers and a barbed comment on the church and its support for the war.

"They"

The Bishop tells us: "When the boys come back
They will not be the same; for they'll have fought
In a just cause: they lead the last attack
On Anti-Christ; their comrades' blood has bought
New right to breed an honourable race,
They have challenged Death and dared him face to face."

"We're none of us the same! the boys reply.
For George lost both his legs; and Bill's stone blind;
Poor Jim's shot through the lungs and like to die;
And Bert's gone syphilitic: you'll not find
A chap who's served that hasn't found *some* change."
And the Bishop said: "The ways of God are strange!"

"A Night Attack"

The rank stench of those bodies haunts me still,
And I remember things I'd best forget.
For now we've marched to a green, trenchless land
Twelve miles from battering guns: along the grass
Brown lines of tents are hives for snoring men;
Wide, radiant water sways the floating sky
Below dark, shivering trees. And living-clean
Comes back with thoughts of home and hours of sleep.

To-night I smell the battle; miles away
Gun-thunder leaps and thuds along the ridge;
The spouting shells dig pits in fields of death,
And wounded men are moaning in the woods.
If any friend be there whom I have loved,
God speed him safe to England with a gash.

It's sundown in the camp; some youngster laughs,
Lifting his mug and drinking health to all
Who come unscathed from that unpitying waste.
(Terror and ruin lurk behind his gaze.)
Another sits with tranquil, musing face,

Puffing his pipe and dreaming of the girl
Whose last scrawled letter lies upon his knee.
The sunlight falls, low-ruddy from the west,
Upon their heads; last week they might have died;
And now they stretch their limbs in tired content.

One says 'The bloody Bosche has got the knock;
And soon they'll crumple up and chuck their games.
We've got the beggars on the run at last!'
Then I remembered someone that I'd seen
Dead in a squalid, miserable ditch,
Heedless of toiling feet that trod him down.
He was a Prussian with a decent face,
Young, fresh, and pleasant, so I dare to say.
No doubt he loathed the war and longed for peace,
And cursed our souls because we'd killed his friends.
One night he yawned along a half-dug trench
Midnight; and then the British guns began
With heavy shrapnel bursting low, and 'hows'
Whistling to cut the wire with blinding din.
He didn't move; the digging still went on;
Men stooped and shovelled; someone gave a grunt,
And moaned and died with agony in the sludge.
Then the long hiss of shells lifted and stopped.

He stared into the gloom; a rocket curved,
And rifles rattled angrily on the left
Down by the wood, and there was noise of bombs.
Then the damned English loomed in scrambling haste
Out of the dark and struggled through the wire,
And there were shouts and curses; someone screamed
And men began to blunder down the trench
Without their rifles. It was time to go:
He grabbed his coat; stood up, gulping some bread;
Then clutched his head and fell.

I found him there
In the gray morning when the place was held.
His face was in the mud; one arm flung out

426

As when he crumpled up; his sturdy legs
Were bent beneath his trunk; heels to the sky.

"Counter-Attack"

We'd gained our first objective hours before
While dawn broke like a face with blinking eyes,
Pallid, unshaved and thirsty, blind with smoke.
Things seemed all right at first. We held their line,
With bombers posted, Lewis guns well placed,
And clink of shovels deepening the shallow trench.

The place was rotten with dead; green clumsy legs
High-booted, sprawled and grovelled along the saps
And trunks, face downward, in the sucking mud,
Wallowed like trodden sand-bags loosely filled;
And naked sodden buttocks, mats of hair,
Bulged, clotted heads slept in the plastering slime.
And then the rain began,—the jolly old rain!

A yawning soldier knelt against the bank,
Staring across the morning blear with fog;
He wondered when the Allemands would get busy;
And then, of course, they started with five-nines
Traversing, sure as fate, and never a dud.
Mute in the clamour of shells he watched them burst
Spouting dark earth and wire with gusts from hell,
While posturing giants dissolved in drifts of smoke.
He crouched and flinched, dizzy with galloping fear,
Sick for escape,—loathing the strangled horror
And butchered, frantic gestures of the dead.

An officer came blundering down the trench:
'Stand-to and man the fire-step!' On he went . . .
Gasping and bawling, 'Fire-step . . . counter-attack!'
Then the haze lifted. Bombing on the right
Down the old sap: machine-guns on the left;
And stumbling figures looming out in front.
'O Christ, they're coming at us!' Bullets spat,

427

And he remembered his rifle . . . rapid fire . . .
And started blazing wildly . . . then a bang
Crumpled and spun him sideways, knocked him out
To grunt and wriggle: none heeded him; he choked
And fought the flapping veils of smothering gloom,
Lost in a blurred confusion of yells and groans . . .
Down, and down, and down, he sank and drowned
Bleeding to death. The counter-attack had failed.

"The Rear-Guard"

Groping along the tunnel, step by step,
He winked his prying torch with patching glare
From side to side, and sniffed the unwholesome air.

Tins, boxes, bottles, shapes too vague to know,
A mirror smashed, the mattress from a bed;
And he, exploring fifty feet below
The rosy gloom of battle overhead.

"The Glory Of Women"

You love us when we're heroes, home on leave,
Or wounded in a mentionable place.
You worship decorations; you believe
That chivalry redeems the war's disgrace.
You make us shells. You listen with delight,
By tales of dirt and danger fondly thrilled.
You crown our distant ardours while we fight,
And mourn our laurelled memories when we're killed.
You can't believe that British troops "retire"
When hell's last horror breaks them, and they run,
Trampling the terrible corpses—blind with blood.
O German mother dreaming by the fire,
While you are knitting socks to send your son
His face is trodden deeper in the mud.

"Atrocities"

You told me, in your drunken-boasting mood,
How once you butchered prisoners. That was good!
I'm sure you felt no pity while they stood
Patient and cowed and scared, as prisoners should.

How did you do them in? Come, don't be shy:
You know I love to hear how Germans die,
Downstairs in dug-outs. "Camerad!" they cry;
Then squeal like stoats when bombs begin to fly.

And you? I know your record. You went sick
When orders looked unwholesome: then, with trick
And lie, you wangled home. And here you are,
Still talking big and boozing in a bar.

"The Redeemer"

Darkness: the rain sluiced down; the mire was deep;
It was past twelve on a mid-winter night,
When peaceful folk in beds lay snug asleep;
There, with much work to do before the light,
We lugged our clay-sucked boots as best we might
Along the trench; sometimes a bullet sang,
And droning shells burst with a hollow bang;
We were soaked, chilled and wretched, every one;
Darkness; the distant wink of a huge gun.

I turned in the black ditch, loathing the storm;
A rocket fizzed and burned with blanching flare,
And lit the face of what had been a form
Floundering in mirk. He stood before me there;
I say that He was Christ; stiff in the glare;
And leaning forward from His burdening task,
Both arms supporting it; His eyes on mine
Stared from the woeful head that seemed a mask
Of mortal pain in Hell's unholy shine.

429

No thorny crown, only a woollen cap
He wore—an English soldier, white and strong,
Who loved his time like any simple chap,
Good days of work and sport and homely song;
Now he has learned that nights are very long,
And dawn a watching of the windowed sky.
But to the end, unjudging, he'll endure
Horror and pain, not uncontent to die
That Lancaster on Lune may stand secure.

He faced me, reeling in his weariness,
Shouldering his load of planks, so hard to bear.
I say that He was Christ, who wrought to bless
All groping things with freedom bright as air,
And with His mercy washed and made them fair.
Then the flame sank, and all grew black as pitch,
While we began to struggle along the ditch;
And someone flung his burden in the muck,
Mumbling: "O Christ Almighty, now I'm stuck!"

"Christ and the Soldier"

I

The straggled soldier halted—stared at Him—
Then clumsily dumped down upon his knees,
Gasping, "O blessed crucifix, I'm beat!"
And Christ, still sentried by the seraphim,
Near the front-line, between two splintered trees,
Spoke him: "My son, behold these hands and feet."

The soldier eyed Him upward, limb by limb,
Paused at the Face; then muttered, "Wounds like these
Would shift a bloke to Blighty just a treat!"
Christ, gazing downward, grieving and ungrim,
Whispered, "I made for you the mysteries,
Beyond all battles moves the Paraclete."

II

The soldier chucked his rifle in the dust,
And slipped his pack, and wiped his neck, and said—

"O Christ Almighty, stop this bleeding fight!"
Above that hill the sky was stained like rust
With smoke. In sullen daybreak flaring red
The guns were thundering bombardment's blight.

The soldier cried, "I was born full of lust,
With hunger, thirst, and wishfulness to wed.
Who cares today if I done wrong or right?"
Christ asked all pitying, "Can you put no trust
In my known word that shrives each faithful head?
Am I not resurrection, life and light?"

III

Machine-guns rattled from below the hill;
High bullets flicked and whistled through the leaves;
And smoke came drifting from exploding shells.
Christ said, "Believe; and I can cleanse your ill.
I have not died in vain between two thieves;
Nor made a fruitless gift of miracles."

The soldier answered, "Heal me if you will,
Maybe there's comfort when a soul believes
In mercy, and we need it in these hells.
But be you for both sides? I'm paid to kill
And if I shoot a man his mother grieves.
Does that come into what your teaching tells?"

A bird lit on the Christ and twittered gay;
Then a breeze passed and shook the ripening corn.
A Red Cross waggon bumped along the track.
Forsaken Jesus dreamed in the desolate day—
Uplifted Jesus, Prince of Peace forsworn—
An observation post for the attack.

"Lord Jesus, ain't you got no more to say?"
Bowed hung that head below the crown of thorns.
The soldier shifted, and picked up his pack,
And slung his gun, and stumbled on his way.
"O God," he groaned, "why ever was I born?"…
The battle boomed, and no reply came back.

"The Hero"

'Jack fell as he'd have wished,' the Mother said,
And folded up the letter that she'd read.
'The Colonel writes so nicely.' Something broke
In the tired voice that quavered to a choke.
She half looked up. 'We mothers are so proud
Of our dead soldiers.' Then her face was bowed.

Quietly the Brother Officer went out.
He'd told the poor old dear some gallant lies
That she would nourish all her days, no doubt.
For while he coughed and mumbled, her weak eyes
Had shone with gentle triumph, brimmed with joy,
Because he'd been so brave, her glorious boy.

He thought how 'Jack', cold-footed, useless swine,
Had panicked down the trench that night the mine
Went up at Wicked Corner; how he'd tried
To get sent home, and how, at last, he died,
Blown to small bits. And no one seemed to care
Except that lonely woman with white hair.

Patrick Shaw-Stewart (1888–1917)

Patrick Shaw-Stewart is a British soldier-poet, once regarded as one of the greatest academic brilliance. He joined the army in 1914, and was killed in December 1917. The poem "I saw a man this morning" was penned in 1915 during a period of rest before fighting at Gallipoli and published after his death. It contains allusions to Greek literature, notably Homer's *Iliad*.

"I saw a man this morning"

I saw a man this morning
    Who did not wish to die:
I ask, and cannot answer,
    If otherwise wish I.

Fair broke the day this morning
    Against the Dardanelles;

The breeze blew soft, the morn's cheeks
    Were cold as cold sea-shells.

But other shells are waiting
    Across the Aegean Sea,
Shrapnel and high explosive,
    Shells and hells for me.

O hell of ships and cities,
    Hell of men like me,
Fatal second Helen,
    Why must I follow thee?

Achilles came to Troyland
    And I to Chersonese:
He turned from wrath to battle,
    And I from three days' peace.

Was it so hard, Achilles,
    So very hard to die?
Thou knowest and I know not—
    So much the happier I.

I will go back this morning
    From Imbros over the sea;
Stand in the trench, Achilles,
    Flame-capped, and shout for me.

T. P. Cameron Wilson (1889–1918)

T. P. Cameron Wilson is a British poet and novelist of the First World War. He joined the armed forces in August 1914, reached the Western Front in February 1916, and was horrified by what he saw. He was killed in action by a machine-gun bullet on March 23, 1918, at the age of 29. The excerpt "Magpies in Picardy" is his best-know poem written in 1916 but published posthumously in 1919.

"Magpies in Picardy"

The magpies in Picardy
Are more than I can tell.

They flicker down the dusty roads
And cast a magic spell
On the men who march through Picardy,
Through Picardy to hell.

(The blackbird flies with panic,
The swallow goes like light,
The finches move like ladies,
The owl floats by at night;
But the great and flashing magpie
He flies as artists might.)

A magpie in Picardy
Told me secret things—
Of the music in white feathers,
And the sunlight that sings
And dances in deep shadows—
He told me with his wings.

(The hawk is cruel and rigid,
He watches from a height;
The rook is slow and sombre,
The robin loves to fight;
But the great and flashing magpie
He flies as lovers might.)

He told me that in Picardy,
An age ago or more,
While all his fathers still were eggs,
These dusty highways bore
Brown singing soldiers marching out
Through Picardy to war.

Isaac Rosenberg (1890–1918)

Isaac Rosenberg is a British poet and painter, best known for his "trench poems" of great imaginative power and originality in imagery. He grew up in extreme poverty, working as apprentice engraver a part-time. Characterised by a profound combination of compassion, clarity, stoicism, and irony, his most representative "trench poems" were written between 1916 and 1918. Some critics say that he is influenced by the Imagists, but his poems also show a more distinctive and mature style. Without any job prospects, when the war in Germany was heating up, he enlisted in the Bantam Battalion of 12 Suffolk Regiment and was sent to the Western Front in 1916. He was killed in battle in 1918, but his body was never found. His poems were posthumously collected and published in London in 1922. All of his poems and other genres of work were collected and published in *The Collected Works of Isaac Rosenberg: Poetry, Prose, Letters, Painting, and Drawings* in 1979.

"On Receiving News of the War"

Snow is a strange white word;
No ice or frost
Have asked of bud or bird
For Winter's cost.

Yet ice and frost and snow
From earth to sky
This Summer land doth know,
No man knows why.

In all men's hearts it is.
Some spirit old
Hath turned with malign kiss
Our lives to mould.

Red fangs have torn His face.
God's blood is shed.
He mourns from His lone place
His children dead.

O! ancient crimson curse!
Corrode, consume.
Give back this universe
Its pristine bloom.

"Break of Day in the Trenches"

The darkness crumbles away.
It is the same old druid Time as ever,
Only a live thing leaps my hand,

A queer sardonic rat,

As I pull the parapet's poppy

To stick behind my ear.

Droll rat, they would shoot you if they knew

Your cosmopolitan sympathies.

Now you have touched this English hand

You will do the same to a German

Soon, no doubt, if it be your pleasure

To cross the sleeping green between.

It seems you inwardly grin as you pass

Strong eyes, fine limbs, haughty athletes,

Less chanced than you for life,

Bonds to the whims of murder,

Sprawled in the bowels of the earth,

The torn fields of France.

What do you see in our eyes

At the shrieking iron and flame

Hurled through still heavens?

What quaver—what heart aghast?

Poppies whose roots are in men's veins

Drop, and are ever dropping;

But mine in my ear is safe,

Just a little white with the dust.

"Louse Hunting"

Nudes—stark and glistening,

Yelling in lurid glee. Grinning faces

And raging limbs

Whirl over the floor one fire.

For a shirt verminously busy

Yon soldier tore from his throat, with oaths

Godhead might shrink at, but not the lice.

And soon the shirt was aflare

Over the candle he'd lit while we lay.

Then we all sprang up and stript

To hunt the verminous brood.

Soon like a demons' pantomime

The place was raging.

See the silhouettes agape,

See the gibbering shadows

Mixed with the battled arms on the wall.

See gargantuan hooked fingers

Pluck in supreme flesh

To smutch supreme littleness.

See the merry limbs in hot Highland fling

Because some wizard vermin

Charmed from the quiet this revel

When our ears were half lulled

By the dark music

Blown from Sleep's trumpet.

"Returning, We Hear the Larks"

Sombre the night is:
And though we have our lives, we know
What sinister threat lies there.

Dragging these anguished limbs, we only know
This poison-blasted track opens on our camp—
On a little safe sleep.

But hark! Joy—joy—strange joy.
Lo! Heights of night ringing with unseen larks:
Music showering our upturned listening faces.

Death could drop from the dark
As easily as song—
But song only dropped,
Like a blind man's dreams on the sand
By dangerous tides;
Like a girl's dark hair, for she dreams no ruin lies there,
Or her kisses where a serpent hides.

"August 1914"

What in our lives is burnt
In the fire of this?
The heart's dear granary?
The much we shall miss?

Three lives hath one life—
Iron, honey, gold.
The gold, the honey gone—
Left is the hard and cold.

Iron are our lives
Molten right through our youth.
A burnt space through ripe fields,
A fair mouth's broken tooth.

"Dead Man's Dump"

The plunging limbers over the shattered track
Racketed with their rusty freight,
Stuck out like many crowns of thorns,
And the rusty stakes like sceptres old
To stay the flood of brutish men
Upon our brothers dear.

The wheels lurched over sprawled dead
But pained them not, though their bones crunched,
Their shut mouths made no moan,
They lie there huddled, friend and foeman,
Man born of man, and born of woman,
And shells go crying over them
From night till night and now.

Earth has waited for them
All the time of their growth
Fretting for their decay:
Now she has them at last!
In the strength of their strength

Suspended—stopped and held.

What fierce imaginings their dark souls lit?
Earth! have they gone into you?
Somewhere they must have gone,
And flung on your hard back
Is their souls' sack ,
Emptied of God-ancestralled essences.
Who hurled them out? Who hurled?

None saw their spirits' shadow shake the grass,
Or stood aside for the half-used life to pass
Out of those doomed nostrils and the doomed mouth,
When the swift iron burning bee
Drained the wild honey of their youth.

What of us, who flung on the shrieking pyre,
Walk, our usual thoughts untouched,
Our lucky limbs as on ichor fed,
Immortal seeming ever?
Perhaps when the flames beat loud on us,
A fear may choke in our veins
And the startled blood may stop.

The air is loud with death,
The dark air spurts with fire
The explosions ceaseless are.
Timelessly now, some minutes past,
These dead strode time with vigorous life,
Till the shrapnel called 'an end!'
But not to all. In bleeding pangs
Some borne on stretchers dreamed of home,
Dear things, war-blotted from their hearts.

A man's brains splattered on
A stretcher-bearer's face;
His shook shoulders slipped their load,
But when they bent to look again
The drowning soul was sunk too deep

For human tenderness.

They left this dead with the older dead,
Stretched at the cross roads.
Burnt black by strange decay,
Their sinister faces lie;
The lid over each eye,
The grass and coloured clay
More motions have then they,
Joined to the great sunk silences .

Here is one not long dead;
His dark hearing caught our far wheels,
And the choked soul stretched weak hands
To reach the living word the far wheels said,
The blood-dazed intelligence beating for light,
Crying through the suspense of the far torturing wheels
Swift for the end to break,
Or the wheels to break,
Cried as the tide of the world broke over his sight.

Will they come? Will they ever come?
Even as the mixed hoofs of the mules,
The quivering-bellied mules,
And the rushing wheels all mixed
With his tortured upturned sight,
So we crashed round the bend,
We heard his weak scream,
We heard his very last sound,
And our wheels grazed his dead face.

Ivor Gurney (1890–1937)

Ivor Bertie Gurney is a British poet and composer. He composed about 300 songs and numerous chamber and instrumental works. He joined the Army in 1917 and served in France, during which he was twice wounded, but he went through a period of intense creativity in the late 1910s until his mental state deteriorated by 1921. He spent the rest of his life in institutions and died of tuberculosis. His most representative collection of poetry includes *Severn and Somme* (1917) and *War's Embers* (1919), from which the excerpts come.

"To His Love"

He's gone, and all our plans
    Are useless indeed.
We'll walk no more on Cotswold
    Where the sheep feed
    Quietly and take no heed.

His body that was so quick
    Is not as you
Knew it, on Severn river
    Under the blue
    Driving our small boat through.

You would not know him now...
    But still he died
Nobly, so cover him over
    With violets of pride
    Purple from Severn side.

Cover him, cover him soon!
    And with thick-set
Masses of memoried flowers—
    Hide that red wet
    Thing I must somehow forget.

"First Time In"

After the dread tales and red yarns of the Line
Anything might have come to us; but the divine
Afterglow brought us up to a Welsh colony
Hiding in sandbag ditches, whispering consolatory
Soft foreign things. Then we were taken in
To low huts candle-lit, shaded close by slitten
Oilsheets, and there but boys gave us kind welcome,
So that we looked out as from the edge of home.
Sang us Welsh things, and changed all former notions
To human hopeful things. And the next day's guns
Nor any Line-pangs ever quite could blot out

That strangely beautiful entry to War's rout;
Candles they gave us, precious and shared over-rations—
Ulysses found little more in his wanderings without doubt.
'David of the White Rock', the 'Slumber Song' so soft, and that
Beautiful tune to which roguish words by Welsh pit boys
Are sung—but never more beautiful than here under the guns' noise.

"The Silent One"

Who died on the wires, and hung there, one of two—
Who for his hours of life had chattered through
Infinite lovely chatter of Bucks accent:
Yet faced unbroken wires; stepped over, and went
A noble fool, faithful to his stripes—and ended.
But I weak, hungry, and willing only for the chance
Of line—to fight in the line, lay down under unbroken
Wires, and saw the flashes and kept unshaken,
Till the politest voice—a finicking accent, said:
'Do you think you might crawl through there: there's a hole.'
Darkness, shot at: I smiled, as politely replied—
'I'm afraid not, Sir.' There was no hole no way to be seen,
Nothing but chance of death, after tearing of clothes.
Kept flat, and watched the darkness, hearing bullets whizzing —
And thought of music—and swore deep heart's deep oaths
(Polite to God) and retreated and came on again,
Again retreated—and a second time faced the screen.

"To the Poet before Battle"

Now, youth, the hour of thy dread passion comes;
Thy lovely things must all be laid away;
And thou, as others, must face the riven day
Unstirred by rattle of the rolling drums,
Or bugles' strident cry. When mere noise numbs
The sense of being, the sick soul doth sway,
Remember thy great craft's honour, that they may say
Nothing in shame of poets. Then the crumbs
Of praise the little versemen joyed to take
Shall be forgotten; then they must know we are,

For all our skill in words, equal in might

And strong of mettle as those we honoured; make

The name of poet terrible in just war,

And like a crown of honour upon the fight.

Arthur Graeme West (1891–1917)

Arthur Graeme West is remembered for his *The Diary of a Dead Officer* (1919), which, comprising his literary remains, contains just ten poems, along with letters and diary entries covering the period from his enlistment in early 1915 until his death near Bapaume on 3 April 1917.

"The Night Patrol"

Over the top! The wire's thin here, unbarbed

Plain rusty coils, not staked, and low enough:

Full of old tins, though—'When you're through, all three,

Aim quarter left for fifty yards or so

Then straight for that new piece of German wire;

See if it's thick, and listen for a while

For sounds of working; don't run any risks;

About an hour; now, over!'

        And we placed

Our hands on the topmost sand-bags, leapt, and stood

A second with curved backs, then crept to the wire,

Wormed ourselves tinkling through, glanced back, and dropped.

The sodden ground was splashed with shallow pools,

And tufts of crackling cornstalks, two years old,

No man had reaped, and patches of spring grass.

Half-seen, as rose and sank the flares, were strewn

With the wrecks of our attack: the bandoliers,

Packs, rifles, bayonets, belts, and haversacks,

Shell fragments, and the huge whole forms of shells

Shot fruitlessly—and everywhere the dead.

Only the dead were always present—present

As a vile sickly smell of rottenness;

The rustling stubble and the early grass,

The slimy pools—the dead men stank through all,

Pungent and sharp; as bodies loomed before,

And as we passed, they stank: then dulled away

443

To that vague fœtor, all encompassing,

Infecting earth and air. They lay, all clothed,

Each in some new and piteous attitude

That we well marked to guide us back: as he,

Outside our wire, that lay on his back and crossed

His legs Crusader-wise; I smiled at that,

And thought on Elia and his Temple Church.

From him, at quarter left, lay a small corpse,

Down in a hollow, huddled as inbed,

That one of us put his hand on unawares.

Next was a bunch of half a dozen men

All blown to bits, an archipelago

Of corrupt fragments, vexing to us three,

Who had no light to see by, save the flares.

On such a trail, so lit, for ninety yards

We crawled on belly and elbows, till we saw

Instead of lumpish dead before our eyes,

The stakes and crosslines of the German wire.

We lay in shelter of the last dead man,

Ourselves as dead, and heard their shovels ring

Turning the earth, then talk and cough at times.

A sentry fired and a machine-gun spat;

They shot a flare above us, when it fell

And spluttered out in the pools of No Man's Land,

We turned and crawled past the remembered dead:

Past him and him, and them and him, until

For he lay some way apart, we caught the scent

Of the Crusader and slid past his legs,

And through the wire and home, and got our rum.

Vera Brittain (1893–1970)

Vera Brittain is a British poet, writer, and lifelong pacifist. She served as a nurse in the Voluntary Aid Detachment hospitals in London and France during the War. Her first poetry collection, *Verses of a V.A.D* was published in 1918, and in 1934 she turned out *Poems of the War and After*. She also wrote several novels such as *Honourable Estate* (1936) and several historical studies such as *Lady into Woman: a History of Women from Victoria to Elizabeth II* (1953).

"St. Pancras Station, August 1915"

One long, sweet kiss pressed close upon my lips,
      One moment's rest on your swift-beating heart,
And all was over, for the hour had come
      For us to part.

A sudden forward motion of the train,
      The world grown dark although the sun still shone,
One last blurred look through aching tear-dimmed eyes—
      And you were gone.

"To My Brother" (*In Memory of July 1st, 1916*)

Your battle-wounds are scars upon my heart,
      Received when in that grand and tragic "show"
You played your part,
      Two years ago,

And silver in the summer morning sun
      see the symbol of your courage glow—
That Cross you won
      Two years ago.

Though now again you watch the shrapnel fly,
      And hear the guns that daily louder grow,
As in July
      Two years ago,

May you endure to lead the Last Advance
      And with your men pursue the flying foe
As once in France
      Two years ago.

Wilfred Owen (1893–1918)

Wilfred Owen is a British poet, widely recognised as one of the greatest voices and one of the most admired poets of the First World War, though few of his poems appeared in print during his lifetime. He enlisted in the Artists Rifles in 1915, and was commissioned as a second lieutenant in the Manchester Regiment in 1916. He was killed at the age of 25—

just one week before the Armistice was declared. The earliest collection of his poetry, *Poems of Wilfred Owen*, was published in December 1920, with an introduction by Sassoon, in the preface of which he says, "This book is not about heroes. English Poetry is not yet fit to speak of them. Nor is it about deeds or lands, nor anything about glory, honour, dominion or power". His poetry, as some critic says, has "graphically illustrated the horrors of warfare, the physical landscapes that surrounded him, and the human body in relation to those landscapes", standing "in stark contrast to the patriotic poems of war written by earlier poets such as Rupert Brooke.

"1914"

War broke: and now the Winter of the world
With perishing great darkness closes in.
The foul tornado, centred at Berlin,
Is over all the width of Europe whirled,
Rending the sails of progress. Rent or furled
Are all Art's ensigns. Verse wails. Now begin
Famines of thought and feeling. Love's wine's thin.
The grain of human Autumn rots, down-hurled.

For after Spring had bloomed in early Greece,
And Summer blazed her glory out with Rome,
An Autumn softly fell, a harvest home,
A slow grand age, and rich with all increase.
But now, for us, wild Winter, and the need
Of sowings for new Spring, and blood for seed.

"Anthem for Doomed Youth"[10]

What passing-bells for these who die as cattle?
    Only the monstrous anger of the guns.
    Only the stuttering rifles' rapid rattle
Can patter out their hasty orisons.

---

10 The poem's representative phrase "die as cattle" symbolizes the ways most people living in capitalist societies are treated as animals and as expendable commodities, highlighting the stark contrasts between the empty formalities of meaningless religious observances and the real brutalities of war. It also suggests that religion provides no real help in preventing or coping with war, and thus can be read as an implied satire on the hollowness of religious explanations and consolations.

No mockeries now for them; no prayers nor bells,
    Nor any voice of mourning save the choirs,—
The shrill, demented choirs of wailing shells;
    And bugles calling for them from sad shires.

What candles may be held to speed them all?
    Not in the hands of boys, but in their eyes
Shall shine the holy glimmers of good-byes.
    The pallor of girls' brows shall be their pall;
Their flowers the tenderness of patient minds,
And each slow dusk a drawing-down of blinds.

"Arms and the Boy"

Let the boy try along this bayonet-blade
How cold steel is, and keen with hunger of blood;
Blue with all malice, like a madman's flash;
And thinly drawn with famishing for flesh.

Lend him to stroke these blind, blunt bullet-heads
Which long to nuzzle in the hearts of lads.
Or give him cartridges of fine zinc teeth,
Sharp with the sharpness of grief and death.

For his teeth seem for laughing round an apple.
There lurk no claws behind his fingers supple;
And God will grow no talons at his heels,
Nor antlers through the thickness of his curls.

"Disabled"

He sat in a wheeled chair, waiting for dark,
And shivered in his ghastly suit of grey,
Legless, sewn short at elbow. Through the park
Voices of boys rang saddening like a hymn,
Voices of play and pleasure after day,
Till gathering sleep had mothered them from him.

About this time Town used to swing so gay

447

When glow-lamps budded in the light-blue trees
And girls glanced lovelier as the air grew dim,
—In the old times, before he threw away his knees.
Now he will never feel again how slim
Girls' waists are, or how warm their subtle hands,
All of them touch him like some queer disease.

There was an artist silly for his face,
For it was younger than his youth, last year.
Now he is old; his back will never brace;
He's lost his colour very far from here,
Poured it down shell-holes till the veins ran dry,
And half his lifetime lapsed in the hot race,
And leap of purple spurted from his thigh.
One time he liked a bloodsmear down his leg,
After the matches carried shoulder-high.
It was after football, when he'd drunk a peg,
He thought he'd better join. He wonders why . . .
Someone had said he'd look a god in kilts.

That's why; and maybe, too, to please his Meg,
Aye, that was it, to please the giddy jilts,
He asked to join. He didn't have to beg;
Smiling they wrote his lie; aged nineteen years.
Germans he scarcely thought of; and no fears
Of Fear came yet. He thought of jewelled hilts
For daggers in plaid socks; of smart salutes;
And care of arms; and leave; and pay arrears;
Esprit de corps; and hints for young recruits.
And soon, he was drafted out with drums and cheers.

Some cheered him home, but not as crowds cheer Goal.
Only a solemn man who brought him fruits
Thanked him; and then inquired about his soul.
Now, he will spend a few sick years in Institutes,
And do what things the rules consider wise,
And take whatever pity they may dole.
To-night he noticed how the women's eyes
Passed from him to the strong men that were whole.

How cold and late it is! Why don't they come
And put him into bed? Why don't they come?

"Dulce Et Decorum Est"

Bent double, like old beggars under sacks,
Knock-kneed, coughing like hags, we cursed through sludge,
Till on the haunting flares we turned our backs,
And towards our distant rest began to trudge.
Men marched asleep. Many had lost their boots
But limped on, blood-shod. All went lame; all blind;
Drunk with fatigue; deaf even to the hoots
Of tired, outstripped Five-Nines that dropped behind.

Gas! GAS! Quick, boys!—An ecstasy of fumbling,
Fitting the clumsy helmets just in time;
But someone still was yelling out and stumbling,
And flound'ring like a man in fire or lime . . .
Dim, through the misty panes and thick green light,
As under a green sea, I saw him drowning.

In all my dreams, before my helpless sight,
He plunges at me, guttering, choking, drowning.

If in some smothering dreams, you too could pace
Behind the wagon that we flung him in,
And watch the white eyes writhing in his face,
His hanging face, like a devil's sick of sin;
If you could hear, at every jolt, the blood
Come gargling from the froth-corrupted lungs,
Obscene as cancer, bitter as the cud
Of vile, incurable sores on innocent tongues,—
My friend, you would not tell with such high zest
To children ardent for some desperate glory,
The old Lie: *Dulce et decorum est Pro patria mori.*

"Futility"

Move him into the sun—

Gently its touch awoke him once,

At home, whispering of fields half-sown.

Always it woke him, even in France,

Until this morning and this snow.

If anything might rouse him now

The kind old sun will know.

Think how it wakes the seeds—

Woke once the clays of a cold star.

Are limbs, so dear-achieved, are sides

Full-nerved, still warm, too hard to stir?

Was it for this the clay grew tall?

O what made fatuous sunbeams toil

To break earth's sleep at all?

"Strange Meeting"[11]

It seemed that out of the battle I escaped

Down some profound dull tunnel, long since scooped

Through granites which Titanic wars had groined.

Yet also there encumbered sleepers groaned,

Too fast in thought or death to be bestirred.

Then, as I probed them, one sprang up, and stared

With piteous recognition in fixed eyes,

Lifting distressful hands as if to bless.

And by his smile, I knew that sullen hall—

By his dead smile I knew we stood in Hell.

With a thousand pains that vision's face was grained;

Yet no blood reached there from the upper ground,

And no guns thumped, or down the flues made moan.

"Strange friend," I said, "Here is no cause to mourn."

"None," said that other, "save the undone years,

The hopelessness. Whatever hope is yours,

Was my life also; I went hunting wild

---

11 In the poem "Strange Meeting," war and peace are hard to keep separate, as are life and death, friend and enemy, safety and danger, earth and hell. In this poem, physical descent results in a kind of moral and spiritual ascent, and escape from pain results in pain of a different sort.

After the wildest beauty in the world,

Which lies not calm in eyes, or braided hair,

But mocks the steady running of the hour,

And if it grieves, grieves richlier than here.

For by my glee might many men have laughed,

And of my weeping something had been left,

Which must die now. I mean the truth untold,

The pity of war, the pity war distilled.

Now men will go content with what we spoiled,

Or, discontent, boil bloody, and be spilled.

They will be swift with swiftness of the tigress,

None will break ranks, though nations trek from progress.

Courage was mine, and I had mystery;

Wisdom was mine, and I had mastery:

To miss the march of this retreating world

Into vain citadels that are not walled.

Then, when much blood had clogged their chariot-wheels

I would go up and wash them from sweet wells,

Even with truths that lie too deep for taint.

I would have poured my spirit without stint

But not through wounds; not on the cess of war.

Foreheads of men have bled where no wounds were.

I am the enemy you killed, my friend.

I knew you in this dark; for so you frowned

Yesterday through me as you jabbed and killed.

I parried; but my hands were loath and cold.

Let us sleep now . . ."

"Exposure"

Our brains ache, in the merciless iced east winds that knive us…

Wearied we keep awake because the night is silent…

Low, drooping flares confuse our memory of the salient…

Worried by silence, sentries whisper, curious, nervous,

　　　　　　　But nothing happens.

Watching, we hear the mad gusts tugging on the wire,

Like twitching agonies of men among its brambles.

Northward, incessantly, the flickering gunnery rumbles,
Far off, like a dull rumour of some other war.
　　　　　　　　What are we doing here ?

The poignant misery of dawn begins to grow…
We only know war lasts, rain soaks, and clouds sag stormy.
Dawn massing in the east her melancholy army
Attacks once more in ranks on shivering ranks of grey,
　　　　　　　　But nothing happens.

Sudden successive flights of bullets streak the silence.
Less deathly than the air that shudders black with snow,
With sidelong flowing flakes that flock, pause, and renew;
We watch them wandering up and down the wind's nonchalance,
　　　　　　　　But nothing happens.

Pale flakes with fingering stealth come feeling for our faces—
We cringe in holes, back on forgotten dreams, and stare, snow-dazed,
Deep into grassier ditches. So we drowse, sun-dozed,
Littered with blossoms trickling where the blackbird fusses,
　　　　　　　　—Is it that we are dying?

Slowly our ghosts drag home: glimpsing the sunk fires, glozed
With crusted dark-red jewels; crickets jingle there;
For hours the innocent mice rejoice: the house is theirs;
Shutters and doors, all closed: on us the doors are closed,—
　　　　　　　　We turn back to our dying.

Since we believe not otherwise can kind fires burn;
Nor ever suns smile true on child, or field, or fruit.
For God's invincible spring our love is made afraid;
Therefore, not loath, we lie out here; therefore were born,
　　　　　　　　For love of God seems dying.

Tonight, this frost will fasten on this mud and us,
Shrivelling many hands, puckering foreheads crisp.
The burying-party, picks and shovels in shaking grasp,
Pause over half-known faces. All their eyes are ice,
But nothing happens.

"Insensibility"

I

Happy are men who yet before they are killed

Can let their veins run cold.

Whom no compassion fleers

Or makes their feet

Sore on the alleys cobbled with their brothers.

The front line withers.

But they are troops who fade, not flowers,

For poets' tearful fooling:

Men, gaps for filling:

Losses, who might have fought

Longer; but no one bothers.

II

And some cease feeling

Even themselves or for themselves.

Dullness best solves

The tease and doubt of shelling,

And Chance's strange arithmetic

Comes simpler than the reckoning of their shilling.

They keep no check on armies' decimation.

III

Happy are these who lose imagination:

They have enough to carry with ammunition.

Their spirit drags no pack.

Their old wounds, save with cold, can not more ache.

Having seen all things red,

Their eyes are rid

Of the hurt of the colour of blood for ever.

And terror's first constriction over,

Their hearts remain small-drawn.

Their senses in some scorching cautery of battle

Now long since ironed,

Can laugh among the dying, unconcerned.

IV

Happy the soldier home, with not a notion

How somewhere, every dawn, some men attack,

And many sighs are drained.

453

Happy the lad whose mind was never trained:

His days are worth forgetting more than not.

He sings along the march

Which we march taciturn, because of dusk,

The long, forlorn, relentless trend

From larger day to huger night.

V

We wise, who with a thought besmirch

Blood over all our soul,

How should we see our task

But through his blunt and lashless eyes?

Alive, he is not vital overmuch;

Dying, not mortal overmuch;

Nor sad, nor proud,

Nor curious at all.

He cannot tell

Old men's placidity from his.

VI

But cursed are dullards whom no cannon stuns,

That they should be as stones.

Wretched are they, and mean

With paucity that never was simplicity.

By choice they made themselves immune

To pity and whatever moans in man

Before the last sea and the hapless stars;

Whatever mourns when many leave these shores;

Whatever shares

The eternal reciprocity of tears.

"The Sentry"

We'd found an old Boche dug-out, and he knew,

And gave us hell; for shell on frantic shell

Lit full on top, but never quite burst through.

Rain, guttering down in waterfalls of slime,

Kept slush waist-high and rising hour by hour,

And choked the steps too thick with clay to climb.

What murk of air remained stank old, and sour

With fumes from whizz-bangs, and the smell of men

454

Who'd lived there years, and left their curse in the den,
If not their corpses…

        There we herded from the blast
Of whizz-bangs; but one found our door at last,—
Buffeting eyes and breath, snuffing the candles,
And thud! flump! thud! down the steep steps came thumping
And sploshing in the flood, deluging muck,
The sentry's body; then his rifle, handles
Of old Boche bombs, and mud in ruck on ruck.
We dredged it up, for dead, until he whined,
'O sir—my eyes,—I'm blind,—I'm blind,—I'm blind.'
Coaxing, I held a flame against his lids
And said if he could see the least blurred light
He was not blind; in time they'd get all right.
'I can't,' he sobbed. Eyeballs, huge-bulged like squids',
Watch my dreams still,—yet I forgot him there
In posting Next for duty, and sending a scout
To beg a stretcher somewhere, and flound'ring about
To other posts under the shrieking air.

Those other wretches, how they bled and spewed,
And one who would have drowned himself for good,—
I try not to remember these things now.
Let Dread hark back for one word only: how,
Half-listening to that sentry's moans and jumps,
And the wild chattering of his shivered teeth,
Renewed most horribly whenever crumps
Pummelled the roof and slogged the air beneath,—
Through the dense din, I say, we heard him shout
'I see your lights!'—But ours had long gone out.

"Spring Offensive"

Halted against the shade of a last hill
They fed, and eased of pack-loads, were at ease;
And leaning on the nearest chest or knees
Carelessly slept.
        But many there stood still

To face the stark blank sky beyond the ridge,

Knowing their feet had come to the end of the world.

Marvelling they stood, and watched the long grass swirled

By the May breeze, murmurous with wasp and midge;

And though the summer oozed into their veins

Like an injected drug for their bodies' pains,

Sharp on their souls hung the imminent ridge of grass,

Fearfully flashed the sky's mysterious glass.

Hour after hour they ponder the warm field

And the far valley behind, where buttercups

Had blessed with gold their slow boots coming up;

When even the little brambles would not yield

But clutched and clung to them like sorrowing arms.

They breathe like trees unstirred.

Till like a cold gust thrills the little word

At which each body and its soul begird

And tighten them for battle. No alarms

Of bugles, no high flags, no clamorous haste,—

Only a lift and flare of eyes that faced

The sun, like a friend with whom their love is done.

O larger shone that smile against the sun,—

Mightier than his whose bounty these have spurned.

So, soon they topped the hill, and raced together

Over an open stretch of herb and heather

Exposed. And instantly the whole sky burned

With fury against them; earth set sudden cups

In thousands for their blood; and the green slope

Chasmed and deepened sheer to infinite space.

Of them who running on that last high place

Breasted the surf of bullets, or went up

On the hot blast and fury of hell's upsurge,

Or plunged and fell away past this world's verge,

Some say God caught them even before they fell.

But what say such as from existence' brink

Ventured but drave too swift to sink,

The few who rushed in the body to enter hell,

And there out-fiending all its fiends and flames

With superhuman inhumanities,

Long-famous glories, immemorial shames—

And crawling slowly back, have by degrees

Regained cool peaceful air in wonder—

Why speak not they of comrades that went under?

Herbert Read (1893–1968)

Herbert Read is a British poet, literary and art critic, and thinker. He fought in the First World War, during which he served with the Yorkshire Regiment in France and Belgium. He wrote two volumes of poetry based upon these experiences in such poems as *Songs of Chaos* (1915) and *Naked Warriors* (1919). After the Second World War outbreak, he became an outspoken pacifist. In the 1950s and 1960s, he had become a renowned critic of literature and the arts. His final volume, *Collected Poems*, was published in 1966. The excerpt "Refugees" was written in 1914.

"The Refugees"

Mute figures with bowed heads

They travel along the road:

Old women, incredibly old

and a hand cart of chattels.

They do not weep:

their eyes are too raw for tears.

Past them have hastened

processions of returning gunteams

baggage wagons and swift horsemen.

Now they struggle along

with the rearguard of a broken army.

We shall hold the enemy towards nightfall

and they will move

mutely into the dark behind us,

only the creaking cart disturbing their sorrowful serenity.

Charles Sorley (1895–1915)

Charles Sorley is a Scottish soldier-poet. He once studied in Germany up until the outbreak of the First World War. Returning to England, He joined the Suffolk Regiment and later rose to the rank of Captain at the mere age of twenty. On October 13th, 1915, he was shot in the head by a sniper at the Battle of Loos. He has left to us all together 37 complete poems, which were collected in his posthumous *Marlborough and Other Poems* (1916). Some critics say that Sorley's poetry serves as the forerunner to Sassoon and Owen, but his style is less sentimental than Rupert Brooke's.

"To Germans"

You are blind like us. Your hurt no man designed,
And no man claimed the conquest of your land.
But gropers both through fields of thought confined
We stumble and we do not understand.
You only saw your future bigly planned,
And we, the tapering paths of our own mind,
And in each other's dearest ways we stand,
And hiss and hate. And the blind fight the blind.

When it is peace, then we may view again
With new-won eyes each other's truer form
And wonder. Grown more loving-kind and warm
We'll grasp firm hands and laugh at the old pain,
When it is peace. But until peace, the storm
The darkness and the thunder and the rain.

"All the Hills and Vales Along"

All the hills and vales along
Earth is bursting into song,
And the singers are the chaps
Who are going to die perhaps.
  O sing, marching men,
  Till the valleys ring again.
  Give your gladness to earth's keeping,
  So be glad, when you are sleeping.

Cast away regret and rue,
Think what you are marching to.
Little live, great pass.
Jesus Christ and Barabbas

Were found the same day.
This died, that went his way.

> So sing with joyful breath,
> For why, you are going to death.
> Teeming earth will surely store
> All the gladness that you pour.

Earth that never doubts nor fears,
Earth that knows of death, not tears,
Earth that bore with joyful ease
Hemlock for Socrates,
Earth that blossomed and was glad
'Neath the cross that Christ had,
Shall rejoice and blossom too
When the bullet reaches you.

> Wherefore, men marching
> On the road to death, sing!
> Pour your gladness on earth's head,
> So be merry, so be dead.

From the hills and valleys earth
Shouts back the sound of mirth,
Tramp of feet and lilt of song
Ringing all the road along.
All the music of their going,
Ringing swinging glad song-throwing,
Earth will echo still, when foot
Lies numb and voice mute.

> On, marching men, on
> To the gates of death with song.
> Sow your gladness for earth's reaping,
> So you may be glad, though sleeping.
> Strew your gladness on earth's bed,
> So be merry, so be dead.

"When You See Millions of the Mouthless Dead"

When you see millions of the mouthless dead
Across your dreams in pale battalions go,

Say not soft things as other men have said,

That you'll remember. For you need not so.

Give them not praise. For, deaf, how should they know

It is not curses heaped on each gashed head?

Nor tears. Their blind eyes see not your tears flow.

Nor honour. It is easy to be dead.

Say only this, 'They are dead.' Then add thereto,

'Yet many a better one has died before.'

Then, scanning all the o'ercrowded mass, should you

Perceive one face that you loved heretofore,

It is a spook. None wears the face you knew.

Great death has made all his for evermore.

Chapter VIII

The Anglo-American Poetry of the Spanish Civil War and World

War II (1918–1945)

The First World War left this world a world of looming crises, among which waves of rampant civil and inter-state wars were rearing their ugly heads. The 1920s marked a relatively peaceful period for the world to recuperate itself, but the 1930s were immediately encountered by turbulent events that would shape the contemporary course of history: the worldwide economic depression, the Spanish Civil War, and the beginnings of World War II.

The Spanish Civil War witnessed an internal conflict, or a military revolution fighting between the Republicans, known as the left side supported by the Soviet Union and the European democracies, which was formed by the Spanish government together with unions, communists, anarchists, workers, and peasants, and the Nationalists, as were called the Rebels aided by Fascist Italy and Nazi Germany and supported by the bourgeoisie, the landlords, and, generally, the upper classes. In 1936, General Francisco Franco (1892–1975) headed a coup d'état that interrupted the democratically elected government of the Second Republic (1931–1936). Winning the revolution, Franco took power and thus inaugurated the longest dictatorship in the history of modern Europe (1939–1975).

The war was closely linked to the European context of the time, where a multitude of foreign factors are also involved. The struggle between the Republican and National Forces engaged the imagination and the conscience of many writers and intellectuals from around the world. The polarisation of political and social values that characterised the war represented the defining struggle of the age: a clash not just between the opposing political ideologies of socialism and fascism, but between civilisation and barbarism, and good and evil. For

461

the Anglo-American world, thousands of volunteers went to Spain. For instance, "The International Brigades" were organized as military units made up of volunteers from different countries, who travelled to Spain to fight for the Second Spanish Republic.

Both British and American poets of the period had played a considerable part, because to many people the struggle of the Republicans has seemed a struggle for the conditions without which the writing and reading of poetry are almost impossible in modern society. Those poets fighting in Spain developed a political and moral awareness through painful experiences and the harsh realities of the war. Representatives from Britain include Stephen Spender, W. H. Auden, George Orwell, Julian Bell, Christopher Caudwell, John Cornford, Sylvia Townsend Warner, George Barker, Rex Warner, and Ralph Fox, many of whom also experienced the Second World War.

While atrocities of the Spanish Civil War committed in the name of ideology were being published daily, and a looming fatalism in many parts of society echoed with the threat of another European war looming large—the Second World War, which fought on almost every continent from 1939 to 1945, and most countries, including all of the great powers, fought as part of two military alliances: the "Axis" (the Rome-Berlin-Tokyo Axis), the alliance of Nazi Germany, Fascist Italy and Japan that was established in 1936, and the "Allies", the coalition of countries including Poland, France, and the United Kingdom formed in 1939 while the British Commonwealth of Canada, Australia, New Zealand, South Africa, and Newfoundland joined soon after the outbreak of war, the Soviet Union joined the group in mid-1941, and the United States joined after Japan's attack on Pearl Harbor. The War was fought as a "total war", meaning all resources a country had, no matter if they were civilian or military ones, had been used in the war efforts. It in fact killed more civilians than soldiers and displaced millions more, included the Holocaust and the systematic extermination of other targeted populations in both Europe and Asia, and concluded with the explosion of two atomic warheads in Japan. In Marxian perspective, if World War I had been an inter-imperialist war in which the rival imperialist powers re-divided the world, the Second World War could be understood as such: It developed in two stages, the first was from its commencement form 1939 to 1941 as an inter-imperialist war, a battle for spoils between rival bourgeoisies, while the second stage, was from 1941 to 1949, changed into an anti-fascist war, a war for human and national liberation.

The poetry of World War II continued to sing war's glooming experiences, but compared with World War I, not many Anglo-American poets produced this war representation. For the British poets of the War, Marina Mackay writes in her *The Cambridge Companion to the Literature of World War II* (2009): "The Second World War is now recognised as a watershed for British poetry, breaking the dominance of high modernist orthodoxies (signalled by the death of Yeats), transforming the openly political poetics of the Auden group into a war poetry of symptom and reportage (inaugurated by the emigration of Auden and Isherwood to the US), releasing a contained and self-censored British surrealism in the form of the New Apocalypse, and seeing the redefinition of formal genres such as the religious ode, sonnet sequence, elegy, and ballad within a range of new registers, from Rilkean-Jungian (Sidney Keyes) to psychoanalytic-demotic (G. S. Fraser)."[1] Those poets include the groups of British poets called respectively the Oxford Poets and Apocalyptic Poets: W.H. Auden, Christopher Isherwood, C. Day-Lewis, and Louis MacNeice, and Stephen Spender, members of the generation of British poets who came to prominence in the 1930s. They already knew the awfulness of armed conflict and came from a society that already knew about its horrors.

For the American poets of the genre, Marina Mackay also wrote in the monograph: "the American poetry of World War II is extremely diverse both formally and thematically. As a result, it defies ready classification and frustrates any sense of coherence."[2] Thematically, combat soldiers could express anti-military sentiments and complaints of national hypocrisy in addition to their patriotism; African American soldiers defended a nation that had abused and continued to abuse them; Jewish soldiers fought Nazi brutality against European Jews; bomber pilots and the infantryman had different genres of warfare with differing ethical dimensions.[3] Representatives of these diverse poets include Louis Simpson, Richard Hugo, Randall Jarrell, Harvey Shapiro, Howard Nemerov, Gwendolyn Brooks, W.H. Auden, Robert Lowell, and Marianne Moore.

1. Poetry of the Spanish Civil War

The Spanish Civil War produced a substantial volume of poetry in English because a number of English-speaking poets served in the War on both sides, making it a distinctive episode in British literary history: Volunteers in the International Brigades fighting for the Republicans' side include such poets as Tom Wintringham, Clive Branson, John Cornford, Charles Donnelly, and Alex McDade, and sometimes Sylvia Townsend Warner and Valentine Ackland; on the Nationalist side, the most famous English language poet of the Spanish Civil War is the South African Roy Campbell.

Roy Campbell (1901–1957)

Roy Campbell is a South African poet. He fought with the Nationalists in the Spanish Civil War. And during World War II, he served in East and North Africa until being disabled from the war. Campbell's first long poem, *The Flaming Terrapin* was published in 1924. His other works include *The Wayzgoose* (1928), a satire on South African intellectuals; *The*

---

1 Marina Mackay, *The Cambridge Companion to the Literature of World War II*. Cambridge and New York: Cambridge University Press, 2009, p.13.
2 Marina Mackay, *The Cambridge Companion to the Literature of World War II*. Cambridge and New York: Cambridge University Press, 2009, p.43.
3 Marina Mackay, *The Cambridge Companion to the Literature of World War II*. Cambridge and New York: Cambridge University Press, 2009, pp.44-45.

Georgiad (1931), an attack on the Bloomsbury group; and his lyrical works, *Adamastor* (1930), *Flowering Reeds* (1933), and *Talking Bronco* (1946).

Excerpt from *Flowering Rifle*

And curse the Soldier, him, the human brand,

That came to lop the sacrilegious Hand,

And root the godless vermin from the land:

For wounds are wings for those who know where God is,

Junkers and Fiats are our slaughtered bodies,

It was not we who lead-swung to the Pities,

When half the loveliest of our ancient cities

Were in the clouds rebuilt- if flames could take them

And rushing smoke restore them in the sky,

When rivers were alive- if blood could make them,

Our blood that had not had the time to die!

Since their intention was not, as they've sworn

To finish off the idle and outworn,

But (as we've proved it openly enough)

To exterminate the valiant, strong, and tough

And by a sudden knifetwist in the scruff!

That the most abject might assume the Seat

And heads be trampled by their dirty feet,

That crime might flourish, sodomy abound,

And Love be crushed forever to the ground:

"Dawn on the Sierra of Gredos"

While those of us by Tagus stray

Whom careless Valkyries forgot

Or stayed behind with on the spot

(Your hair the night, your face the day!)

And others ride the Milky Way

Whose hearts with 'greater love' were shot-

In what new Tercio, what battalion,

Serves now our recent Alferez,

The Legionary angel, Death,

The rider of the pale grey stallion,

Who paid the godless hordes their tallion,
And made their wrath a waste of breath?

The last of four tall shades, he's ridden,
Along the eastward mountain-track,
Their faces in sombreros hidden
Though by their horses they were known -
The riders of the White, the Black,
The Colorado, and his own.

He will return, but not to harm,
Rather to rest us, and relieve.
He will come back, but as on leave
Or visiting some friendly farm -
No more in the thunderclouds to sleeve
The lightning of his strong right arm.

Like young Morato's eagle heart
His own grew wings, and would not stay
When all our best had got the start,
Outstripped the flesh, their service done.
And joined new Tercios in the Sun
To guard the frontiers of the Day.

High on the Gredos near the sky
His iron hand our own we clapped in
Returning earthwards, Life and I.
When on his way we wished him well
Now in the Seraphry to Captain
Promoted for contempt of Hell.

The shades of night began to trickle
Away, like those whom late the Sickle
And Hammer led to shame and loss
By their own emblems laid quiescentSo
deftly Sickled by the Crescent,
So soundly Hammered with the Cross.

There where the Gredos drops so sheer,

Rearing my horse to wave goodbye,
I caught my lifted cattle-spear
Entangled in the dawn-lit sky
As though some canopy to rear
Or streaming oriflamme to fly.

From Africa away to France,
Flag-tethered to so frail a lance,
It tugged and thundered in my hold -
A whole horizon of horizons
Where crimson clouds, like herded bisons.
Migrated over wastes of gold.

Like the tall sloe-stem that towers
To herd the sunsets as they die
Till (once a century) it flowers
And gives them back to later days
From lion-throated blooms ablaze
To roar its fragrance through the sky.

Like that lit stem, my lance outbroke
With clouds of pollen for its smoke
Igniting into tongues of praise,
While birds, the solar Aviation,
Like morning stars at the creation
Exulting magnified the rays.

Range over range around us rolled
With snow-peaks turning green and gold
And crimson. Nearer to the eye
The Guadarramas rose, like surges
Serrated, when the northwind scourges
Their tops, and makes the spindrift fly.

A swift arcade of poplars white,
The steep Alberche swerved from sight
And in the Tagus sought its father,
And now the day itself showed white
Like winged Victory poised for flight

Upon the wreck of the Alcazarl

Down where the lyddite and the 'nitro'
Had scorched the base of the sierras,
Blossoming almonds, row on white row,
And flowering peaches, row on red row,
Shelved glimmering down by tier and terrace
To the Arenas of San Pedro.

I felt as one who bears the dais,
At Corpus, when our King's proud way is,
And wondrous light around him waves,
A rose-red nimbus, trawling fire,
It harps each dark street like a lyre
As water harps the walls of caves.

Toledo's streets those fissured kloofs
Appeared: those ranges scanned her walls,
With woods for people on the roofs,
With cliffs for balconies, for shawls,
The flowering orchards in their falls,
Descending from our horses' hoofs.

The day, exultant and serene,
In slow procession passed between
Till like a Phoenix, bleeding fire,
Shot through with arrows of desire,
The Monstrance in the sun was seen
To flame with love as Hell with ire-

The sun, with resurrected brow,
Who dies each day, to teach *us* how,
Who feeds his blaze with deaths of men
Until it shall devour the sky,
And make the abyss one huge round eye
Of wonder to adorn it then.

I know that blaze, though worlds should shatter,
Its afterclothing for the sprite,

The flesh, when it has taken flight.
For light's the absolute of Matter,
And what the light is to the latter,
The Intellect is to the light.

It is the stuff our comrades burn to
Like incense rising from the mire.
It is the source our bodies yearn to
And our crusading hearts aspire,
Out of the dust that they return to
Translated into song and fire.

We gazed into that light primordial
That filled with love the whole vast region
Whereunto death had passed from here:
So comradely, so frank, so cordialLike
re-enlisting in the Legion
It made the thought of death appear.

Freed from the locustries of Marx,
The plain sent up a myriad larks,
And Life and I, with time to spare,
Rode homeward down the slope abreast,
And hung our rifles up to rest
And yoked the oxen to the share.

George Orwell (1903–1950)[4]

From his prose *Looking Back on the Spanish War*

The Italian soldier shook my hand
Beside the guard-room table;
The strong hand and the subtle hand
Whose palms are only able

To meet within the sound of guns,

---

4 For George Orwell's brief biography, see the preceding chapters' introduction. George Orwell also occasionally wrote poetry that has been largely anti-war in such excerpts as follows. The excerpt is from his prose published in 1939.

But oh! what peace I knew then
In gazing on his battered face
Purer than any woman's!

For the fly-blown words that make me spew
Still in his ears were holy,
And he was born knowing what I had learned
Out of books and slowly.

The treacherous guns had told their tale
And we both had bought it,
But my gold brick was made of gold—
Oh! who ever would have thought it?

Good luck go with you, Italian soldier!
But luck is not for the brave;
What would the world give back to you?
Always less than you gave.

Between the shadow and the ghost,
Between the white and the red,
Between the bullet and the lie,
Where would you hide your head?

For where is Manuel Gonzalez,
And where is Pedro Aguilar,
And where is Ramon Fenellosa?
The earthworms know where they are.

Your name and your deeds were forgotten
Before your bones were dry,
And the lie that slew you is buried
Under a deeper lie;

But the thing that I saw in your face
No power can disinherit:
No bomb that ever burst
Shatters the crystal spirit.

Alex McDade (1905–1937)

Alex McDade, sometimes spelled as "Alex McDude", was a Glasgow labourer who went to Spain to fight with the International Brigade in the Spanish Civil War. He was a political commissar with the British Battalion and was wounded at the Battle of Jarama in February 1937. He was killed on the first day of the Battle of Brunete on 6 July 1937. His representative poem is "Jarama Valley".

"Jarama Valley"

There's a valley in Spain called Jarama,
That's a place that we all know so well,
For 'tis there that we wasted our manhood
And most of our old age as well.

From this valley they tell us we're leaving.
But don't hasten to bid us adieu,
For e'en though we make our departure,
We'll be back in an hour or two.

Oh, we're proud of our British Battalion,
And the marathon record it's made,
Please do us this little favour,
And take this last word to Brigade:

You will never be happy with strangers,
They would not understand you as we,
So remember the Jarama Valley
And the old men who wait patiently.

Rupert John Cornford (1915–1936)

Rupert John Cornford is a British poet and communist. He has been neglected for too long. In 1935, he became a full member of the Communist Party of Great Britain. During the Spanish Civil War, he was recruited in Cambridge for the International Brigade, and fought in the war himself, first as a member of the POUM militia and later the International Brigades. He died while fighting against the Nationalists. His best-known work was published after his death, such as *The Last Mile to Huesca* (1938) and *Poems from Spain* (1938), from which the following excerpts come.

"A Letter from Aragon"

This is a quiet sector of a quiet front.

We buried Ruiz in a new pine coffin,
But the shroud was too small and his washed feet stuck out.
The stink of his corpse came through the clean pine boards
And some of the bearers wrapped handkerchiefs round their faces.
Death was not dignified.
We hacked a ragged grave in the unfriendly earth
And fired a ragged volley over the grave.

You could tell from our listlessness, no one much missed him.

This is a quiet sector of a quiet front.
There is no poison gas and no H. E.

But when they shelled the other end of the village
And the streets were choked with dust
Women came screaming out of the crumbling houses,
Clutched under one arm the naked rump of an infant.
I thought: how ugly fear is.

This is a quiet sector of a quiet front.
Our nerves are steady; we all sleep soundly.

In the clean hospital bed, my eyes were so heavy
Sleep easily blotted out one ugly picture,
A wounded militiaman moaning on a stretcher,
Now out of danger, but still crying for water,
Strong against death, but unprepared for such pain.

This on a quiet front.

But when I shook hands to leave, an Anarchist worker
Said: 'Tell the workers of England
This was a war not of our own making
We did not seek it.
But if ever the Fascists again rule Barcelona

It will be as a heap of ruins with us workers beneath it.'

"Full Moon at Tierz: Before the Storming of Huesca"

I

The past, a glacier, gripped the mountain wall,

And time was inches, dark was all.

But here it scales the end of the range,

The dialectic's point of change,

Crashes in light and minutes to its fall.

Time present is a cataract whose force

Breaks down the banks even at its source

And history forming in our hand's

Not plasticine but roaring sands,

Yet we must swing it to its final course.

The intersecting lines that cross both ways,

Time future, has no image in space,

Crooked as the road that we must tread,

Straight as our bullets fly ahead.

We are the future. The last fight let us face.

II

Where, in the fields by Huesca, the full moon

Throws shadows clear as daylight's, soon

The innocence of this quiet plain

Will fade in sweat and blood, in pain,

As our decisive hold is lost or won.

All round the barren hills of Aragon

Announce our testing has begun.

Here what the Seventh Congress said,

If true, if false, is live or dead,

Speaks in the Oviedo mausers tone.

Three years ago Dimitrov fought alone

And we stood taller when he won.

But now the Leipzig dragon's teeth

Sprout strong and handsome against death

And here an army fights where there was one.

We studied well how to begin this fight,

Our Maurice Thorez held the light.

But now by Monte Aragon

We plunge into the dark alone,

Earth's newest planet wheeling through the night.

III

Though Communism was my waking time,

Always before the lights of home

Shone clear and steady and full in view—

Here, if you fall, there's help for you—

Now, with my Party, I stand quite alone.

Then let my private battle with my nerves,

The fear of pain whose pain survives,

The love that tears me by the roots,

The loneliness that claws my guts,

Fuse in the welded front our fight preserves.

O be invincible as the strong sun,

Hard as the metal of my gun,

O let the mounting tempo of the train

Sweep where my footsteps slipped in vain,

October in the rhythm of its run.

IV

Now the same night falls over Germany

And the impartial beauty of the stars

Lights from the unfeeling sky

Oranienburg and freedom's crooked scars.

We can do nothing to ease that pain

But prove the agony was not in vain.

England is silent under the same moon,

From Clydeside to the gutted pits of Wales.

The innocent mask conceals that soon

Here, too, our freedom's swaying in the scales.

O understand before too late

Freedom was never held without a fight.

Freedom is an easily spoken word

But facts are stubborn things. Here, too, in Spain

Our fight's not won till the workers of all the world

Stand by our guard on Huesca's plain

Swear that our dead fought not in vain,

Raise the red flag triumphantly

For Communism and for liberty.

"To Margot Heinemann"

Heart of the heartless world,
Dear heart, the thought of you
Is the pain at my side,
The shadow that chills my view.

The wind rises in the evening,
Reminds that autumn's near.
I am afraid to lose you,
I am afraid of my fear.

On the last mile to Huesca,
The last fence for our pride,
Think so kindly, dear, that I
Sense you at my side.
And if bad luck should lay my strength
Into the shallow grave,
Remember all the good you can;
Don't forget my love.

2. World War II Poets: British and Commonwealth

According to its thematic orientation and formal structuring, World War II British poets can be classified as the war poets of the two "Schools". The first is called the Apocalyptic School: Henry Treece (1911–1966) is a British poet and novelist, who, with others, initiated a poetic movement known as the New Apocalypse, serving as a literary reaction against the politically oriented left-wing Auden group and the machine-age literature and surrealist poetry of the 1930s. From 1940 to 1946, he joined the volunteer reserve of the Royal Air Force, serving as an intelligence officer. His important poetic collections include *The Black Seasons* (1945) and *The Exiles* (1952). Another important representative is J. F. Hendry, whose collection, *The Bombed Happiness*, provides a superb prospectus of the horrors and unconscious dream work inflicted by the War.

The second school is War poets of the Oxford School, or "Oxford Poets", which emerged from the colleges and later joined the army: C. S. Lewis, J. R. R. Tolkien, Sidney Keyes, and Keith Douglas. C. S. Lewis, or "Clive Staples Lewis" (1898–1963), is mainly known throughout the world as the author of *The Chronicles of Narnia* fantasy series. He carried pieces of shrapnel from World War I, some of which were surgically removed in 1944, thus did not fight in World War II. He served World War II as a popular morale-building Christian apologist. His major poetic collection include *Spirits in Bondage: A Cycle of Lyrics* (1919) and *Dymer* (1926), a long narrative poem. J. R. R. Tolkien, in full John Ronald Reuel Tolkien (1892–1973), is a British writer and scholar who achieved fame with his children's book *The Hobbit* (1937) and his richly inventive epic fantasy *The Lord of the Rings* (1954–1955).

And there are other war poets addressed the topics of the concerned wars: Bernard Gutteridge, who served in Burma, wrote one of the best long poems of the war, "Burma Diary" (1948), as collected in *Old Damson-Face: Poems 1934 to 1974*; G. S. Fraser served in the Middle East while his war poems had been collected in *Home Town Elegy* (1944) and *The Traveller has Regrets* (1948); The South African poet F. T. Prince did not experience combat, but served in the Intelligence Corps of the British Army in the Middle East and Italy. Other service poets include: Emanuel Litvinoff, who served in West Africa, and whose three collections, *Conscripts* (1941), *The Untried Soldier* (1942), and *Crown for Cain* (1948), are a powerful expression of Jewish anger and denunciation; Herbert Mallalieu, who served in Africa and Italy, wrote some of the best love poetry of the war, and the elegy to war-ravaged Greece, "Greece 1945"; Sorley MacLean, who was severely wounded at El Alamein, wrote the finest Gaelic poetry of the war.

Edith Sitwell (1887–1964)

Edith Sitwell is a British poet, critic, and writer. She was a legendary figure in her lifetime for her outspoken manner and rebellion against the accepted modes of behavior. Her collections of poetry include *The Mother and Other Poems* (1915), *The Wooden Pegasus* (1920), *Façade* (1922), *Variations on a Theme* (1933), *Green Song and Other Poems* (1944), *The Canticle of the Rose: Selected Poems 1920–1947* (1950). She was also a writer, known for her *Pacific 13* (1956), *About Religion* (1956), and *Camera Three* (1955). The excerpt is subtitled "The raids, 1940. Night and Dawn", written in 1942.

"Still Falls the Rain"

Still falls the Rain—
Dark as the world of man, black as our loss—
Blind as the nineteen hundred and forty nails
Upon the Cross.

Still falls the Rain
With a sound like the pulse of the heart that is changed to the hammer-beat
In the Potter's Field, and the sound of the impious feet
On the Tomb:

Still falls the Rain

In the Field of Blood where the small hopes breed and
the human brain
Nurtures its greed, that worm with the brow of Cain.

Still falls the Rain
At the feet of the Starved Man hung upon the Cross.
Christ that each day, each night, nails there,
have mercy on us—
On Dives and on Lazarus:
Under the Rain the sore and the gold are as one.

Still falls the Rain—
Still falls the Blood from the Starved Man's wounded Side:
He bears in His Heart all wounds,—those of the light that died,
The last faint spark
In the self-murdered heart, the wounds of the sad
uncomprehending dark,
The wounds of the baited bear,—
The blind and weeping bear whom the keepers beat
On his helpless flesh…the tears of the hunted hare.

Still falls the Rain—
Then—O Ile leape up to my God: who pulles me doune—
See, see where Christ's blood streames in the firmament:
It flows from the Brow we nailed upon the tree
Deep to the dying, to the thirsting heart
That holds the fires of the world,—dark-smirched with pain
As Caesar's laurel crown.

Then sounds the voice of One who like the heart of man
Was once a child who among beasts has lain—
'Still do I love, still shed my innocent light, my Blood, for thee.'

Herbert Read[5] (1893–1968)

"To a Conscript of 1940"

Qui n'a pas une fois désespéré de l'honneur, ne sera
jamais un héros.

Georges Bernanos

A soldier passed me in the freshly fallen snow
His footsteps muffled, his face unearthly grey;

And my heart gave a sudden leap
As I gazed on a ghost of five-and-twenty years ago.

I shouted Halt! and my voice had the old accustomed ring
And he obeyed it as it was obeyed
In the shrouded days when I too was one
Of an army of young men marching

Into the unknown. He turned towards me and I said:
'I am one of those who went before you
Five-and-twenty years ago: one of the many who never returned,
Of the many who returned and yet were dead.

'We went where you are going, into the rain and the mud;
We fought as you will fight
With death and darkness and despair;
We gave what you will give—our brains and our blood.

'We think we gave in vain. The world was not renewed.
There was hope in the homestead and anger in the streets
But the old world was restored and we returned
To the dreary field and workshop, and the immemorial feud

'Of rich and poor. Our victory was our defeat.
Power was retained where power had been misused
And youth was left to sweep away

---

5 For Herbert Reed's biography, see the preceding chapters' section, and the excerpted poem war written in
1944 about the Second World War.

The ashes that the fires had strewn beneath our feet.
'But one thing we learned: there is no glory in the deed

Until the soldier wears a badge of tarnished braid;
There are heroes who have heard the rally and have seen
The glitter of a garland round their head.

'Theirs is the hollow victory. They are deceived.
But you, my brother and my ghost, if you can go
Knowing that there is no reward, no certain use
In all your sacrifice, then honour is reprieved.

'To fight without hope is to fight with grace,
The self reconstructed, the false heart repaired.'
Then I turned with a smile, and he answered my salute
As he stood against the fretted hedge, which was like white lace.

C. Day-Lewis (1904–1972)

C. Day-lewis is an Irish-born British poet and novelist, serving as the poet laureate of Great Britain from 1967 to 1972. During the 1930s, he was associated with the W. H. Auden group of the leftist poets, and was a member of the Communist Party from 1935 to 1938. His collection of verses include *Transitional Poem* (1929), *Collected Poems 1929–1933* (1935), *Overtures to Death* (1938), *Short Is the Time* (1945), *Collected Poems* (1954), *Pegasus and Other Poems* (1957), *The Room and Other Poems* (1965), and *The Whispering Roots and Other Poems* (1970). Generally speaking, his early poetry is marked by didacticism and a preoccupation with social activism while his later volumes show a conservative belief.

"The Stand-To"

Autumn met me today as I walked over Castle Hill.
The wind that had set our corn by the ears was blowing still:
Autumn, who takes the leaves and the long days, crisped the air
With a tang of action, a taste of death; and the wind blew fair

From the east for men and barges massed on the other side—
Men maddened by numbers or stolid by nature, they have their pride
As we in work and children, but now a contracting will
Crumples their meek petitions and holds them poised to kill.

Last night a Stand-To was ordered. Thirty men of us here
Came out to guard the star-lit village—my men who wear
Unwitting the season's beauty, the received truth of the spade—
Roadmen, farm labourers, masons, turned to another trade.

A dog barked over the fields, the candle stars put a sheen
On the rifles ready, the sandbags fronded with evergreen:
The dawn wind blew, the stars winked out on the posts where we lay,
The order came, Stand Down, and thirty went away.

Since a cold wind from Europe blows back the words in my teeth,
Since autumn shortens the days and the odds against our death,
And the harvest moon is waxing and high tides threaten harm,
Since last night may be the last night all thirty men go home,

I write this verse to record the men who have watched with me—
Spot who is good at darts, Squibby at repartee,
Mark and Cyril, the dead shots, Ralph with a ploughman's gait,
Gibson, Harris and Long, old hands for the barricade,

Whiller the lorry-driver, Francis and Rattlesnake,
Fred and Charl and Stan—these nights I have lain awake
And thought of my thirty men and the autumn wind that blows
The apples down too early and shatters the autumn rose.

Destiny, History, Duty, Fortitude, Honour—all
The words of the politicians seem too big or too small
For the ragtag fighters of lane and shadow, the love that has grown
Familiar as working-clothes, faithful as bone to bone.

Blow, autumn wind, upon orchard and rose! Blow leaves along
Our lanes, but sing through me for the lives that are worth a song!
Narrowing days have darkened the vistas that hurt my eyes,
But pinned to the heart of darkness a tattered fire-flag flies.

"Where are the War Poets?"

They who in folly or mere greed
Enslaved religion, markets, laws,

Borrow our language now and bid
Us to speak up in freedom's cause.

It is the logic of our times,
No subject for immortal verse—
That we who lived by honest dreams
Defend the bad against the worse.

Norman Cameron (1905–1953)

Norman Cameron is a British poet, whose background has been little known. The excerpted poem has been frequently anthologised in various digital archives.

"Green, Green is El Aghir"

Sprawled on the crates and sacks in the rear of the truck,
I was gummy-mouthed from the sun and the dust of the track,
And the two Arab soldiers I'd taken on as hitch-hikers
At a torrid petrol-dump, had been there on their hunkers
Since early morning. I said, in a kind of French
'On m'a dit, qu'il y a une belle source d'eau fraîche,
Plus loin, à El Aghir'…

   It was eighty more kilometres
Until round a corner we heard a splashing of waters,
And there, in a green, dark street, was a fountain with two faces
Discharging both ways, from full-throated faucets
Into basins, thence into troughs and thence into brooks.
Our negro corporal driver slammed his brakes,
And we yelped and leapt from the truck and went at the double
To fill our bidons and bottles and drink and dabble.
Then, swollen with water, we went to an inn for wine.
The Arabs came, too, though their faith might have stood between.
'After all,' they said, 'it's a boisson,' without contrition.
Green, green is El Aghir. It has a railway-station,
And the wealth of its soil has borne many another fruit,
A mairie, a school and an elegant Salle de Fêtes.
Such blessings, as I remarked, in effect, to the waiter,
Are added unto them that have plenty of water.

Louis MacNeice (1907–1963)

Louis MacNeice is a British poet and playwright. He was a member of "a group whose low-keyed, un-poetic, socially committed, and topical verse" called in the 1930s "New Poetry", including such left-wing poets as W.H. Auden, C. Day-Lewis, and Stephen Spender. His first poetic collection, *Blind Fireworks*, appeared in 1929, followed by other volumes: *Poems* (1935), *The Earth Compels* (1938), *Autumn Journal* (1939), *The Last Ditch* (1940), *Plant and Phantom* (1941), *Springboard, Poems 1941–1944* (1944), and *Holes in the Sky, Poems 1944–1947* (1948), *Collected Poems, 1925–1948* (1949), *Ten Burnt Offerings* (1952), *Autumn Sequel: A Rhetorical Poem* (1954), and the posthumous *The Burning Perch* (1963). He was also a prolific scriptwriter while serving as producer with the BBC and creating more than 150 scripts, most of which are radio dramas. The two excerpts are written respectively in 1939 and 1948, alluding to the Spanish Civil War and the Second World War.

Excerpts from *Autumn Journal*

And I remember Spain
  At Easter ripe as an egg for revolt and ruin
Though for a tripper the rain
  Was worse than the surly or the worried or the haunted faces
With writings on the walls—
  Hammer and sickle, Boicot, Viva, Muerra;
With café-au-lait brimming the waterfalls,
  With sherry, shellfish, omelettes.
With fretted stone the Moor
  Had chiselled for effects of sun and shadow;
With shadows of the poor,
  The begging cripples and the children begging.
The churches full of saints
  Tortured on racks of marble—
The old complaints
  Covered with gilt and dimly lit with candles.
With powerful or banal
  Monuments of riches or repression
And the Escorial
  Cold for ever within like the heart of Philip.
With ranks of dominoes
  Deployed on café tables the whole of Sunday;
With cabarets that call the tourist, shows
  Of thighs and eyes and nipples.

481

With slovenly soldiers, nuns,

    And peeling posters from the last elections

Promising bread or guns

    Or an amnesty or another

Order or else the old

    Glory veneered and varnished

As if veneer could hold

    The rotten guts and crumbled bones together.

And a vulture hung in air

    Below the cliffs of Ronda and below him

His hook-winged shadow wavered like despair

    Across the chequered vineyards.

And the boot-blacks in Madrid

    Kept us half an hour with polish and pincers

And all we did

    In that city was drink and think and loiter.

And in the Prado half-wit princes looked from the canvas they had paid for

(Goya had the laugh—

    But can what is corrupt be cured by laughter?)

And the day at Aranjuez

    When the sun came out for once on the yellow river

With Valdepeñas burdening the breath

    We slept a royal sleep in the royal gardens;

And at Toledo walked

    Around the ramparts where they throw the garbage

And glibly talked

    Of how the Spaniards lack all sense of business.

And Avila was cold

    And Segovia was picturesque and smelly

And a goat on the road seemed old

    As the rocks or the Roman arches.

And Easter was wet and full

    In Seville and in the ring on Easter Sunday

A clumsy bull and then a clumsy bull

    Nodding his banderillas died of boredom.

And the standard of living was low

    But that, we thought to ourselves, was not our business;

All that the tripper wants is the *status quo*

    Cut and dried for trippers.

And we thought the papers a lark
> With their party politics and blank invective;

And we thought the dark
> Women who dyed their hair should have it dyed more often.

And we sat in trains all night
> With the windows shut among civil guards and peasants

And tried to play piquet by a tiny light
> And tried to sleep bolt upright;

And cursed the Spanish rain
> And cursed their cigarettes which came to pieces

And caught heavy colds in Cordova and in vain
> Waited for the right light for taking photos.

And we met a Cambridge don who said with an air
> 'There's going to be trouble shortly in this country,'

And ordered anis, pudgy and debonair,
> Glad to show off his mastery of the language.

But only an inch behind
> This map of olive and ilex, this painted hoarding,

Careless of visitors the people's mind
> Was tunnelling like a mole to day and danger.

And the day before we left
> We saw the mob in flower at Algeciras

Outside a toothless door, a church bereft
> Of its images and its aura.

And at La Linea while
> The night put miles between us and Gibraltar

We heard the blood-lust of a drunkard pile
> His heaven high with curses;

And next day took the boat
> For home, forgetting Spain, not realising

That Spain would soon denote
> Our grief, our aspirations;

Not knowing that our blunt
> Ideals would find their whetstone, that our spirit

Would find its frontier on the Spanish front,
> Its body in a rag-tag army.

"The Streets of Laredo"

O early one morning I walked out like Agag,
Early one morning to walk through the fire
Dodging the pythons that leaked on the pavements
With tinkle of glasses and tangle of wire;

When grimed to the eyebrows I met an old fireman
Who looked at me wryly and thus did he say:
'The streets of Laredo are closed to all traffic,
We won't never master this joker today.

'O hold the branch tightly and wield the axe brightly,
The bank is in powder, the banker's in hell,
But loot is still free on the streets of Laredo
And when we drive home we drive home on the bell.'

Then out from a doorway there sidled a cockney,
A rocking-chair rocking on top of his head:
'O fifty-five years I been feathering my love-nest
And look at it now—why, you'd sooner be dead.'

At which there arose from a wound in the asphalt,
His big wig a-smoulder, Sir Christopher Wren
Saying: 'Let them make hay of the streets of Laredo;
When your ground-rents expire I will build them again.'

Then twangling their bibles with wrath in their nostrils
From Bonehill Fields came Bunyan and Blake:
'Laredo the golden is fallen, is fallen;
Your flame shall not quench nor your thirst shall not slake.'

'I come to Laredo to find me asylum',
Says Tom Dick and Harry the Wandering Jew;
'They tell me report at the first police station
But the station is pancaked—so what can I do?'

Thus eavesdropping sadly I strolled through Laredo
Perplexed by the dicta misfortunes inspire

Till one low last whisper inveigled my earhole—
The voice of the Angel, the voice of the fire:

O late, very late, have I come to Laredo
A whimsical bride in my new scarlet dress
But at last I took pity on those who were waiting
To see my regalia and feel my caress.

Now ring the bells gaily and play the hose daily,
Put splints on your legs, put a gag on your breath;
O you streets of Laredo, you streets of Laredo,
Lay down the red carpet—My dowry is death.

John Jarmain (1911–1944)

John Jarmain is a British poet and writer. He joined up and became a young artillery officer in the British Army in September 1939. While active in service, he wrote some of his most famous poems. He fought at El Alamein and Normandy as an anti-tank gunner for the 51st Highland Division, killed by shrapnel in 1944. He loved the desert, and sent back his poems in numbered airmail letters to his wife. These poems were published posthumously. The excerpt was written in Mareth, in Tunisia, March 1943.

"El Alamein"

There are flowers now, they say, at Alamein;
Yes, flowers in the minefields now.
So those that come to view that vacant scene,
Where death remains and agony has been
Will find the lilies grow—
Flowers, and nothing that we know.

So they rang the bells for us and Alamein,
Bells which we could not hear:
And to those that heard the bells what could it mean,
That name of loss and pride, El Alamein?
—Not the murk and harm of war,
But their hope, their own warm prayer.

It will become a staid historic name,
That crazy sea of sand!

Like Troy or Agincourt its single fame
Will be the garland for our brow, our claim,
On us a fleck of glory to the end:
And there our dead will keep their holy ground.

But this is not the place that we recall,
The crowded desert crossed with foaming tracks,
The one blotched building, lacking half a wall,
The grey-faced men, sand powdered over all;
The tanks, the guns, the trucks,
The black, dark-smoking wrecks.

So be it: none but us has known that land:
El Alamein will still be only ours
And those ten days of chaos in the sand.
Others will come who cannot understand,
Will halt beside the rusty minefield wires
And find there—flowers.

Dylan Thomas (1914–1953)

Dylan Thomas is a British poet and writer. He considered filing for conscientious objector status, but later served as an anti-aircraft gunner. During the war years, he was able to secure employment writing documentary scripts for the BBC. To avoid the air raids, he and his dancer wife left London in 1944 and settled in the Boat House at Laugharne. His poetic collection includes *18 Poems* (1934), *Twenty-Five Poems* (1936), *The World I Breath* (1939), *The Map of Love* (1939), *New Poems* (1943), *Deaths and Entrances* (1946), *In Country Sleep, And Other Poems* (1952), and *Poems* (1971), all of which were written with its intense lyricism and highly charged emotion, a revival of Romantic tradition in the new context.

"The Hand that Signed the Paper"

The hand that signed the paper felled a city;
Five sovereign fingers taxed the breath,
Doubled the globe of dead and halved a country;
These five kings did a king to death.

The mighty hand leads to a sloping shoulder,
The finger joints are cramped with chalk;
A goose's quill has put an end to murder

That put an end to talk.

The hand that signed the treaty bred a fever,
And famine grew, and locusts came;
Great is the hand that holds dominion over
Man by a scribbled name.

The five kings count the dead but do not soften
The crusted wound nor stroke the brow;
A hand rules pity as a hand rules heaven;
Hands have no tears to flow.

"A Refusal to Mourn the Death, by Fire, of a Child in London"

Never until the mankind making
Bird beast and flower
Fathering and all humbling darkness
Tells with silence the last light breaking
And the still hour
Is come of the sea tumbling in harness

And I must enter again the round
Zion of the water bead
And the synagogue of the ear of corn
Shall I let pray the shadow of a sound
Or sow my salt seed
In the least valley of sackcloth to mourn

The majesty and burning of the child's death.
I shall not murder
The mankind of her going with a grave truth
Nor blaspheme down the stations of the breath
With any further
Elegy of innocence and youth.

Deep with the first dead lies London's daughter,
Robed in the long friends,
The grains beyond age, the dark veins of her mother,
Secret by the unmourning water

Of the riding Thames.
After the first death, there is no other.

"Deaths and Entrances"

On almost the incendiary eve
Of several near deaths,
When one at the great least of your best loved
And always known must leave
Lions and fires of his flying breath,
Of your immortal friends
Who'd raise the organs of the counted dust
To shoot and sing your praise,
One who called deepest down shall hold his peace
That cannot sink or cease
Endlessly to his wound
In many married London's estranging grief.

On almost the incendiary eve
When at your lips and keys,
Locking, unlocking, the murdered strangers weave,
One who is most unknown,
Your polestar neighbour, sun of another street,
Will dive up to his tears.
He'll bathe his raining blood in the male sea
Who strode for your own dead
And wind his globe out of your water thread
And load the throats of shells
with every cry since light
Flashed first across his thunderclapping eyes.

On almost the incendiary eve
Of deaths and entrances,
When near and strange wounded on London's waves
Have sought your single grave,
One enemy, of many, who knows well
Your heart is luminous
In the watched dark, quivering through locks and caves,
Will pull the thunderbolts

To shut the sun, plunge, mount your darkened keys

And sear just riders back,

Until that one loved least

Looms the last Samson of your zodiac.

Alun Lewis (1915–1944)

Alun Lewis is a Welsh-born British poet and soldier, known as one of the most well-known poets of World War II. He enlisted in the army in 1940, travelled with his battalion to India, and finally to Burma to face the Japanese. He committed suicide by shooting himself because of his spiritual bewilderment and depression. He published his poetry collection *Raiders' Dawn* (1942), focusing on the experiences of the army life of British soldiers in training camps. His collection of short stories *The Last Inspection* (1942) and *Ha! Ha! Among the Trumpets* (1945) contain the verses he wrote after leaving England for military duty in the East, describing his experiences as an enlisted man and then an officer during World War II. *His Letters from India* (1946) and *Selected Poetry and Prose* (1966) were published posthumously.

"All Day it Has Rained"

All day it has rained, and we on the edge of the moors

Have sprawled in our bell-tents, moody and dull as boors,

Groundsheets and blankets spread on the muddy ground

And from the first grey wakening we have found

No refuge from the skirmishing fine rain

And the wind that made the canvas heave and flap

And the taut wet guy-ropes ravel out and snap.

All day the rain has glided, wave and mist and dream,

Drenching the gorse and heather, a gossamer stream

Too light to stir the acorns that suddenly

Snatched from their cups by the wild south-westerly

Pattered against the tent and our upturned dreaming faces.

And we stretched out, unbuttoning our braces,

Smoking a Woodbine, darning dirty socks,

Reading the Sunday papers—I saw a fox

And mentioned it in the note I scribbled home;—

And we talked of girls, and dropping bombs on Rome,

And thought of the quiet dead and the loud celebrities

Exhorting us to slaughter, and the herded refugees;

—Yet thought softly, morosely of them, and as indifferently

As of ourselves or those whom we
For years have loved, and will again
Tomorrow maybe love; but now it is the rain
Possesses us entirely, the twilight and the rain.

And I can remember nothing dearer or more to my heart
Than the children I watched in the woods on Saturday
Shaking down burning chestnuts for the schoolyard's merry play,
Or the shaggy patient dog who followed me
By Sheet and Steep and up the wooded scree
To the Shoulder o' Mutton where Edward Thomas brooded long
On death and beauty—till a bullet stopped his song.

"Dawn on the East Coast"

From Orford Ness to Shingle Street
The grey disturbance spreads
Washing the icy seas on Deben Head.

Cock pheasants scratch the frozen fields,
Gulls lift thin horny legs and step
Fastidiously among the rusted mines.

The soldier leaning on the sandbagged wall
Hears in the combers' curling rush and crash
His single self-centred monotonous wish;

And time is a froth of such transparency
His drowning eyes see what they wish to see;
A girl laying his table with a white cloth.
.   .   .

The light assails him from a flank,
Two carbons touching in his brain
Crumple the cellophane lanterns of his dream.

And then the day, grown feminine and kind,
Stoops with the gulfing motion of the tide
And pours his ashes in a tiny urn.

From Orford Ness to Shingle Street
The grey disturbance lifts its head
And one by one, reluctantly,
The living come back slowly from the dead.

"Goodbye"

So we must say Goodbye, my darling,
And go, as lovers go, for ever;
Tonight remains, to pack and fix on labels
And make an end of lying down together.

I put a final shilling in the gas,
And watch you slip your dress below your knees
And lie so still I hear your rustling comb
Modulate the autumn in the trees.

And all the countless things I shall remember
Lay mummy-cloths of silence round my head;
I fill the carafe with a drink of water;
You say 'We paid a guinea for this bed,'

And then, 'We'll leave some gas, a little warmth
For the next resident, and these dry flowers,'
And turn your face away, afraid to speak
The big word, that Eternity is ours.

Your kisses close my eyes and yet you stare
As though God struck a child with nameless fears;
Perhaps the water glitters and discloses
Time's chalice and its limpid useless tears.

Everything we renounce except our selves;
Selfishness is the last of all to go;
Our sighs are exhalations of the earth,
Our footprints leave a track across the snow.

We made the universe to be our home,
Our nostrils took the wind to be our breath,

Our hearts are massive towers of delight,
We stride across the seven seas of death.

Yet when all's done you'll keep the emerald
I placed upon your finger in the street;
And I will keep the patches that you sewed
On my old battledress tonight, my sweet.

"Song (On seeing dead bodies floating off the Cape[6])"

The first month of his absence
I was numb and sick
And where he'd left his promise
Life did not turn or kick.
The seed, the seed of love was sick.

The second month my eyes were sunk
In the darkness of despair,
And my bed was like a grave
And his ghost was lying there.
And my heart was sick with care.

The third month of his going
I thought I heard him say
'Our course deflected slightly
On the thirty-second day—'
The tempest blew his words away.

And he was lost among the waves,
His ship rolled helpless in the sea,
The fourth month of his voyage
He shouted grievously
'Beloved, do not think of me.'

The flying fish like kingfishers
Skim the sea's bewildered crests,
The whales blow steaming fountains,

---

6 The Cape of Good Hope, South Africa.

The seagulls have no nests
Where my lover sways and rests.

We never thought to buy and sell
This life that blooms or withers in the leaf,
And I'll not stir, so he sleeps well,
Though cell by cell the coral reef
Builds an eternity of grief.

But oh! the drag and dullness of my Self;
The turning seasons wither in my head;
All this slowness, all this hardness,
The nearness that is waiting in my bed,
The gradual self-effacement of the dead.

Keith Douglas (1920–1944)

Keith Douglas is one of the foremost British poets of World War II, best known for describing his experiences as a tank commander in North Africa. He believes that military service and battle experience would be the most relevant literary topic of his time, and that only a soldier could write authentically about war. With the advent of war in 1939, he volunteered for military duty and was eventually transferred to a tank regiment in Egypt. He was later sent to the European front, but was killed during the invasion of Normandy. He wrote his war experiences while in active service with a poetic of "extrospectiveness", focusing on external impressions rather than inner emotions to expose war's atrocities. His *Collected Poems* was published posthumously in 1951.

"John Anderson"

John Anderson, a scholarly gentleman
advancing with his company in the attack,
received some bullets through him as he ran.

So his creative brain whirled, and he fell back
in the bloody dust—it was a fine day there
and warm. Blood turned his tunic black

while past his desperate final stare
the other simple soldiers run
and leave the hero unaware.

Apt epitaph or pun
he could not hit upon, to grace
a scholar's death; he only eyed the sun.

But I think, the last moment of his gaze
beheld the Father of Gods and Men,
Zeus, leaning from heaven as he dies.

Whom in his swoon he hears again
summon Apollo in the Homeric tongue:
Descend Phoebus and cleanse the stain

of dark blood from the body of John Anderson.
Give him to Death and Sleep,
who'll bear him as they can

out of the range of darts, to the broad vale
of Lycia; there lay him in a deep
solemn content on some bright dale.

And the brothers, Sleep and Death
lift up John Anderson at his last breath.

"Gallantry"

The Colonel in a casual voice
spoke into the microphone a joke
which through a hundred earphones broke
into the ears of a doomed race.

Into the ears of the doomed boy, the fool
whose perfectly mannered flesh fell
in opening the door for a shell
as he had learnt to do at school.

Conrad luckily survived the winter:
he wrote a letter to welcome
the auspicious spring: only his silken
intentions severed with a single splinter.

Was George fond of little boys?
We always suspected it,
but who will say: since George was hit
we never mention our surmise.

It was a brave thing the Colonel said,
but the whole sky turned too hot
and the three heroes never heard what
it was, gone deaf with steel and lead.

But the bullets cried with laughter,
the shells were overcome with mirth,
plunging their heads in steel and earth—
(the air commented in a whisper).

"Vergissmeinnicht"[7]

Three weeks gone and the combatants gone
returning over the nightmare ground
we found the place again, and found
the soldier sprawling in the sun.

The frowning barrel of his gun
overshadowing. As we came on
that day, he hit my tank with one
like the entry of a demon.

Look. Here in the gunpit spoil
the dishonoured picture of his girl
who has put: *Steffi. Vergissmeinnicht*
in a copybook gothic script.

We see him almost with content,
abased, and seeming to have paid
and mocked at by his own equipment

---

7 "Vergissmeinnicht" ("forget me not") is perhaps Douglas's most acclaimed poem, in which he described in exacting detail his discovery in the desert of a dead German soldier carrying with him a photograph of his sweetheart. While commenting on the War's threat to both life and personal identity, he contrasted the woman's perception of her lover with the killer he had become.

that's hard and good when he's decayed.

But she would weep to see today
how on his skin the swart flies move;
the dust upon the paper eye
and the burst stomach like a cave.

For here the lover and killer are mingled
who had one body and one heart.
And death who had the soldier singled
has done the lover mortal hurt.

"Aristocrats"

The noble horse with courage in his eye
clean in the bone, looks up at a shellburst:
away fly the images of the shires
but he puts the pipe back in his mouth.

Peter was unfortunately killed by an 88:
it took his leg away, he died in the ambulance.
I saw him crawling on the sand, he said
It's most unfair, they've shot my foot off.

How can I live among this gentle
obsolescent breed of heroes, and not weep?
Unicorns, almost,
for they are fading into two legends
in which their stupidity and chivalry
are celebrated. Each, fool and hero, will be an immortal.

These plains were their cricket pitch
and in the mountains the tremendous drop fences
brought down some of the runners. Here then
under the stones and earth they dispose themselves,
I think with their famous unconcern.
It is not gunfire I hear, but a hunting horn.

"How to Kill"

Under the parabola of a ball,
a child turning into a man,
I looked into the air too long.
The ball fell in my hand, it sang
in the closed fist: Open Open
Behold a gift designed to kill.

Now in my dial of glass appears
the soldier who is going to die.
He smiles, and moves about in ways
his mother knows, habits of his.
The wires touch his face: I cry
NOW. Death, like a familiar, hears

And look, has made a man of dust
of a man of flesh. This sorcery
I do. Being damned, I am amused
to see the centre of love diffused
and the wave of love travel into vacancy.
How easy it is to make a ghost.

The weightless mosquito touches
her tiny shadow on the stone,
and with how like, how infinite
a lightness, man and shadow meet.
They fuse. A shadow is a man
when the mosquito death approaches.

"Desert Flowers"

Living in a wide landscape are the flowers -
Rosenberg I only repeat what you were saying -
the shell and the hawk every hour
are slaying men and jerboas, slaying
the mind: but the body can fill
the hungry flowers and the dogs who cry words
at nights, the most hostile things of all.

But that is not news. Each time the night discards

draperies on the eyes and leaves the mind awake

I look each side of the door of sleep

for the little coin it will take

to buy the secret I shall not keep.

I see men as trees suffering

or confound the detail and the horizon.

Lay the coin on my tongue and I will sing

of what the others never set eyes on.

Sidney Keyes (1922–1943)

Sidney Keyes is a major British poet of World War II, and also one of the representative Oxford Poets. He joined the British Army and served in the Queen's Own Royal West Kent Regiment in 1942, but in 1943, he was killed in Tunisia while covering his platoon's retreat. His first collection, *The Iron Laurel*, appeared in 1942, and his second volume of poems, *The Cruel Solstice*, was posthumously published in 1943. His poetic representation of the War depicts death as a real presence to which the serviceman must submit courageously.

Excerpts from *The Foreign Gate*

The moon is a poor woman.

The moon returns to weep with us. The crosses

Burn raw and white upon the night's stiff banners.

The wooden crosses and the marble trees

Shrink from the foreign moon.

The iron gate glitters. Here the soldiers lie.

Fold up the flags, muffle the soldier's drum;

Silence the calling fife. O drape

The soldier's drum with heavy crêpe;

With mourning weeds muffle the soldier's girl.

It's a long way and a long march

To the returning moon and to the soil

No time at all.

      O call

The soldier's glory by another name:

Shroud up the soldier's common shame

And drape the soldier's drum, but spare

The steel-caged brain, the feet that walk to war.

Once striding under a horsehair plume
Once beating the taut drums for war
The sunlight rang from brass and iron;
History was an angry play—
The boy grew tall and rode away;
The door hung slack; the pale girl wept
And cursed the company he kept.
And dumb men spoke
Through the glib mouths of smoke;
The servile learned to strike
The proud to shriek;
And strangled in their lovers' lips
The young fell short of glory in the sand
Raking for graves among the scattered sand;
The tattered flags strained at the wind
Scaring the thrifty kite, mocking the dead.
But muffle the soldier's drum, hide his pale head,
His face a spider's web of blood. O fold
The hands that grip a splintered gun.
    The glittering gate
Baffles him still, his starvecrow soul. O drape
The soldier's drum and cry, who never dare
Defy the ironbound brain, the feet that walk to war.

The cold hand clenches. The stupid mouth
Writhes like a ripple. Now the field is full
Of noises and dead voices…
    'My rags flap
Though the great flags are trampled…'
      'My mouth speaks
Terror and truth, instead of hard command.'
'Remember the torn lace, the fine coats slashed
With steel instead of velvet. Künersdorf
Fought in the shallow sand was my relief.'
'I rode to Naseby'…'And the barren lan d
Of Tannenberg drank me. Remember now
The grey and jointed corpses in the snow,
The struggle in the drift, the numb hands freezing
Into the bitter iron…'

'At Dunkirk I

Rolled in the shallows, and the living trod

Across me for a bridge...'

                'Let me speak out

Against this sham of policy, for pain

Alone is true. I was a general

Who fought the cunning Africans, returned

Crowned with harsh laurel, frantically cheered

Through Roman streets. I spoke of fame and glory.

Women grabbed at my robe. Great poets praised me.

I died of cancer, screaming, in a year.'

'I fell on a black Spanish hillside

Under the thorn-hedge, fighting for a dream

That troubled me in Paris; vomited

My faith and courage out among the stones...'

'I was a barb of light, a burning cross

Of wood and canvas, falling through the night.'

'I was shot down at morning, in a yard.'

The moon regards them without shame. The wind

Rises and twitters through the wreck of bone...

                   'It is so hard to be alone

Continually, watching the great stars march

Their circular unending route; sharp sand

Straying about the eyes, blinding the quick-eyed spirit.'

A soldier's death is hard;

There's no prescribed or easy word

For dissolution in the Army books.

The uniform of pain with pain put on is straiter

Than any lover's garment; yet the death

Of these is different, and their glory greater.

Once men, then moving figures on a map,

Patiently giving time and strength and vision

Even identity

Into the future's keeping;

Nourished on wounds and weeping

Faces and laughing flags and pointed laurels,

Their pain cries down the noise of poetry.

So muffle the soldier's drum, forget the battles;

Remember only fame's a way of living:
The writing may be greater than the speaking
And every death for something different
From time's compulsion, is a written word.
Whatever gift, it is the giving
Remains significant: whatever death
It is the dying matters.
                    Emblematic
Bronze eagle or bright banner or carved name
Of fighting ancestor; these never pardon
The pain and sorrow. It is the dying pardons,
For something different from man or emblem.
Then drape the soldier's drum
And carry him down
Beyond the moon's inspection, and the noise
Of bands and banners and the striking sun.
Scatter the soldier's emblems and his fame:
Shroud up the shattered face, the empty name;
Speak out the word and drape the drum and spare
The captive brain, the feet that walk to war
The ironbound brain, the hand unskilled in war
The shrinking brain, sick of an inner war.

"Timoshenko"[8]

Hour ten he rose, ten-sworded, every finger
A weighted blade, and strapping round his loins
The courage of attack, he threw the window
Open to look on his appointed night.

Where lay, beneath the winds and creaking flares
Tangled like lovers or alone assuming
The wanton postures of the drunk with sleep,
An army of twisted limbs and hollow faces
Thrown to and fro between the winds and shadows.
O hear the wind, the wind that shakes the dawn.
And there before the night, he was aware

---

8 The Russian Marshal Semyon Konstantinovich Timoshenko was appointed commissar for defense in 1940.

Of the flayed fields of home, and black with ruin
The helpful earth under the tracks of tanks.
His bladed hand, in pity falling, mimicked
The crumpled hand lamenting the broken plow;
And the oracular metal lips in anger
Squared to the shape of the raped girl's yelling mouth.
He heard the wind explaining nature's sorrow
And humming in the wire hair of the dead.

He turned, and his great shadow on the wall
Swayed like a tree. His eyes grew cold as lead.
Then, in a rage of love and grief and pity,
He made the pencilled map alive with war.

Excerpts from *The Wilderness*

The red rock wilderness
Shall be my dwelling-place.

Where the wind saws at the bluffs
And the pebble falls like thunder
I shall watch the clawed sun
Tear the rocks asunder.

The seven-branched cactus
Will never sweat wine:
My own bleeding feet
Shall furnish the sign.

The rock says 'Endure.'
The wind says 'Pursue.'
The sun says 'I will suck your bones
And afterwards bury you.'
Here where the horned skulls mark the limit
Of instinct and intransigent desire
I beat against the rough-tongued wind
Towards the heart of fire.

So knowing my youth, which was yesterday,

And my pride which shall be gone tomorrow,
I turn my face to the sun, remembering gardens
Planted by others—Longinus, Guillaume de Lorris
And all love's gardeners, in an early May.
O sing, small ancient bird, for I am going
Into the sun's garden, the red rock desert
I have dreamt of and desired more than the lilac's promise.
The flowers of the rock shall never fall.

O speak no more of love and death
And speak no word of sorrow:
My anger's eaten up my pride
And both shall die tomorrow.

Knowing I am no lover, but destroyer,
I am content to face the destroying sun.
There shall be no more journeys, nor the anguish
Of meeting and parting, after the last great parting
From the images of dancing and the gardens
Where the brown bird chokes in its song:
Until that last great meeting among mountains
Where the metal bird sings madly from the fire.

O speak no more of ceremony,
Speak no more of fame:
My heart must seek a burning land
To bury its foolish pain.

By the dry river at the desert edge
I regret the speaking rivers I have known;
The sunlight shattered under the dark bridge
And many tongues of rivers in the past.
Rivers and gardens, singing under the willows,
The glowing moon…
                    And all the poets of summer
Must lament another spirit's passing over.
O never weep for me, my love,
Or seek me in this land:
But light a candle for my luck

And bear it in your hand.

"War Poet"

I am the man who looked for peace and found

My own eyes barbed.

I am the man who groped for words and found

An arrow in my hand.

I am the builder whose firm walls surround

A slipping land.

When I grow sick or mad

Mock me not nor chain me:

When I reach for the wind

Cast me not down:

Though my face is a burnt book

And a wasted town.

3. World War II Poets: Americans

Unlike its late entry into World War I, the United States plunged into the thick of World War II actively and comprehensively. As some historian says, the Japanese attack on Pearl Harbor further created a massive consensus in the USA about the moral and political necessity of fighting against the Japanese military hegemony in Asia and its fascist European allies. As for its poetic production, Walter Hölbling wrote in *The Cambridge Companion to War Writing*: "Many more American poets wrote about the Second World War more than about the First, though there is little of the heroic idealist rhetoric and personal drama... In poetry (unlike fiction), the modernist aesthetics that flowered between the wars are continued and developed. The new style is mostly nonchalant, cool, sometimes laconic, with a preference for brevity and minimalism, often reminiscent of the complex compactness of imagism and occasionally of e. e. cummings's linguistic experiments."[9]

H. D. (1886–1961)

Hilda Doolittle is an American poet and writer, initially known as an Imagist who emphasises direct treatment, economy of expression, and musicality of sequence. She is also a translator, novelist, playwright, and self-proclaimed "pagan mystic." Her husband Aldington joined the British Amy and left to serve in World War I in 1916. Her first volume of verse, *Sea Garden* (1916), established her as an important voice among the radical young Imagist poets.

---

9 Kate Mcloughlin, ed., *The Cambridge Companion to War Writing*. Cambridge: Cambridge University Press, 2009, p.219.

Her subsequent poetic collection includes *Hymen* (1921), *Heliodora and Other Poems* (1924), *Red Roses for Bronze* (1931), and *The Walls Do Not Fall* (1944), *Tribute to the Angels* (1945), *Flowering of the Road* (1946), and the posthumous *Helen in Egypt* (1961). The excerpted poem employs a variety of objects and allusions to address the consequences of all wars, including World War Two.

Excerpts from *The Walls do not Fall*

An incident here and there,
and rails gone (for guns)
from your (and my) old town square:

mist and mist-grey, no colour,
still the Luxor bee, chick and hare
pursue unalterable purpose

in green, rose-red, lapis;
they continue to prophesy
from the stone papyrus:

there, as here, ruin opens
the tomb, the temple; enter,
there as here, there are no doors:

the shrine lies open to the sky,
the rain falls, here, there
sand drifts; eternity endures:

ruin everywhere, yet as the fallen roof
leaves the sealed room
open to the air,

so, through our desolation,
thoughts stir, inspiration stalks us
through gloom:

unaware, Spirit announces the Presence;
shivering overtakes us,
as of old, Samuel:

trembling at a known street-corner,

we know not nor are known;

the Pythian pronounces—we pass on

to another cellar, to another sliced wall

where poor utensils show

like rare objects in a museum;

Pompeii has nothing to teach us,

we know crack of volcanic fissure,

slow flow of terrible lava,

pressure on heart, lungs, the brain

about to burst its brittle case

(what the skull can endure!):

over us, Apocryphal fire,

under us, the earth sway, dip of a floor,

slope of a pavement

where men roll, drunk

with a new bewilderment,

sorcery, bedevilment:

the bone-frame was made for

no such shock knit within terror,

yet the skeleton stood up to it:

the flesh? it was melted away,

the heart burnt out, dead ember,

tendons, muscles shattered, outer husk dismembered,

yet the frame held:

we passed the flame: we wonder

what saved us? what for?

Marianne Moore (1887–1972)

Marianne Moore is one of the foremost American poetesses. She published *Selected Poems* in 1935, and her other works include *The Pangolin and Other Verse* (1936), *What Are Years*

(1941), *Nevertheless* (1944), and *Collected Poems* (1951). Her anti-war poems "Keeping their World Large" and "In Distrust of Merits" are sometimes considered the best of poetry to come out of World War II.

"Keeping their World Large"

I should like to see that country's tiles, bedrooms,
stone patios
    and ancient wells: Rinaldo
Caramonica's the cobbler's, Frank Sblendorio's
    and Dominick Angelastro's country
    the grocer's, the iceman's, the dancer's—the
beautiful Miss Damiano's; wisdom's

    and all angels' Italy, this Christmas Day
this Christmas year.
    A noiseless piano, an
innocent war, the heart that can act against itself. Here,
    each unlike and all alike, could
    so many-stumbling, falling, multiplied
    till bodies lay as ground to walk on-say

    "If Christ and the apostles died in vain, I'll
die in vain with them"
against this way of victory? Stem after stem
    of what we call the tree-set, row
    on row; that forest of white crosses; the
    vision makes us faint. My eyes won't close to it. While

    the knife was lifted, Isaac the offering
lay mute.
    These, laid like animals for sacrifice,
like Isaac on the mount, were their own substitute.
    And must they all be harmed by those
    whom they have saved. Tears that don't fall are what
    they wanted. Belief in belief marching
    marching marching-all alone, all similar,
spurning pathos,
    clothed in fear-marching to death

marching to life; it was like the cross, is like the cross.
    Keeping their world large, that silent
    marching marching marching and this silence
    for which there is no description, are

    the voices of fighters with no rests between,
who would not yield;
    whose spirits and whose bodies
all too literally were our shield, are still our shield.
    They fought the enemy, we fight
    fat living and self-pity. Shine, o shine
    unfalsifying sun, on this sick scene.

"In Distrust of Merits"

Strengthened to live, strengthened to die for
    medals and positioned victories?
They're fighting, fighting, fighting the blind
    man who thinks he sees, —
Who cannot see that the enslaver is
enslaved; the hater, harmed. O shining O
    firm star, O tumultuous
    ocean lashed till small things go
    as they will, the mountainous
    wave makes us who look, know

depth. Lost at sea before they fought! O
    star of David, star of Bethlehem,
O black imperial lion
    of the Lord-emblem
of a risen world-be joined at last, be
joined. There is hate's crown beneath which all is
    death; there's love's without which none
    is king; the blessed deeds bless
    the halo. As contagion
    of sickness makes sickness,

contagion of trust can make trust. They're
    fighting in deserts and caves, one by

one, in battalions and squadrons;
        they're fighting that I
may yet recover from the disease, My
Self; some have it lightly; some will die. "Man's
        wolf to man" and we devour
        ourselves. The enemy could not
        have made a greater breach in our
        defenses. One piloting a blind man can escape him, but
        Job disheartened by false comfort knew
that nothing can be so defeating
        as a blind man who
can see. O alive who are dead, who are
proud not to see, O small dust of the earth
        that walks so arrogantly,
        trust begets power and faith is
        an affectionate thing. We
        vow, we make this promise

to the fighting-it's a promise—"We'll
        never hate black, white, red, yellow, Jew,
Gentile, Untouchable." We are
        not competent to
make our vows. With set jaw they are fighting,
fighting, fighting-some we love whom we know,
        some we love but know not-that
        hearts may feel and not be numb.
        It cures me; or am I what
        I can't believe in? Some

in snow, some on crags, some in quicksands,
        little by little, much by much, they
are fighting fighting fighting that where
        there was death there may
be life. "When a man is prey to anger,
he is moved by outside things; when he holds
        his ground in patience patience
        patience, that is action or
        beauty," the soldier's defense
        and hardest armor for

the fight. The world's an orphans' home. Shall
    we never have peace without sorrow?
without pleas of the dying for
    help that won't come? O
quiet form upon the dust, I cannot
look and yet I must. If these great patient
    dyings-all these agonies
    and wound-bearings and bloodshedcan
    teach us how to live, these
    dyings were not wasted.

Hate-hardened heart, O heart of iron,
    iron is iron till it is rust.
There never was a war that was
    not inward; I must
fight till I have conquered in myself what
causes war, but I would not believe it.
    I inwardly did nothing.
    O Iscariot-like crime!
    Beauty is everlasting
    and dust is for a time.

E. E. Cummings[10] (1894–1962)

"why must itself up every of a park"

why must itself up every of a park

anus stick some quote statue unquote to
prove that a hero equals any jerk
who was afraid to dare to answer "no"?

quote citizens unquote might otherwise
forget (to err is human;to forgive
divine) that if the quote state unquote says
"kill" killing is an act of christian love.

---

10 For E. E. Cummings' brief introduction, see the preceding chapters.

"Nothing" in 1944 AD

"can stand against the argument of mil
itary necessity"(generalissimoe)
and echo answers "there is no appeal

from reason" (freud)—you pays your money and
you doesn't take your choice. Ain't freedom grand.

"neither awake"

neither awake
(there's your general
yas buy gad)
nor asleep

booted & spurred
with an apish grin
(extremely like
but quite absurd

gloved fist on hip
& the scowl of a cannibal)
there's your mineral
general animal

(five foot five)
neither dead
nor alive
(in real the rain)

"where's Jack Was"

Where's Jack Was
General Was
the hero of the Battle of Because
        he's squatting
in the middle of remember
with his rotten old forgotten

full of why
>   (rub-her-bub)
>   bub?
>   (bubs)

where's Jim Soon
Admiral Soon
the saviour of the Navy of the Moon
>   he's swooning
at the bottom of the ocean
of forever with a never
in his fly
>   (rub-her-bub)
>   bub?
>   (bubs)

Where's John Big
Doughgob Big
pastmaster of the Art of Jigajig
>   sitting pretty
on the top of notwithstanding
with his censored up a wench's
rock-a-bye
>   (rub-her-bub)
>   bub?
>   (bubs)

when your honest redskin toma
hawked and scalped his victim,

not to save a world for stalin
was he aiming;

spare the child and spoil the rod
quoth the palmist.

Randall Jarrell (1914–1965)

Randall Jarrell is an American poet, literary essayist, and poetry critic. He enlisted in the United States Army Air Corps, working as a tower operator and instructor in Tucson, Arizona, for navigators serving on bombing missions. The Second World War witnessed a turning point for his poetry, during which he published *Blood for a Stranger* (1942), *Little Friend, Little Friend* (1945), and *Losses* (1948), all of which are based on his experiences as an Air Force navigator, bitterly and dramatically documenting the intense fears and moral struggles of young soldiers and thus establishing his reputation. His highly acclaimed *The Woman at the Washington Zoo* (1960) won the National Book Award. His other collection includes *The Seven-League Crutches* (1951), *Selected Poems* (1955), and *The Lost World* (1965). The following excerpts were written respectively from the early 1940s to the late 1950s.

"Eighth Air Force"

If, in an odd angle of the hutment,
A puppy laps the water from a can
Of flowers, and the drunk sergeant shaving
Whistles O *Paradiso!* —shall I say that man
Is not as men have said: a wolf to man?
The other murderers troop in yawning;

Three of them play Pitch, one sleeps, and one
Lies counting missions, lies there sweating
Till even his heart beats: One; One; One.
O murderers! …Still, this is how it's done:

This is a war… But since these play, before they die,
Like puppies with their puppy; since, a man,
I did as these have done, but did not die—
I will content the people as I can
And give up these to them: Behold the man!

I have suffered, in a dream, because of him,
Many things; for this last saviour, man,
I have lied as I lie now. But what is lying?
Men wash their hands, in blood, as best they can:
I find no fault in this just man.

"A Camp in the Prussian Forest"

I walk beside the prisoners to the road.
Load on puffed load,

Their corpses, stacked like sodden wood,

Lie barred or galled with blood

By the charred warehouse. No one comes today

In the old way

To knock the fillings from their teeth;

The dark, coned, common wreath

Is plaited for their grave—a kind of grief.

The living leaf

Clings to the planted profitable

Pine if it is able;

The boughs sigh, mile on green, calm, breathing mile,

From this dead file

The planners ruled for them... One year

They sent a million here:

Here men were drunk like water, burnt like wood.

The fat of good

And evil, the breast's star of hope

Were rendered into soap.

I paint the star I sawed from yellow pine—

And plant the sign

In soil that does not yet refuse

Its usual Jews

Their first asylum. But the white, dwarfed star—

This dead white star—

Hides nothing, pays for nothing; smoke

Fouls it, a yellow joke,

The needles of the wreath are chalked with ash,

A filmy trash

Litters the black woods with the death

Of men; and one last breath

Curls from the monstrous chimney... I laugh aloud

Again and again;

The star laughs from its rotting shroud

Of flesh. O star of men!

"A Front"

Fog over the base: the beams ranging

From the five towers pull home from the night

The crews cold in fur, the bombers banging
Like lost trucks down the levels of the ice.
A glow drifts in like mist (how many tons of it?),
Bounces to a roll, turns suddenly to steel
And tires and turrets, huge in the trembling light.
The next is high, and pulls up with a wail,
Comes round again—no use. And no use for the rest
In drifting circles out along the range;
Holding no longer, changed to a kinder course,
The flights drone southward through the steady rain.
The base is closed… But one voice keeps on calling,
The lowering pattern of the engines grows;
The roar gropes downward in its shaky orbit
For the lives the season quenches. Here below
They beg, order, are not heard; and hear the darker
Voice rising: *Can't you hear me? Over. Over* —
All the air quivers, and the east sky glows.

"Losses"

It was not dying: everybody died.
It was not dying: we had died before
In the routine crashes—and our fields
Called up the papers, wrote home to our folks,
And the rates rose, all because of us.
We died on the wrong page of the almanac,
Scattered on mountains fifty miles away;
Diving on haystacks, fighting with a friend,
We blazed up on the lines we never saw.
We died like aunts or pets or foreigners.
(When we left high school nothing else had died
For us to figure we had died like.)

In our new planes, with our new crews, we bombed
The ranges by the desert or the shore,
Fired at towed targets, waited for our scores—
And turned into replacements and woke up
One morning, over England, operational.

It wasn't different: but if we died
It was not an accident but a mistake
(But an easy one for anyone to make.)
We read our mail and counted up our missions—
In bombers named for girls, we burned
The cities we had learned about in school—
Till our lives wore out; our bodies lay among
The people we had killed and never seen.
When we lasted long enough they gave us medals;
When we died they said, 'Our casualties were low.'

They said, 'Here are the maps'; we burned the cities.

It was not dying—no, not ever dying;
But the night I died I dreamed that I was dead,
And the cities said to me: 'Why are you dying?
We are satisfied, if you are; but why did I die?'

"The Death of the Ball Turret Gunner"

From my mother's sleep I fell into the State,
And I hunched in its belly till my wet fur froze.
Six miles from earth, loosed from its dream of life,
I woke to black flak and the nightmare fighters.
When I died they washed me out of the turret with a hose.

4. Further Readings of Representing the Two Wars

A number of poets' works should have been included in this critical anthology, but due to the volume constraint and copyright limit, the following academic summary could only provide a preliminary examination for further reading and research of these poets and their works writing these two wars. For the British side, there are such as Tom Wintringham, Clive Branson, Charles Donnelly, and others:

Tom Wintringham (1898–1949) is a British writer, poet, and social activist. He enlisted on his 18th birthday, and on 5th June 1916, he joined the Royal Flying Corps during the First World War. Like many social activists, Wintringham was very concerned about the large-scale unemployment following the War. He joined the Communist Party of Great Britain in 1923, and became the leading Marxist expert on military affairs. He wrote a series of pamphlets, including *War and the Way to Fight Against It* (1932) and *Air Raid Warning* (1934). In 1935, he published *The Coming World War*. In August 1936, Wintringham went to Spain, and soon developed the idea of a volunteer international legion to fight on the side of the Republican Army. He was the first commander of the British Battalion of the International Brigade. He was an important figure in the formation of the Home Guard during World War II and one of the founders of the Common Wealth Party. After the war, he continued his course until his death.

Clive Branson, or **Clive Ali Chimmo Branson (1907–1944)**, was an English artist and poet, and active communist in the 1930s. He was a recruiter for the International Brigade, and fought in the Spanish Civil War. In 1938, he was taken as a prisoner of war at the Nationalist camp of San Pedro de Cardeña. He died in action in Burma on 25 February 1944 during the Second World War, where he was serving as a Sergeant in the British Army, as part of the 54th Training Regiment of the Royal Armoured Corps. During and after the Spanish civil war, he wrote a number of poetic pieces.

Charles Donnelly (1914–1937) is an Irish poet and left-wing political activist. In July 1934, he was arrested and imprisoned for two weeks for his role in picketing a Dublin bakery with other Congress members. After this, his father expelled him from the family home and he spent a period sleeping rough in parks around Dublin. In February 1935, he left Ireland for London, where he worked for the Republican Congress London branch. In July 1936, on the outbreak of the Spanish Civil War, he urged to send fighters to the International Brigades, and by the end of 1936, he had gone again to London and joined the Brigades. He had come to Spain to fight on the Republican side, while he and his comrades were attached to the American Abraham Lincoln Battalion. Later, he was killed in the fighting.

For the American side, there are such as Robert Lowell, Gwendolyn Brooks, Howard Nemerov, and others:

Robert Lowell (1917–1977) is a unique American poet and a conscientious objector during the Second World War that earned him five months in prison after he refused to be inducted in 1943. He acted in protest of the Allied bombing of German cities, the policy of unconditional surrender, and the US alliance with the Soviet Union. His poetic collections include *Land of Unlikeness* (1944), *Lord Weary's Castle* (1946), *Life Studies* (1959), *The Old Glory* (1965), and *For the Union Dead* (1964).

Other poets include the much-honoured African American poetess, **Gwendolyn Brooks (1917–2000)**, and **Howard Nemerov (1920–1991)**, a highly acclaimed American poet, who enlisted in the Royal Canadian Air Force, and was later allowed to transfer to the American Air Force in early 1944 as a pilot. Many works of his poetry included *Guide to Ruins* (1950); *The Salt Garden* (1955); *The Winter Lightning; Selected Poems* (1968); *The Collected Poems of Howard Nemerov* (1977) *Sentences* (1980); and *Trying Conclusions: New and Selected Poems 1961–1991* (1991).

An American poet of the Pacific Northwest, **Richard Hugo (1923–1982)**, served in the Army Air Corps as a bombardier in the Mediterranean between 1943 and 1945. His major poetry collections include *A Run of Jacks* (1961), *Selected Poems* (1979), *31 Letters and 13 Dreams* (1977), *What Thou Lovest Well, Remains American* (1975), *The Lady in Kicking Horse Reservoir* (1973), *Good Luck in Cracked Italian* (1969), *Death of the Kapowsin Tavern* (1965), and *A Run of Jacks* (1961).

And finally, the famous American poet, editor and academic who edited the anthology *Poets of World War II* (2003), **Harvey Shapiro (1924–2013)**, served in World War II as an Air Force tail gunner. His poetic collections include *The Eye* (1953), *Battle Report: Selected Poems* (1966), *This World* (1971), *National Cold Storage: New and Selected Poems* (1988) and *The Sights along the Harbor* (2006).

Chapter IX

The Anglo-American War Poetry after World War II (1945–   )

Following the collapse of the Nazi and quasi-Nazi regimes across the globe at the close of World War II in 1945, the uneasy wartime alliance between the United States and the Soviet Union and their respective allies began to unravel, and gradually turned into the open yet restricted rivalry waged along those political, economic, and propaganda fronts with limited recourse to weapons. The Cold War loomed large. The English writer George Orwell published an article in 1945, which predicted that there would be a nuclear stalemate called the "Cold War" between "two or three monstrous super-states, each possessed of a weapon by which millions of people can be wiped out in a few seconds." In March 1946, Winston Churchill (1874–1965), the then British prime minister who rallied the British people and led Britain from the brink of defeat to victory, spoke at Fulton, Missouri, U. S.: "From Stettin in the Baltic to Trieste in the Adriatic, an iron curtain has descended across the Continent." During the Cold War, the Iron Curtain was not only marked by the physical construction of the Berlin Wall and extended to the airwaves unfolding ideological propaganda, but also witnessed a number of direct military confrontations and armed conflicts such as the Korean War (1950–1953), Cuban Missile Crisis (1962), the Vietnam War (1965–1973), and other military or quasi-war operations such as those in former East Germany, Hungary, Czechoslovakia, Afghanistan, Guatemala, Cuba, the Dominican Republic, and Grenada. The "West-East Confrontation" came to a close as the Soviet Union terminated in the early 1990s. Ever since then, contemporary warfare with Anglo-American involvement evolved into a new age with such wars as the Iraqi War and its subsequent waves of "Wars on Terror".

The two early wars with overwhelming Anglo-American involvement are the wars in Korea and Vietnam, which had largely much in common. These two "Cold-War conflicts" conceived as limited, non-nuclear wars to halt the spread of so-called communism in the eyes of the capitalist West and to safeguard the revolutionary fruit of socialism in the perspectives of the socialist East, but both resulted in heavy losses from both parties: 36,000 US troops died in Korea, and 58,000 in Vietnam.[1] Both the British and Americans learned traumatic lessons in the new realities of warfare. The Korean War, although fought under the auspices of the United Nations, is often regarded as a "forgotten war", which thus generated only a small fraction of poetic representation such as the American war poets Rolando Hinojosa and William Wantling. The Vietnam War, however, produced much more poetic responses, in such poets as William Childress, Michael Casey, W. D. Ehrhart, Yusef Komunyakaa, Bruce Weigl, James Magner Jr., Reg Saner, and Keith Wilson. The Iraqi War and "Wars on Terror" produced Brian Turner and others.

The most important feature of the war poetry after the Second World War is that most of them wrote with two or more war subjects in mind, all with a kind of anti-war sentiment and mood of elegy. Kate McLoughlin's edited *The Cambridge Companion to War Writing* (2009) draws such a conclusion: "Literary output from the Korean War is modest compared with that generated by the Vietnam conflict. In literature, as in life, Vietnam still exerts a posttraumatic stress effect, reminding Americans of a failed military enterprise and warning of the dangers of ill-thought-out foreign policy. For most writers who fought in Korea or Vietnam, the memory of hundreds of thousands of Korean, Chinese, and Vietnamese deaths remains on their conscience. For readers, literature of the Korean and Vietnam Wars offers prescient comment on America's subsequent military engagements, such as her lengthening involvement in Iraq and Afghanistan."[2]

In their *Writing between the Lines: An Anthology on War and Its Social Consequences*, Kevin Bowen and Bruce Weigl write: "More than forty poets, fiction writers, and nonfiction writers from Vietnam, the United States, Puerto Rico, Nicaragua, and Guatemala have participated as faculty or as visiting writers. Notably, they have worked not as antagonists of their various traditions but as contributors to and refiners of those traditions. This anthology then is an homage to them, and to their students, and it is a celebration of what the workshop has come to stand for: the power of the word in the face of that which threatens the word."[3] The current critical anthology has the identical purpose.

---

1 There are many statistics about the casualties in these two wars; the above two numbers are one of those most popular statistics.

2 Kate Mcloughlin, ed., *The Cambridge Companion to War Writing*. Cambridge: Cambridge University Press, 2009, p. 237.

3 Kevin Bowen, and Bruce Weigl. *Writing between the Lines: An Anthology on War and Its Social Consequences*. Amherst: University of Massachusetts Press, 1997, pp. xix-xx.

1. Poetry from the Korean War to "Wars on Terror"

Far less Korean War poetry has been produced, making it difficult to locate and systematically anthologize. In the poet and scholar W. D. Ehrhart's anthology and criticism *Retrieving Bones: Stories and Poems of the Korean War* (collaborated with Philip K. Jason, 1999), a dozen of poets are discussed for their representation and elegy of this "Wrong War" (just to evoke Omar Nelson Bradley's terminology[4]) , including Rolando Hinojosa, the prolific Spanish-American poet with Texas Mexican cultures, writing his America odyssey both in the War and his turbulent society; William Childress, who often conflates the two conflicts of Korea and Vietnam attacking generals and politicians for their cowardice and self-seeking in such of his famous "The Long March"; William Wantling, who died at in his forties from drug addiction as haunted by his illusion of what he perceived as the war crimes he had committed; Reg Saner, who had tried avoid confrontation with Korea and later Vietnam memories, but was constantly possessed by those familiar images of hunting, school-days, or driving mixed with traumas of war atrocity; and so do James Magner, Jr., and Keith Wilson.

The Vietnam War has been equally controversial and divisive. Soldiers coming home did not meet the welcoming crowds that filled World War II newsreels. Called "baby killers", they had few official support systems to help them return to a society that has dispossessed of them. To a great extent, the War is "an America's shame" and "the search for literary expression" has always witnessed such a sentiment: Loss of the self-esteem, crumble of national virtue, and widespread of guilt and elegy. This sentiment is worsened by the military defeat and public opinion that has turned irrevocably against the War, thus leaving a horrifying distortion of its national psyche with possessed physical and psychological trauma as can be read in contradictory poetic patterns of its literary production. These patterns can be found in those war poems anthologized and discussed in Larry Rottmann, Jan Barry and Basil T. Paquet's edited *Winning Hearts and Minds* (1972), James F. Mersmann's *Out of the Vietnam Vortex* (1974), Jan Barry and W. D. Ehrhart's *Demilitarized Zones* (1976), and the later poet's two anthologies, *Carrying the Darkness* (1985) and *Unaccustomed Mercy* (1989). Representative poets are D. F. Brown, Michael Casey, David Huddle, Bryan Alec Floyd, Yusef Komunyakaa, Basil T. Paquet, D. C. Berry, and Gerald McCarthy. Just for monograph space and copyright limit, this critical anthology only selects some of the most representative poetic pieces for illustration and for readers' further research upon this topic.

Denise Levertov (1923–1997) is a British poetess. her poetry reflected such beliefs as an artist and a humanist. In her "What Were They Like?" (1967), she attacked the global involvement in the Vietnam War with the following lines:

---

4 Omar Nelson Bradley (1893–1981), the former Chairman of the Joint Chiefs of Staff (JCS)

Did the people of Vietnam
  use lanterns of stone?
Did they hold ceremonies
  to reverence the opening of buds?
Were they inclined to quiet laughter?
Did they use bone and ivory,
  jade and silver, for ornament?
Had they an epic poem?
Did they distinguish between speech and singing?
Sir, their light hearts turned to stone.
  It is not remembered whether in gardens
  stone lanterns illumined pleasant ways.
Perhaps they gathered once to delight in blossom,
  but after the children were killed
  there were no more buds.
Sir, laughter is bitter to the burned mouth.
A dream ago, perhaps. Ornament is for joy.
  All the bones were charred.
It is not remembered. Remember,
  most were peasants; their life
  was in rice and bamboo.
  When peaceful clouds were reflected in the paddies
  and the water buffalo stepped surely along terraces,
  maybe fathers told their sons old tales.
  When bombs smashed those mirrors
  there was time only to scream.
There is an echo yet
  of their speech which was like a song.
  It was reported their singing resembled
  the flight of moths in moonlight.
  Who can say? It is silent now.

Rolando Hinojosa (1929–2022) is a prolific Spanish-American poet, who, together with his fiction for he is one of the most prolific and well-respected contemporary Hispanic novelists, provided a copious source of somewhat prosaic narrative.

Another similar poet and writer is Adrian Mitchell (1932–2008), a British poet and dramatist. It has been said that his work demonstrates a powerful social conscience, and he has been described as the "shadow poet laureate". In his "To Whom It May Concern" (1968), he has repeatedly questioned the significance of all wars:

I was run over by the truth one day.
Ever since the accident I've walked this way
       So stick my legs in plaster
       Tell me lies about Vietnam.

Heard the alarm clock screaming with pain,
Couldn't find myself so I went back to sleep again
       So fill my ears with silver
       Stick my legs in plaster

Tell me lies about Vietnam.
Every time I shut my eyes all I see is flames.
Made a marble phone book and I carved all the names
       So coat my eyes with butter
       Fill my ears with silver
       Stick my legs in plaster
     Tell me lies about Vietnam.

I smell something burning, hope it's just my brains.
They're only dropping peppermints and daisy-chains
       So stuff my nose with garlic
       Coat my eyes with butter
       Fill my ears with silver
       Stick my legs in plaster
       Tell me lies about Vietnam.

Where were you at the time of the crime?
Down by the Cenotaph drinking slime
So chain my tongue with whisky
     Stuff my nose with garlic
     Coat my eyes with butter
     Fill my ears with silver
     Stick my legs in plaster
     Tell me lies about Vietnam.

You put your bombers in, you put your conscience out,
You take the human being and you twist it all about
     So scrub my skin with women
     Chain my tongue with whisky

Stuff my nose with garlic
Coat my eyes with butter
Fill my ears with silver
Stick my legs in plaster
Tell me lies about Vietnam.

Walter McDonald (1934–　) is an American poet and scholar. He served in the Air Force and is a veteran of the Vietnam War. He earned his PhD from the University of Iowa and later taught at Texas Tech University. He published more than 20 books of poetry, part of which were some of the war's most enduring poems as he drew upon his service in Vietnam: *Caliban in Blue* (1976), *The Flying Dutchman* (1987), *After the Noise of Saigon* (1988), *Night Landings* (1989), and *Counting Survivors* (1995). He also published other poems such as *Climbing the Divide* (2003), *A Thousand Miles of Stars* (2004), and *Faith is a Radical Master* (2005). For instance, in his "Digging in a Footlocker", he combined all of his reflections of the past wars including the First, Second World Wars and Vietnam War as a kind of remembrance:

Crouched before dismantled guns,
we found war souvenirs
our uncle padlocked in the attic,
a brittle latch easily pried off.

Stiff uniforms on top, snapshots
of soldiers young as our cousins,
a velvet box of medals
as if he fought all battles.
…

As a conscientious objector of the War, **John Balaban (1943–　)** went to Vietnam through the International Volunteer Services and recounted his experiences of horrors. He taught in Vietnam but was wounded during the 1968 Tet Offensive, which was vividly depicted of how his life changed when he was wounded in his collection *After the War* (1974). His other poetic collection includes *Blue Mountain* (1982), *Words for My Daughter* (1991), which places the Vietnam War in the contexts of oriental, classical, and western European culture, *Locusts at the Edge of Summer: New and Selected Poems* (1997), and *Path, Crooked Path* (2006). In his poem "After Our War," he writes his meditation about the peace agreement signed between the United States and North Vietnam in 1973 with an apocalyptic vision:

After our war, the dismembered bits
—all those pierced eyes, ear slivers, jaw splinters,

gouged lips, odd tibias, skin flaps, and toes—
came squinting, wobbling, jabbering back.
The genitals, of course, were the most bizarre,
inching along roads like glowworms and slugs.
The living wanted them back but good as new.
The dead, of course, had no use for them.
And the ghosts, the tens of thousands of abandoned souls
who had appeared like swamp fog in the city streets,
on the evening altars, and on doorsills of cratered homes,
also had no use for the scraps and bits
because, in their opinion, they looked good without them.

John Balaban also produced other literary outputs: The novel *Coming Down Again* (1985, 1989), the juvenile fable *The Hawk's Tale* (1988), the nonfiction *Vietnam: The Land We Never Knew* (1989), the memoir *Remembering Heaven's Face: A Moral Witness in Vietnam* (1991). In his works, he often offers from his experiences during the Vietnam War a deep concern for humanity on the brink of annihilation, for instance, in the first two stanzas of *In Celebration of Spring* (1997):

Our Asian war is over; others have begun.
Our elders, who tried to mortgage lies,
are disgraced, or dead, and already
the brokers are picking their pockets
for the keys and the credit cards.

In delta swamp in a united Vietnam,
a Marine with a bullfrog for a face,
rots in equatorial heat. An eel
slides through the cage of his bared ribs.
At night, on the old battlefield, ghosts,
like patches of fog, lurk into villages
to maunder on doorsills of cratered homes,
while all across the U.S.A.
the wounded walk about and wonder where to go.

Yusef Komunyakaa (1947–) is an African American poet, who served in Vietnam, not only depicted a nightmarish scene of jungle warfare, but also wrote about the atrocities and costs of serving a nation that doesn't recognize all its soldiers as its own citizens. In his poetry, he weaves together personal narrative, jazz rhythms, and vernacular language to create complex images of life in peace and in war, for instance in his *Facing It* (1988) and *Starlight Scope Myopia* (1988). In the following excerpts, Komunyakaa creates an atmosphere of horrors alluding to the prospect of peace, for instance, the title poem from *Facing It* with the following lines:

My black face fades,
hiding inside the black granite.
I said I wouldn't
dammit: No tears.
I'm stone. I'm flesh.
My clouded reflection eyes me
like a bird of prey, the profile of night
slanted against morning. I turn
this way—the stone lets me go.
I turn that way—I'm inside
the Vietnam Veterans Memorial
again, depending on the light
to make a difference.
I go down the 58,022 names,
half-expecting to find
my own in letters like smoke.
I touch the name Andrew Johnson;
I see the booby trap's white flash.
Names shimmer on a woman's blouse
but when she walks away
the names stay on the wall.
Brushstrokes flash, a red bird's
wings cutting across my stare.
The sky. A plane in the sky.
A white vet's image floats
closer to me, then his pale eyes
look through mine. I'm a window.
He's lost his right arm
inside the stone. In the black mirror
a woman's trying to erase names:
No, she's brushing a boy's hair.

Peter Wyton (1944–   ) is a contemporary American poet. The excerpt "Unmentioned in Dispatches" write about the American warring involvement in the Middle East, especially in

Iraq:

Some of them never come home to fanfares,
they dump their kitbags down at the door,
kiss their wives and let their children
wrestle them down to the kitchen floor,
switch the telly on, pour out a whiskey,
search for the local football score.

Some of them skip the quayside welcome,
dodge the bunting and cannonade,
make their landfall in silent harbours,
nod to the coastguard, but evade
the searchlight of public scrutiny
like those engaged in the smuggling trade.

Some of them land at lonely airfields
far removed from the celebration,
hang their flying gear in a locker,
cadge a lift to the railway station,
make for home and take for granted
the short-lived thanks of a grateful nation.

Some of them miss the royal salute,
the victory parade along the Mall,
the fly-past, the ships in formation passing
the cheering crowds on the harbour wall.
Remembered only by friends and relatives,
some of them never come home at all.

W. D. Ehrhart (1948–   ) served shortly with an infantry battalion from 1967 to 1968 in Vietnam and was wounded in the battle during the Tet Offensive of 1968. When he was discharged, he went on to Swarthmore College, becoming very active in the antiwar movement. His initial collection of Vietnam War poetry, *Winning Hearts and Minds* (1972), gained him national recognition as a famous war poet. After the war, he produced a great succession of volumes of poetry with identical themes, such as including *A Generation of Peace* (1975), *To Those Who Have Gone Home Tired* (1984), *The Distance We Travel* (1993), *Beautiful Wreckage* (1999), and *Sleeping with the Dead* (2006), all combining a critique of America's other military interventions abroad with political courage as well as perseverance.

In his "Beautiful Wreckage" (1999), he writes in the latter part of the poem:

> …
>
> In Vietnamese, Con Thien means
> *place of angels.* What if it really was
> instead of the place of rotting sandbags,
> incoming heavy artillery, rats and mud.
>
> What if the angels were Ames and Ski,
> or the lady, the man, and the boy,
> and they lifted Gaffney out of the mud
> and healed his shattered knee?
>
> What if none of it happened the way I said?
> Would it all be a lie?
> Would the wreckage be suddenly beautiful?
> Would the dead rise up and walk?

Another poet of the same inclination is **Bruce Weigl (1949–   )**, an American poet, writer and scholar. He enlisted in the Army and served in Vietnam for only one year, but the war "ruined" his life. His early poetry was engaged directly with the horror of his experience of war with a complex narrative and visionary patterns, relating the evolving history of the War and giving voice to thousands of soldiers who saw action in the Vietnam War during the late 1960s and early 1970s: *Executioner* (1976), *Like a Sack Full of Old Quarrels* (1976), *The Monkey Wars* (1984), and *Song of Napalm* (1988). He also published translations of Vietnamese and Romanian poetry and edited or co-edited several anthologies of war poetry, including *Writing Between the Lines: An Anthology on War and Its Social Consequences* (1997), *Mountain River: Vietnamese Poetry from the Wars, 1948–1993* (1998), and *A Bilingual Collection* (1998). His more recent are entitled *The Abundance of Nothing* (2012) and *On the Shores of Welcome Home* (2019). For instance, in his "Song of Napalm," he begins with a bucolic description of horses that the speaker and his wife watch while suddenly visions from his war experiences intrude once again:

> Still I close my eyes and see the girl
> Running from her village, napalm
> Stuck to her dress like jelly,
> Her hands reaching for the no one
> Who waits in waves of heat before her.
>
> …

And finally flashes with the denouement of war horrors:
Burning bodies so perfectly assume. Nothing
Can change that; she is burned behind my eyes
And not your good love and not the rain-swept air
And not the jungle green
Pasture unfolding before us can deny it.

Brian Turner (1967–   ) is an American poet and scholar. He joined the Army in 1997 and served in Iraq as a team leader with the 3rd Stryker Brigade Combat Team, the 2nd Infantry in 2003, widely known as "Sergeant T" or "The Professor". In his recent memoir *My Life as a Foreign Country* (2015), he relates his war experience and homecoming to aftermath, combining free self-indulgence with self-glorification and seeking "parallels in the histories of others who have gone to war, especially his grandfather in World War II," and painting "a devastating portrait of what it means to be a soldier and a human being." In his famous "The Hurt Locker" (2005), he chronicled chilling lessons from Iraq when he crossed the line of departure with a convoy of soldiers headed into the Iraqi desert. As he imagines himself in his poem, he became "a drone aircraft, hovering over the terrains of Bosnia and Vietnam, Iraq and Northern Ireland, the killing fields of Cambodia and the death camps of Europe—a landscape of ongoing violence, revealing all that man has done to man":

Nothing but hurt left here.
Nothing but bullets and pain
and the bled-out slumping
and all the *fucks* and *goddamns*
and *Jesus Christs* of the wounded.
Nothing left here but the hurt.

Believe it when you see it.
Believe it when a twelve-year-old
rolls a grenade into the room.
Or when a sniper punches a hole
deep into someone's skull.
Believe it when four men
step from a taxicab in Mosul
to shower the street in brass
and fire. Open the hurt locker
and see what there is of knives
and teeth. Open the hurt locker and learn
how rough men come hunting for souls.

2. The Cold War Confrontation and Anti-war Reflections

The First World War produced poetry that still resonated down the years, but the Second World War produced poetry that came from disillusion, a war spawned by what Auden called the "Low Dishonest Decade". During and after the age of the Cold War, from the 1950s to the new millennium, the Anglo-American poetic arena on the war had been largely conceived in an anti-war sentiment. Nearly all war writings have dwelled heavily on anti-war reflections. For instance, one of the most important such poets is **Robert Lowell (1917–1977)**, the American poet best known for his volume *Life Studies* (1959), which forever changed the landscape of modern poetry, much as Eliot's *The Waste Land* had three decades before. He had a profound interest in history and politics. In his poetry, he juxtaposed self and history in ways that illuminated both. The excerpt "Fall 1961" (1965) writes the horrors of all wars in the beginning stanzas:

> Back and forth, back and forth
> goes the tock, tock, tock
> of the orange, bland, ambassadorial
> face of the moon
> on the grandfather clock.
>
> All autumn, the chafe and jar
> of nuclear war;
> we have talked our extinction to death.
> I swim like a minnow
> behind my studio window.
> …

Another good poet with an anti-war reflection is the American poet **Lincoln Kirstein (1907–1996)**, and also among the most influential figures in American dance. Kirstein's poetry collections include *Low Ceilings* (1935) and *Rhymes of a Pfc.* (1963), the two of which include experiences and reflections from his years in the U.S. Army during World War II. In his poetic satire "Rank" (1964), he wrote:

> Differences between rich and poor, king and queen,
> Cat and dog, hot and cold, day and night, now and then,
> Are less clearly distinct than all those between
> Officers and us: enlisted men.
>
> Not by brass may you guess nor their private latrine

Since distinctions obtain in any real well-run war;
It's when off duty, drunk, one acts nice or mean
In a sawdust-strewn bistro-type bar.

Ours was on a short street near the small market square;
Farmers dropped by for some beer or oftener to tease
The Gargantuan bartender Jean-Pierre
About his sweet wife, Marie-Louise.

GI's got the habit who liked French movies or books,
Tried to talk French or were happy to be left alone;
It was our kinda club; we played chess in nooks
With the farmers. We made it our own.

To this haven one night came an officer bold;
Crocked and ugly, he'd had it in five bars before.
A lurid luster glazed his eye which foretold
He'd better stay out of our shut door,

But did not. He barged in, slung his cap on the zinc:
'Dewbelle veesky,' knowing well there was little but beer.
Jean-Pierre showed the list of what one could drink:
'What sorta jerk joint you running here?'

Jean-Pierre had wine but no whisky to sell.
Wine loves the soul. Hard liquor hots up bloody fun,
And it's our rule noncommissioned personnel
Must keep by them their piece called a gun.

As well we are taught, enlisted soldiers may never
Ever surrender this piece—MI , carbine, or rifle—
With which no mere officer whomsoever
May freely or foolishly trifle.

A porcelain stove glowed in its niche, white and warm.
Jean-Pierre made jokes with us French-speaking boys.
Marie-Louise lay warm in bed far from harm;
Upstairs, snored through the ensuing noise.

This captain swilled beer with minimal grace. He began:
'Shit. What you-all are drinkin's not liquor. It's piss.'
Two privates (first class) now consider some plan
To avoid what may result from this.

Captain Stearnes is an Old Army joe. Eighteen years
In the ranks, man and boy; bad luck, small promotion;
Without brains or cash, not the cream of careers.
Frustration makes plenty emotion.

'Now, Mac,' Stearnes grins (Buster's name is not Mac; it is Jack),
'Toss me your gun an' I'll show you an old army trick;
At forty feet, with one hand, I'll crack that stove, smack.'
'Let's not,' drawls Jack back, scared of this prick.

'You young punk,' Stearnes now storms, growing moody but mean,
'Do you dream I daren't pull my superior rank?'
His hand snatches Jack's light clean bright carbine.
What riddles the roof is no blank.

The rifle is loaded as combat zones ever require.
His arm kicks back without hurt to a porcelain stove.
Steel drilling plaster and plank, thin paths of fire
Plug Marie-Louise sleeping above.

Formal enquiry subsequent to this shootin'
Had truth and justice separately demanded.
Was Stearnes found guilty? You are darned tootin':
Fined, demoted. More: reprimanded.

The charge was not murder, mayhem, mischief malicious,
Yet something worse, and this they brought out time and again:
Clearly criminal and caddishly vicious
Was his: Drinking With Enlisted Men.

I'm serious. It's what the Judge Advocate said:
Strict maintenance of rank or our system is sunk.
Stearnes saluted. Jean-Pierre wept his dead.
Jack and I got see-double drunk.

Reflections on the Second World War are also conceived by the British poet **Charles Causley (1917–2003)**. For instance, in his two poems of 1957, he wrote the date of significance in the poem "Armistice Day" with these ironic terms:

> I stood with three comrades in Parliament Square
> November her freights of grey fire unloading,
> No sound from the city upon the pale air
> Above us the sea-bell eleven exploding.
>
> Down by the bands and the burning memorial
> Beats all the brass in a royal array,
> But at our end we are not so sartorial:
> Out of (as usual) the rig of the day.
>
> Starry is wearing a split pusser's flannel
> Rubbed, as he is, by the regular tide;
> Oxo the ducks that he ditched in the Channel
> In June, 1940 (when he was inside).
>
> Kitty recalls his abandon-ship station,
> Running below at the Old Man's salute
> And (with a deck-watch) going down for duration
> Wearing his oppoe's pneumonia-suit.
>
> Comrades, for you the black captain of carracks
> Writes in Whitehall his appalling decisions,
> But as was often the case in the Barracks
> Several ratings are not at Divisions.
>
> Into my eyes the stiff sea-horses stare,
> Over my head sweeps the sun like a swan.
> As I stand alone in Parliament Square
> A cold bugle calls, and the city moves on.

And accordingly, he wrote the deaths with sorrows in the poem "At the British War Cemetery, Bayeux" with such overwhelming gloom:

> I walked where in their talking graves
> And shirts of earth five thousand lay,

When history with ten feasts of fire
Had eaten the red air away.

I am Christ's boy, I cried, I bear
In iron hands the bread, the fishes.
I hang with honey and with rose
This tidy wreck of all your wishes.

On your geometry of sleep
The chestnut and the fir-tree fly,
And lavender and marguerite
Forge with their flowers an English sky.

Turn now towards the belling town
Your jigsaws of impossible bone,
And rising read your rank of snow
Accurate as death upon the stone.

About your easy heads my prayers
I said with syllables of clay.
What gift, I asked, shall I bring now
Before I weep and walk away?

Take, they replied, the oak and laurel.
Take our fortune of tears and live
Like a spendthrift lover. All we ask
Is the one gift you cannot give.

The American Poet, **Howard Nemerov (1920–1991)** , also deserves attention in this aspect. As introduced in the preceding sections, Nemerov's numerous collections of poetry include *Trying Conclusions: New and Selected Poems, 1961–1991* (1991), *War Stories: Poems About Long Ago and Now* (1987), *Inside the Onion* (1984), *Sentences* (1980), *The Collected Poems of Howard Nemerov* (1977) that won the Pulitzer Prize, the National Book Award, and the Bollingen Prize, *Gnomes and Occasions* (1973), *The Winter Lightning: Selected Poems* (1968), *The Blue Swallows* (1967), *Mirrors and Windows* (1958), *The Salt Garden* (1955), *Guide to the Ruins* (1950), and *The Image and the Law* (1947). In 1987, he wrote the poem "The War in the Air" with the following lines:

For a saving grace, we didn't see our dead,

Who rarely bothered coming home to die
But simply stayed away out there
In the clean war, the war in the air.

Seldom the ghosts came back bearing their tales
Of hitting the earth, the incompressible sea,
But stayed up there in the relative wind,
Shades fading in the mind,

Who had no graves but only epitaphs
Where never so many spoke for never so few:
Per ardua, said the partisans of Mars,
Per aspera, to the stars.

That was the good war, the war we won
As if there were no death, for goodness' sake,
With the help of the losers we left out there
In the air, in the empty air.

Alan Ross (1922–2001) is a British poet and editor, who served first as a minesweeper and then on the destroyers that accompanied the Arctic convoys safely through the seas, ended his service in Germany overseeing the break-up of the German fleet, de-nazification, the identifying of war criminals, and the Belsen Trials. In his poem "Off Brighton Pier" (1958), Ross wrote about the horrifying living conditions of the veteran soldiers, which is an illustration of the tragic effects of wars.

I saw him a squat man with red hair,
Grown into sideburns, fishing off Brighton pier:
Suddenly he bent, and in a lumpy bag
Rummaged for bait, letting his line dangle,
And I noticed the stiffness of his leg
That thrust out, like a tripod, at an angle.
Then I remembered: the sideburns, that gloss
Of slicked-down ginger on a skin like candy floss.
He was there, not having moved, as last,
On a windless night, leaning against the mast,
I saw him, groping a bag for numbers.
And the date was the 17th of September,
15 years back, and we were playing Tombola

During the last Dog, someone beginning to holler
'Here you are' for a full card, and I remember
He'd just called 'Seven and six, she was worth it,'
When—without contacts or warning—we were hit.
Some got away with it, a few bought it.
And I recall now, when they carried him ashore,
Fishing gear lashed to his hammock, wishing
Him luck, and his faint smile, more
To himself than to me, when he saluted
From the stretcher, and, cadging a fag,
Cracked 'I'm quids in, it's only one leg,
They'll pension me off to go fishing.'

James Dickey (1923–1997) is one of the major mid-century American poets. His numerous poetry collections include *The Whole Motion: Collected Poems, 1945–1992*, *The Eagle's Mile* (1990), *The Strength of Fields* (1979), *Buckdancer's Choice* (1965) that received both the National Book Award and the Melville Cane Award, *Helmets* (1964), and *Into the Stone, and Other Poems* (1960).

Another poet of similar themes is the American poet, Anthony Hecht (1923–2004). Hecht's work combined a deep interest in form with a passionate desire to confront the horrors of 20th century history, with the Second World War, in which he fought, and the Holocaust being recurrent themes in his work. In his "More Light! More Light!" (1967), he wrote:

Composed in the Tower before his execution
These moving verses, and being brought at that time
Painfully to the stake, submitted, declaring thus:
'I implore my God to witness that I have made no crime.'

Nor was he forsaken of courage, but the death was horrible,
The sack of gunpowder failing to ignite.
His legs were blistered sticks on which the black sap
Bubbled and burst as he howled for the Kindly Light.

And that was but one, and by no means one of the worst;
Permitted at least his pitiful dignity;
And such as were by made prayers in the name of Christ,
That shall judge all men, for his soul's tranquility.

We move now to outside a German wood.

Three men are there commanded to dig a hole
In which the two Jews are ordered to lie down
And be buried alive by the third, who is a Pole.

Not light from the shrine at Weimar beyond the hill
Nor light from heaven appeared. But he did refuse.
A Lüger settled back deeply in its glove.
He was ordered to change places with the Jews.

Much casual death had drained away their souls.
The thick dirt mounted toward the quivering chin.
When only the head was exposed the order came
To dig him out again and to get back in.

No light, no light in the blue Polish eye.
When he finished a riding boot packed down the earth.
The Lüger hovered lightly in its glove.
He was shot in the belly and in three hours bled to death.

No prayers or incense rose up in those hours
Which grew to be years, and every day came mute
Ghosts from the ovens, sifting through crisp air,
And settled upon his eyes in a black soot.

The American poet and teacher, **W. D. Snodgrass (1926–2009)**, is one of the central figures of the Confessional mode, wrote the returning-home soldiers in his "Returned to Frisco, 1946" (1959):

We shouldered like pigs along the rail to try
And catch that first gray outline of the shore
Of our first life. A plane hung in the sky
From which a girl's voice sang: '…you're home once more.'
For that one moment, we were dulled and shaken
By fear. What could still catch us by surprise?
We had known all along we would be taken
By hawkers, known what authoritative lies
Would plan us as our old lives had been planned.
We had stood years and, then, scrambled like rabbits
Up hostile beaches; why should we fear this land

Intent on luxuries and its old habits?

A seagull shrieked for garbage. The Bay Bridge,

Busy with noontime traffic, rose ahead.

We would have liberty, the privilege

Of lingering over steak and white, soft bread

Served by women, free to get drunk or fight,

Free, if we chose, to blow in our back pay

On smart girls or trinkets, free to prowl all night

Down streets giddy with lights, to sleep all day,

Pay our own way and make our own selections;

Free to choose just what they meant we should;

To turn back finally to our old affections,

The ties that lasted and which must be good.

Off the port side, through haze, we could discern

Alcatraz, lavender with flowers. Barred,

The Golden Gate, fading away astern,

Stood like the closed gate of your own backyard.

The British poet, **Thom Gunn (1929–2004)**, wrote a verse notable for its adroit, terse language and counterculture themes, combined with historical nightmares and traumas, as in his *"Claus Von Stauffenberg of the bomb-plot on Hitler, 1944"* (1961):

What made the place a landscape of despair,

History stunned beneath, the emblems cracked?

Smell of approaching snow hangs on the air;

The frost meanwhile can be the only fact.

They chose the unknown, and the bounded terror,

As a corrective, who corrected live

Surveying without choice the bounding error:

An unsanctioned present must be primitive.

A few still have the vigour to deny

Fear is a natural state; their motives neither

Of doctrinaire, of turncoat, nor of spy.

Lucidity of thought draws them together.

The maimed young Colonel who can calculate

On two remaining fingers and a will,

Takes lessons from the past, to detonate
A bomb that Brutus rendered possible.

Over the maps a moment, face to face:
Across from Hitler, whose grey eyes have filled
A nation with the illogic of their gaze,
The rational man is poised, to break, to build.

And though he fails, honour personified
In a cold time where honour cannot grow,
He stiffens, like a statue, in mid-stride
—Falling toward history, and under snow.

Ted Hughes (1930–1998) is a British poet and fiction writer. He is also considered as one of the giants of the 20th century British poetry. He never joined in any wars, but once served in the Royal Air Force for two years as a ground wireless mechanic. His poetry include *The Hawk in the Rain* (1957), *Crow* (1971), *Cave Birds* (1979), *Moortown* (1980), *Flowers and Insects* (1986), *Wolfwatching* (1990), and *The Birthday Letters* (1998). His posthumous publications include *Selected Poems 1957–1994* (2002) and *Collected Poems* (2003), the latter two of which had resurrected new waves of Highes studies. The excerpt, "Platform One" (1995)[5], illustrate Hughes' reflections of wars.

Holiday squeals, as if all were scrambling for their lives,
Panting aboard the "Cornish Riviera".
Then overflow of relief and luggage and children,
Then ducking to smile out as the station moves.

Out there on the platform, under the rain,
Under his rain-cape, helmet and full pack,
Somebody, head bowed reading something,
Doesn't know he's missing his train.

He's completely buried in that book.
He's forgotten utterly where he is.
He's forgotten Paddington, forgotten

---

5 On platform number one of London's Paddington Station, Charles Sargeant Jagger's larger-than-life-size bronze statue of the soldier described in this poem stands as a memorial to the "Men and Women of the Great Western Railway who gave their Lives for King and Country" in the World Wars of 1914–1918 and 1939–1945.

Timetables, forgotten the long, rocking

Cradle of a journey into the golden West,
The coach's soft wingbeat—as light
And straight as a dove's flight.
Like a graveyard statue sentry cast

In blackened old bronze. Is he reading poems?
A letter? The burial service? The raindrops
Beaded along his helmet rim are bronze.
The words on his page are bronze. Their meanings bronze.

Sunk in his bronze world he stands, enchanted.
His bronze mind is deep among the dead.
Sunk so deep among the dead that, much
As he would like to remember us all, he cannot.

Similar to Ted Hughes' mythical framework in poetic production, the British poet and novelist **George MacBeth (1932–1992)** wrote a kind of verse ranged from moving personal elegies, highly contrived poetic jokes, and loosely structured dream fantasies to macabre satire, as can be seen from his "The Land-Mine" (1967):

It fell when I was sleeping. In my dream
    It brought the garden to the house
And let it in. I heard no parrot scream
    Or lion roar, but there were flowers
And water flowing where the cellared mouse
Was all before. And air moved as in bowers

Of cedar with a scented breath of smoke
    And fire. I rubbed scales from my eyes
And white with brushed stone in my hair half-woke
    In fear. I saw my father kneel
On glass that scarred the ground. And there were flies
Thick on that water, weeds around his heel

Where he was praying. And I knew that night
    Had cataracted through the wall
And loosed fine doors whose hinges had been tight

And made each window weep glass tears
That clawed my hands. I climbed through holes. My hall
Where I had lain asleep with stoppered ears

Was all in ruins, planted thick with grime
      Of war. I walked as if in greaves
Through fire, lay down in gutters choked with lime
      And spoke for help. Alas, those birds
That dived in light above me in the leaves
Were birds of prey, and paid no heed to words.

Now I was walking, wearing on my brow
      What moved before through fireless coal
And held my father's head. I touch it now
      And feel my dream go. And no sound
That flying birds can make, or burrowing mole,
Will bring my garden back, or break new ground.

The war is over and the mine has gone
      That filled the air with whinnying fire
And no more nights will I lie waiting on
      Cold metal or cold stone to freeze
Before it comes again. That day of ire,
If it shall come, will find me on my knees.

3. Poetry of War Remembrance and Commemoration

War Remembrance, or "War Commemoration", is a historic occasion in the social and cultural history of humanity. It is also a political and extraordinary cultural appetite for history as memory to address those issues of how wars and the loss of life in wars have been remembered collectively in the aftermath of armed conflicts. In their co-edited *War and Remembrance in the Twentieth Century* (1999), the two scholars Jay Winter and Emmanuel Sivan say:

Collective remembrance is a public recollection. It is the act of gathering bits and pieces of the past, and joining them together in public. The 'public' is the group that produces, expresses, and consumes it. What they create is not a cluster of individual memories; the whole is greater than the sum of the parts. Collective memory is constructed through the action of groups and individuals in the light of day. Passive memory—understood as the personal recollections of a silent individual—is not collective memory, though the way we talk about our own memories is socially bounded. When

541

people enter the public domain, and comment about the past—their own personal past, their family past, their national past, and so on—they bring with them images and gestures derived from their broader social experience.[6]

The two historians propose that war is always mediated through knowledge and feeling. Lenses and perspective are mediated to filter out some of its blinding, terrifying light, but they are not fixed in that they change over time. As different social agencies, different creative arts have framed our meditations on war, and those mediated images of war in turn circulate through language to constitute our "cultural memory" of war.

To recall history and remembrance of history, commemorate martyrs, cherish peace, and send a warning to the future, we inaugurate the present and future, but only if lessons from history are kept in mind. In his *War beyond Words: Languages of Remembrance from the Great War to the Present* (2017), Jay Winter writes that "What we know of war is always mediated knowledge and feeling" and that "each language carries its own lexicon about war, in which are imprinted traces of the experience of armed conflict."[7] War has inspired poets since humankind began telling stories from antiquity. Whether to honour those who have fallen in battle or to mourn the senseless destruction that such conflict causes, poetic representation of wars has captured the darkest moments in human history, explored a broad range of experiences, celebrated victories, mourned the losses, and reported the atrocities. This genre of poetry has encoded all later modes of record and remembrance, including revisionist twists and deconstructionist suspicion.

War Remembrance Poetry, as a vehicle for remembrance and reflection of war written on "Remembrance Day", or "Commemoration Day", or an occasion to review the past violence, or Veterans' recollection, has reflected the rich patchwork that the later generation wished to cherish and preserve. The tradition serves as a cultural touchstone in relation to which we position and measure the past military engagements, acting as a locus around which the many epistemological, ontological, and heuristic questions. These writings are vehicles for remembrance, written in constantly newer contexts, juxtaposing familiar images of the war with newly revealed dimensions.

To present memory of war, war remembrance or commemoration can be initiated from a collective entity or a private individual, thus there can be many different memories: global memory, international memory, national or state memory, any collective or communal memory, and finally individual memory such as a poet. For instance, the American poet Robert Lowell's poem "For the Union Dead" (1964) writes about the American Civil War, but it can be regarded as a war remembrance poem for all war reflections. The poem is subtitled "Relinquunt Omnia Servare Rem Publicam". Lowell altered the inscription on the Shaw

---

6 Jay Winter and Emmanuel Sivan. *War and Remembrance in the Twentieth Century*. Cambridge and New York: Cambridge University Press, 1999, p. 6.

7 Jay Winter, *War beyond Words: Languages of Remembrance from the Great War to the Present*. New York: Oxford University Press, 2017, p. 1.

Memorial that reads "*Omnia Reliquit Servare Rem Publicam*" ("He leaves all behind to serve the Republic") to his epigraph that reads "*Relinquunt Omnia Servare Rem Publicam*" ("They give up everything to serve the Republic").

The poem was written in 1960 for the Boston Arts Festival where Lowell first read it in public. The title references the 1928 poem "Ode to the Confederate Dead" by Lowell's former teacher and mentor Allen Tate. The public monument is Colonel Robert Gould Shaw, who led the 54th Massachusetts Volunteer Infantry Regiment, a regiment of African-American soldiers raised for the Union Army from freed blacks and escaped slaves, in the American Civil War. He died at the battle for Fort Wagner in South Carolina in July 1863. In the poem, he thinks about Shaw and recounts the history of his regiment and the memorial monument, before reflecting on the civil rights movement and school integration protests emerging in the late 1950s and early 1960s, as can be seen in the following stanzas:

> The old South Boston Aquarium stands
> in a Sahara of snow now. Its broken windows are boarded.
> The bronze weathervane cod has lost half its scales.
> The airy tanks are dry.
>
> Once my nose crawled like a snail on the glass;
> my hand tingled
> to burst the bubbles
> drifting from the noses of the cowed, compliant fish.
>
> My hand draws back. I often sigh still
> for the dark downward and vegetating kingdom
> of the fish and reptile. One morning last March,
> I pressed against the new barbed and galvanized
>
> fence on the Boston Common. Behind their cage,
> yellow dinosaur steamshovels were grunting
> as they cropped up tons of mush and grass
> to gouge their underworld garage.
>
> Parking spaces luxuriate like civic
> sandpiles in the heart of Boston.
> A girdle of orange, Puritan-pumpkin colored girders
> braces the tingling Statehouse,
>
> shaking over the excavations, as it faces Colonel Shaw

and his bell-cheeked Negro infantry
on St. Gaudens' shaking Civil War relief,
propped by a plank splint against the garage's earthquake.

Two months after marching through Boston,
half the regiment was dead;
at the dedication,
William James could almost hear the bronze Negroes breathe.

Their monument sticks like a fishbone
in the city's throat.
Its Colonel is as lean
as a compass-needle.

He has an angry wrenlike vigilance,
a greyhound's gentle tautness;
he seems to wince at pleasure,
and suffocate for privacy.

He is out of bounds now. He rejoices in man's lovely,
peculiar power to choose life and die—
when he leads his black soldiers to death,
he cannot bend his back.

On a thousand small town New England greens,
the old white churches hold their air
of sparse, sincere rebellion; frayed flags
quilt the graveyards of the Grand Army of the Republic.

The stone statues of the abstract Union Soldier
grow slimmer and younger each year—
wasp-waisted, they doze over muskets
and muse through their sideburns...

Shaw's father wanted no monument
except the ditch,
where his son's body was thrown
and lost with his 'niggers.'

The ditch is nearer.
There are no statues for the last war here;
on Boylston Street, a commercial photograph
shows Hiroshima boiling

over a Mosler Safe, the 'Rock of Ages'
that survived the blast. Space is nearer.
When I crouch to my television set,
the drained faces of Negro school-children rise like balloons.

Colonel Shaw
is riding on his bubble,
he waits
for the blessèd break.

The Aquarium is gone. Everywhere,
giant finned cars nose forward like fish;
a savage servility
slides by on grease.

In this aspect, the celebrated British poet, **Ted Hughes (1930–1998)**, also wrote "Remembrance Day", which as one critic explains, Hughes "develops his identification with his father. No easy commemoration rituals for either of them. The poet damns the poppy, the symbol of so much suffering, and of so many unshakable memories from which no one escaped."[8] These lines are as follows:

The poppy is a wound, the poppy is the mouth
        Of the grave, maybe of the womb searching—
A canvas-beauty puppet on a wire
        Today whoring everywhere. It is years since I wore one.

It is more years
The shrapnel that shattered my father's paybook
        Gripped me, and all his dead
Gripped him to a time

He no more than they could outgrow, but, cast into one, like iron,

---

8 Jay Winter, *War Beyond Words: Languages of Remembrance from the Great War to the Present*. New York: Oxford University Press, 2017, p. 196.

Hung deeper than refreshing of ploughs
In the woe-dark under my mother's eye—
One anchor

Holding my juvenile neck bowed to the dunkings of the Atlantic.
So goodbye to that bloody-minded flower.
You dead bury your dead.
Goodbye to the cenotaphs on my mother's breasts.
Goodbye to all the remaindered charms of my father's survival.
Let England close. Let the green sea-anemone close.

Similarly, the American poet, **James Tate (1943–   )**, wrote a private remembrance for his father *"The Lost Pilot for My Father, 1922–1944"* (1967). In his tragic, comic, absurdist, ironic, hopeful, haunting, lonely, and surreal reflection, he lamented both his private loss and national catastrophe:

Your face did not rot
like the others—the co-pilot,
for example, I saw him

yesterday. His face is corn—
mush: his wife and daughter,
the poor ignorant people, stare

as if he will compose soon.
He was more wronged than Job.
But your face did not rot

like the others—it grew dark,
and hard like ebony;
the features progressed in their

distinction. If I could cajole
you to come back for an evening,
down from your compulsive

orbiting, I would touch you,
read your face as Dallas,
your hoodlum gunner, now,

with the blistered eyes, reads
his braille editions. I would
touch your face as a disinterested

scholar touches an original page.
However frightening, I would
discover you, and I would not

turn you in; I would not make
you face your wife, or Dallas,
or the co-pilot, Jim. You

could return to your crazy
orbiting, and I would not try
to fully understand what

it means to you. All I know
is this: when I see you,
as I have seen you at least

once every year of my life,
spin across the wilds of the sky
like a tiny, African god,

I feel dead. I feel as if I were
the residue of a stranger's life,
that I should pursue you.

My head cocked toward the sky,
I cannot get off the ground,
and, you, passing over again,

fast, perfect, and unwilling
to tell me that you are doing
well, or that it was mistake

that placed you in that world,
and me in this; or that misfortune
placed these worlds in us.

The British poet and journalist, **James Fenton (1949–   )**, who was remarked upon for his facility with a wide variety of verse styles and for the liberal political views threading his oeuvre, also wrote with the same sentiments in his "Dead Soldiers" (1982):

When His Excellency Prince Norodom Chantaraingsey
Invited me to lunch on the battlefield
I was glad of my white suit for the first time that day.
They lived well, the mad Norodoms, they had style.
The brandy and the soda arrived in crates.
Bricks of ice, tied around with raffia,
Dripped from the orderlies' handlebars.

And I remember the dazzling tablecloth
As the APCs fanned out along the road,
The dishes piled high with frogs' legs,
Pregnant turtles, their eggs boiled in the carapace,
Marsh irises in fish sauce
And inflorescence of a banana salad .

On every bottle, Napoleon Bonaparte
Pleaded for the authenticity of the spirit.
They called the empties Dead Soldiers
And rejoiced to see them pile up at our feet.

Each diner was attended by one of the other ranks
Whirling a table-napkin to keep off the flies.
It was like eating between rows of morris dancers—
Only they didn't kick.
On my left sat the prince;
On my right, his drunken aide.
The frogs' thighs leapt into the sad purple face
Like fish to the sound of a Chinese flute.
I wanted to talk to the prince. I wish now
I had collared his aide, who was Saloth Sar's brother.
We treated him as the club bore. He was always
Boasting of his connections, boasting with a head-shake
Or by pronouncing of some doubtful phrase.
And well might he boast. Saloth Sar, for instance,
Was Pol Pot's real name. The APCs

Fired into the sugar palms but met no resistance.

In a diary, I refer to Pol Pot's brother as the Jockey Cap.
A few weeks later, I find him 'in good form
And very skeptical about Chantaraingsey.'
'But one eats well there,' I remark.
'So one should,' says the Jockey Cap:
'The tiger always eats well,
It eats the raw flesh of the deer,
And Chantaraingsey was born in the year of the tiger.
So, did they show you the things they do
With the young refugee girls?'

And he tells me how he will one day give me the gen.
He will tell me how the prince financed the casino
And how the casino brought Lon Nol to power.
He will tell me this.
He will tell me all these things.
All I must do is drink and listen.

In those days, I thought that when the game was up
The prince would be far, far away —
In a limestone faubourg, on the promenade at Nice,
Reduced in circumstances but well enough provided for.
In Paris, he would hardly require his private army.
The Jockey Cap might suffice for café warfare,
And matchboxes for APCs.

But we were always wrong in these predictions.
It was a family war. Whatever happened,
The principals were obliged to attend its issue.
A few were cajoled into leaving, a few were expelled,
And there were villains enough, but none of them
Slipped away with the swag.

For the prince was fighting Sihanouk, his nephew,
And the Jockey Cap was ranged against his brother
Of whom I remember nothing more
Than an obscure reputation for virtue.

I have been told that the prince is still fighting

Somewhere in the Cardamoms or the Elephant Mountains.

But I doubt that the Jockey Cap would have survived his good connections.

I think the lunches would have done for him—

Either the lunches or the dead soldiers.

In the Anglo-American world, there are a great number of "remembrance day" or "commemoration day", for instance in the US, there is the "Memorial Day," which is an annual federal holiday observed in the United States on the last Monday of May. Originally known as Decoration Day, it comes as a commemoration of those who lost their lives while fighting in the Civil War. But today, it evolved into a more general celebration of American military personnel who have died in all wars.

Poetry written on these occasions varies differently. It makes up an important portion of Anglo-American war poetry. The most recent American young poet, Nathaniel Fick, wrote as an ex-soldier's take on recent war poetry. He served as a Marine Corps infantry officer in Afghanistan and Iraq. After serving tours of duty in both Afghanistan and Iraq, he looks at recent war-themed collections of poetry and sees how they stack up in his excellent prose, "When Yellow Ribbons and Flag-Waving Aren't Enough": "Soldiers and Marines today know it as well. Yellow ribbons and flag-waving aren't much. Even aboard a commercial flight on a bright day, I know it too. If, in two hours, a bomb goes off on the airport road, or if, tonight, a lucky mortar round falls into the camp, no one will cry except my family. Despite the very real comradeship and teamwork, soldiering is, in the end, the loneliest of professions." "Maybe this explains", as he continues. "the solemn solidarity that exists between warriors and civilians who've lived through the war. They have more in common with each other than with their counterparts who've only known peace."[9] In reading these "poems to honour and remember", all must be conceived in peace.

---

9 https://www.poetryfoundation.org/articles/68931/when-yellow-ribbons-and-flag-waving-arent-enough

Epilogue

As can be seen in this critical anthology, there have been all kinds of wars, and there have been diverse kinds of war poetry. The first is "poetry of firsthand war experiences": war poets were not necessarily soldiers, but the First World War brought a series of new poetry by soldiers whose writing from the trenches and battlefields for the global conflict had stirred a tidal wave of patriotism and an unprecedented call to arms; those "soldier-poets" offered firsthand knowledge of war; many finest war poems about the atrocities of war were written by real warriors in uniform; those poetic writings created by "soldier-poets" recounts their mental and physical suffering; for them, war mixed in sulfur mustard and trenches were not an abstract principle or a political motivation for the nobler good but daily occurrences.

The second is "poetry of indirect war experiences": those poets have written on war without having a direct experience of it, for instance, Homer's *Iliad* recounts the progress of the Trojan War. In the 20th century, it became obvious that armed conflicts, such as open wars, border disputes, skirmishes, and others, had been affecting the lives of the general population. War poetry has been written by many "civilians" caught up in the conflict in other ways, for instance, W. H Auden in the Spanish Civil War and other poets in the Second World War.

The third is "war songs", those related to war especially accompanying a war dance that incites military ardour. The fourth is "poetry of witness": those painful writings of those who endured war, imprisonment, exile, repression, and human rights violations. The fifth is what has often called the war remembrance or commemoration poetry.

The 20th Century has passed. It had been "a bloody century": 9 million soldiers died in World War I, 17 million in World War II, and 58,000 Americans and 3 million Vietnamese in America's war against Vietnam, but what is unfortunate is this: "opposing sides have a remarkable capacity not to see war as death and suffering, blocking that view before, during, and after hostilities with a more palatable vision of noble and always defensive manliness." The critic continued, "Many ordinary citizens all over Europe, Allied and Central Powers alike, actually welcomed World War I."[1] This is what we called the "pathology" of war culture.

The Critique of "Cultural Pathology" advocated a critical strategy of "Fragmented Reading", or "Fragmentation of Reading", for instance, *Beowulf* is itself contradictory because the former part of Beowulf's dragon-slaying narrative evidently tried to legitimate the later part of Beowulf's "natural becoming" of the King, which is an ideological infiltration of power manipulation in cultural formation. Emily Dickinson once wrote: "Tell All the Truth/ But Tell It Slant." Poets tell the truth, but due to those social taboos, censorships, moral constraints, they often tell the truth "*Slant*", that is, here and there "artistically" in their text. So focusing on deconstruction of power, critical reading can be a fragmented reading in which power can be focused on, and the constructive ethics of such criticism is to expose the corruption of power.

To deconstruct the legitimacy of power to generate a war, we have to understand its discourse for legitimacy. In his *The Language of War: Literature and Culture in the U.S. from the Civil War through World War II*, James Dawes wrote: "War is the limit case for understanding violence. War is violence maximized and universalized. In its 'ideal' or theoretical form, Carl von Clausewitz famously argued, war achieves unlimited violence: The logic of combat is mutual escalation, as cultures sacrifice blood and treasure in ever-increasing volume in their efforts to match and overmaster one another." He summarized that the warmonger "treats language both as a disciplinary regime premised on the use of force and as a method of disciplining and controlling violence in order to concentrate its effects."[2]

Because war has frequently been considered as pathology of culture, modern and contemporary Anglo-American war poetry leans heavily on the antiwar formulations, having cast off those sublime representations such as in "The Star-Spangled Banner": "And the rockets' red glare, the bombs bursting in air, /Gave proof through the night that our flag was still there." Of course, there was "patriotic war poetry", such as Alfred Tennyson's "The Charge of the Light Brigade", Ralph Waldo Emerson's "Concord Hymn" for the Independence Day celebration, Julia Ward Howe's "Battle Hymn of the Republic" about the American Civil War. There was also "Anti-war poetry", as poets believe that words, not weapons and war, solve conflicts; those soldiers, veterans, and war victims expose overwhelming disturbing realities, and their poetry becomes a social movement and an outcry against military conflicts.

Some critic once said, "Any launch of war is a crime, for which victory brings no atonement." According to his advice, what is equally crucial for us is to find the words for war and to interrogate them at every stage. War finally becomes a "myth" in which, due to the scientific invention of black powder and the first chemical explosive, advancements in military

---

1 Kathy J. Phillips, *Manipulating Masculinity: War and Gender in Modern British and American Literature*. New York: Palgrave Macmillan, 2006, p.1.

2 James Dawes. *The Language of War: Literature and Culture in the U.S. From the Civil War through World War II*. Massachusetts and London: Cambridge University Press, 2002, pp. 1-2.

technology, the modern invention of insensate destruction, it became difficult for war poets to speak in the same enthusiasm: destructive weapon systems became accessible for warring sides to exploit, and millions of soldiers were wounded or died. Those honours, braveries, masculinities, leaderships, prides, patriotism, sublimity tested and developed in war poetry, have become the ideology of "sheer power". The Horacian discourse "Dulce et Decorum Est" ("It is sweet and appropriate to die for one's country") has already become Wilfred Owen's "The old Lie: *Dulce et decorum est pro patria mori*".

We have to reassess the old sweet word "patriotism". It should witness a new meaning, for instance, as a "Trinity of Affection, Defense, and Alertness" (TADA): Affection for its People, Defense of its Land, and Alertness on those rulers both domestic and foreign. As recorded in James Boswell's *The Life of Johnson* (1791), Samuel Johnson (1709–1784) gave the most frequently quoted words about its common denomination: "Patriotism is the last refuge of a scoundrel. But let it be considered, that he did not mean a real and generous love of our country, but that pretended patriotism which so many, in all ages and countries, have made a cloak for self-interest."

We have to sing highly of those with antiwar sensibilities, for instance, in *We Who Dared to Say No to War* (2008), Murray Polner and et al "bring[s] together some of the most memorable, if largely neglected, writings and speeches by those Americans who have opposed our government's addiction to war, from the War of 1812 to the present," having "assembled some of the most compelling, vigorously argued, and just plain interesting speeches, articles, poetry, and book excerpts."[3]

We have to reassess such concepts as the State, the Nation, the Society, even the Truth, the Good and the Beauty. In dominant ideological discourse, for instance, "truth" is in itself lying, or it is "lying by truth" or "lying by fact". Any truth or fact has its totality, and any representation of a truth or fact is inevitably ideological. The only objective of dominant ideological discourse is to legitimate its reproduction of power, thus any truth or fact represented in dominant ideological discourse is "a lie". Thus in the critique of cultural pathology, fragmentation is one feature of its totality. This critical judgement comes from the New Historicism's "Difference" reading strategy in the perspective of the materialism of signification: Language and literature are always the product of a specific time and place. The connections between different cultures and different periods can be established only *on the basis of analogy*, not identity. For instance, the tragedies of Sophocles and of Shakespeare may appear to fulfil a similar function within their respective cultures, but there can be only a likeness between them, not equality. It is the differences between the two forms that are more significant than the similarities. This leads to a refusal of the overarching conceptual explanations.

This illuminating concept comes from the poststructuralist idea that any structure or

---

3 Murray Polner, and Thomas, E. Woods, Jr., *We Who Dared to Say No to War: American Antiwar Writing from 1812 to Now.* New York: Basic Books, 2008, p.1.

system would be affected through differential and socially coded relations, or structure or system is always historically contingent and socially encoded. New historicism has become the dominant mode of literary criticism in the Anglophone world since its emergence in the 1980s. The term itself is often attributed to Stephen Greenblatt (he has frequently expressed a preference for the term "cultural poetics", e.g. in his *The Forms of Power and The Power of Forms in the English Renaissance*, 1982). It is Greenblatt's own text, *Renaissance Self-Fashioning* (1980), that is frequently taken to be the first major contribution to the new historicist enterprise, and his work remained inseparable from any attempt to define its rejection of the "traditional historicism and New Criticism." The former approach, Greenblatt maintained, sought to impose an artificial unity, making them internally coherent and reflective of an equally organic world view, both of which tended to legitimize dominant modes of power. The latter, in its good purpose, focused exclusively on a de-historicized text, repressing its political meaning.

The history that New Historicist critics evoke is thus discontinuous, fragmentary, and unstable, always seen to be in a process of change that is neither progressive nor declining since it is not fundamentally linear. The new method thus emphasized the contradictions within the cultural formation of each historical moment, indeed making these contradictions their subject, stressing the interdependent nature of cultural forms and institutions, and reading all traces of the past as texts and narratives to be interpreted. Its emphasis upon the marginal texts is a good case in point. It is easy to see the attraction of the experiences of the marginalized for those wishing to open up traditional historical narratives to alternative voices and images; at the same time, it is clear where a practice that emphasizes upon the importance of the non-canonical text and the neglected documents or object holds an appeal for those who wish to expand the range of materials available to the cultural critic.

And finally, its emphasis upon "incompleteness" and "anecdotes" also illustrates the point. Incompleteness is part of its utility as a form, which is mirrored by another recurrent feature, the use of anecdotes. Depending on these counter-historical anecdotes, traces of "power" in textual formation can be searched, and they open up the accepted narratives of history to forms of resistance. More importantly, such literary texts as poetry are consequently seen to be similarly discontinuous, being able to reveal its negotiation with multivalent power.

Appendices

1. British Rulers or Monarchs and American Presidents

British Rulers or Monarchs[1]		American Presidents
The Celts, 900 BC—55 BC		
The Romans, 55 BC—AD 450		
The Anglo-Saxons, AD 450—AD 1066		
House of Wessex		
Egbert	802–839	
Aethelwulf	839–858	
Aethelbald	858–860	
Aethelberht	860–866	
Aethelred I	866–871	
Saxon Kings		
Alfred the Great	871–899	
Edward the Elder	899–925	
Athelstan	925–939	
Edmund the Magnificent	939–946	
Eadred	946–955	
Eadwig	955–959	
Edgar the Peaceable	959–975	
Edward the Martyr	975–978	
Ethelred the Readiless		
Ethelred II the Unready	978–1016	
Edmund Ironside	1016	

1 After the Act of Union in 1707, the king or queen is more correctly called the monarch of Great Britain.

Danish Kings	
Svein Forkbeard	1014
Cnut (Canute)	1016–1035
Harold I	1035–1040
Hardicanute (Harthacnut)	1040–1042
Saxon Kings	
Edward the Confessor	1042–1066
Harold II (Godwinson)	1066
House of Normandy	
William I the Conqueror	1066–1087
William II Rufus	1087–1100
Henry I Beauclerc	1100–1135
Stephen	1135–1154
Empress Matilda Queen Maud	1141
House of Plantagenet	
Henry II	1154–1189
Richard I Coeurde Lion	1189–1199
John Lackland	1199–1216
Henry III	1216–1272
Edward I	1272–1307
Edward II	1307–1327
Edward III	1327–1377
Richard II	1377–1399
House of Lancaster	
Henry IV	1399–1413
Henry V	1413–1422
Henry VI	1422–1461
House of York	
Edward IV	1461–1483
Edward V	1483
Richard III	1483–1485
House of Tudor	
Henry VII	1485–1509
Henry VIII	1509–1547
Edward VI	1547–1553
Mary I	1553–1558
Elizabeth I	1558–1603

House of Stuart		
James I of England and VI of Scotland	1603–1625	
Charles I	1625–1649	
Commonwealth (declared 1649)		
Oliver Cromwell, Lord Protector	1653–1658	
Richard Cromwell	1658–1659	
House of Stuart (Restored)		
Charles II	1660–1685	
James II	1685–1688	
William II and Mary II (Mary d. 1694)	1689–1702	
Anne	1702–1714	
House of Hanover		
George I	1714–1727	
George II	1727–1760	
George III	1760–1820	George Washington, 1789–1797 John Adams, 1797–1801 Thomas Jefferson, 1801–1809 James Madison, 1809–1817
George IV	1820–1830	James Monroe, 1817–1825 John Quincy Adams, 1825–1829
William IV	1830–1837	Andrew Jackson, 1829–1837
Victoria	1837–1901	Martin Van Buren, 1837–1841 William Henry Harrison, 1841 John Tyler, 1841–1845 James Knox Polk, 1845–1849 Zachary Taylor, 1849–1850 Millard Fillmore, 1850–1853 Franklin Pierce, 1853–1857 James Buchanan, 1857–1861 Abraham Lincoln, 1861–1865 Andrew Johnson, 1865–1869 Ulysses Simpson Grant, 1869–1877 Rutherford Birchard Hayes, 1877–1881 James Abram Garfield, 1881 Chester Alan Arthur, 1881–1885 Grover Cleveland, 1885–1889 Benjamin Harrison, 1889–1893 Grover Cleveland, 1893–1897 William McKinley, 1897–1901
House of Saxe-Coburg-Gotha		
Edward VII	1901–1910	Theodore Roosevelt, 1901–1909

House of Windsor		
George V	1910–1936	William Howard Taft, 1909–1913
		Woodrow Wilson, 1913–1921
		Warren Gamaliel Harding, 1921–1923
		Calvin Coolidge, 1923–1929
		Herbert Clark Hoover, 1929–1933
Edward VIII	1936	Franklin Delano Roosevelt, 1933–1945
George VI	1936–1952	Harry S. Truman, 1945–1953
Elizabeth II	1952–	Dwight D. Eisenhower, 1953–1961
		John F. Kennedy, 1961–1963
		Lyndon B. Johnson, 1963–1969
		Richard M. Nixon, 1969–1974
		Gerald Ford, 1974–1977
		Jimmy Carter, 1977–1981
		Ronald Reagan, 1981–1989
		George Bush, 1989–1993
		Bill Clinton, 1993–2001
		George W. Bush, Jr., 2001–2007
		Barack Hussein Obama, 2007–2017
		Donald John Trump, 2017–2020
		Joseph Robinette Biden 2021–

2. Chart of Major Wars with British and American Involvement

The British and Americans have been involved with wars both large and small since before their national formation. This "Chart of Major Wars with British and American Involvement" lists major wars both that they involved and especially that their poets have frequently responded. In addition to the named wars and conflicts listed, members of the two nations have played small but active roles in many other national or international conflicts.

Timeline	Wars and Combatants
43–61 CE	The Roman Conquest of Britain
c. 205–369 CE	The Saxon Raids
c. 395–405 CE	The Irish Raids in Britain
c. 407–c. 550 CE; c. 550–577 CE	The Saxon Raids
593–616 C.E.	Aethelfrith's Wars
793–870 CE	The Early Viking Raids in England
871–896 CE	The Viking Raids against Alfred
899–1016 CE	The Later Viking Raids in England
937 CE	The Viking Defeat at Brunanburh
1066	The Norman Conquest
1072	William I's Invasion of Scotland

1076	William I's Invasion of Normandy
1079–1080	The Anglo-Scottish War
1109–1113; 1116–1119; 1123–1135	The Anglo-French War
1138–1154	The English Dynastic War
1159–1189; 1202–1204; 1213–1214; 1214–1216	The Anglo-French War
1215–1217	The English Civil War
1242–1243; 1294–1298; 1300–1303	The Anglo-French War
1314–1328	The Scottish War
1337–1457	The Hundred Years' War
1394–1399	The English Invasions of Ireland
1413	The Battle of Flodden
1415	The Battle of Agincourt
1428–1429	The Siege of Orleans
1455–1485	The Wars of the Roses
1568–1648	The Eighty Years' War
1587–1604	The Anglo-Spanish War
1588	The Defeat of the Spanish *Armada*
1618–1648	The Thirty Years' War
1622	Jamestown Massacre: The English Colonies vs. Native Indians
1622–1644	The Powhatan War: The English Colonies vs. Native Indians
1637	The Pequot War: The English Colonies vs. Native Indians of Connecticut included the Narragansetts, Mohegans, Wampanoags, Nipmucks, Pocumtucks, Abenakis and Pequots
1640–1701	The Beaver Wars, also known as the Iroquois Wars or the French and Iroquois Wars
1642–1646	The First or Great English Civil War
1648–1651	The Second English Civil War
1655–1659	The Anglo-Spanish War
1655	The Peach Tree War, also known as the Peach War: The Susquehannock Nation and allied Native Americans on several New Netherland settlements centered on New Amsterdam
1664–1665	The Anglo-Dutch War in West Africa
1675–1677	King Philip's War: New England Colonies vs. Wampanoag, Narragansett, and Nipmuck Indians and others; So named after Metacomet of the Wampanoag tribe, who was called Philip by the English; More than one third of America's white population was wiped out
1687	The Anglo-Siamese War
1688	The Glorious Revolution
1689–1697	King William's War: The English Colonies vs. France
1701–1714	Queen Anne's War (The War of Spanish Succession): The English Colonies vs. France
1744–1748	King George's War (The War of Austrian Succession): The French Colonies vs. Great Britain
1756–1763	French and Indian War (The Seven Years War): The French Colonies vs. Great Britain
1759–1761	Cherokee War: English Colonists vs. Cherokee Indians

1764	Pontiac's Rebellion: The Ottawa Chief Pontiac (1720–1769) led a rebellion of a number of tribes against the British
1773	The Boston Tea Party: Massachusetts patriots dressed as Mohawk Indians protest against the British Tea Act by dumping crates of tea into Boston Harbor
1775–1783	The American Revolution: English Colonists vs. Great Britain
1782–1810	The Hawaiian Wars
1798–1800	The Franco-American Naval War: United States vs. France
1792–1802	The French Revolutionary Wars
1703–1815	The Napoleonic Wars: The series of conflicts fought between France a shifting number of European nations.
1801–1805; 1815	Barbary Wars: United States vs. Morocco, Algiers, Tunis, and Tripoli
1812–1815	The War of 1812: United States vs. Great Britain
1813–1814	Creek War: United States vs. Creek Indians
1824–1826	The First Anglo-Burmese War
1836	The War of Texas Independence: Texas vs. Mexico
1839–1842	The First Afghan War
1839–1842	The First Opium War
1846–1848	The Mexican-American War: United States vs. Mexico
1853–1856	The Crimean War: the Russians vs. the British, French, and Ottoman Turkish
1856–1857	The Anglo-Persian War
1856–1860	The Second Opium War
1861–1865	The U.S. Civil War: Union vs. Confederacy; The surrender of Robert E. Lee on April 9, 1865 signaled the end of the Confederacy
1880–1881; 1899–1902	The Boer Wars: or the South African Wars between the British and the descendants of the Dutch settlers (Boers) in Africa.
1898	The Spanish-American War: United States vs. Spain
1900–1915	The British Colonial Wars in Africa
1914–1918	World War I: Triple Alliance: Germany, Italy, and Austria-Hungary vs. Triple Entente: Britain, France, and Russia; The United States joined on the side of the Triple Entente in 1917
1916–1921	The Anglo-Irish Civil War
1925–1933	The Nicaraguan Civil War: The US vs. the Natives
1936–1939	The Spanish Civil War: Military revolt against the Republican government of Spain while the Nationalists supported by Fascist Italy and Nazi Germany and the Republicans by the Soviet Union and the International Brigades composed of volunteers from Europe and the United States
1939–1945	World War II: Axis Powers: Germany, Italy, Japan vs. Major Allied Powers: United States, Great Britain, France, and Russia
1950–1953	The Korean War: United States (as part of the United Nations) and South Korea vs. North Korea and China
1960–1975	Vietnam War: United States and South Vietnam vs. North Vietnam
1961	The Bay of Pigs Invasion: United States vs. Cuba
1969–1998	The Northern Ireland Civil War
1982	Falkland Islands/Islas Malvinas War: Britain vs. Argentina
1983	The US Invasion of Grenada: United States Intervention
1989	The US Invasion of Panama: United States vs. Panama
1990–1991	The Persian Gulf War: United States and Coalition Forces vs. Iraq
1995–1996	The Intervention in Bosnia and Herzegovina: United States as part of NATO acted peacekeepers in former Yugoslavia
2001–	Invasion of Afghanistan: United States and Coalition Forces vs. the Taliban regime in Afghanistan to fight terrorism.

2003–2011	Invasion of Iraq: United States and Coalition Forces vs. Iraq
2004–	War in Northwest Pakistan: United States vs. Pakstan
2007–	Somalia and Northeastern Kenya: United States and Coalition forces vs. al-Shabaab militants
2009–2016	Operation Ocean Shield (Indian Ocean): NATO allies vs. Somali pirates
2011	The Intervention in Libya: US and NATO allies vs. Libya
2011–2017	The Lord's Resistance Army: US and allies against the Lord's Resistance Army in Uganda
2014–2017	The US-led Intervention in Iraq: US and coalition forces against the Islamic State of Iraq and Syria
2014–	The US-led intervention in Syria: US and coalition forces against al-Qaeda, Isis, and Syria
2015–	The Yemeni Civil War: Saudi-led coalition and US, France and Kingdom against the Houthi rebels, Supreme Political Council in Yemen and allies
2015–	The US intervention in Libya: US and Libya against ISIS

Bibliography

1. Books

Aaron, Daniel. *The Unwritten War: American Writers and the Civil War* [M]. New York: Knopf, 1973.

Adams, R. J. Q. *The Great War 1914–18: Essays on the Military, Political and Social History of the First World War* [C]. London: Macmillan, 1990.

Anderson, B. *Imagined Communities: Reflections on the Origin and Spread of Nationalism* [M]. London: Verso, 2008.

Baird, Jay W. *Hitler's War Poets: Literature and Politics in the Third Reich* [C]. New York: Cambridge University Press, 2008.

Baker, Kenneth. *The Faber Book of War Poetry* [C]. London: Faber and Faber, 1996.

Baring, Maurice. *Poems: 1914–1919* [C]. London: Martin Secker, 1920.

Barrett, Faith. *To Fight Aloud Is Very Brave: American Poetry and the Civil War [M]*. Amherst: University of Massachusetts Press, 2012.

Bates, Scott. *Poems of War Resistance from 2300 B.C. to the Present* [C]. New York: Grossman, 1969.

Beidler, Philip D. *Re-Writing America: Vietnam Authors in Their Generation* [M]. Athens: University of Georgia Press, 1991.

Bennett, Martyn. *The Civil Wars Experienced: Britain and Ireland, 1638–1661* [M]. London: Routledge, 2000.

Boland, Eavan. *After Every War: Twentieth-Century Women Poets* [C]. Princeton, NJ: Princeton University Press, 2004.

Bowen, Kevin, and Bruce Weigl. *Writing Between the Lines: An Anthology on War and Its Social Consequences* [C]. Amherst: University of Massachusetts Press, 1995.

Brantlinger, Patrick. *Rule of Darkness: British Literature and Imperialism, 1830–1914* [M]. Ithaca, NY: Cornell University Press, 1988.

Brewer, John. *The Sinews of Power: War, Money and the English State, 1688–1783* [M]. New

York: Knopf, 1989.

Brooks, Cleanth, and Robert Penn Warren. *Understanding Poetry* [C]. Fort Worth, Tex.: Heinle & Heinle, 2003.

Brownlee, James Henry. *War-Time Echoes: Patriotic Poems, Heroic and Pathetic, Humorous and Dialectic, of the Spanish-American War* [C]. New York and Chicago: The Werner Company, 1989.

Carey, Gary, and Mary Ellen Snodgrass. *A Multicultural Dictionary of Literary Terms* [C]. Jefferson, N.C.: McFarland, 1999.

Caute, David. *The Dancer Defects: The Struggle for Cultural Supremacy during the Cold War* [C]. Oxford: Oxford University Press, 2005.

Chaliand, Gérard. *The Art of War in World History from Antiquity to the Nuclear Age* [M]. Berkeley: University of California Press, 1994.

Chattarji, Subarno. *Memories of a Lost War: American Poetic Responses to the Vietnam War* [C]. New York: Oxford University Press, 2001.

Chomsky, Noam. *9–11* [M]. New York: Seven Stories, 2001.

Clarke, George Herbert. *A Treasury of War Poetry: British and American Poems of the World War, 1914–1917* [C]. Boston: Houghton Mifflin, 1917.

Colley, Linda. *Britons: Forging the Nation 1707–1837* [M]. New Haven, CT: Yale University Press, 1992.

Cullen, Jim. *The Civil War in Popular Culture: A Reusable Past* [M]. (Washington, DC: Smithsonian Institution Press, 1995.

Cunningham, Valentine. *British Writers of the Thirties* [M]. Oxford University Press,1988.

Cunningham, Valentine. *Spanish Front, Writers on the Civil War* [C]. Oxford University Press, 1986.

Cunningham, Valentine. *The Penguin Book of Spanish Civil War Verse* [C]. Penguin, 1980.

Das, Santanu. *Touch and Intimacy in First World War Literature* [M]. Cambridge University Press, 2003.

Dawes, James. *The Language of War: Literature and Culture in the U.S. from the Civil War through World War II* [M]. Boston, MA: Harvard University Press, 2002.

Day, Gary. *Literary Criticism: A New History*. Edinburgh: Edinburgh University Press, 2008.

Deutsch, Babette. *Poetry Handbook: A Dictionary of Terms* [C]. New York: Funk& Wagnalls, 1974.

Drury, John. *The Poetry Dictionary* [C]. Cincinnati, Ohio: Story Press, 1995.

Dwivedi, Amitabh Vikram. War Poetry [C]// Paul Joseph. *The Sage Encyclopedia of War: Social Science Perspectives*. Thousand Oaks: SAGE Publications, 2017.

Eberhart, Richard and Selden Rodman. *War and the Poet: An Anthology of Poetry Expressing Man's Attitude to War from Ancient Times to the Present* [C]. New York: Devin-Adair, 1945.

Eby, Cecil Degrotte. *The Road to Armageddon: The Martial Spirit in English Popular*

Literature, 1870–1914 [M]. Durham, NC: Duke University Press, 1987.

Eggleston, George Cary. *American War Ballads and Lyrics: A Collection of the Songs and Ballads of the Colonial Wars, the Revolution, the War of 1812–1815, the War with Mexico and the Civil War* [C]. *Volume I.* New York and London: The Knickerbocker Press, 1889.

Ehrhart, W. D. *Carrying the Darkness: Poetry of the Vietnam War* [C]. Lubbock: Texas Tech UP, 1989.

Faust, Drew Gilpin. *This Republic of Suffering: Death and the American Civil War* [M]. New York: Knopf, 2008.

Featherstone, Simon. *War Poetry: An Introductory Reader* [C]. London & NY: Routledge, 1995.

Ferguson, John. *War and the Creative Arts: An Anthology* [C]. London and Basingstoke: The Open University, 1972.

Ferguson, Margaret, and et al. *The Norton Anthology of Poetry* [C]. London and New York: W. W. Norton & Company, 2005.

Friedman, Thomas. *Longitudes and Attitudes: Exploring the World after September11* [M]. New York: Farrar Straus Giroux, 2002.

Fussell, Paul. *The Great War and Modern Memory* [M]. Oxford: Oxford University Press, 1985.

Fussell, Paul. *The Norton Book of Modern War* [C]. New York: Norton, 1991.

Fussell, Paul. *Wartime: Understanding and Behavior in the Second World War* [M]. Oxford University Press, 1989.

Gat, Azar. *War in Human Civilization* [M]. Oxford University Press, 2006.

Goldensohn, Lorrie. *American War Poetry: An Anthology* [C]. New York: Columbia University Press, 2006.

Gotera, Vicente F. *Radical Visions: Poetry by Vietnam Veterans* [M]. Athens: University of Georgia Press, 1994.

Graham, Desmond. *Poetry of the Second World War: An International Anthology* [C]. Pimlico, 1998.

Habib, M. A. R. *A History of Literary Criticism: From Plato to the Present* [M]. Malden, Mass.: Wiley-Blackwell, 2005.

Hale, J. R. *Renaissance War Studies* [M]. London: Hambledon, 1983.

Hanley, Lynne. *Writing War: Fiction, Gender, and Memory* [M]. Amherst: University of Massachusetts Press, 1991.

Harari, Yuval Noah. *Renaissance Military Memoirs: War, History, and Identity, 1450–1600* [M]. Woodbridge: Boydell, 2004.

Harries, Meirion, and Susie Harries. *The Last Days of Innocence: America at War, 1917–1918* [M]. New York: Vantage, 1997.

Hazen, Edith P., ed. *Columbia Granger's Index to Poetry.* 10th ed. NewYork: Columbia University Press, 1994.

Hoffman, Herbert H., and Rita Ludwig Hoffman. *International Index to Recorded Poetry* [C]. New York: H. W. Wilson, 1983.

Howard, Michael. *War in European History* [M]. Oxford: Oxford University Press, 1976.

James, Jennifer C. *A Freedom Bought with Blood: African American War Literature from the Civil War to World War II* [M]. Chapel Hill: University of North Carolina Press, 2007.

Jason, Philip K. *Acts and Shadows: The Vietnam War in American Literary Culture* [M]. Lanham, MD: Rowman and Littlefield, 2000.

Jason, Philip K., ed. *Masterplots II: Poetry Series* [C]. Pasadena, Calif.: Salem Press, 2002.

Jump, Jim. *Poets from Spain: British and Irish International Brigadiers on the Spanish Civil War* [C]. London: Lawrence & Wishart, 2006.

Kaufman, Will. *The Civil War in American Culture* [M]. Edinburgh University Press, 2006.

Keen, Maurice. *Chivalry* [M]. New Haven, CT: Yale University Press, 1984.

Kendall, Tim. *Modern English War Poetry* [M]. Oxford: Oxford University Press, 2006.

Kendall, Tim. *Poetry of the First World War: An Anthology* [C]. New York: Oxford University Press, 2013.

Kendall, Tim. *The Oxford Handbook of British and Irish War Poetry* [C]. Oxford: Oxford University Press, 2007.

Kennedy, David M. *Over Here: The First World War and American Society* [M]. *Oxford:* Oxford University Press, 1980.

Kinzie, Mary. *A Poet's Guide to Poetry* [C]. Chicago: University of Chicago Press, 1999.

Klaus, H. Gustav. *Strong Words Brave Deeds: The Poetry, Life and Times of Thomas O'Brien, Volunteer in the Spanish Civil War* [C]. Dublin: O'Brien, 1994.

Lalumia, Matthew Paul. *Realism and Politics in Victorian Art of the Crimean War* [M]. Ann Arbor, MI: UMI Research Press, 1984.

Lázaro, Alberto. *The Road from George Orwell: His Achievement and Legacy* [C]. Bern: Peter Lang, 2001.

Lehman, David. *The Oxford Book of American Poetry* [C]. Oxford and New York: Oxford University Press, 2006.

Lennard, John. *The Poetry Handbook: A Guide to Reading Poetry for Pleasure and Practical Criticism* [C]. New York: Oxford University Press, 1996.

Linn, Brian McAllister. *The Echo of Battle: The Army's Way of War* [M]. Boston, MA: Harvard University Press, 2007.

Lodge, David, and Nigel Wood. *Modern Criticism and Theory* [C]. New York: Longman, 2008.

Looby, Christopher. *Voicing America: Language, Literary Form, and the Origins of the United States* [M]. Chicago University Press, 1996.

Magill, Frank N. *Magill's Bibliography of Literary Criticism* [C]. Englewood Cliffs, N.J.: Salem Press, 1979.

Mahony, Philip. *From Both Sides Now: The Poetry of the Vietnam War and Its Aftermath* [C].

NY: Scribner, 1998.

Matterson, Stephen, and Darryl Jones. *Studying Poetry* [M]. New York: Oxford University Press, 2000.

McLoughlin, Kate. *Authoring War: The Literary Representation of War from the "Iliad" to Iraq* [M]. Cambridge: Cambridge University Press, 2011.

McLoughlin, Kate. *The Cambridge Companion to War Writing* [C]. Cambridge, New York: Cambridge University Press, 2009.

Moore, Frank. *Songs and Ballads of the Southern People.1861–1865* [C]. New York: D. Appleton And Company, 1886.

Morley, Christopher. *Modern Essays* [C]. Noston: Harcourt, Brace and Company, Inc., 1921.

Munton, Alan. *English Fiction of the Second World War* [M]. London: Faber, 1989.

Packard, William. *The Poet's Dictionary: A Handbook of Prosody and Poetic Devices* [C]. New York: Harper & Row, 1989.

Padgett, Ron. *The Teachers and Writers Handbook of Poetic Forms* [C]. New York: Teachers & Writers Collaborative, 2000.

Patterson, Samuel White. *The American Revolution as Revealed in the Poetry of the Period: A Study of American Patriotic Verse from 1760–1783* [C]. Boston: Richard G. Badger, 1915.

Piette, Adam. *Imagination at War* [M]. London: Papermac, 1995.

Pinsky, Robert. *The Sounds of Poetry: A Brief Guide* [C]. New York: Farrar, Straus and Giroux, 1998.

Polner, Murray, and Thomas E. Woods. *We Who Dared to Say No to War: American Antiwar Writing from 1812 to Now* [C]. New York: Basic Books, 2008.

Pratt, John H. *Chaucer and War* [M]. Lanham, MD: University Press of America, 2000.

Preminger, Alex, and T. V. F. Brogan. *New Princeton Encyclopedia of Poetry and Poetics* [C]. Princeton, N.J.: Princeton University Press, 1993.

Preminger, Alex, et al. *The New Princeton Encyclopedia of Poetry and Poetics* [C]. Princeton, N.J.: Princeton University Press, 1993.

Quinn, Patrick. *British Poets of the Great War: Brooke, Rosenberg, Thomas: A Documentary Volume* [C]. Detroit: Gale Group, 2000.

Reilly, Catherine W. *English Poetry of the Second World War: A Biobibliography* [M]. Boston: G.K. Hall, 1986.

Reisman, Rosemary M. Canfield. *Critical Survey of Poetry War Poets* [C]. Ipswich, Massachusetts: Salem Press, 2012.

Rowe, John Carlos, and Rick Berg. *The Vietnam War and American Culture* [C]. New York: Columbia University Press, 1991.

Roy, Pinaki. *The Scarlet Critique: A Critical Anthology of War Poetry* [C]. New Delhi: Sarup Book Publishers Pvt. Ltd., 2010.

Saunders, Corinne, and Françoise Le Saux, Neil Thomas. *Writing War: Medieval Literary Responses to Warfare* [C]. Cambridge: D. S. Brewer, 2004.

Scarry, Elaine. *The Body in Pain: The Making and Unmaking of the World* [M]. Oxford University Press, 1985.

Selmer, Louis. *Boer War Lyrics*. London, New York, and Montreal: The Abbey Press, 1903.

Seymour-Smith, Martin, and Andrew C. Kimmens, eds. *World Authors, 1900–1950*. Wilson Authors Series. 4 vols. New York: H. W. Wilson, 1996.

Shapiro, Harvey. *Poets of World War II* [C]. New American Library, 2003.

Shipley, Joseph Twadell, ed. *Dictionary of World Literary Terms, Forms, Technique, Criticism* [C]. Boston: George Allen and Unwin, 1979.

Silkin, Jon. *Penguin Book of First World War Poetry* [C]. NY: Penguin, 1997.

Smith, Angela K. *The Second Battlefield: Women, Modernism and the First World War* [M]. Manchester University Press, 2000.

Stallworthy, Jon. *The New Oxford Book of War Poetry* [C]. New York: Oxford University Press, 2014.

Stallworthy, Jon. *The Oxford Book of War Poetry*. New York: Oxford University Press, 1984.

Steiner, George. *Language and Silence* [M]. Harmondsworth: Penguin, 1969.

Strachan, Hew. *Carl von Clausewitz's On War: A Biography* [M]. London: Atlantic, 2007.

Stradling, Robert. *History and Legend: Writing the International Brigades* [M]. Cardiff: University of Wales Press, 2003.

Tatum, James. *The Mourner's Song: War and Remembrance from The Iliad to Vietnam* [M]. Chicago: University of Chicago Press, 2003.

Tatum, James. *The Mourner's Song: War and Remembrance from The Iliad to Vietnam* [M]. Chicago: University of Chicago Press, 2003.

The Vigilantes Books. *Fifes and Drums: A Collection of Poems of America at War* [C]. New York: George H. Doran Company, 1917.

Thompson, Clifford. *World Authors, 1990–1995* [C]. Wilson Authors Series. New York: H. W. Wilson, 1999.

Turco, Lewis. *The NewBook of Forms: A Handbook of Poetics* [C]. Hanover, N.H.: University Press of New England, 1986.

Vale, Malcolm. *War and Chivalry: Warfare and Aristocratic Culture in England, France and Burgundy at the End of the Middle Ages* [M]. London: Duckworth, 1981.

Vedder, Polly. *World Literature Criticism Supplement: A Selection of Major Authors from Gale's Literary Criticism Series* [C]. Detroit: Gale Research, 1997.

Wakeman, John. *World Authors, 1950–1970* [C]. New York: H. W. Wilson, 1975.

Wakeman, John. *World Authors, 1970–1975* [C]. New York: H. W. Wilson, 1991.

Walsh, Jeffrey. *American War Literature, 1914 to Vietnam* [M]. London and Basingstoke: Macmillan, 1982.

Weigley, Russell F. *The American Way of War: A History of United States Military Strategy and Policy* [M]. New York: Macmillan, 1973.

Willhardt, Mark, and Alan Michael Parker. *Who's Who in Twentieth Century World Poetry* [C].

New York: Routledge, 2000.

Williams, Miller. *Patterns of Poetry: An Encyclopedia of Forms* [C]. Baton Rouge: Louisiana State University Press, 1986.

Winn, James Anderson. *The Poetry of War* [M]. Cambridge: Cambridge University Press, 2008.

Winter, Jay, and Emmanuel Sivan. *War and Remembrance in the Twentieth Century* [C]. Cambridge and New York: Cambridge University Press, 1999.

Young, Alfred. *The Shoemaker and the Tea Party: Memory and the American Revolution* [C]. Boston, MA: Beacon, 1999.

Young, Elizabeth. *Disarming the Nation: Women's Writing and the American Civil War* [M]. Chicago: University of Chicago Press, 1999.

2. Websites

http://andromeda.rutgers.edu/~jlynch/Lit (Literary Resources on the Net)

http://famouspoetsandpoems.com/poets/joaquin_miller/biography

http://litweb.net

http://poetsagainstthewar.org/ (The Global Movement of Poets: Poets Against the War)

http://rpo.library.utoronto.ca (Representative Poetry Online)

http://theotherpages.org/poems (Poet's Corner)

http://voices.cla.umn.edu/ (Voices from the Gaps)

http://vos.ucsb.edu (Voice of the Shuttle)

http://warpoetry.org (The Dean Echenberg War Poetry Collection)

http://ww1lit.nsms.ox.ac.uk/ww1lit/

http://ww1lit.nsms.ox.ac.uk/ww1lit/collections/jones

http://ww2f.com/threads/world-war-2-poetry.58517/

http://www.america.gov/publications/books/outline-of-american-literature.html (Outline of American Literature)

http://www.bartleby.com

http://www.contemporarywriters.com/authors (Contemporary British Writers)

http://www.england-history.org/category/00-early-period/

http://www.greatwar.co.uk/poems/

http://www.gutenberg.org

http://www.literaryhistory.com

http://www.luminarium.org/ (Anthology of English Literature online)

http://www.poetpatriot.com/

http://www.poetry.org/

http://www.poetry-archive.com/

http://www.poetry-archive.com/collections/poems_on_war.html

http://www.poetryfountain.com/

http://www.poetrywar.com/

http://www.poets.org (Academy of American Poets)

http://www.poetsandwar.com/

http://www.themodernword.com/authors.html (The Modern Word: Authors of the Libyrinth)

http://www.vietnamwar.net/poetry.htm

http://www.warpoets.org/

http://www.warpoets.org/home/ [The War Poets Association (WPA)]

https://classicalpoets.org/

https://poetryarchive.org/

https://poetshouse.org/

https://rpo.library.utoronto.ca/poems/french-revolution

https://sourcebooks.fordham.edu/mod/1914warpoets.asp

https://war-poems.com/

https://worldwarpoetry.com/

https://worldwarpoetry.com/

https://www.biographyonline.net/

https://www.firstworldwar.com/poetsandprose/

https://www.poemhunter.com/poems/war/page-1/31639/#content

https://www.poetryfoundation.org/ (Poetry Foundation)

https://www.poetryinvoice.com/poems/war

https://www.thoughtco.com/great-war-poems-4163585

https://www.warpoetry.uk/

Index